CONVENIENCE FOODS

CONVENIENCE FOODS
Recent Technology

Philip M. Robbins

NOYES DATA CORPORATION
Park Ridge, New Jersey, U.S.A.
1976

Copyright © 1976 by Noyes Data Corporation
No part of this book may be reproduced in any form
without permission in writing from the Publisher.
Library of Congress Catalog Card Number: 76-24147
ISBN: 0-8155-0641-4
Printed in the United States

Published in the United States of America by
Noyes Data Corporation
Noyes Building, Park Ridge, New Jersey 07656

FOREWORD

The detailed, descriptive information in this book is based on U.S. patents issued since 1972 that deal with convenience foods. This includes one reissue.

This book serves a double purpose in that it supplies detailed technical information and can be used as a guide to the U.S. patent literature in this field. By indicating all the information that is significant, and eliminating legal jargon and juristic phraseology, this book presents an advanced, technically oriented review of the commercial preparation of convenience foods.

The U.S. patent literature is the largest and most comprehensive collection of technical information in the world. There is more practical, commercial, timely process information assembled here than is available from any other source. The technical information obtained from a patent is extremely reliable and comprehensive; sufficient information must be included to avoid rejection for "insufficient disclosure." These patents include practically all of those issued on the subject in the United States during the period under review; there has been no bias in the selection of patents for inclusion.

The patent literature covers a substantial amount of information not available in the journal literature. The patent literature is a prime source of basic commercially useful information. This information is overlooked by those who rely primarily on the periodical journal literature. It is realized that there is a lag between a patent application on a new process development and the granting of a patent, but it is felt that this may roughly parallel or even anticipate the lag in putting that development into commercial practice.

Many of these patents are being utilized commercially. Whether used or not, they offer opportunities for technological transfer. Also, a major purpose of this book is to describe the number of technical possibilities available, which may open up profitable areas of research and development. The information contained in this book will allow you to establish a sound background before launching into research in this field.

Advanced composition and production methods developed by Noyes Data are employed to bring our new durably bound books to you in a minimum of time. Special techniques are used to close the gap between "manuscript" and "completed book." Industrial technology is progressing so rapidly that time-honored, conventional typesetting, binding and shipping methods are no longer suitable. We have bypassed the delays in the conventional book publishing cycle and provide the user with an effective and convenient means of reviewing up-to-date information in depth.

The Table of Contents is organized in such a way as to serve as a subject index. Other indexes by inventor, patent number and company help in providing easy access to the information contained in this book.

15 Reasons Why the U.S. Patent Office Literature Is Important to You —

1. The U.S. patent literature is the largest and most comprehensive collection of technical information in the world. There is more practical commercial process information assembled here than is available from any other source.

2. The technical information obtained from the patent literature is extremely comprehensive; sufficient information must be included to avoid rejection for "insufficient disclosure."

3. The patent literature is a prime source of basic commercially utilizable information. This information is overlooked by those who rely primarily on the periodical journal literature.

4. An important feature of the patent literature is that it can serve to avoid duplication of research and development.

5. Patents, unlike periodical literature, are bound by definition to contain new information, data and ideas.

6. It can serve as a source of new ideas in a different but related field, and may be outside the patent protection offered the original invention.

7. Since claims are narrowly defined, much valuable information is included that may be outside the legal protection afforded by the claims.

8. Patents discuss the difficulties associated with previous research, development or production techniques, and offer a specific method of overcoming problems. This gives clues to current process information that has not been published in periodicals or books.

9. Can aid in process design by providing a selection of alternate techniques. A powerful research and engineering tool.

10. Obtain licenses — many U.S. chemical patents have not been developed commercially.

11. Patents provide an excellent starting point for the next investigator.

12. Frequently, innovations derived from research are first disclosed in the patent literature, prior to coverage in the periodical literature.

13. Patents offer a most valuable method of keeping abreast of latest technologies, serving an individual's own "current awareness" program.

14. Copies of U.S. patents are easily obtained from the U.S. Patent Office at 50¢ a copy.

15. It is a creative source of ideas for those with imagination.

CONTENTS AND SUBJECT INDEX

INTRODUCTION 1
CEREALS. 2
  Ready-to-Eat Items. 2
    Inert Material Added to Improve Texture 2
    Clustered Product 4
    Laminated Product 6
    Flaked Cereal Resembling Biscuit 8
    Coating Composition to Improve Mouthfeel and Bowl Life 10
    Simultaneous Extrusion and Coating Process 11
    Oat Cereal Biscuit 12
  "Instant" Reconstitutable Products 14
    Textured Infant Cereal 14
    Low Salt Precooked Cereal 16
    Fried Swelled Cereal Particles 18
    Uniform Textured Cereal 19
    Instant Corn Grits 21
  Nutritionally Improved Products. 22
    Palatability Improvement Using Yeast and Malt with Soy Additive. 22
    Additive-Free Product. 23
    Sodium Caseinate Used as High Protein Additive 24
    Puffed Item Having up to 60% Protein 26
    Soy Protein and Sodium Bicarbonate Additives 30
    Iron-Fortified Grain 32
    Corticated Oat Kernels and Flakes 33
    Vitamin Coated Cereal Which Retains Crispness 36
    Vitamin Coated Ready-to-Eat Cereal. 39
  Ready-to-Eat Sweetened Products. 41
    Emulsified Oil and Sugar Coating 41
    Artificially Sweetened Cereal Using L-Aspartic Acid to Avoid
      "Hot Spots" 43
    Use of Hard Butter and Crystalline Sugar 44
    Use of Syrup Solution. 45

Contents and Subject Index

POTATO AND OTHER SNACK FOODS 47
  Potato Chip Processes 47
    Forming Rippled Chips 47
    Unique Packaging Design 48
    Extruded Puffed Stick 49
    Expanded Item 50
    Preparation Using α-Amylase 52
    Using Variable Potato Stock Made into Dough 54
    Two Stage Frying Process 56
    Use of Low Grade Potato Material 59
    Use of Potato Flakes in Flour Matrix 61
  Starch-Based Snacks 62
    Chip Fracturing from Fried Ribbon 62
    Wetting Dough Surface Prior to Frying to Eliminate Blistering 63
    Shaping Fried Dough Product After Frying 64
    Low Density Puffed Product Using Protein Gel 67
    Using Starch with Specified Abrasion Rating 69
    Extruded Item Requiring No Further Cooking 73
    Acylated High Amylose Starch as Expansion Prevention Agent ... 74
    Process for Aerating Batter and Casting into Thin Film 77
    Granular Modified Starch Binder for Dough Forming 79
  Rice-Flour-Based Snacks 80
    Rice Starch Snack Food 80
    Rice Flour Expanded Snack 82
  Nutritionally Enhanced Products 85
    Protein Snack Food 85
    High Protein Expanded Food 86
    Protein Fortified Snack 89
    Protein Coated Potato Chips 92

CONVENIENCE POTATO AND GRAIN PRODUCTS 95
  "Instant" Potato Processes 95
    Ambient Temperature Storage-Stable Item 95
    Preformed Potato Pieces 98
    Reconstituted Rapid Drying Granules 101
    Method for Removing Peels for Dehydrated Flakes 105
    Vitamin Enriched Flakes 107
    Dehydrated Granular Product with High Cold Water Adsorption ... 110
  Fried Potato Processes 113
    Water Leaching Prefried Potato Slices 113
    French Fried Potatoes from Potato Dough 114
    Unrefrigerated Shelf Stable French Fried Potatoes 116
    Frozen French Fried Potatoes Surface Coated with Atomized Fat
      Globules 117
    French Fried Potatoes with Reduced Oil Content 118
    EDTA Esters to Reduce Oil Darkening 120
    Freeze-Thaw Stable French Fry Potato Product 121
  Rice and Grain Processes 125
    Frozen Cooked Rice 125
    Quick-Cooking Brown Rice 127
    Quick-Cooking Whole Grain Rice 128
    Prefried Grain Product 131
    Quick-Cooking Rice Prepared by Preliminary Frying Process 134

Contents and Subject Index

SYNTHETIC FOOD PROCESSES 136
   High Protein Items Resembling Meat Product.......................136
      Quick Cooking Foodstuff..136
      Food Flavor Pellets..139
      Textured Expanded Food...142
   Puffing Procedures..145
      Moist Food Puffing Using Inert Noncondensible Gas...............145
      Gaseous Conveyor Heating.......................................149
   Other Simulated Food Products.....................................150
      Meat, Fish or Dairy Item from Fermented Vegetable Product.......150
      Artificial Caviar..153
   Simulated Nutmeat Products..155
      Process Using Vacuum Treatment.................................155
      Particle Bonding Using Pressure................................158

FILLED FOOD PRODUCTS..160
   Meat-Containing Convenience Items.................................160
      Shelf Stable High Moisture Product.............................160
      Meat Roll..161
   Toaster Sandwiches..162
      Dielectric Sealing Method......................................162
      Method of Preparation..166

COATING PREPARATIONS..168
   Starch Batters..168
      Batters Suitable for Use on Frozen Food........................168
      Baked Coating Resembling Deep-Fat-Fried Coating................172
   Specialty Coatings..173
      Coating Suitable for Imparting Flavor to Snack Foods...........173
      Vitamins A and C Coating for Food Particles....................175
      Coating for Use on Dehydrated Foods............................177
      Amylose Coating for Deep Fried Potatoes........................178
   Specific Purpose Meat Coatings....................................180
      Coating for Texture Improvement................................180
      Dry Powder Coating to Impart Glaze.............................182
   Apparatus...184
      Continuous Application of Wet Batter and Dry Coating...........184

MEAT AND DAIRY PRODUCTS...185
   Precooked Bacon Items...185
      Process and Apparatus for Precooking Bacon.....................185
      Precooked Shelf Stable Bacon Product...........................185
   Pork Snack Products...187
      Puffed Unfried Pork Rind.......................................187
      Puffed Pork Skin Pellets.......................................189
      Crispy Fried Pork Product......................................189
   Stable Food Items from "Waste" Protein Sources....................190
      Achieving Structural Integrity Without Use of Supplemental Binders in
         Shaped Food Items..190
      Use of Waste Fish Material in Edible Fish Stick................191
      Thermoplastic Meat Patty.......................................194
      Simulated Meat Pieces from Expanded Meat and Vegetable Protein
         Source...196

Contents and Subject Index

Meat Product Adjuvants 197
    Barbecue Sauce with Tenderizer 197
    Concentrated Meat Extract and Flavoring. 198
Ready-to-Eat Meat Product Enhancement Processes. 201
    Inhibiting Gel Formation in Meat-in-Gravy Product 201
    Microbial Stabilization of a Meat, Vegetable and Gravy Product. 203
Dairy Products 207
    Apparatus for Making Expanded Dairy Item. 207
    Snack Size Extruded Cheese Item 209
    Shelf Stable Low-Fat Biologically Fermented Dairy Product 212

FOOD BARS. 217
    Nutritionally Oriented Food Bars 217
        Meat and Vegetable Stocks ("Junior" Food). 217
        Granola Product 219
        Balanced Diet Product. 220
        Bar Product with Protein Rich Filling. 224
        High Protein Product. 228
    Dehydrated Reconstitutable Bars 231
        Directly Edible, Readily Hydratable Product 231
        Compressed Compounded Reconstitutable Product 233
        Directly Edible Compacted Dehydrated Fruit Product 235

EGG AND WAFFLE PRODUCTS. 237
    Eggs, Omelets and Pancakes 237
        Cooked Frozen Egg Products 237
        Controlled Portion Product. 240
    Waffles 241
        Apparatus for Making Waffles. 241
        Shelf Stable Product 242

FRUIT AND DESSERT TYPE ITEMS 245
    Fruit and Nut Products. 245
        Dehydrated Fried Snack Food from Apples 245
        Dehydrated Fruit to Add to Powdered Instant Food 246
        Nutmeat Confection Coating. 249
        Layered Jelly Dessert 251
    "Instant" and "Ready-to-Eat" Desserts. 254
        Dessert Powder for "Instant" Cooked Pudding. 254
        Spoonable Gelatin Dessert Concentrate. 256
        Canned Fruit Pudding. 258
    Baking and Baked Products. 260
        Dough and Icing Combination Packaging Method. 260
        Flavor Bits for Cake Mixes 262

POPCORN PROCESSES. 264
    Flavorings. 264
        Flavored Popcorn Using Encapsulated Flavoring Substances. 264
        Popcorn Flavored by Using Oil-in-Water Emulsion Containing Flavor
          Ingredient 266
    Packaging Method and Popping Apparatus 268
        Popcorn Package. 268
        Separately Packaged Popcorn Confection for Making Popcorn Balls. . . . 269

Automatic Popcorn Popping Method	270
Specialized Processes	271
Popped Corn in Dough Matrix Snack Food	271
Sugar Coated Popcorn Coating Method	274

ETHNIC AND SPECIALTY FOOD ITEMS 276

Fried Products	276
Fried Tofu	276
Apparatus for Dough Sheets for Rolled Foods	278
Frittaten	280
Tortillas	282
Shelf Stable Tortillas	282
Extending Shelf Life of Tortillas	284
Peanut Products	285
Peanut Flakes	285
Peanut Butter	288
Combination Nut and Jelly Spread	291
Vegetable and Salad Products	294
Stable Avocado Base	294
Dehydrated Ready Mix Tabouly Salad	297
French Fried Onion Product	297
Snack Products	299
Heat-Sensitive Condiment-Containing Fatty Particle	299
Dough Covered Nutmeat Snack Food	303

MISCELLANEOUS PROCESSES 305

Specialty Products and Processes	305
Quickly Soluble Gelatinized Powdered Starch	305
Distributing Food Dye on Protein Seed	306
Food Preservation by Immersion Cooking in Stabilizing Solution	307
Flavorings	311
Potato Chip Flavor Concentrate	311
Potato Chip Flavor and Aroma	314
Popcorn Flavorant	317
Adjuvants	319
Salts of Acetyl Amino Acids as Water Binders	319
Hydrocolloidal Food Thickener	320
Specialty Nutritive Products	322
Encapsulated Nutrients	322
High Protein Chocolate Snack	323
Protein Enriched Low Shortening, Low Sugar Baked Product	325
Hydratable Translucent Proteinaceous Product	327

COMPANY INDEX 332
INVENTOR INDEX 334
U.S. PATENT NUMBER INDEX 337

INTRODUCTION

Patterns of food preparation and consumption have altered radically in the recent past. Ready-to-eat, "instant," and synthetic foods have become commonplace. The ready acceptance of these "fast" foods by consumers is accompanied by an increase in the research and development of newer and better processes for their preparation. This fact is confirmed by the large number of patents issued over the last three years (some 150) which relate to both convenience and "snack" type foods.

In terms of snack food, nutritional concern over "empty" calories has spurred interest in making these highly popular items more nutritionally sound. This is proven by noting that a large part of the thrust in snack food technology appears to be in nutritional enhancement along with improved processing technology.

Both ready-to-eat foods and instant foods, i.e., those which require a minimum of preparation time by the consumer, also experienced large increases in technological expertise judging by the number of patented processes for improved methods for their preparation. These products range most literally from soup to nuts, with cereals, starches, main courses and desserts in between.

Scarcities and high prices of particular kinds of foods, i.e., meat and fish, have served to make the increased use of cheaper and more abundant sources of protein prepared as "synthetic" substitutes much more attractive. The new technology which has contributed much to their improved quality is in very large part a factor in their increased consumption and use.

This updated volume concerning all that is new and relevant in this food field will serve the industry well.

CEREALS

READY-TO-EAT ITEMS

Inert Material Added to Improve Texture

A.H. Rosenquest, A.J. Knipper and R.W. Wood; U.S. Patent 3,927,222; Dec. 16, 1975; assigned to Nabisco, Inc. describe a process in which expanded ready-to-eat cereal products of improved texture are produced by mixing with milled grain between 0.2 and 2% of finely divided, insoluble, inert, nonreactive material and processing the mixture through a high-temperature and high-pressure cooking extruder. The inert materials are selected from the group consisting of titanium dioxide, calcium silicate, silicon dioxide, and aluminum oxide. The resulting products have a structure composed of cells which are substantially all of uniform small size and are of a tender friable texture.

The milled grain may be corn, oats, wheat, rice or a combination of these grains. The grains are preferably milled to a flour; however, coarser grinds may be used provided the cooking and working of the grains within the extruder is sufficient to break down the grain particles and disperse the inert material uniformly throughout the dough.

The quantity of inert material added to the grain is between about 0.2 and about 2% of the total weight of the grain. The particle size of the major portion of the material is about 4 microns or smaller. The inert material may be titanium dioxide, calcium silicate, silicon dioxide, aluminum oxide or a combination of these compounds. Optional ingredients such as sugar, salt, vitamins, etc. may be added to the mixture. All the ingredient materials may be mixed together to a batch before addition to the cooking extruder or they may each be added to the extruder continuously at a metered rate for continuous production.

The mixture of dry materials fed to the extruder normally contains about 10 to 12% water, and additional water is added within the extruder to bring the moisture content of the dough to between 12 and 20%. In the extrusion head, the dough is subjected to a high pressure and a temperature which is above the boiling point of water and generally above 300°F.

The dough is extruded in strands through a plurality of orifices. A rotating knife is normally mounted on the extrusion head to cut the strands into short pieces. As the dough emerges from the extrusion orifices, it expands as a result of the sudden drop in pressure.

The products produced were found to have a cellular structure wherein substantially all of the cells were uniform in size and were significantly smaller than the cells formed in products subjected to the same processing but without the incorporation of an inert ingredient. For example, the addition of the inert ingredient at a level of 0.5% was generally found to reduce the cell size from about 110 to about 35 microns.

Although the cell size of the products produced was reduced, the bulk density of the products were generally comparable to or less than that of conventionally formed products. Where the bulk density increased, the increase was not great and the product was of acceptable density. The product is considerably more tender and friable than conventional products made with high-pressure, high-temperature cooking extruders.

It is believed that the small cell size and tender structure of these products produced is caused by a reduction in the strength and/or stretchability of the dough as a result of the presence of the inert material. When the moisture in the dough flashes to the gaseous state upon extrusion, the weakened dough forming the walls of the cell breaks while the cells are still small. The weakened dough would also account for the tenderness of the product.

The inert ingredient may weaken the dough by physically interfering with starch gelatinization or by holding water so as to deprive the starch of some of the water needed for complete gelatinization. Each individual particle of inert ingredient may tend to hold a small amount of water, thus forming nuclei for the cells and at the same time depriving the starch of water.

In three separate trials, titanium dioxide, calcium silicate, and aluminum oxide were individually added to identical formulas which consisted of 26 lb rice flour, 24 lb yellow corn flour, 9 lb sugar, 0.5 lb salt, and 4 oz mono- and diglycerides. The trials were conducted using a Wenger Model X-25 extruder having a medium shaft, a cut flight screw, a straight ribbed casing, and a die containing ten $3/16$" holes two of which were plugged. A control trial run was first conducted using this formula without an inert ingredient. The product produced had relatively large cells, of about 100 microns in diameter, had a bulk density of 6.6 lb/ft^3, and was brittle and glassy in texture.

In the second run 12 oz of titanium dioxide was mixed with the above-described formula. The product had smaller and more uniform cells of about 30 microns in diameter. It was tender and friable and had a bulk density of 5.9 lb/ft^3. In the third run 12 oz of calcium silicate was mixed with the basic formula. The product was essentially identical to that produced by run number 2 and its bulk density was 5.2 lb/ft^3. In the last trial 13 oz of aluminum oxide was added to the basic formula. The product produced was of very light and tender texture with small and uniform cells, and had a bulk density of 4.5.

In the three trials employing inert ingredients described above, the inert ingredients accounted for the following percentage of the total formula on a weight basis: titanium dioxide, 1.25%; calcium silicate, 1.25%; and aluminum oxide, 1.35%. In another test, silicon dioxide was added in different amounts to identical formulas consisting of 26 lb rice flour, 24 lb yellow corn flour, 7 lb sugar, 0.5 lb salt, and 1 lb of monoglycerides. The trials were conducted using a Wenger Model X-25 extruder having a medium shaft, cut flight screw, straight ribbed jacket, and a die containing ten $3/16"$ holes, eight of which were plugged. A control trial run was first conducted using this formula without an inert ingredient. The product produced by the control run had moderately open cells of a diameter of about 100 microns and a bulk density of 4.3 lb/ft^3.

In the next run, 1 oz of silicon dioxide (0.1% by weight) was added to the formula. The product produced had the same cell size and bulk density of 5.0 lb/ft^3. In the final run 5 oz of silicon dioxide (0.52% by weight) was added to the basic formula. The product produced by this run had a smaller cell size of about 60 microns and a more tender and friable texture. The bulk density of this product was 6.3 lb/ft^3 which is commercially acceptable.

In another test, calcium silicate was added in three different amounts to a formula consisting of 50 lb yellow corn flour, 20 lb rice flour, 35 lb wheat flour, 9.5 lb sugar, 1 lb salt, and 0.35 lb monoglycerides. The trials were conducted using a Wenger Model X-25 extruder having a medium shaft, cut flight screw, straight ribbed jacket, and using a 10-holed $3/16"$ die plate. Control runs at both the beginning and end of the trial were made using no calcium silicate, and once the run was begun, no changes were made to the extruder as the formulas were fed in one by one. Thus, any changes in product produced was due solely to the ingredients in the formula. The results of these runs are as follows:

Formula	Puff Description	Cell Size, microns
Control	Hard, glossy	110
4 oz calcium silicate	More tender	65
8 oz calcium silicate	Very tender	32
12 oz calcium silicate	Very tender	25
Control	Hard, glossy	115

All of the above products had a commercially acceptable bulk density of between 4 and 7 lb/ft^3.

Clustered Product

A ready-to-eat cereal product is described by *G.A. Decelles and V.M. Larson; U.S. Patent 3,868,471; February 25, 1975; assigned to The Pillsbury Company* which comprises clusters or agglomerates of a base consisting of rolled or flattened substantially whole cereal grains such as wheat, rye or oats together with minor amounts of other cereals, cereal parts or seeds such as wheat germ, sesame seeds, cocoanut and the like. These products are first coated with an edible oil or fat in the amount from 3 to 18% which is allowed to penetrate their surfaces.

After the lipid coating has been applied, the second coating is applied consisting of syrup formed from water which is an edible mono- or disaccharide, or mixtures thereof so that the syrup coats the cereals to form a substantially continuous and separate, i.e., discrete film thereon. Additional optional ingredients such as nutmeats are then added and the product is roasted at a temperature between 300° to 450°F for 10 to 20 minutes until the product has obtained a golden brown color and a cooked odor and taste and the moisture content is reduced to less than 5%, typically 2%. Additional optional ingredients such as dried fruit can then be added.

The product is prepared by mixing the cereals as well as the cereal parts and nuts if any, impregnating at least the surfaces of the cereal with the fat and thereafter applying the sugar syrup with stirring to distribute the syrup as a continuous film over the surfaces of the solid particles. The product is then roasted and the moisture content is reduced to about 5% or less.

To begin production, the base cereal, e.g., crushed or rolled cereal such as wheat, rye or oats or mixtures thereof is placed in a suitable mixer and dry blended with minor solid ingredients such as cocoanut, seeds or cereal parts, nutmeats, etc. This can be done, for example, at 25 rpm for 15 seconds or until fairly uniformly blended without breaking up the oats.

An edible oil or fat is then introduced in the amount of 3.5 to 8% by weight of the total mix before it is dried, i.e., on a wet basis. The amount of oil will determine the softness of the product, with the greater amounts of oil producing a softer product. No more should be added in any event than can be absorbed by the cereal. When 3% or less is used, the product tends to be rather hard or tough when chewed.

Mixing of the oil should continue preferably for only about 10 to 15 seconds to minimize the breaking of oats. It is at this point after the oil has been added and penetrates at least the surface layer of the cereal that the syrup is added.

The syrup is used in the amount of about 15 to 25% wet weight basis as a portion of the total wet finished product. The syrup can be formed from any mono- or disaccharide or mixtures thereof. An especially good syrup is made up by dissolving brown sugar, which consists of crystalline sucrose and a small amount of molasses to form a syrup having a 68 to 72% solids basis. This syrup is heated if desired, but not above boiling, to control viscosity. Generally, the syrup should not be warmed so much that it penetrates the cereal to any extent, the object being simply to form a substantially continuous surface layer or envelope over the layer of oil-impregnated material on the surface of the cereal.

The minimum amount of syrup that can be used is determined by rancidification and it has been found that the continuous film of syrup over the oil is instrumental in reducing rancidification. For this reason, good shelf life cannot be obtained with amounts of syrup ranging less than about 10% solids by weight in the finished product. On the other hand, if the amount of syrup is too great it will tend to run off the product or stay in the mixer or otherwise separate. The fat layer prevents syrup penetration and hence tends to extend the effectiveness of the syrup.

After the syrup has been added and agitated, the product is roasted for 16 minutes in a zone heater of decreasing temperature beginning at about 450°F and ending 16 minutes later at 350°F. Other forms of heating can, of course, be used including microwave heating and the like. The roasting accomplishes a number of objectives. It imparts a brown and preferably a golden brown color to the product, a nutty flavor and cooks the product. The raw grain taste is removed during roasting and moisture is reduced to 5% or less, preferably 2% or less. Following roasting, additional optional ingredients can be added such as dried fruit and the like.

Examples 1 through 6: [All quantities and percentages herein are on a wet weight basis, i.e., before roasting and drying (% by weight)].

Example Number	1	2	3	4	5	6
Rolled Oats (wheat or rye)	62.50	53.50	51.2	65.2	77.7	37.7
Vegetable oil	8.50	8.50	18.0	3.0	8.5	8.5
Wheat Germ	1.00	10.00	3.8	3.8	3.8	3.8
Syrup[1]	28.00	28.00	27.8	28.0	10.0	50.0

[1] Syrup—70% solids **brown sugar** slurry. Honey or corn syrup can be substituted for any or all the brown sugar syrup.

Additional syrup formulations and usage levels are as follows:

	A	B	C
Brown Sugar	63.91	70.98	72.03
Water	21.28	23.61	24.02
Honey	13.85	4.43	3.95
Sea Salt	0.96	1.09	

Syrup formula A can be used in the amount of about 26% in Examples 1 through 6 and optionally with cinnamon flavoring in the amount of about 29% in any of Examples 1 through 6 in place of the syrup indicated. Formulas B and C can also be used either with or without added flavoring such as cinnamon flavoring in the amount from about 25 to 28% in place of the syrup designated in Examples 1 through 6.

Laminated Product

J.L. Rossen, R.C. Miller and G. Gellman; U.S. Patent 3,851,084; November 26, 1974; assigned to Nabisco, Inc. describe a method of producing laminated cereal and snack food products which retain their integrity during packaging, shipping and handling wherein a plurality of dissimilar homogeneous viscous molten doughs containing free starch molecules are coextruded under high pressure and total laminar flow conditions to produce a bond between two contacting layers which is stronger than the internal bond strength of the weaker of the two layers.

It has been found that the layers of different doughs are securely bonded together with each layer of dough being of uniform consistency up to the line of junction. There is no visible intermixing of the contacting layers, each layer terminating abruptly at the junction line. Tests have shown that the bond between the contacting layers is stronger than the weaker of the two layers. It is believed that the bond between the layers results from intermeshing and/or hydrogen bonding of the starch, and perhaps protein, molecules at the contacting surface.

The coextrusion of two dough layers is believed to result in a weaving of the molecules of the one dough with the molecules of the other dough along the junction line of the two doughs to produce a bond which is stronger than the bond between the molecules of the weaker material. It is possible that such a weaving of molecules could be produced or enhanced by the relative motion of the two doughs along the line of contact as they are brought into contact. Relative movement along the contact line would give the surface molecules an opportunity to catch and interlock.

Another factor which is believed to contribute to molecular intermeshing at the junction line is that the longer molecules tend to become aligned during laminar flow extrusion. As the two doughs flow, the laminar flow condition tends to align the long molecules parallel to the direction of flow. Since the molecules of the different dough streams are aligned in the same direction, when the two streams are brought into contact, the surface molecules of each stream have the same orientation as the spaces between the aligned molecules at the surface of the other stream. When, as the contacting surfaces move with respect to each other, a molecule at one surface registers with a space in the opposing surface, the molecule would tend to move into the space under the high pressure acting on the dough streams.

The alignment of the molecules during extrusion also increases the possibility of hydrogen bonding and bonds resulting from Van Der Waals forces being formed between the molecules of the contacting surfaces. The hydrogen atoms are positioned along the sides of the long molecules, and therefore, when the long molecules at both surfaces are aligned in the same direction, the greatest number of hydrogen atoms are positioned to bond with other molecules. The relative movement of the contacting surfaces increases the opportunity of such hydrogen bonds being formed.

A number of different combinations of dough formulations have been utilized to produce laminated comestible products. A strong bond was achieved between the layers of the products produced from each of these combinations. In each case, attempts made to peel the layers apart by hand were unsuccessful.

In producing these products, both cooking and forming extruders were used. The extruders were operated at various speeds to produce flow rates of extrudate from the coextrusion head of between 1 and 3 lb/min. The doughs were introduced into the coextrusion head at pressures ranging from 500 to 1,200 psi. The ratio of flow rates used were within the range of 1 to 4 and 4 to 1, that is the flow rate of one layer was between one-fourth and four times the flow rate of the other layer. The temperature range of the extrudate as it emerged from the die was between 120° and 180°F.

Example:

Layer A Ingredients

Rice flour	12 lb 8 oz
Wheat flour	8 lb 12 oz
Wheat starch	2 lb
Mono-diglyceride	2 oz
Sugar	2 lb
Salt	8 oz
Citric acid	2 oz
Red coloring	0.25 gram
Water	10 lb

Layer B Ingredients

Rice flour	12 lb 8 oz
Wheat flour	8 lb 12 oz
Wheat starch	2 lb
Mono-diglyceride	2 oz
Sugar	2 lb
Salt	8 oz
Citric acid	2 oz
Yellow coloring	0.40 gram
Water	10 lb

The layer A (red formulation) ingredients were mixed, cooked in a cooking extruder and collected. The layer B (yellow formulation) ingredients were mixed, cooked in the cooking extruder and fed directly from that extruder into the coextrusion head while the cooked layer A dough was fed to the head by a forming extruder. The density of these doughs was approximately 80 lb/ft^3.

The bond strength was tested on this extrudate produced. The forming extruder was run at 30 rpm and the cooking extruder at 68 rpm during the coextrusion. A pressure of 500 psi was developed in the zone immediately downstream of the nozzles and the flow rate of the extrudate was 2 lb/min total or ⅔ lb/min per orifice.

Test samples were prepared by taking a section of the two layer extrudate, and, with a razor blade, carefully cutting along the full width of the bond for a distance of ¾" from one end of the section. The free ends of the individual separated layers were each placed in one of the two pairs of jaws of an Instron tensile tester. The two pairs of jaws were initially spaced 1" apart and during the test were moved away from each other at a rate of 2"/min in an attempt to peel the two layers apart. This test was performed twice and each time layer B (the yellow layer) failed in tension with no apparent further separation or peeling of the two layers along the bond line. The unit strength of layer B was approximately 1.5 lb/in of width. The tests on the two samples were conducted 9 and 14 minutes respectively after extrusion.

The average viscosity of the extruded stream was computed to be 72.1 lb/in sec and the Reynolds number of the layered flow was computed to be 2.57×10^{-4}. The Reynolds number for turbulent flow is approximately 2100; therefore, it can be seen that the flow under consideration was seven orders of magnitude below the turbulent region.

Flaked Cereal Resembling Biscuit

S.H. Reesman; U.S. Patent 3,845,232; October 29, 1974; assigned to General Foods Corporation describes a means for producing a breakfast-type cereal that closely resembles a biscuit in textural and eating qualities without the disadvantages of such a biscuit product. The product, while resembling a prior art flaked product in appearance, more closely resembles a biscuit in characteristics other than appearance. It is well recognized that a cereal biscuit, particularly wheat, has entirely different taste properties than its flake form.

In the process, it is necessary to form a wheat source, such as flour or berry, into a pellet prior to shredding. The wheat is cooked and such cooking may take place either before or after pelletizing. Cooking is customarily undertaken by steaming the cereal in a pressure cooker at elevated pressures such as 5 to 30 psig. The shaping technique of pelletizing is well-known in the art and refers to extrusion of the cereal dough as through a conventional, commercial pelletizing machine.

As an optional step that is preferred, although not essential, the shaped cooked pellet prior to flaking is heated at a temperature of 100° to 300°F for 1 to 3 minutes. This heating step warms the inside of the pellet while the surface or case hardens. The pellet, while in the heated condition, is mechanically flaked through shredding rolls. A critical feature of the process is the type of shredding rolls that are employed. While one of the shredding rolls may be smooth, it is required that at least one of the rolls must be corrugated.

Corrugation of the rolls parallel to the roll direction of travel is preferable. With a transverse direction of roll indentation, sticking of the wheat to the roll may take place under specific operating conditions and a coating on the roll having antistick properties, as Teflon, may be necessary. The shredding rolls should be closely spaced to cause indentation on the flake, but should not totally sever the pressed pellets, since otherwise only shreds would form. The rippled flakes of uneven thickness after formation are toasted and then dried. As an alternate procedure, the low temperature drying step may take place prior to toasting.

In the toasting operation, low velocity air is employed with elevated temperature to bring the desired brown color. A temperature within the range of 300° to 550°F is generally employed in toasting for a period of about 1 to 2 minutes. However, since oven puffing is not needed, low velocity air is employed, which velocity is preferably about 50 ft/min or less. High velocity air with toasting temperatures results in puffing which is not necessary and undesirable in forming a flaked breakfast cereal resembling in eating characteristics a cereal in biscuit form.

A separate lower temperature drying operation in addition to toasting brings the final moisture content to a level between 1.0 to 7.0%. The drying temperature is several hundred degrees lower than the toasting temperature. A moisture content of 1 to 7% in a cereal such as wheat lends a range of textural properties when the cereal is eaten. At the lower range of about 1% moisture, the product will be dry and brittle. At the upper range of about 7%, with a substantially greater moisture content, increased chewiness will be introduced. The toasted and dried product with adjusted moisture content is cooled and packaged.

For consumption, the flaked product is intended primarily to be eaten with milk, although this liquid is not required. For example, the flakes may be eaten directly as a snack item. When the flakes are mixed with milk, the interconnecting thin membrane of the flakes will dissolve in the milk to produce shreds of the cereal. Thus, in this way interconnecting threads of a biscuit would be duplicated. Generally speaking, the connecting membrane of the flake should dissolve in a period of less than about 3 minutes with an optimum time range downward to about 1 minute. The time of dissolving of the membrane will be dependent upon its thickness.

With decreasing membrane thickness, the dissolving time of the membrane is reduced. The time necessary for the shred formation may be directly controlled by prior processing steps primarily with the flaking rolls. The maximum thickness of the thin membrane will vary depending upon the cereal employed, since cereals will vary in their ability to withstand being dissolved in milk. In the case of wheat, it has been found that membrane thickness in the range of 0.003 to 0.10 inch is satisfactory and desirable.

Example: A source of ingredients in specific concentration was used as follows:

Whole wheat flour, lb	7
Salt, oz	6
Water, lb	2

These ingredients were blended uniformly in a mixer. The composition was pelletized. The wheat-containing material was cooked in a pressure cooker at 20 psi for 22 minutes. The mix was cooled, repelletized through a die having 3/32" holes, and shredded. The corrugated roll was not cross cut and the roll was spaced so as to indent and not cut the pressed pellet. The shredded flake produced had a corrugated shape of uneven thickness. The flake could be considered to be a a series of shreds connected by a thin membrane. The shred portion of the flakes was measured and was found to have a thickness between 0.020 to 0.025 inch with a width of 0.020 to 0.025 inch.

The connecting membrane had a measured thickness between 0.003 to 0.010 inch and a width of 0.020 to 0.047 inch. The flakes were toasted at a temperature of 420°F with about a 100 ft/min air velocity for a duration of 60 seconds. The flakes were dried at 225°F to a moisture content of about 3%.

The product was tested by adding milk. The connecting membrane readily dissolved producing a series of distinct, separated shreds. The shredded product when eaten has the wheat texture, flavor and mouthfeel of a biscuit of shredded wheat.

Coating Composition to Improve Mouthfeel and Bowl Life

Cereals and snacks may have a relatively low density and be extremely porous as exemplified by puffed cereals, or they may comprise cereal doughs with relatively high density such as corn flakes. Normally when eaten with milk, these materials absorb liquids rapidly and become mushy. However, if they are coated with a mixture of ingredients comprising sucrose, fat, water, coloring, flavors, salt, spices, and other ingredients, they remain dry and crispy in liquids such as milk for a larger period of time.

Snacks and cereals having a rich apparent mouthfeel as well as satisfactory bowl life are produced by incorporating a hexitol such as sorbitol or mannitol with a fat-containing coating composition such that the weight ratio of hexitol/fat ranges between 0.03 to 2 in a process described by *D.T. Rusch and M.J. Lynch; U.S. Patent 3,769,438; October 30, 1973; assigned to ICI America Inc.*

The process is usually practiced by first preparing an aqueous solution of a hexitol such as mannitol, sorbitol, or mixtures of the two; however, any method which incorporates the hexitol into the mix is suitable. Incorporation of these materials is hastened by heating the mixture to about 120°F. Into this heated mixture are added sugars or sweeteners of various types, salt, flavors, and in some cases emulsifiers, and finally fat. Usually the mixture is heated to a temperature of 180°F to form a free-flowing syrup.

The coating is applied as an aqueous syrup (10 to 25% water) to the snack in conventional coating pans by allowing a hot syrup to flow over the tumbling snack particles. The tumbling is permitted to continue for periods of about 10 minutes until the surface of each particle becomes more or less uniformly covered. The coated particles are then removed from the pan and are dried in conventional means such as a forced-air drying oven for a time sufficient to reduce the water content of the final product to a range of 1.5 to 4% by weight based on the total particle weight. The coating on the dry particle ranges between 25 to 75% but more frequently in the range of 40 to 60% by weight of the total.

The composition of the coating on the dry particle can be about 0.5 to 15% hexitol, 5 to 20% fat, with a hexitol/fat weight ratio of 0.03 to 2, and preferably 0.1 to 1, with the remainder being sweeteners, flavors, salt, seasonings, coloring agent, etc. The coating syrup used in preparing the coated particle has hexitol/fat in the same weight ratio but differs in water content. The hexitol used is preferably sorbitol, dulcitol, and especially mannitol, and mixtures thereof.

The fat material can be an edible fat or oil of natural origin which may if desired be a partially or completely hydrogenated product resulting from oils of coconut, soy, cottonseed, corn, etc., and fats such as tallow, or blends of these. Sweetening agents and sugars other than sucrose may be used such as dextrose, fructose, unrefined sugars such as brown sugar, maple syrup, honey, and artificial sweeteners such as saccharin, etc. Various seasonings in addition to salt may be useful as well as artificial flavorings and colors.

Example: To 171 grams of distilled water add 10 grams of mannitol. Heat to about 120°F and stir until mannitol is dissolved and thereafter add 620 grams of sucrose, 45 grams brown sugar, 14 grams of salt, and heat to 180°F with stirring. To this add 70 grams of 76° coconut oil and mix well for 10 minutes.

Load 200 grams of expanded base into a coating pan. With pan running, slowly add 186 grams of hot syrup into the tumbling cereal base. Allow the cereal base and syrup to continue to tumble for an additional 10 minutes while breaking up twins. Place the dry coated cereal into a forced-air oven heated to a temperature of 25°F to drive the moisture content of the final product down to 2 to 2½%.

Simultaneous Extrusion and Coating Process

Coating of cereal products is desirable in order to add flavoring ingredients, such as sugar, or nutritional ingredients, such as vitamins. Conventionally, cereal products have been coated by tumbling in a drum and adding the coating thereto, or by some type of spraying of the coating material in conjunction with a tumbling operation. After coating, it has been conventional to dry the coated material to the desired packaging levels. *L.J. Henthorn and F.R. Kings; U.S. Patent 3,764,715; October 9, 1973; assigned to The Quaker Oats Company* describe a process for coating a cereal product where the exact amount of coating for each particle can be carefully determined, and where the product does not need excessive tumbling to insure uniformity of the coating.

This object is achieved according to the following method. A hot cooked cereal dough is first extruded under puffing conditions through a first die thereby forming an expanded cereal extrudate. A syrup-like liquid is simultaneously extruded through a second die, the second die being positioned within the orifice of the first die in such a manner that the extrudate from the first die completely surrounds the extrudate from the second die and in such a manner that the direction of flow of the second extrudate is the same as the direction of flow of the first extrudate, the syrup-like liquid being heated as it is being extruded within the first die extrudate.

The resulting extrudate is then cut into segments in the moments in which the puffed cereal extrudate is in a plastic, adhesive condition. The cutting of the resulting extrudate also seals the ends of the segments, thereby encapturing the syrup-like liquid totally within the puffed cereal extrudate. The syrup-like liquid is forced through the puffed cereal extrudate by heating the cut segments, thereby substantially evacuating the center of the puffed cereal extrudate leaving it essentially hollow. The cut segments are dried by further heating them, which forces the syrup-like liquid to the outside of the puffed cereal extrudate to form a coating thereon.

Preferably, the syrup-like liquid used for center filling and subsequent coating comprises from 7½ to 9 parts by weight sugar solids and from 1 to 2½ parts by weight water.

In producing this novel coated cereal product a syrupy filling and surrounding hot plastic cereal dough are first extruded simultaneously. The dough is then crimped at the ends and cut to form a pillow-like cereal particle having a syrupy interior. This particle is then dried to an extent sufficient to bring the syrupy interior to the exterior of the cereal product and dry it as a coating thereon. Usually a temperature of about 315° to 350°F is sufficiently high to produce the required drying and glazing when left for a time sufficient to reduce the moisture in the final product to a level of about 2 to 3%. It has been found that drying for a period of from 40 to 50 seconds at 315°F to produce a final moisture content of 3%, makes a very acceptable product.

Example: A cereal mixture was prepared by mixing 80 parts by weight corn flour, 10 parts by weight oat flour, 5 parts by weight sugar, 5 parts by weight rice flour and 2 parts by weight flavoring ingredients. This mixture was then mixed with water to bring the moisture to about 16 to 20% by weight. A filling was prepared by mixing 16 parts by weight water, 36 parts by weight granulated sugar, 36 parts by weight powdered sugar, and a minor portion of flavoring ingredients. The mixtures were then properly extruded in the previously described extrusion equipment and toasted for from 40 to 50 seconds at 315°F. The resulting product was a pleasant-tasting, uniformly coated, ready-to-eat cereal.

Oat Cereal Biscuit

J.G. Poat and N.F. Smith; U.S. Patent 3,732,109; May 8, 1973; assigned to The Quaker Oats Company produce a ready-to-eat oat cereal biscuit comprising finely subdivided oat flakes and syrup compressed together and dried to a moisture content of 4 to 5% by weight.

The first step in the process comprises mixing oat flour with water. While it is acceptable to use a mixture comprising only oat flour and water, other products can be added to enhance the flavor while still not detracting from the oat flour flavor and texture. For instance, the oat flour mixture can be 100% oat flour or it can comprise a major portion of oat flour along with minor portions of corn flour, wheat flour and rice flour. If desired, it may also include up to about 10% by weight of a protein concentrate such as soy protein concentrate to enhance nutrition.

It may also include added vitamins and minerals to enhance nutrition. The oat flour and water are mixed in an amount sufficient to produce a moisture content in the oat flour of from 10 to 25% by weight. Substantial deviation from these percentages will provide a mixture incapable of being subjected to the other processing conditions which follow.

The next step is subjecting the oat flour-water mixture to a water boiling temperature and a superatmospheric pressure. This is customarily accomplished by use of cereal extruders. When such an extruder is used, the temperature of a product may vary from just above the boiling point of water up to the neighborhood of about 400°F. While the pressure on the product may vary from just over atmospheric pressure to a much larger amount, it is customary to operate the extruder up to a pressure of approximately 3,000 psi in order that release of the pressure will produce the desired effect.

After the oat flour-water mixture has been subjected to a water boiling temperature and a superatmospheric pressure sufficient to gelatinize a portion of the starch in the oat flour, the pressure is suddenly released from the mixture in the cereal extruder. This is accomplished by passing the mixture through an orifice into the atmosphere. The mixture is then formed into flake-shaped pieces. This is accomplished normally by having the mixture pass through an orifice which is in the shape of a thin slit and then cutting the extruded portion into small pieces.

After the flake-shaped pieces are formed, they are dried to a moisture content of 2 to 6% by weight water with this drying being accomplished in an air stream having a temperature of 400° to 800°F by any well-known commercial method. At this point it is preferable, although not critical, to have the bulk density of the flaked pieces from 0.32 to 0.362 oz/in^3. After the oat flakes have been produced, they are subdivided until a substantial portion of the subdivided pieces will pass through a 3.5 mesh U.S. Standard Sieve.

After the subdivided pieces are prepared, they are mixed with a syrup. The syrup should have from 2 to 7 parts by weight of sugar with from 1 to 4 parts by weight water. A preferred syrup has 4 parts by weight of common table sugar, 1 part by weight brown sugar, 1 part by weight honey and 4 parts by weight water with a very small portion of vegetable oil added thereto. The syrup should be mixed with the subdivided pieces in an amount such that the weight ratio of the syrup to the subdivided oat flake pieces is from 1:2 to 1:3. Substantial deviation from these ranges will provide a mixture which either cannot be formed or else which will not retain its shape once it is formed.

After the subdivided pieces are mixed with the syrup they are compacted into a form of a biscuit. This can best be accomplished by placing the mixture in a mold, pressing the mixture into the mold and then removing the biscuit from the mold. After the formed biscuits are prepared, they are then dried to a moisture content of from about 4 to 5% by weight and packaged.

Example: An oat flour mixture was prepared comprising 6 parts by weight oat flour with 3.5 parts by weight wheat flour and 1 part by weight sugar. The moisture was adjusted by adding water thereto until the moisture content of the flour was about 20% by weight. The mixture was then introduced into a cereal extruder where it was raised to a temperature of about 350°F and a pressure of from 2,600 to 2,750 psi.

After approximately 3 minutes' residence time in the extruder, the mixture was passed through a thin slit and immediately cut into particles having a length of about one-fourth to one-half inch and very closely resembling oat flakes. This material was immediately dropped into an air stream of about 550°F and conveyed therein until the moisture content of the flakes was about 4% by weight. After the flakes left the air stream, they lost another 1% by weight water. The flakes were then passed through a set of breaker rolls to subdivide them and give a screen analysis as follows:

U.S. Standard Sieve	Amount, % by wt
on 3.5 mesh	0.6
on 8.0 mesh	55.6
on 14 mesh	21.9
on 30 mesh	7.3
through 30 mesh	14.6

A syrup mixture was next prepared by mixing 4 parts by weight sugar, 1 part by weight brown sugar, and 1 part by weight honey with 4 parts by weight water. One part by weight of the syrup was then mixed with 2 parts by weight of the subdivided oat flakes. This mixture was then placed in a mold and compressed until the volume was approximately reduced in half. The biscuits were then removed from the mold and dried to a moisture content of 4.5% by weight. The resulting product was placed in a cereal bowl and milk was added thereto. The result was a highly delicious and extremely nutritional product.

"INSTANT" RECONSTITUTABLE PRODUCTS

Textured Infant Cereal

The process described by *L.L. Cloud, V.J. Kelly and W.J. Smalligan; U.S. Patent 3,956,506; May 11, 1976; assigned to Gerber Products Company* relates to the preparation of a precooked, dehydrated, grain cereal product that is rapidly reconstitutable with liquid to form a coarse textured cereal mass suitable for infant feeding. It has been found that instant-type cereals that have a coarse texture can be formed by modifications in formulation composition and processing prior to conventional drying treatment on a drum dryer.

By providing for reducing sugars in an amount from 12 to 30 wt % of the grain cereal slurry and subjecting the slurry to sterilization conditions of greater temperature and line pressure, the resulting drum-dried product possesses the desired coarse texture, yet remains fully assimilable by an infant between six months and two years of age.

Cereals

In one embodiment, the product is made from a slurry having a significantly higher malt concentration than any previously employed. More particularly, a malt concentration in excess of 3% by weight, such as 3 to 7% by weight is preferred. Essential to this embodiment is to first subject such a modified cereal slurry to starch hydrolysis through the use of malt enzyme (diastase) digestion at 140° to 160°F for 10 to 30 minutes in order to convert at least part of the starch to reducing sugars, 12 to 30%, preferably 18 to 24%. Other diastatic enzymes that appear to be useful for starch reduction include the mixture of α-amylase and β-amylase from fungal, bacterial or animal sources.

In a second embodiment, dextrose is added to the initial slurry ingredients in an amount sufficient to provide the aforementioned concentration of reducing sugar. Under these conditions, starch hydrolysis can be eliminated or at least minimized.

In either embodiment, it has been found to be essential to heat the resulting slurry to 240° to 270°F, while applying a line pressure of 35 to 55 psig, while holding the heated slurry under these conditions of temperature and pressure for 45 seconds. It has been found that the resulting drum-dried product can be reconstituted to have a mouthfeel heretofore unobtainable by conventional techniques. It has been found desirable to control the fat level of the product in the range of 7 to 9% by weight. With respect to protein level, it has been found necessary in forming the product to adjust protein level to 17 to 19% by weight.

The use of up to 10% of a high-protein material, such as soy flour, in combination with a slurry of at least one cereal grain has been found to further enhance the texture of the reconstituted product. It has been found that when the concentration of soy flour is increased so that the protein content of the cereal is at least 25%, with the obvious decrease in the other cereal ingredients, here again the initial step of enyzme hydrolysis is not necessary. Heating such a slurry under the aforementioned conditions of temperature and pressure (200° to 308°F, 30 to 55 psig) for about 45 seconds produces the desired texture.

Example: Oatmeal Cereal — In a dry ingredient blender were mixed 100 lb of oat flour, 5 lb of malted barley flour, 1.6 lb of calcium sulfate, 1.5 lb of vanilla sugar, 0.25 lb of vitamin mix (containing niacinamide, riboflavin, pyridoxine hydrochloride, and thiamine mononitrate) and 0.06 lb of electrolytic iron. The blended ingredients were then passed through a finisher where 60 gallons of water were slurried therewith.

The slurry was heated for about 20 minutes at 140°F in a cook tank and thereafter transferred through a tangential heater maintained at 240°F where the slurry was subjected to a sterilization line pressure of 50 psig. The pressure was accomplished by providing a girdler valve within the sterilization line and adjusted to 50 psig. The resulting gelatinized sterilized slurry was fed to a conventional double drum dryer, with the drums operating at about 50 psig internal pressure. The drums rotated at 4 rpm, and the dried sheets were removed with doctor blades. The sheets were then flaked to the desired size, screened and packaged. The size of the flakes was in the range of 0.25" to 1.0".

The above-described cereal was prepared for eating by placing 1 oz of the cereal in a bowl and adding ½ to ⅔ cup hot or cold water, milk or formula. Upon addition of water, the instant cereal rapidly reconstituted to a porridge having the desired flavor and coarse texture.

Low Salt Precooked Cereal

V.J. Kelly, L.L. Cloud and W.J. Smalligan; U.S. Patent 3,930,027; December 30, 1975; assigned to Gerber Products Company describe a process which relates to the preparation of a precooked, dehydrated grain cereal product that can be either salt-free or contain a low salt content, as well as higher conventional levels of salt. The process provides a dehydrated product that is rapidly reconstitutable with liquid to form a homogeneous smooth-textured cereal mass with the distinctive flavor of the original cereal grain and is especially suitable for infant or geriatric feeding.

It has been found that the salt concentration of the grain cereal slurry can be substantially reduced or actually entirely eliminated, without adversely affecting the ultimate product quality or overall efficiency of product dehydration, by completely hydrolyzing a portion, e.g., from 30 to 70% by weight of the total starch in the slurry composition.

Futhermore, it has been found that improved results are obtained whether the remaining nonhydrolyzed starch is separated prior to initial gelatinization and then returned to the slurry in an ungelatinized form prior to enzyme hydrolysis, or separated after total gelatinization from the slurry portion to be hydrolyzed and thereafter readded to the hydrolyzed portion of the slurry when enzyme conversion has been completed. With either procedure, the resulting slurry is readily dried and exhibits highly desirable reconstitution characteristics including an appetizing flavor.

Grain starch granules are formed of two basic types of starch molecule, i.e., the linear maltose polymer-amylose and the branched maltose polymer-amylopectin. The size of the maltose polymer and the amount of each type of the polymer that is present in the starch granule determine the specific properties of the individual starch. Both types are normally synthesized by and are present in plants. Most starch granules, as produced by nature, contain approximately 20 to 30% of the amylose-type molecule, with the balance being amylopectin-type molecules.

The starch granules are formed by attractive forces between these large carbohydrate molecules, i.e., the linear portions of the molecule tend to associate together into micelles which bind the various molecules together into a crystalline-like structure. Such a structure is fairly rigid and insoluble in cold water. However, when the temperature of a suspension of starch in water is increased to or above a critical point, called the gelatinization temperature, water penetrates the granules, causing them to swell and produce a viscous mass. Gelatinization temperatures vary from about 140° to 167°F depending upon the particular type of starch involved. By increasing the temperature above that required for gelatinization, i.e., to about 220°F, adequate gelatinization of the cereal grain is thus insured.

Treatment of gelatinized starches with an enzyme such as amylase converts the starch, i.e., hydrolyzes it, to produce lower viscosity types of molecules such as dextrins and maltose. Ultimate enzyme conversion with an enzyme such as amylase results in the starch molecule being depolymerized to maltose and, depending upon the structure of the starch, various higher sugars such as maltotriose, maltotetrose, etc. This process involves conventional gelatinization and subsequent hydrolysis, but in a manner whereby the ultimate portion reduced to dextrin and maltose is readily controlled within the concentration required to obtain satisfactory slurry properties and reconstitution characteristics, even in the absence of conventional concentrations of salt.

The susceptibility of the ultimate packaged cereal product to caking when subjected to storage humidities in excess of 70% RH is directly related to the maltose content. By employing this process, maltose concentration is readily controlled at the optimum concentration of about 14%. Thus, when the enzyme is allowed to react on previously gelatinized starch molecules, cooled to a temperature in the range of normal enzyme activity, the time of reaction, the enzyme concentration and the temperature of the reaction do not require the precise control previously found mandatory in conventional gelatinization/hydrolysis cereal processes.

It appears that enzyme hydrolysis is limited to that portion of the cereal slurry starch that has previously been gelatinized. Furthermore, by heating the starch slurry to a temperature significantly above the gelatinization temperature of the starch, i.e., in about the range of 160° to 220°F, not only will all the starch present be gelatinized, but any naturally occuring enzymes will be in part permanently inactivated or destroyed. The process is particularly useful where the grain requires high-temperature gelatinization, higher than the inactivation temperature of most diastatic enzyme systems. Thus grains such as long grain rice can be utilized more readily in cereal preparation.

As a result, subsequent quantity control of the amount of gelatinized starch that is allowed to be subjected to enzyme conversion will enable the hydrolysis to be conducted without stringent process conditions, i.e., hydrolysis of the gelatinized starch can go to completion. The ultimate effect of such uniformly complete hydrolysis appears to be that the dextrins are more completely hydrolyzed. Therefore, dehydration is not dependent on the presence of salt as an aid thereto.

Example 1: A formulation was prepared in the following proportions:

Ingredient	Quantity Percent by Weight*
Rice flour	70.0
Rice polish	25.0
Dicalcium phosphate	2.6
Sodium iron pyrophosphate	0.8
Rice oil	0.7
Vitamin mix	0.2
Malt	0.7

*Solids content only

Sufficient water was added to reduce the overall solids content to about 22.6%. The slurry at about room temperature was pumped through a line strainer having a screen size of 0.060" to an agitating heater at a temperature of about 210°F and held for about 15 minutes. The slurry was then removed and approximately two-thirds, by weight thereof, transferred to a holding tank and the temperature adjusted to about 90°F.

After about 17 minutes at this temperature, the slurry containing hydrolyzed starch was recombined with the portion containing gelatinized starch and fed to a conventional double drum dryer, each drum operating at an interval pressure of 80 psig. The drums were rotated at 5 rpm and the dried sheet easily removed with doctor blades. The resulting sheet was nonplastic, continuous and had a film thickness of about 5 mils. Similar tests were conducted with corn, barley, wheat and oat and mixtures thereof.

Example 2: Using the slurry formulation of Example 1, a quantity of slurry was divided into 2 portions in about a 2 to 1 weight ratio. The larger portion was subjected to gelatinization as in Example 1, at 170°F. Thereafter, the remaining ungelatinized slurry, still at room temperature, was added thereto, lowering the temperature to about 120°F. Hydrolysis was allowed to occur for about 20 minutes. The resulting slurry was again drum dried and the dehydrated sheet easily removed from the drum surfaces.

In each of Examples 1 and 2, the resulting cereal was found to have excellent reconstitution characteristics and a highly appetizing taste.

Fried Swelled Cereal Particles

M. Takatsu, F. Ohnishi and J. Minami; U.S. Patent 3,914,454; October 21, 1975; assigned to Nissin Shokuhin Kaisha, Ltd., Japan provide a method for preparing cereal foods which can be cooked readily and in a very short period of time. Swelled cereal particles are partially dehydrated to a water content of 8 to 25% by weight and are thereafter fried for a short period of time. Immediately and before cooling, oil is removed from the fried particles.

Cereals are washed with water to remove foreign materials, dipped in water, and then freed of water. When the cereals have a strong offensive odor, they are first subjected to a deodorizing treatment by dipping them in a 0.3 to 1.0% solution of H_2O_2, a 0.5 to 2.0% solution of sodium bicarbonate or a 0.3 to 1.0% solution of phosphoric acid, and then freed of water.

Afterwards the cereals are coated uniformly with a nontoxic substance, such as an edible surfactant or edible oil, and then heated to gelatinize. Either normal steam-cooking or pressurized steam-cooking will be carried out to gelatinize the whole interior of the cereal particles. The addition of edible surfactants or edible oil is intended to prevent the agglomeration of cereal particles in the course of drying after steam-cooking; thus it is sufficient to add a small amount, i.e., 0.1 to 1.0% by weight of such substances.

Next, the particles which have been gelatinized are dried at 20° to 100°C by means of hot air until a water content of the kernel particles is decreased to 8 to 25%. The range of the water content of the dried particles should strictly be controlled because it has a considerable effect on the degree of swelling during subsequent frying and on the quality of cooked cereal foods.

The cereals after being dried to 8 to 25% of water content, are then subjected to a frying treatment for as short a time as about 5 to 30 seconds in an edible oil previously heated to a temperature at least as high as 150° to 220°C to obtain swelled cereals. Water in them is rapidly removed by this frying treatment, resulting in the formation of swelled and porous particles. This treatment must be carried out with special attention.

What is essential to the treatment is to maintain the edible oil at a high temperature of 150° to 220°C. For example, temperatures below 150°C cause a lower degree of swelling, thereby reducing the quality of cooked cereal foods, and temperatures above 220°C cause the so-called browning reaction, thereby adversely affecting their appearance. Oil attached to the fried particles thus obtained penetrates into the swelled kernels in part to replace part of the water; however in a large part the oil sticks to the surface.

The next treatment is a deoiling process in which oil attached to the particles are reduced to less than 16.5% by weight based upon the weight of the particles from the fried particles. This deoiling can generally be carried out by using centrifugal force, hot air, or chemical solvents such as ethyl alcohol, and may also be carried out by means of vacuum. Thus, it is sufficient to be able to reduce the oil content by any conventional technique.

When the oil content in the swelled cereal particles is reduced by the deoiling treatment, water is allowed to penetrate into the particles rapidly during cooking, thereby accelerating the restoration of the particles. And the small amount of oil still remaining in the particles after deoiling acts effectively to improve the quality of cooked cereal foods and provides a quality superior to that of conventional puffed cereal foods.

When cooked cereal foods such as cooked rice, pilaff and fried rice, are made from the cereal food prepared by the above-described process, it is sufficient for good taste to place the kernels in a frying pan or cooker, add water and heat for 3 minutes.

Uniform Textured Cereal

In a process described by *V.J. Kelly and W. Smalligan; U.S. Patent 3,887,714; June 3, 1975; assigned to Gerber Products Company,* instant-type grain cereals are provided which are rapidly reconstituted into smooth, uniform porridges and are substantially free of other than the specific grain cereal and desirable food supplements, e.g., iron and vitamins and, optionally, fruit. A mixture of a minor amount of pregelatinized flakes of the cereal is combined with a major amount of quick cooking cereal flakes which, upon the addition of boiling water, is reconstituted to a uniform, desirably textured and flavored product.

In one method, oat bits are allowed to pass downwardly through a laterally tapering long vessel, whose lower walls are inclined inwardly so as to feed the oat bits to a grooved roller which feeds the oat bits between flaking rollers. The oat bits are fed at a rate so as to keep the steamer vessel filled. Steam pipes, which extend downwardly through the vessel, have openings near the central portion of the vessel so that steam is brought in contact with the oat bits as they move downwardly through the vessel. Ordinarily, the oats are steamed in the vessel for about 8 to 10 minutes. After flaking, the product is quick oats or baby oats, depending on the degree of fineness of the flakes.

Various pretreatments of the oats include dehulling oats, steel cutting the resultant groats, and the like. The treatment may include both dehydration and hydration steps. Desirably, the final oats will vary in size from 0.05 to 0.25 inch cross section.

The quick cooking wheat flake is prepared in substantially the same manner as the oat flake, which is considered to be representative of cereal flakes generally.

The pregelatinized base flake will normally be made from the appropriate cereal flour and a mineral supplement. Salts, such as sodium chloride, calcium phosphate or calcium carbonate, and other minor additives including malt, vitamins, phosphatides, e.g., lecithin, vegetable oils, food acids, and the like may be included. Optionally, a major amount of a fruit puree may be added, such as bananas, prunes, strawberries, apples and the like.

Conveniently, a mixture containing 80 to 95 wt % of the appropriate grain cereal flour, from 4 to 8 wt % of a mineral supplement such as calcium carbonate, and from 0.5 to 1.5 wt % of malt are mixed. In addition, minor amounts of food supplements may be added, normally being in the range of 0.1 to 2 wt % in total amount, individual amounts varying from 0.01 to 0.5. Furthermore, when desired, from 6 to 10 wt % of salt can be included.

The dry mixture may then be slurried with from about 2.5 to 10.0 times its weight of water to provide a slurry. The slurry is then heated in the range of 190° to 205°F, in conventional equipment. The time employed is sufficient to ensure the gelatinization of the cereal flour. Alternatively, the heating can be eliminated and gelatinization accomplished by drying the cold slurry on a drying surface as hereinafter described.

Drying is accomplished by any conventional equipment. The dehydrated base material can be removed from the drying surface as a continuous sheet, usually having a thickness of about 4 to 7 mils. The particles may then be flaked in accordance with the desired size.

When it is desired to include a fruit flavoring in the instant cereal, the pregelatinized grain flakes will be employed as the medium for providing the fruit flavoring. Usually, a composition as described above, containing the flour, salt and other ingredients, will be combined with about 2 to 4 times by weight the amount of a fruit puree to provide a final product with the addition of water, having about 25 wt % solids. The slurry is then dried as described previously.

To provide the final cereal, the pregelatinized base flakes and the quick cooking cereal flakes are combined, with or without the addition of other additives, such as flavorings, food supplements, or the like. The weight ratio of the quick cooking cereal flakes to the pregelatinized base flakes will generally be in a weight ratio 1.5 to 4:1. In addition, it is desirable to add from 0.01 to 0.10 wt % of the total mixture of electrolytic iron as a food supplement. Where a fruit flavored pregelatinized base is employed, sugar will also be desirably added in relatively large amounts, usually from about 10 to 30 wt % of the final composition.

Example: In the mixing vessel are slurried together 50 lb of oat flour, 5 lb of salt, 3.95 lb of calcium carbonate, 0.63 lb of malt, and 0.28 lb of vitamin mix (containing niacinamide, riboflavin, pyridoxine hydrochloride, and thiamin mononitrate), with 33 gallons of water. The slurry is then heated for a short time with mixing at a temperature of from about 140° to 160°F and then fed to a conventional double drum dryer, with the drums operating at about 80 psig internal pressure. The drums rotate at 3 rpm, and the dried sheets are removed with doctor blades. The sheets are then flaked to the desired size and screened.

Approximately 5 lb of quick cooking oat flakes are blended with 0.036 lb of electrolytic iron, followed by adding 70 lb of quick cooking oat flakes and 25 lb of the oatmeal base flakes, and the entire mixture blended together. The size of the two different flakes is in the range of 0.05" to 0.25".

The cereal is prepared for eating by placing 1 oz of the cereal in a bowl and adding one-half to two-thirds cup of boiling water. The cereal retains a uniform composition during storage and handling. Upon addition of water, the instant cereal rapidly reconstitutes to a homogeneous, smooth-textured porridge having the desired flavor and texture of a cooked porridge.

Instant Corn Grits

It is the object of a process described by *R.G. Hyldon; U.S. Patent 3,792,956; February 19, 1974; assigned to The Quaker Oats Company* to produce an instant corn grits product which may be prepared as corn grits by the mere addition of warm water to the product in a serving bowl, which product then acquires the texture and flavor characteristics of conventionally cooked corn grits. The so-produced corn grits product is also free of emulsifier.

The process comprises mixing corn grits, critical amounts of water and critical amounts of polysaccharide gum, rapidly heating the mixture to 71° to 100°C within 30 seconds of the time the corn grits, water, and gum are substantially mixed together, immediately drying the heated mixture in the form of a thin sheet on a drum dryer and collecting the dried sheet of product and comminuting it to form an instant-type product.

The polysaccharide gums used must be capable of hydrating rapidly with the addition of water and must be edible. Edible polysaccharide gums include both true gums of vegetable origin and synthetic gums such as carboxymethylcellulose, methylcellulose, and other cellulose derivatives which approximate the vegetable gums in physical and chemical properties.

In general, to be satisfactory, any gum employed must be edible, have no undesirable flavor, and disperse rapidly in hot water. The concentration of the polysaccharide gum is critical. The polysaccharide gum must be present in an amount preferably from 1.0 to 3.0% by weight of the finished corn grits product. The elimination of an emulsifier is accomplished by a rapid heating step followed by an immediate drying step.

This product is different from those made by inclusion of emulsifiers. This difference is most dramatically illustrated by a comparison of the density of the two products. If the process uses emulsifiers to obtain a product, the volume of a normal 24-gram serving of the grits (before water is added to the bowl) will be about ¼ cup which is a density of about 1,536 g/gal. The product produced by this process, however, has a volume of about ⅓ cup for a 24-gram serving which is a density of about 1,152 g/gal. This product is therefore about 25% less dense than prior known products. The product is further distinguished by its extremely fast cooking time, that is, by the fact that it reaches a very high viscosity within seconds of the time it is mixed with boiling water.

Example: A metering system can be employed to mix corn grits, carboxymethylcellulose and water at room temperature and immediately inject the mixture into a steam injector. The metering system is adjusted such that the mixture is comprised of 100 parts by weight water, 50 parts by weight corn grits, and 0.028 parts by weight carboxymethylcellulose. Steam is injected rapidly into the mixture as it passes through the steam injector and within about 20 seconds of the time that the materials are mixed together the mixture has a temperature of 95°C.

The mixture at the 95°C temperature is immediately deposited in the trough of a drum dryer. Within about 2 minutes of the time that the mixture reaches the 95°C temperature substantially all of the mixture is passed through the nip of the dryer. The heated mixture forms a thin sheet on the internally heated rotating double drum dryer and the product is then removed in a thin sheet having a thickness of about 0.025" and comminuted to the particle size of corn grits.

⅓ cup (about 24.0 grams) of the corn grits product are placed in a bowl. ½ cup water (preferably boiling) is poured over the product and stirred until blended and seasoned to taste. The product is found to have the taste and texture characteristics of normally prepared corn grits.

NUTRITIONALLY IMPROVED PRODUCTS

Palatability Improvement Using Yeast and Malt with Soy Additive

G.J. Haas; U.S. Patent 3,920,852; November 18, 1975; assigned to General Foods Corporation describes a process in which the palatability of breakfast cereals containing soy products is improved by mixing dried inactive yeast and malt with the soy. The soy being treated may include raw, cooked or debittered soybeans, soy grits, soy flakes, soy meal, soy flour, soy protein isolates and concentrates, and the like. The soy may be defatted or not.

The supplement of this process is particularly useful in ready-to-eat and other breakfast cereals. Dried, inactive yeast is added directly to the soy to prepare a flavorful supplement or is added to the food product containing the soy. In preparing cereal products it is preferred to heat the cereal formulation after addition of soy and dried, inactive yeast such as by cooking, baking, toasting or combinations thereof well-known in the cereal field. Heating insures the development of optimum flavor.

The dried, inactive yeast may be any commercially available product such as yeast flakes, Torula yeast or *Saccharomyces fragilis* or equivalent which has been dried and inactivated with heat. The quantity of dried, inactive yeast that is mixed with the soy may be regulated to give mixtures having various degrees of flavor and protein value. Up to 50% by weight dried, inactive yeast by weight of soy may be employed although 0.05 to 25% is normally sufficient to reduce the beany-bitter flavor of the soy. It is preferred to employ from 3 to 20% dried, inactive yeast by weight of soy.

Soy may be employed at a level of 0.5 to 30% of the food with 1 to 25% of concentrated soy preferred for breakfast cereal formulations. For use as an ingredient in breads, biscuits, rolls, cookies, cakes, doughnuts, pancakes, soup bases, gravy bases or meat extracts up to 30% soy may be used.

Example 1: A dry blend of 217.6 grams rice flour, 64 grams corn flour, 12.3 grams wheat gluten, 7.9 grams wheat germ, 44 grams Promine D soy and a mixture of 3.1 grams dry Torula yeast and 5 grams primary yeast flakes is prepared in a Hobart mixer. A wet mix containing 30.3 grams sucrose, 9.5 grams sodium chloride and 26 grams conventional malt syrup (regular malt water extract) is prepared and added to the dry mix gradually with 124 grams of distilled water so that a uniform distribution of liquid is obtained.

The mixture is extruded through a metal die into cereal ropes and then autoclaved at 15 psig for 20 minutes. The cereal ropes are then cut and pressed into flakes. The flakes are dried to a crisp texture at 66°C and toasted at 176°C to a golden color. When 16 grams of Munich malt or caramel malt is used to replace the 5 grams of yeast flakes there is obtained an equally palatable debittered cereal.

Example 2: A dry mix is prepared as in Example 1 except that the Promine D and dried, inactive yeast (Torula and the flakes) is replaced by 60 grams of a supplement prepared as follows: To 50 grams of Promine D in a quart jar is added 10 grams of Torula yeast flour. The jar is rotated by hand for about two minutes until a uniform blend is obtained, the degree of blend readily determined by appearance. After moistening, the mix is treated as in Example 1 to prepare a debittered cereal.

Additive-Free Product

W.A. Bonner, M.R. Gould and T.E. Milling; U.S. Patent 3,876,811; April 8, 1975; assigned to The Quaker Oats Company describe a ready-to-eat cereal product of natural ingredients which is distinguished in that it is substantially free from additives and from severe processing conditions. The cereal has a base made of cereal flakes, coconut, milk solids, and edible nuts, with a coating made of brown sugar, pure nonhydrogenated vegetable oil, and sugar solution with a specified density and moisture content.

The process for preparing this cereal is as follows. A base is prepared by mixing 22 to 28 parts by weight oat flakes, 8 to 22 parts by weight wheat flakes, 7 to 9 parts by weight almonds, 6 to 8 parts by weight coconut, and 6 to 8 parts by weight milk solids. A coating material is prepared by mixing 17 to 20 parts by weight brown sugar, 7 to 13 parts by weight coconut oil, and ¼ to 2½ parts by weight honey, with sufficient water to make the coating liquid. The coating material is heated to 140° to 160°F. The coating material is enrobed onto the base, and the enrobed base is dried to below 3½% by weight moisture to give a product having a density of 0.15 to 0.35 oz/in^3. The coated base, or ready-to-eat cereal product may also include from 5 to 25 parts by weight dehydrated fruit. The dehydrated fruit is optional but is highly desirable.

If dehydrated fruit is to be included in the ready-to-eat cereal, then the dehydrated fruit is mixed with the dried enrobed base and 5 to 25 parts by weight of the dehydrated fruits are added to the dried coated base. The final moisture of the product, including the fruit, must then fall within the range of 1.0 to 5.0% by weight. An unusually good product can be produced by a process wherein the coated base is formed into a sheet, such as by depositing it on a moving belt, prior to drying and then subdivided to an average particle size of about one-fourth inch after drying. The resulting texture is excellent and the product is uniform in particle size and devoid of dust and fines which diminish acceptance.

Example: A cereal base was prepared by mixing 31 parts by weight oat flakes, 15 parts by weight wheat flakes, 8 parts by weight almonds, 7½ parts by weight coconut, and 7½ parts by weight nonfat dry milk solids. These ingredients were thoroughly mixed in a mixer. A coating syrup was prepared by mixing 19 parts by weight brown sugar with 11 parts by weight coconut oil, 1½ parts by weight honey, and 10 parts by weight water. This coating material was mixed together and heated to a temperature of about 150°F. After the ingredients had been thoroughly mixed at the temperature, the base and coating were placed in a cereal enrober and the coating enrobed onto the cereal base. The product was then dried in an oven to a moisture content of about 3% by weight. The drying was accomplished in an oven having inlet air temperatures of between 270° and 290°F but the temperature of the cereal was never high enough to substantially degrade either the cereal base or the coating thereon. The product thus produced was a highly desirable ready-to-eat cereal product of natural ingredients unadulterated by chemical addition.

Sodium Caseinate Used as High Protein Additive

E.C. Schwab, W.D. Petersen and E. Bumbiers; U.S. Patent 3,873,748; March 25, 1975; assigned to General Mills, Inc. describe a process for making high protein ready-to-eat puffed breakfast cereals having unique textural properties.

In the process, a cooked, dried and ground dough of cereal flour, selected from corn flour, rice flour and mixtures thereof, is mixed with dry sodium caseinate and the mixture added to water in amounts sufficient to bring the overall moisture content to about 26 to 29% by weight of the mixture. The dry dough and the sodium caseinate compete for and tenaciously hold the water. The mixture is very stiff. Severe mechanical work in the form of kneading and pulling is applied to the mixture under conditions which hold the temperature of the mass below about 145°F until a stiff, viscous, sticky, opaque, homogeneous, semiplastic mass is obtained.

Working the dough into a state of opaque, homogeneous semiplasticity prior to extrusion is essential. The worked dough is then extruded at temperatures below about 165°F and the resulting rope is cut into pellets. The material after extrusion is translucent and semiplastic. The change from opaqueness to translucency of the dough indicates that some type of change in the dough occurred during extrusion. Following the extrusion step, the pellets are cooled and preferably sheeted. The sheeted material is slit and cut into pieces which are dried and subsequently puffed and toasted in an air flow fluid bed oven.

In the process, it is found that to obtain the unique puffed texture which characterizes this ready-to-eat breakfast food, the cereal dough should contain corn flour or rice flour or mixtures thereof. It is also found that after reconstitution of the mixture of dry dough and dry sodium caseinate, the moisture level of 26 to 27% by weight of the reconstituted mass was essential. Moisture levels below 26% by weight of the mixture produce bubbling in the final product. Moisture levels below 25% by weight of the mixture produce a final product which is gummy and rubbery. At moisture levels above 29%, handling of the mix is difficult. In addition, it was found that from among the many known protein sources, sodium caseinate was vastly superior in producing good flavor and puffed characteristics in a fluid bed puffed ready-to-eat breakfast cereal. Other proteins such as soy protein can be used to some extent in conjunction with the sodium caseinate. Soy protein, however, does not provide the degree of puffing obtained from sodium caseinate.

Finally it was found that the mixture of dry cereal dough, sodium caseinate and water should be worked into a homogeneous semiplastic mass prior to extrusion and preliminary to fluid bed drying. By semiplastic mass is meant a mass capable of being molded or receiving form when a pressure greater than 200 psig is applied. Severe working of the dough at this point develops sufficient plasticity in the dough that a high degree of puffing and smoothing of the pieces is obtained in the fluid bed. Working the dough to a state of plasticity prior to extrusion requires severe working conditions and a considerable power input. The form of work is kneading and pulling the dough. Best results were obtained by working the dough with counterrotating, rigid fingers. After working, the dough is characteristically opaque, homogeneous and semiplastic.

In a preferred formula, the cereal component may contain, in addition to corn and/or rice flour, regular crystalline sugar for sweetness, brown sugar for flavor, salt, malt or corn syrup and a small amount of oil. It can also contain natural or artificial flavors and small amounts of vitamins. A small amount of wheat or corn starch can be added as a puffing aid. These additive type ingredients may make up as much as about 40% by weight of the cereal component. The moisture level of the initial cereal component is preferably about 7 to 10% by weight.

The product has a uniform bubbled interior structure. There are substantially no off flavors due to protein heating. Furthermore, the final product is substantially resistant to liquids and does not become soggy.

Example: The dry ingredients in the initial cereal component were screened to remove large pieces and foreign material from the mix. The dry ingredients were then fed to a cooker and mixed. The fluid ingredients were then added and mixed with the dry ingredients. The complete cereal base had the following formulation:

Ingredient	Percent
Corn meal degermed yellow corn	51.336
Rice flour	18.000
Sucrose	15.000
Wheat starch	4.000
Sugar, brown	4.000
Salt, cereal	3.250
Malt syrup	2.000
Coconut oil 92°	2.000
Vitamins	0.414

The cereal base was mixed in the cooker. Water was added at the exit end of the agitator section and at the entrance to the extrusion auger. The agitator temperature was 210°F at a feed rate of about 8 lb/min. The cereal base was moved by the auger through a die. The die temperature was about 310° to 350°F. The cereal base was extruded through $9/32$" holes. Two ropes were extruded. The ropes fell onto a feed belt which transfers them to a temper belt. The temper belt carried the ropes to a cutter where they were cut into pieces approximately ¾" in length. The pieces were conveyed to a drier. At temperatures of approximately 190°F and belt speeds of 15 fpm on the heating sections, the pieces were dried down to about 6.5 to 8.5% moisture based on the weight of the mixture. The dried pieces were then ground in a hammer mill and ground through a 1/32" round-holed screen. The ground cereal base was then mixed with sodium caseinate. The proportions were about 23.1% sodium casinate by weight based on the weight of the mixture and about 76.9% ground, dried dough by weight based on the weight of the mixture.

The cereal base-sodium caseinate mixture was conveyed into a high powered kneader mixer with counterrotating, rigid fingers and a power rate usage of 15 to 20 kw/hr. After a period of dry working 1.9 lb of water were added per 7.1 lb dry mix to bring the moisture level of the mixture to about 26.5%. The mixer jacket was cooled with water to maintain the temperature of the mixture below about 145°F. The moistened mixture was then worked until a homogeneous semiplastic, opaque dough was obtained.

Once the above dough condition was obtained the dough was extruded through a breaker plate having 3/32" holes and then through a die having 3/16" holes. The temperature of the die head was about 175°F. Actual dough temperature at extrusion was about 167°F. The extrusion pressure was 650 to 850 psig. The extruder operated at 14.5 rpm. The extruded rope was cut into pellets about 3/16" long.

The pellets were cooled to about 95°F in an air enrober and then moved to a surge belt. The surge belt provided a constant feed rate to an agitator hopper. The agitator hopper fed the dough pellets onto shred rolls, one of which was corrugated. The shred rolls were cooled with cold water. The shred roll pressure was 1,000 psig. The shred rolls were set at 40 fpm. The sheet was slit into 7/16" wide strips which were subsequently cut into 5/8" flat rectangular pellets with corrugations on one side. The pellets were cooled with an air blast in an enrober. The pellets were then dried in a helix drier in two stages.

The first stage was at a temperature of about 140°F for a period of 30 minutes. The second stage was at a temperature of about 134°F for a period of 180 minutes. During the drying the pellets were case hardened. The pellets were then conveyed to a fluid bed where they were puffed in two stages. The first stage was at a temperature of about 450°F for a period of 54.5 seconds. The second stage was at a temperature of about 330°F for a period of 28 seconds. The volume of the final product was 5 oz/128 in^3. The final moisture was 2.0%. The final product was crisp and retained its crispness in milk. There were no off flavors. The bubbled interior structure was uniform.

Puffed Item Having up to 60% Protein

Protein is an essential component of human growth. Attempts have been made to utilize various nonmeat protein sources to provide adequate protein for purposes of nutrition. Unfortunately many of the high-quality nonmeat protein sources are of minimal palatability. For this reason these proteins have been combined with other foods. For example, several attempts have been made to produce a so-called protein-fortified breakfast cereal. This type of breakfast cereal, usually, has protein from a vegetable-derived product such as soy or other oil seeds or has milk-derived protein such as casein or refined whey fractions.

Cereals

So far, attempts to produce fortified, ready-to-eat breakfast cereals have centered around making of flakes having protein coated on the surface.

One of the problems with this approach is that the proteins are characterized by somewhat objectionable flavors and by concentrating the protein on the outside of the ready-to-eat breakfast cereal the flavor intensity of the protein is also increased. Another problem associated with coating the cereal flakes with a supplemental protein source is the change in rehydration characteristics. These rehydration characteristics are vastly altered when protein is added to the surface at a level of say 20%. Because of this, the amount of protein which can be added to a flake-type breakfast cereal is severely limited, e.g., one part protein to two parts of cereal with this protein being adhered to the outside of the flake. However, the preferred maximum when soy (one of the preferred protein sources) is used, is only half of the above level.

W.R. Malzahn; U.S. Patent 3,852,491; December 3, 1974; assigned to Ralston Purina Company describes a process by which a puffed ready-to-eat breakfast cereal containing up to about 60% protein is made by blending a bland edible protein material and a farinaceous material, adding moisture to a level of 17 to 30%, kneading the mixture and extruding it at pressures greater than about 1,000 psig at a temperature greater than the boiling point of water.

There are a variety of factors which influence the degree of puffing. The most important of these factors are the amount of moisture in the dough, the presence and type of nonfarinaceous additives, temperature and pressure. A puffed ready-to-eat breakfast cereal is herein defined as an expanded product with a bulk density of 0.046 to 0.135 g/cc having a farinaceous matrix and a cellular structure which will rapidly lose its structure when compared to a product having a proteinaceous fiber-like component, upon subjection to agitation in boiling water.

For the production of this product moisture added to form the dough immediately prior to its entrance into the extruder is in the range of 10 to 30% by weight of the ingredients. (The ingredients themselves will generally contain from 8 to 10% by weight of moisture; therefore, the total moisture is somewhat higher than the figures represented by adding moisture.)

Pressure needed to produce the product is at least about 1,000 psig at protein levels of 35 to 40% (lower pressures can be used for the higher protein levels within the range of the product). Maximum pressures used are dependent mostly on the capabilities of the extruder although pressures up to 3,000 to 5,000 psig are adequate and are easily obtainable on common food extruders.

Maximum temperature need be only slightly above that of boiling water. It has been found that a product temperature greater than 230°F is sufficient to produce a puffed product within the definition given above when protein is added at a level of 55% ingredient weight at a pressure of 1,500 psig.

Maximum temperature is generally determined by that which will decompose or biologically inhibit the ingredients; however, when the higher protein levels of this process are used, maximum values are established by another criterion. For example, at protein levels of 55% the formation of a fiber-like protein structure becomes apparent where product temperature measured in the exit orifice exceeds 315°F with an added moisture level of about 30% at a pressure of 1,500 psig.

In another instance with the same protein level, lower moisture, i.e., 17% by weight and 2,200 psig, dough temperatures greater than about 345°F were needed to induce formation of a proteinaceous fiber. In both cases other extrusion conditions were identical.

While temperatures greater than boiling are required and temperatures much greater than 350°F will cause some damage to the product, other maximum and minimum conditions are not so easily established. In general, formation of fiber-like proteinaceous strands is dependent on the severity of the extrusion. As either temperature, pressure screw pitch or screw rpm increases the possibility of fiber-like formations also increases. Also, the lower the moisture level the more likely the extrudate is to form fibers. Therefore, the lowest temperature and pressure to produce expansion should be used at the higher protein levels within the ranges described above.

The farinaceous source material for the product may be virtually any grain with the understanding that materials which are difficultly gelatinizable are not preferred because they have a tendency to scorch, e.g., unmodified corn starch. Some modified corn starches will, of course, be suitable because some of the treatments involved aid in the ease of gelatinization.

Certainly, pregelatinized corn starch as a farinaceous source material will provide no problem. For reasons of nutrition it is preferred that there is a minimum amount of reducing sugar present in the farinaceous material. The reducing sugars react with certain amino acids which are present in proteinaceous materials and which are necessary for nutrition, particularly lysine. This reaction is known as the Maillard or protein browning reaction and inhibits the biological activity of the amino acids.

The choice of protein will depend primarily on economics. Although soy and other oil seed proteins are generally somewhat more objectionable from a flavor standpoint, the process tends to minimize the objectionable flavors and sweetened cereals especially exhibit almost no discernible beany taste.

Whey as a protein source, is reasonable economically, but has problems which are related to the Maillard reaction described above. Whey protein is very seldom available in pure form and carries substantial amounts of lactose, a fairly strong reducing sugar as it is sold commercially. This, of course, limits the practicality of the use of whey as the sole protein source.

However, as a matter of economics, whey may be added in conjunction with the vegetable-derived proteins or possibly in conjunction with casein. For purposes of nutrition, various amino acids may be added at some stage in the process to more perfectly balance the amino acid content in the particular proteinaceous material chosen. For example, most vegetable protein is deficient in lysine; however, soy protein has ample lysine but is deficient in another amino acid, methionine. For proper nutrition therefore, supplementation with the proper amino acids is desirable.

In all examples the proteinaceous source and the farinaceous material were mixed together in a dry state, although containing their natural moisture. The moisture in the ingredients of the dry blend is between 8 and 10%. This dry blending was then followed by mixing with water. The moistened mixture was then extruded through a six zone extruder containing a constant pitch screw having a variable root diameter with a length to diameter ratio of 24:1 through a circular extruder orifice with a diameter of 0.172". The rpm on the auger screw was maintained between 90 and 120 to help maintain a continuous extrudate flow.

The product temperature was measured as the product exited thorugh the extruder orifice. It has been found that temperatures in the sixth or outermost zone are 5° to 15°F higher than the product temperature measured at the extruder orifice as the temperature increased from 250° to 300°F. In the temperature range from 300° to 350°F in the sixth zone the product exit temperature is 15° to 40°F lower than the temperature in the sixth zone.

Example 1: The following formulation was prepared as described above.

Ingredient	Percentage
Soy isolate, spray dried	55
Wheat starch	33
Oat flour	10.5
Salt	1.5

This formulation produced a calculated protein level of 55%. The extrusion took place with the maximum pressure being maintained between 1,000 and 1,500 psig. The temperature in the highest temperature zone, i.e., zone 6 in this example was 355°F. The dough temperature measured at the exit port was increased until a temperature of 315°F was obtained. As the temperature reached this level the dough started to change character and when the dough temperature was raised above 315°F, the dough exhibited the formation of the fiber-like proteinaceous strands mentioned above.

The extrusion run was continued and the dough temperature consistently lowered until at 225°F, the product produced at the exit port of the extruder was devoid of cellular structuring and could no longer be considered expanded. Temperature at zone 6, at the time the dough temperature was measured at 225°F was 230°F. The level of added moisture in this example was 29.85%. The structure on the product made between 225° and 315°F which was cereal-like in appearance, puffed and frangible was similar to other extruded cereal products with the degree of the expansion increasing with increasing temperature.

Example 2: Moisture is a known lubricant and puffing aid for farinaceous systems; therefore, a decrease in moisture, everything being equal, should narrow the temperature range in which the product of this process can be produced. In this example, however, the maximum pressure applied was increased to a level of 2,200 psig. The moisture level in this example was 17% as added moisture. The ingredients were the same as in the above example.

It was found that when the dough temperature was greater than 345°F production of protein fiber-like masses described in the above example commenced. The increase in maximum extrusion pressure, therefore, more than counteracted the decrease in moisture as far as establishing the breadth of the operating temperature range. When this product was placed in water and the water brought to a boil the product structure started to disintegrate.

Example 3: The same ingredients used in Example 1 were used; however, the percentages were changed to yield a product having 42% by ingredient weight calculated protein. The percentages of ingredients are expressed below.

Ingredient	Percentage
Soy protein isolate, spray dried	35
Wheat starch	13
Oat flour	50.5
Salt	1.5

The product in this example extruded at a maximum pressure of 1,200 psig with the same equipment as in the preceding example. It was found, surprisingly, that the temperature of 250°F was needed to produce the minimum amount of puffing within the definition of a ready-to-eat puffed breakfast cereal indicated in the disclosure above. While generally it had been accepted in the art, that protein was a puff inhibitor for farinaceous extrusion, this example shows that, quite the contrary, protein may actually serve as a puff enhancer.

This product sample was sugar coated with a coating comprised of 54.5% white sugar, 6% brown sugar, 1.5% salt, 8% corn syrup, 12% coconut oils and 18% water to produce a 40% weight coating (dry). The product was dried to remove coating by water and a sweetened breakfast cereal with no discernible beany flavor was produced having a protein content of 20%.

Soy Protein and Sodium Bicarbonate Additives

W.T. Bedenk and E.R. Purves; U.S. Patent 3,814,824; June 4, 1974; assigned to The Procter & Gamble Company describe a process for making palatable ready-to-eat breakfast cereals containing soy protein. The incorporation of from 0.2 to 2.0% sodium bicarbonate in a soy protein-fortified cereal food results in the removal of objectionable soy flavor and the emergence of a high-intensity, well-rounded, pleasant flavor.

The soy protein material is mixed with the cooked cereal grain to form a soy-containing cereal dough. The amount of soy material ranges from 5 to 90% of the total weight of the cereal dough, and the amount of cooked cereal grain ranges from 5 to 90% of the total weight of the cereal dough. Other ingredients such as sugar, salt, flavorings, coloring, spices, vitamins, minerals, and antisticking agents can be added to the dough.

It has been found that the incorporation of from about 0.2 to about 2%, by weight of the total cereal ingredients, of sodium bicarbonate in the above-described breakfast cereal products results in the elimination of the undesirable soy flavor and the emergence of a high-intensity, well-rounded, pleasant flavor. The flavor is not the type of flavor normally associated with sodium bicarbonate. If less than 0.2% sodium bicarbonate is incorporated, the undesirable soy flavor is not eliminated. If more than 2% sodium bicarbonate is incorporated in the cereal product, an undesirable flavor, different from that of the soy material, is obtained.

The sodium bicarbonate may be added at any point in the above-described process, but preferably not during the cooking of the cereal grain if the product color is important. If the sodium bicarbonate is added to the dough while it is being cooked, the dough will become excessively dark in color. The sodium bicarbonate may be added to the soy protein material before it is blended into the cooked cereal grain, the sodium bicarbonate may be added to the cooked cereal grain before it is blended with the soy protein material, or the sodium bicarbonate may be added to the cooked cereal grain dough after the soy protein material has been blended in.

In the production of a cold breakfast cereal, containing soy protein and cooked cereal grains, various general procedures used for making such food products are utilized depending upon the desired form, type, or condition of the final product. Typically, a cereal dough is extruded into strands of a relatively small cross-sectional area and thereafter sliced into small links, thereby forming pellet-like particles. If a flake-type cereal product is desired, the next step after pelletizing is to mechanically modify the pellets to a flake form. This can be accomplished by passing the pellets between a pair of cooperating rollers or a roller and a flat surface spaced apart a distance sufficient to produce the desired flake thickness, which generally is in the range from 0.007" to 0.012".

Generally, the flakes are then puffed to enhance their crispness and tenderness. A cereal is puffed by causing trapped moisture in the flake to expand very rapidly from the liquid state to the vapor phase. Rapid heating or a rapid decrease in the pressure are the methods commonly used to convert dense hard flakes into more palatable porous tender flakes. A toasting operation is generally employed to enhance the color and flavor of the resultant protein-fortified cereal product. Toasting is accomplished by heating the flakes, usually to 200° to 300°F. If a puffed pellet-shaped product is desired, the flaking step should be omitted and a puffing process, such as slow puffing, oven puffing, or gun puffing, should be substituted. The example demonstrates the effect of sodium bicarbonate on the flavor of breakfast cereal flakes made by the above-described process.

Example: 7,480 grams of brewer's corn grits, 220 grams of salt, 200 grams of sugar, and 2,100 grams of water are placed in a preheated rotary cooker at 260°F. The cooker is held at 18 psig pressure for 5 minutes and the cooked grits are discharged. The grits are dried overnight at 145°F to a moisture content of about 4.9%. The dried grits are then hammer milled to a particle size of ¼" and impact milled so that the grits are finer than corn flour. The grits are then combined with Edipro N, a commercially available soy protein isolate (at least 90% protein) to form the base mix. The following cereal formulas are then made by mixing together the following ingredients.

Sample	1	2	3	4	5	6
Base mix:						
Cooked grits (grams)	748	737	721	748	737	721
Edipro N (grams)	288	300	315	288	300	315
Finished formula:						
Base mix (grams)	72.5	70.5	68.3	72.5	70.5	68.3
Malt (grams)	4.0	6.0	8.0	4.0	6.0	8.0
$NaHCO_3$	1.0	1.0	1.0			
L-proline (grams)	0.4	0.4	0.4	0.4	0.4	0.4
Sodium saccharin (milliliters)	73	72	72	72	72	72
Water (grams)	15.3	15.3	15.5	15.3	15.3	15.5

Note that samples 4, 5, and 6 are the same as samples 1, 2 and 3 except that samples 4, 5, and 6 contain no sodium bicarbonate. The samples are extruded into strands with a circular cross section of approximately 3/16". These strands are then sliced into pellets of approximately 3/16" length. These pellets are next passed through a two-roll mill to produce flakes of about 0.008" thickness and dried to a moisture content of about 10.5%. Then the flakes are salt puffed by contacting them with hot salt at 350°F for 10 seconds. The flakes are then toasted in a hot air rotary kiln flake drier for 4 minutes at 260°F.

Samples 1, 2, and 3, which contain sodium bicarbonate, all exhibit a strong toasted malt flavor. Samples 4, 5, and 6, which do not contain sodium bicarbonate, exhibit a slightly toasted malt flavor, but also exhibit an objectionable soy note. These tests show that the addition of sodium bicarbonate depresses the soy flavor and brings out a pleasant toasted flavor in cereal flakes. If the above described samples are slow, oven, or gun puffed instead of flaked, the same flavor advantages are observed in the sodium bicarbonate-containing cereals.

Iron-Fortified Grain

L.P. Carroll, J.C. Novotny and A.W. Richards; U.S. Patent 3,806,613; April 23, 1974; assigned to The Quaker Oats Company seek to provide a grain product fortified with reduced iron which does not separate therefrom during handling.

This is accomplished by dispersing a slurry of reduced iron in an edible fatty acid ester of glycerol or sorbitol on a cereal grain product. The edible ester has a melting point below 125°F and comprises 0.15 to 5.0% by weight of the cereal. Reduced iron is a physiologically available form of iron which is less expensive per unit of iron than any of the usual iron salts, i.e., ferrous sulfate, ferrous gluconate, ferrous fumarate, ferric orthophosphate, sodium iron pyrophosphate, etc., and is less likely to cause problems such as rancidity and off colors.

Cereal grain product includes such products as white rice, corn grits, corn meal, barley and the like. An edible ester of glycerol or sorbitol and a fatty acid includes any animal or vegetable oil, natural or hydrogenated of an edible type and having a melting point preferably below 80°F. The slurry of reduced iron and an edible ester of glycerol or sorbitol may be molecular dispersions (solutions), colloidal dispersions, and particulate or mechanical dispersions.

In general, preferably from 80 to 250 mg of reduced iron per pound of cereal grain product may be applied. It is essential that the slurry contain between 0.15 and 5.0% by weight of the fatty acid ester of glycerol or sorbitol based on the weight of the cereal grain product. If much less than 0.15% of the edible ester is used, the reduced iron will not be effectively bound to the cereal grain product. If much more than 5.0% of the edible ester is used, the ester will interfere with the cook and the visual and organoleptic acceptance of the cereal grain product. That is, if more than 5.0% of the edible ester is used the grain product when coated with the slurry has an unnatural appearance best described as like wet sand. Above the 5.0% level the cereal grain product when cooked is oily and has an unpleasant mouthfeel.

The slurry is preferably prepared by adding the reduced iron to the edible ester of glycerol or sorbitol, holding the mixture at a temperature sufficient to liquefy it, and agitating the mixture to produce the slurry. Other materials such as salt, vitamins, other minerals, antioxidants, colorants, flavorings, flavor enhancers, flavor potentiators, etc. which can be dissolved or suspended in the edible ester may be added. Temperatures above the temperature sufficient to liquefy the slurry can be used but are not necessary. When heat degradable vitamins such as vitamin A, vitamin B, vitamin B_{12}, vitamin C, and vitamin D or other heat unstable materials are added to the slurry heating the slurry to temperatures much above that necessary to liquefy it or for prolonged periods of time should be avoided.

The slurry may be applied in liquid form to the cereal grain product by spraying, by tumble enrobing, or by any other conventional method. In each case the object is to evenly distribute the slurry around the product. After coating the cereal grain product with the slurry, the product is immediately ready for human or animal consumption or for packaging.

Example 1: A slurry was prepared from 0.10 lb of coconut oil having a 75°F MP, 2,500 mg of reduced iron, and 9.0 grams of a vitamin and mineral premix. 10 pounds of corn grits were tumbled with 56.8 grams of the oil slurry prepared above. The corn grits and oil slurry were mixed until the slurry was uniformly distributed over the surface of the cereal product.

The enriched cereal product was packaged and subjected to a 1,000-mile simulated rail trip. To determine the amount of separation of the reduced iron from the corn grits, samples were taken from the top, center, and bottom of the package and analyzed for reduced iron. The results are shown below.

Example 2: 10 lb of corn grits were tumbled with 0.10 lb of coconut oil having a 75°F MP. The corn grits and the oil were mixed until the oil was uniformly distributed over the surface of the cereal product. 2,500 mg of reduced iron and 9.0 grams of a vitamin and mineral premix were then added and mixing continued until the mixture was uniform. The enriched cereal product was then packaged, subjected to the 1,000-mile simulated rail trip, and samples were taken as in Example 1. The results are shown below.

Example No.	Top, mg Fe/lb	Middle, mg Fe/lb	Bottom, mg Fe/lb
1	264	254	278
2	195	213	315

Example 1 when compared with Example 2 demonstrates the benefit of this process. A sample taken from Example 1 shows that substantially no separation of the reduced iron from the cereal grain product occurred during the simulated rail trip. Example 2 shows separation of the reduced iron from the cereal grain product.

Example 1 demonstrates the criticality of the sequence of steps. It is absolutely essential to prepare first a slurry of the reduced iron in the edible ester and second to apply the slurry to the cereal grain product to be enriched. Any other sequence of steps as demonstrated by Example 2 results in an iron enriched cereal product from which the reduced iron separates during handling.

Corticated Oat Kernels and Flakes

Oat food products are not only especially well suited as breakfast foods, but are also especially nutritious. To utilize to the greatest degree possible this favorable dietetic effect, the oat kernel used for the production of food products should be left in the natural state if possible, i.e., for example, the capability of the kernel to germinate should remain intact and all nutritional contents as well as vitamins should be retained in their natural condition, especially the saponin content. Moreover, an improvement in taste is desired for certain purposes, for example, in the case of oat flakes. In conjunction with this problem, as few kernels as possible should be broken during the production operation, since broken kernels lead to bitter and rancid oat products in a short time.

H.-J.F.G. Fritze; U.S. Patent 3,790,690; February 5, 1974 describes a process whereby an oat kernel material capable of germination and left in its natural state is prepared such that all natural nutrient contents and vitamins are retained in the oat kernel as well as in the oat flakes produced therefrom. In so doing, the valuable dietetic properties of the natural grain are retained. The kernel can be stored and is durable for an unlimited interval of time, even after decortication and the oat flakes produced therefrom have a remarkably good taste.

The process for the production of decorticated oat kernels capable of germination and having good keeping qualities and of oat flakes made therefrom comprises: subjecting the oats to a silo and mill cleaning, transporting through trieures, wetting with water and immediately bringing the oats into a silo where they remain until the moisture content amounts to 17 to 21% throughout the entire kernel, then decorticating the kernels in the conventional manner in a centrifugal dehusking machine, then conducting the oats through a vertical airsifter and gravity separator as well as through a centrifugal dust separator and through trieures and finally to the paddy tables.

The oat kernels then proceed to the mantle brush machine and are then kilndried at a temperature of not more than 65°C, preferably 60°C, without supplying steam. The oat kernel prepared in this way can then either be stored and/or transported as long as desired, or directly supplied to the flaking mill to produce oat flakes.

According to a modification of this process the oat kernels after hulling are passed through a rolling mill and in doing so the kernels are pressed with pressure that is higher than the pressure normally used in preparing oat flakes. The flakes produced in this manner are then kiln-dried to a desired moisture content. By this kiln-drying the desired special nut taste is developed. Using this process the kilndrying may be accomplished at somewhat higher temperatures of the flake.

The above modifications may further be modified by passing the oat kernels through a cutter for cutting before being passed through the rolling mill. The natural nutrient contents and vitamins of the oat kernel are in no way damaged by the entire moisturizing operation or the careful kiln-drying operation. The thoroughly moisturized oat kernel acquires throughout its entirety the nut flavor desired for food products, especially for oat flakes, to a surprising degree even though there is no steaming. The oat kernels preserved in this way can be stored, for practical purposes, for an unlimited length of time and do not turn bitter or rancid so that oat flakes do not have to be produced immediately after the preceding steps.

It is essential that the grain and the kernels are thoroughly moisturized. In accordance with a preferred and special modification hereof, the moisturized oat grain and the kernel are allowed to grow biologically until germination begins.

This yields a product having an especially full-grade nutritional value. During this process of growth, the husk is not yet detached, but has started to open. The resultant specific degree of elasticity and softness is of particular advantage for further processing as well. The time interval necessary for the beginning of germination varies according to the origin of the oats, but normally amounts to 36 to 60 hours.

The time necessary to the beginning of germination can easily be determined for a particular batch of oats by actual experiments keeping some small batches in a wet atmosphere in a wooden box for different time periods and cutting the kernels to see whether they are thoroughly moistened and whether growth of the germ has begun. For a specific variety of oats coming from a certain region and having a specific moisture content, there are only slight variations in time of treatment required. Treatment with hot water or steam is avoided in this process and, furthermore, kiln-drying is also carried out at an unusually low temperature, i.e., not more than 60°C. This means a temperature at which there is no denaturation.

Example: 10 tons of raw oats (U.S. No. 2, approximately 12% by weight of moisture) are subjected to a conventional silo cleaning by means of a swing sieve. The oats are then conducted through trieures in parallel, each having an output of 3 tph where the remaining seeds and foreign matter are removed. The oats are then wetted with a conventional wetting apparatus having a wetting screw to achieve the desired moisture content and are then deposited directly from the screw into wooden silos having a capacity of 10 to 25 tons. The oats remain in the silo until germination begins, approximately 48 to 54 hours in the present case.

The oats are then removed and are conducted via an elevator to a number of strato mills having an hourly output of approximately 1.2 tons (MIAG) for the decortication process. A production capacity of 6 tph can be maintained if five strato mills are employed. After decortication, the material is fed into vertical airsifters, gravity separators and centrifugal dust separators to separate kernel, hull and other material and then proceeds to the paddy table for separation of the nondecorticated kernels. Preferably, a trieure is provided prior to the paddy table. The oats then proceed into a mantle brush machine to remove the germhairs which adhere to the oats.

The effective yield can be checked at this point and shows that yields of at least 70% are obtained at normal operating conditions as opposed to approximately 65% using the known methods. The kernels which have moisture contents of 17 to 20% here, are then fed into a kiln apparatus (type MIAG) having a kiln-drying effect where they are dried to a moisture content of 11 to 12% at a temperature of about 60°C. During this operation, the taste is at the same time improved, the oats taking on a distinct and pleasant nut taste. The dried oat kernels obtained in this manner are then led to a roller mill conventional for oat flake production. If desired, the kernels may be passed through a cutter for cutting before rolling.

The process can be carried out continuously or interruptedly according to the silo and machine capacities utilized. It must be noted that the moisture content established in the silo should remain constant until decortication. The residence time in the silo is determined by the beginning of germination. The oats should not be transported pneumatically from the beginning of the wetting operation until after the decortication operation is completed so that the moisture content is not changed too greatly.

The oat kernels which are produced in this process are clean, undamaged and have a moisture content of at least 16% by weight. About 1% by weight of its moisture content could get lost during the husking. They may be dried or kiln-dried to any desired moisture content either before or after processing to oat flakes.

Vitamin Coated Cereal Which Retains Crispness

Various methods for adding vitamins to ready-to-eat cereal products have certain disadvantages. For example, when vitamins have been added to the cereal dough before cooking, vitamins A, B_1, B_{12}, C, and D, which are unstable, partially deactivate during the cooking step. Vitamin degradation is particularly undesirable because of the formation of distasteful odors and flavors, as well as the loss of vitamin activity.

To overcome some of the difficulties associated with mixing the vitamins into the uncooked dough, vitamins have been sprayed in an aqueous solution or oil emulsion on the surface of a cooked dough usually having a moisture content between about 25 and 35%. To reduce the moisture content of the cereal product, to provide the desired crispness, and to develop a desired flavor in the dough, the vitamin-coated dough is subjected to an intensive heat transfer step. This heat transfer step is commonly referred to as drying.

This process suffers from the same difficulties as the process wherein the vitamins are mixed in the uncooked dough. Namely, many of the more heat labile vitamins degrade during the drying step. Further shortcomings peculiar to this process are that there is a large material loss of vitamins during the spraying step due to spray-over and that the distribution of vitamins on the cooked dough is customarily uneven.

Furthermore, as sufficient vitamins are added to the cereal product by these prior art processes to provide the adult minimum daily requirements or the recommended daily allowance established by the U.S. Food and Drug Administration, the ready-to-eat cereal product develops a decidedly and wholly undesirable medicinal flavor.

L.F. Duvall and C.D. Stone; U.S. Patent 3,782,963; January 1, 1974; assigned to The Quaker Oats Company provide a process for applying vitamins to a ready-to-eat cereal product whereby the more heat labile vitamins are not substantially deactivated and wherein there is a low material loss of vitamins.

In the process a precooked cereal having a moisture content between 0.5 and 30% by weight is precoated at 75°F with an aqueous suspension or solution having a viscosity between 100 and 200,000 cp which is comprised substantially of sugar. The precoated cereal is dried until the moisture content is between 0.5 and 3% by weight. The dried cereal is then coated with vitamins while it is hot and tacky, whereby the vitamins adhere to the tacky surface of the cereal.

Furthermore, the vitamins are coated with a fatty composition which is a saturated aliphatic fatty acid having between 12 and 20 carbons, inclusive, or a glyceride having the formula:

$$\begin{array}{l} CH_2-O-R_1 \\ CH-O-R_2 \\ CH_2-O-R_3 \end{array}$$

where R_1 is an acyl radical derived from a saturated aliphatic fatty acid having between 12 and 20 carbons, inclusive, per molecule and R_2 and R_3 are hydrogen or the same as R_1.

The precooked cereal is prepared by any of the known processes, such as extrusion, puffing, or flaking. The grain in the precooked cereal may be rice, wheat, oats, corn, barley, or any combination of two or more such grains. The precooked cereal may be formed into a variety of shapes and sizes by any well-known technique. The sugar may be any blend of mono-, di-, tri-, and other higher saccharides. When the sugar is sucrose, it is preferred that the aqueous suspension comprise 50 to 90% by weight of sucrose and 50 to 10% by weight of water.

It is advantageous to heat the aqueous sugar mixture to just below 200°F to bring about the partial dissolution of the sugar. The partially solubilized sugar in the aqueous mixture does not clog the spray head when the mixture is applied to the precooked cereal by spraying.

While the amount of aqueous suspension is not narrowly critical, the moisture content of the precooked cereal before drying should be between 1 and 35 which therefore limits the amount of aqueous sugar suspension or solution of any given viscosity. The precoated cereal is dried under temperatures and for times as is well-known in the art depending primarily on the nature of the cereal piece and the amount and viscosity of the aqueous sugar suspension or solution. For example, with an aqueous solution of sugar which comprises 20 to 60% by weight of the cereal product after drying, the product requires a period of 3 to 15 minutes at a temperature of 200° to 400°F.

After drying and while it is hot, the precoated cereal is coated with vitamins. The vitamins adhere to the hot cereal product in the glassy, sticky sugar. While the temperature of the dried precoated cereal product during the vitamin coating procedure is not narrowly critical, it should be sufficient to prevent crystallization of the sugar. Much higher temperature than necessary to prevent crystallization of the sugar should be avoided to prevent deactivation of the heat labile vitamins. The precoated dried cereal may be coated with vitamins while the cereal is between 120° and 300°F. After coating the precoated dried cereal product with vitamins, the cereal product is immediately cooled and is ready for human consumption.

As sufficient vitamins are added to the cereal product to provide the adult minimum daily requirements or recommended daily allotments when consumed in an amount reasonably suited for adult consumption, the cereal develops an unpleasant medicinal taste. High levels of vitamins may be added to the cereal by coating the vitamins with a fatty composition which is a saturated aliphatic fatty acid or a glyceride of the above formula without the development of an undesirable flavor. Furthermore, the fatty composition helps anneal the vitamins to the dried, hot cereal piece.

Suitable saturated aliphatic acids include stearic acid, palmitic acid, myristic acid, and lauric acid. The saturated aliphatic fatty acid glyceride may contain between 0 and 2 hydroxy groups inclusive. About 0.05 to 5% by weight based on the weight of the cereal product of the fatty composition is satisfactory.

The vitamins are coated by suspending the particular vitamin in a molten fatty material and chilling the resulting suspension to produce spheroidal particles of the vitamin having a coating of the fatty composition. The coated vitamins may be blown through a small orifice to provide beadlets of vitamins the cross-section of which is determined by the diameter of the orifice.

Vitamins B_1, B_2, niacinamide, C and B_{12} may be coated with the above-described fatty composition. The coating of vitamins A, D, and E with the fatty composition would not be advantageous since these vitamins are not sufficiently soluble in the fatty composition.

While vitamin A and vitamin D are not advantageously coated with the fatty composition, they are often dispersed in gelatin which acts as a protective medium to prevent oxidation thereof whereby the vitamins lose their vitamin activity. The use of gelatin-coated vitamin A and vitamin D is preferred. These vitamins are well-known and commercially available.

While the size of the particles of vitamins is not narrowly critical, they must be no larger than will adhere to the cereal piece. This size is dependent on the melting point of the fatty composition forming the coating if any, the geometry of the particle which need not be perfectly spherical, and the temperature of the dried cereal pieces to which the vitamin particle is annealed.

Example: 50 lb of a precooked cereal product having a moisture content of about 7% by weight was sprayed with an aqueous suspension comprised substantially of sugar which was prepared by mixing together 41 lb of sucrose, 7 lb of vegetable oil, 1 lb of salt, and 11 lb of water. The components of the aqueous suspension were heated to 190°F for 2 minutes and sprayed on the precooked cereal product while the cereal tumbled in an enrober. The precoated precooked cereal product was tumbled sufficiently to provide a uniform distribution of the aqueous sugar suspension around the precooked cereal pieces.

The precoated cereal product was then dried in an oven equipped with tray pans having a volume of approximately 3,000 in^3 and a bed depth of approximately 3". The direction of air flow was upward through the product. A temperature of 280°F was maintained for 160 seconds. After the first 80 seconds elapsed, the tray was shaken vigorously to shatter clumps and redistribute the partially dried product in order to insure uniform drying. At the end of the drying period the moisture content of the dried cereal product was about 2.4% by weight.

While the dried cereal product was at a temperature of 160° to 180°F and the sugar coating still tacky, the cereal was tumbled with 2.7542 lb of a vitamin premix. The vitamin premix was composed of 1.9830 lb of confectioner's sugar and 0.7712 lb of a vitamin blend. Each pound of the vitamin blend was composed of vitamin A palmitate having an activity of 9.0720 M.U. (1 M.U. equals 1,000 I.U.) in combination with vitamin D_2 in gelatin having an activity of 0.9072 M.U., thiamine mononitrate having a glycerol monostearate waxy coat and an activity of 2.2680 grams, riboflavin having a stearic acid waxy coat and an activity of 2.7216 grams, niacinamide having a stearic acid waxy coat and an activity of 22.6800 grams, pyridoxine hydrochloride having a stearic acid waxy coat and an activity of 3.4020 grams, sodium ascorbate having an activity of 68.0400 grams, vitamin B_{12} in gelatin and having an activity of 4.9900 mg, and corn starch to make up the balance to 1 lb. The percentage of the vitamin particles in the premix passing through the given Standard U.S. Mesh sizes is given in the following table.

	Mesh Size, Percent										
	10	20	30	40	50	60	70	80	90	100	200
Vitamin A and D_2 combination	100	–	90	–	–	–	–	25	–	–	–
Thiamine mononitrate	–	–	100	90	–	65	–	–	–	–	50
Riboflavin					(Fine powder)						
Niacinamide	–	–	100	90	–	65	–	–	–	–	50
Pyridoxine hydrochloride	99	–	–	90	–	65	–	–	–	–	50
Sodium ascorbate	–	100	–	–	–	–	–	–	–	–	–
Vitamin B_{12}	–	–	–	–	–	100	–	98	–	–	–

The vitamin coated cereal product was tumbled for 10 seconds after the addition of the vitamin premix to insure even distribution of the vitamins on the surface of each cereal piece. The vitamin coated ready-to-eat cereal product prepared by the above process had the minimum daily adult requirements of vitamins per 1 ounce serving of the product. More specifically on analysis it was found that there is at least 16 mg/lb of thiamine; 480 mg/lb of vitamin C; 6,400 I.U./lb of vitamin D; 64,000 I.U./lb of vitamin A; 160 mg/lb of niacin; 1,912 mg/lb of riboflavin; 24 mg/lb of vitamin B_6; and 35.2 µg/lb of vitamin B_{12}. The product was also subjected to taste evaluation. A comparison of taste of this product obtained with the product obtained by conventional processes showed that the vitamin coated product produced by this process had a superior, nonmedicinal flavor.

Vitamin Coated Ready-to-Eat Cereal

W.L. Keyser and W.J. Zielinski; U.S. Patent 3,767,824; October 23, 1973; assigned to The Quaker Oats Company disclose a process for vitamin coating cereal products, particularly for ready-to-eat breakfast cereals. In the process, a precooked cereal having a moisture content between 1 and 30% by weight is dried until the moisture content thereof is between 0.5 and 3%. The dried cereal is coated with vitamins which themselves have been coated with a fatty composition while the cereal is at a temperature between the melting point of the fatty composition and 300°F, the fatty composition comprising a saturated aliphatic acid having between 12 and 20 carbons inclusive or a glyceride having the formula:

$$\begin{array}{l} CH_2-O-R_1 \\ CH-O-R_2 \\ CH_2-O-R_3 \end{array}$$

where R_1 is an acyl radical derived from a saturated aliphatic acid having between 12 and 20 carbons per molecule and R_2 and R_3 are hydrogen or the same as R_1.

It is essential that all the vitamins be coated with the fatty composition. Suitable saturated acids for coating the vitamins include, for example, stearic, palmitic, myristic, and lauric acids. The saturated aliphatic fatty acid glycerides for coating the vitamins may contain between 0 and 2 hydroxy groups inclusive. The glycerides need not be pure compounds, but can be glycerides from mixtures of the above-mentioned saturated aliphatic fatty acids.

The vitamins are coated by suspending the particular vitamin in a molten fatty material and chilling the resulting suspension or solution to produce particles of the vitamin having a coating of the fatty composition. The coated vitamins may be blown through a small orifice to provide beadlets of vitamins the cross section of which is determined by the diameter of the orifice. Higher temperatures than necessary to form the suspension or solution are preferably avoided to prevent deactivation of the heat labile vitamins. From 0.05 to 5% by weight based on the weight of the cereal product of the fatty composition is preferred.

While the size of the particles of vitamins is not narrowly critical, they must be no larger than will adhere to the cereal piece. This size is dependent on the melting point of the fatty composition forming the coating, the geometry of the particle, and the temperature of the dried cereal piece to which the vitamin particle is annealed. The maximum size can be easily determined by one skilled in the art by a few routine experiments.

The precooked cereal is prepared by any of the known processes, such as extrusion, puffing, or rotary cooking. The grain in the precooked cereal may be rice, wheat, oats, corn, barley, or any combination of two or more such grains. The precooked cereal may be formed into a variety of shapes and sizes by well-known techniques in the art.

The precooked cereal is dried under temperatures and for times as is well-known in the art depending primarily on the nature and size of the cereal piece, humidity and velocity of the air in the drier, and the amount of moisture present in the cereal. For example, a precooked cereal having a moisture content of 20 to 35% by weight required a period of 3 to 15 minutes at a temperature of 200° to 400°F to reduce the moisture content of the cereal to 2.0%. Drying is continued until the moisture content of the precooked cereal is between 0.5 and 3% by weight.

After drying and while it is hot, the precooked cereal is coated with vitamins. The temperature of the dried precooked cereal product during the vitamin coating procedure should be sufficient to soften the fatty coating on the vitamins. Much higher temperatures than necessary to soften the fatty coating should be avoided to prevent deactivation of the heat labile vitamins.

It has been found advantageous to coat the dried cereal with vitamins while the cereal is between 160° and 200°F but temperatures up to 300°F may be used. The fatty coated vitamins may optionally be preheated to a temperature less than necessary to deactivate them before applying them to the hot dried precooked cereal. After coating the precoated dried cereal product with vitamins, the cereal product is immediately cooled and is ready for human consumption.

Sufficient vitamins may be added to the cereal product to provide the adult minimum daily requirements or recommended daily allotments when consumed in an amount reasonably suited for adult consumption without the development of an unpleasant medicinal taste.

Example: 850 grams of an extruded breakfast cereal product having a bulk density of 5.5 oz/121.5 in^3 and a moisture content of 5% by weight was toasted at 400°F for 45 seconds. An air flow was directed upward through the product at the rate of 250 cfm. At the end of the toasting period the dried cereal had a moisture content of 2.0% by weight and weighed 824 grams. The dried cereal was tumbled with a vitamin premix immediately after toasting and while the cereal was at a temperature of 290°F.

The vitamin premix was composed of 69,600 µg of beta-carotene coated with 139,200 µg of a saturated aliphatic acid having between 12 and 20 carbons or a glyceride thereof; 290 mg of niacin coated with 580 mg of stearic acid; 34.8 mg of riboflavin coated with 69.6 mg of stearic acid; 29 mg of thiamin coated with 58 mg of glycerol monostearate; 670 mg of ascorbic acid coated with 1,340 mg of a saturated aliphatic acid having between 12 and 20 carbons or a glyceride thereof; 58 mg of vitamin B_6 coated with 116 mg of stearic acid; 145 mg of vitamin B_{12} coated with 290 mg of a saturated aliphatic acid having between 12 and 20 carbons or a glyceride thereof; 290 µg of vitamin D_2 coated with 580 µg of a saturated aliphatic acid having between 12 and 20 carbons or a glyceride thereof; and 29 grams of powdered sugar as a carrier.

All of the above coated vitamins passed through a Standard U.S. 20 mesh screen. The vitamin coated cereal piece was tumbled for 10 seconds after the addition of the vitamin premix to insure even distribution of the vitamins on the surface of each cereal piece.

The vitamin coated ready-to-eat cereal product prepared by the above process had all the vitamins for which an adult minimum daily requirement has been established and had the recommended daily allotments of vitamins B_6 and B_{12} for an adult male per 1 oz serving of the product.

READY-TO-EAT SWEETENED PRODUCTS

Emulsified Oil and Sugar Coating

A.A. Lyall and R.J. Johnston; U.S. Patents 3,959,498; May 25, 1976; and 3,840,685; October 8, 1974; both assigned to Nabisco, Inc. describe a cereal coating process which comprises, in sequence, the steps of:

(a) applying to prepared cereal particles a syrupy oil-in-water emulsion having a temperature of 170° to 240°F, the emulsion comprising by weight, based on the total weight of emulsion, 5 to 32% of an edible oil- or fat-derived oleaginous material, an aqueous syrup solution containing 60 to 85% by weight of sugar solids, and 0.5 to 5% of an emulsifier consisting essentially of distilled monoglycerides, the emulsion containing, by weight, from 9 to 34% of water, no heating being carried out during the application of the emulsion to the cereal particles; and

(b) drying the coated cereal particles at a temperature and for a time sufficient to reduce the moisture content of the coated cereal particles to a level in the range of 2.0 to 3.0% by weight of the particles, while vigorously agitating the particles throughout the drying step, thereby obtaining discrete, candy-coated cereal particles.

In preparing the coating compositions one can add the appropriate amounts of sugar solids, edible fat or oil, distilled monoglycerides and such other ingredients as coloring and flavoring agents as are desired, simultaneously to water at a temperature of about 140°F. This would effectively drop the temperature of the overall mass to 110° to 115°F. The mass is then heated to about 180°F, at which temperature it is ready for application to cereal substrates.

It is preferred, however, to make up the aqueous syrupy solution first, by adding the sugar solids to water at a temperature of 140° to 150°F, and effecting dissolution of the sugar with constant agitation and with heating to maintain the temperature within the range of 140° to 155°F. Then the edible fat or oil or other edible oleaginous material is added to the syrup solution, while all the while the mass is constantly agitated and heating is maintained. After a short time complete emulsification of the edible fat or oil and water is achieved. Then the mass is heated to a temperature of about 180°F. It is important that the mass be constantly agitated throughout the stages of adding ingredients and heating to the desired temperature for application to cereals.

Consistently successful results are obtained when the emulsifier is selectively added to the mixture of syrup and edible fat or oil at a temperature in the range of 145° to 155°F. It is critical that the emulsifier be added below 156°F; or stated another way, under no circumstances should the emulsifier be added to a syrupy slurry with a temperature reading above 155°F. The final syrup temperature should desirably be maintained between 175° to 180°F. Although temperatures of the syrup emulsion preparatory to coating onto cereals may be raised as high as 240°F without harm to the composition, nevertheless, no advantage with respect to physical characteristics or qualities of the product, is imparted to the formulation by heating it to a temperature in excess of about 180°F.

Example:

	Weight
Water, oz	16
Icing sugar, oz	64
Soybean oil, oz	7
Distilled monoglycerides, oz	1
Honey, oz	12
Artificial food color, gram	0.5

Preparation of coating:

(1) The water, sugar and honey are placed in a hot water jacketed kettle and are heated to 150°F under constant agitation.

(2) The soybean oil is then added and allowed to melt under agitation.

(3) The distilled monoglycerides are added under agitation.

(4) Heating is continued, under agitation, to 180°F, then the food color is added. The coating composition is maintained at this temperature until it is used.

Artificially Sweetened Cereal Using L-Aspartic Acid to Avoid "Hot Spots"

P.A. Baggerly; U.S. Patent 3,955,000; May 4, 1976; assigned to General Foods Corporation describes a process for making a cereal product in which L-aspartic acid derivative sweetening compounds are mixed in aqueous suspension with hydrolyzed amylaceous derivatives comprising predominantly oligosaccharides solids having a low dextrose equivalency and applied as a coating solution to a cereal-base comestible whereby localized "hot spots" are ameliorated and the product has a smooth sweetness, the derivative being uniformly distributed throughout the coating and a portion thereof being present as undissolved crystals.

In the process sweet-tasting dipeptides and like L-aspartic derivatives in the group of which methyl ester of L-aspartyl-L-phenylalanine (APM) is a preferred member (hereafter marked L-aspartic acid derivatives) are combined with a starch hydrolyzate recovered as by the acid or enzymatic hydrolysis of an amylaceous substance typically having a low dextrose equivalency and providing oligosaccharides of elemental monosaccharides, di- and tri-, tetra-, penta- and hexasaccharides which may have a varying dextrose equivalency but commonly would have a DE less than 30. A coating of a dried solution of such an hydrolyzate of cereal solids having a fine dispersion of the L-aspartic acid derivative has been found to smooth out the taste impact generated by any sweetening imbalance attributable to the incomplete solution of the APM or nonuniformity of its dispersion.

Generally, the coating solution will be maintained preferably below 170°F during its preparation and application to the dry comestible, the temperature being low enough to have the sweetening derivative dispersed therein as undissolved hydrated particles. The coated comestible also will be dried at product temperatures that do not exceed 200°F in order to assure that the sweetening compound is not degraded while the coated comestible is dried to a stable moisture, i.e., below 6%.

Example: 9.65 grams of hydrolyzed cereal solids having a dextrose equivalency of 10 to 13 and composed of the following assay of carbohydrates on a dry basis are used to prepare a solution by addition to 14 grams of water at 110°F and 1.08 grams of APM.

DE	10-13
pH	4.5-5.5
Carbohydrate, % db	
Dextrose	1
Disaccharide	4
Trisaccharide	5
Tetrasaccharide	4
Pentasaccharide	4
Hexasaccharide and above	82

Preferably the dextrin solution is prepared by stirring the warm solution to eliminate any lumps and facilitate mixing and insure solution of the dextrin;

the APM is added to the dextrin solution and uniformly mixed and homogenized in a bench-top homogenizer to create a uniform suspension of the APM particles which is allowed to cool to ambient room temperature, say 72°F. The solution is ready for spray application.

The solution thus produced can be sprayed on 444.5 grams of corn flakes and then dried at air temperature of 180°F for 25 minutes until a moisture content of approximately 2.5% is obtained. Homogenizing the mixture in water produces a very discrete finite dispersion of the APM such as would permit application thereof as a fine slurry onto the corn flakes by atomization, 24 grams of the coating being employed to uniformly coat all of the cereal flakes as aforesaid resulting in a coating of sweetening of about 0.24% by weight.

The coated cereal system had a sweetness quite comparable to that of sucrose-coated corn flakes and advantageously did not have the overly frosted appearance that many consumers associate with an undesirable or excessive amount of sucrose; the product when tested, in packaging, will be found to be stable over a period of at least 3 months' storage when tested under accelerated packaging conditions of high and low relative humidity.

Use of Hard Butter and Crystalline Sugar

L.J. Henthorn and F.R. Kincs; U.S. Patent 3,814,822; June 4, 1974; assigned to The Quaker Oats Company describes a process for the preparation of a presweetened, moisture-resistant ready-to-eat breakfast cereal which includes applying a hard butter containing crystalline sugar to the breakfast cereal. The process comprises applying in liquid form to the surface of the cereal product 15 to 40% by weight of a slurry comprising preferably from 15 to 30% by weight of crystalline sugar, and 90 to 60% by weight of a hard butter having a Wiley melting point of 90° to 105°F and a solid fat index as follows:

Temperature, °F	Percent Solids
80	21-59
92	7-23
100	4-5

Ready-to-eat breakfast cereals are those produced from cereal grain and subjected to a starch gelatinization step. The grain may be rice, wheat, oats, corn, barley, or any combination of two or more such grains. Sugar, fat, and a variety of other flavoring materials may be present within the dough or sprayed on the surface of the cereal product. The ready-to-eat breakfast cereal may be formed into a variety of shapes and sized by well-known techniques in the art and may be subjected to a variety of additional processing steps. Some of these are toasting, drying, cooking and puffing, and the like. In order to make these products edible, however, they all must undergo some measure of starch gelatinization.

The hard butters used are vegetable fats or glyceridic oils. These oils are treated by hydrogenation, interesterification, or fractional crystallization, and blending of oils with harder butters so as to stabilize the oils and modify their melting points consistent with the desired melting point temperature range. It is preferred that the hard butter have the additional characteristics shown on the following page.

Cereals

Temperature, °F	Percent Solids
50	30-72
70	24-66

The crystalline sugar preferably should be crystalline sucrose having a relatively coarse granulation. For best results, it is preferred that the particle size be such that at least 60% is retained on a U.S. 100 standard mesh screen. By using crystals which are relatively large, it has been found that a smaller amount of sugar is generally needed than when a noncrystalline sugar, e.g., syrup or pastel confectionery coating is used to coat the cereal piece. The crystalline sugar and the hard butter are applied to the ready-to-eat breakfast cereal in liquid form as a slurry.

Example: A slurry was prepared from 40 parts by weight of granulated sugar and 60 parts by weight of Kaomel. The Kaomel had a Wiley melting point of 97° to 101°F and a solid fat index as follows:

Temperature, °F	Percent Solids
50	72±3
70	66±3
80	59±3
92	23±3
100	5.0

70 parts by weight of a ready-to-eat breakfast cereal and 30 parts of the slurry in liquid form prepared above were tumbled together. The coated cereal when placed in milk had sufficient bowl life that it did not become soggy in the time necessary to consume it. The coated cereal had a pleasant, presweetened flavor when eaten.

Use of Syrup Solution

A.A. Lyall and C.N. Lundy; U.S. Patent 3,792,183; February 12, 1974; assigned to Nabisco, Inc. describe the candy coating of cereal particles, and the provision thereby of a hard, transparent cereal candy coating which is not susceptible to moisture pick-up even under humid conditions.

In the process a syrup solution containing, by weight, 60 to 85% sugar solids, is made up, and is applied to a cereal base without heating. The sugar solids comprise by weight, based on the total sugar solids, on a dry basis, from 80 to 68% sucrose solids and 20 to 32% low dextrose equivalent glucose solids. After coating, the product is subjected to substantial heat in a drying apparatus for 20 to 28 minutes, and the drying is effected with substantial agitation of the coated cereal particles. A hard, glossy, nonhydroscopic transparent cereal coating is obtained which does not crystallize or decrease in glossiness even after extended shelf life.

The cereal particles include all ready-to-eat cereal particles in flaked, shredded, puffed or other forms, such as corn flakes, shredded wheat, puffed wheat, puffed rice, bran flakes, wheat flakes, puffed corn, breakfast cereals in the form of extruded and puffed doughs and the like. Such cereal particles are prepared in the usual manner and may be either toasted or untoasted.

The sucrose content of the syrup to be preferred in any given case is governed to some extent by the nature of the cereal particles being coated. In the case of porous cereal particles such as puffed wheat and other gun-puffed products, a syrup of higher concentration is desirable to reduce the amount absorbed into the cereal particles before a satisfactory external coating is obtained. Soaking into such porous cereal particles can be further reduced, if desired, by the use of thickeners such as dextrins, gums, methylcellulose, gelatinized starches, etc.

In the event that a thickener is used, the amount thereof to be added to the syrup would depend upon the concentration of the syrup, upon the nature of the cereal body and particularly its porosity, and also of course upon the particular thickener employed. Dextrins and corn syrup may be used within the range of 0.5 to 10% (dry basis), above which the coating becomes sticky; whereas gums and methylcellulose and carboxymethylcellulose may be employed within the range of 0.2 to 2%. With dextran and the gelatinized starches the range is about 0.5 to 5%, the upper limit again being that at which the coating becomes sticky.

For porous cereal particles syrups containing 75 to 80% sugars or syrups in which an equivalent viscosity is obtained by using thickeners are preferred. For nonporous cereal particles, on the other hand, syrups containing about 60 to 70% sugars are sufficiently viscous without thickeners.

In the coating composition of this process, it is especially preferred that the aqueous syrup contain about 80% by weight of sugar solids. Preferably the sugar solids are made up of 75% by weight sucrose solids and 25% by weight of low dextrose equivalent (DE) glucose solids. By employing low dextrose equivalent glucose solids in an amount preferably 25% by weight of the total sugar solids of the coating composition, it has been found that a higher than ordinary proportion of sugar coating to cereal base may be used without the end product being unpalatable due to excessive sweetness.

POTATO AND OTHER SNACK FOODS

POTATO CHIP PROCESSES

Forming Rippled Chips

A.D. Curry, L. Levine, and D.W. Rose; U.S. Patent 3,956,517; May 11, 1976; assigned to The Procter & Gamble Company have found that rippled chip-type products can be conveniently prepared by passing a dough sheet between a pair of rollers, one of the rollers having a smooth surface and the other having an annularly grooved surface. The gap between the rollers is adjusted so as to impress a corrugated, or rippled configuration on only one surface of the dough sheet, leaving the other surface substantially smooth. The sheet is cut into desired chip-like portions and further processed, as by deep fat frying, to form chip-type products having alternate arcuate ridges and grooves on both surfaces which provide a rippled effect on both sides of the product.

The material to be treated is a formulated dough suitable for sheeting and subsequent deep-fat frying to form chip-type food products. The dough may be formulated from any of a variety of ingredients, such as farinaceous materials such as potatoes, corn, wheat, rice, oats, etc.; proteinaceous materials such as soy, peanuts or sunflower seed; or any delectable combination thereof. The only requirement is that the material must be able to be formed into a coherent workable dough sheet for further processing according to the process.

Other optional ingredients, such as condiments or spices, natural or artificial flavorings, vitamins, emulsifiers, antioxidants, colorants, or the like can be suitably included in the dough base. The preferred material for treatment is dehydrated potatoes, either granules, flakes, or mixtures thereof. The dough may conveniently be prepared by blending dehydrated potatoes with water, as by mixing in a known manner in a conventional blender or mixer. In the preparation of a formulated potato dough, it is preferred that the moisture content be 25 to 55% of the total dough material.

In the operation of the process, it is important that the surface design impressed on the dough sheet be substantially parallel alternate arcuate grooves and ridges.

If the design impressed onto the dough sheet is other than a rippled design, such as a checkerboard, honeycomb, or other similar pattern, the surface design will not be conveyed to the opposite side of the chip during frying. This difference in design transfer from one surface to both surfaces during cooking is due to dough shrinkage during cooking. With a rippled design, dough shrinkage is restricted along the ridges, due to the dough buildup in the ridges. But shrinkage between the ridges is accentuated, since the dough sheet is thinner and there are no thick dough ridges to restrict shrinkage.

However, if the surface design impressed onto the dough sheet consists of a pattern having substantially transverse ridges, shrinkage upon cooking is restricted in both directions, thus inhibiting the conveyance of a distinct design to the opposite surface of the cooked chip. While both sides of the cooked chips have a distinct rippled effect, the ripples may be slightly more pronounced on the one surface. Chip-type products having a decidedly rippled configuration on both sides can, however, be readily prepared.

Example: A formulated potato dough prepared from dehydrated potatoes and water and having a moisture level of 38% was obtained and placed in a feed hopper having walls converging in a feed opening which was situated immediately above the nip of contrarotating roll mills. The dough sheet formed thereby stuck to one roll mill (the front roll mill) since that roll mill was at a temperature of 60°F higher and was rotating at a 50% faster rate than the other roll mill. As the dough sheet was conveyed along the front roll mill, longitudinal corrugations, or ripples, were impressed in one broad surface of the dough sheet by the use of an embossing roll which was annularly grooved.

The grooves in the embossing roll were spaced 0.090 inch apart and were machined into the surface to a depth of 0.055 inch, each groove having a width at the roll surface of 0.030 inch and having sides converging at an angle of 20°. The annularly grooved roll had a Teflon coating on its peripheral surface. Prior to having the longitudinal ripples impressed therein, the dough sheet was 0.020 inch thick. The dough sheet, still sticking to the front roll mill, was scraped therefrom by means of a doctor blade and was removed from the vicinity of the front roll mill by means of an endless conveyor belt. Thereafter, the rippled dough sheet was processed in accordance with U.S. Patent 3,530,248 to form unique uniformly shaped chip-type products with both broad surfaces thereof having a distinct rippled configuration.

It may thus be seen that with this process, chip-type products having both of their broad surfaces in a rippled configuration may readily be prepared from a formulated coherent workable dough sheet. In addition, these rippled chip-type products may be prepared from such a dough sheet having a rippled configuration impressed in only one broad surface thereof, thus leaving the opposite surface smooth. This then permits the dough sheet to be processed in accordance with conventional processing techniques, especially those particularly adapted for use with a flat dough sheet.

Unique Packaging Design

The packaging of snack chips such as potato chips has in the past involved placing irregularly shaped chips into a bag in a random unoriented manner. Such bags are made typically from one or more sheets of waxed paper or glassine.

Although this type of bag is relatively inexpensive, it provides little protection for the fragile chips during handling and shipping. Thus, it is quite common to have a number of broken chips in the bag.

Another possible package for chip type snacks of uniform shape and size involves vertically stacking the chips one upon the other to form a straight column. The column may be placed within a substantially rigid tubular container. The tubular container may be sealed closed by securing ends thereto. It has been found that when such container is dropped on its bottom (i.e., one of such ends) the chips nearest such end tend to break. Broken chips do not normally meet with consumer acceptance.

Accordingly, *N.J. Beall; U.S. Patent 3,956,510; May 11, 1976* provides a protective package for uniformly shaped fragile chip type snack food products which will prevent breakage of such items while in shipment and during handling. It has been found that chip breakage is reduced when the chips are supported on their edges.

In other words, the chips are disposed in the package with their major surfaces perpendicular to the bottom of the supporting portion of the container. The design contemplates a loop array of nested uniform chips and packaging suitable for maintaining the chips in the loop array. The circular or loop array provides protection regardless of the direction from which the package is dropped.

Extruded Puffed Stick

A method is provided by *R.O. Straughn, G.L. Elofson and R.D. Reinhart; U.S. Patent 3,925,563; December 9, 1975; assigned to General Mills, Inc.* for preparing a puffed snack product resembling a French fried potato stick. Dry ingredients including a meal (e.g., corn grits), potato granules and flavoring may be dry blended. Sufficient water is added to the blend to raise the total moisture content to between 16 and 22%, by weight. The mixture is tempered for between one-half hour and 24 hours. The mixture is treated in a collet type extruder where the temperature is raised to between 255° and 340°F and the pressure is between 800 and 1500 psig. The mixture expands upon extrusion and is cut into pieces which are toasted and enrobed with an edible oil and salt.

Example: A snack was prepared by dry blending, by weight, 75 parts granulated potato solids and 25 parts corn grits. The potato solids had a moisture content of 8 to 10% and the corn grits had a moisture content of 8% by weight. Sufficient moisture was added to raise the total moisture content to about 19%. After the moisture was thoroughly distributed throughout the potato-corn mixture, the mixture was fed to a collet extruder having a bore with an internal diameter of about 3 inches and an effective working length of about 3 inches or, in other words, a length to diameter ratio of 1:1. The extruder was provided with a cooling jacket. The mixture entering the die was maintained at 265°F and a pressure of about 925 psig.

The mixture passed through the collet extruder at the rate of 2.5 lb/min. The extrudate expanded about 4.8 times upon extrusion. The expanded product was square in cross-sectional shape with each side of the square being about $5/16$ inch. The expanded product was cut at the face of the die to provide pieces approximately 2½ inches in length. The pieces were toasted in an oven at about

300°F for about three minutes. The toasted pieces were enrobed with a vegetable oil, namely, coconut oil and salt. The final composition was approximately 53¼% potato solids, 17¼% corn solids, 25% coconut oil, 2.5% salt and 2% moisture, by weight. The process is described in the patent in conjunction with a suitable fully diagrammed apparatus.

Expanded Item

M.J. Willard; U.S. Patent 3,886,291; May 27, 1975 describes a process which provides an expanded potato snack having an appearance or structure distinct from that of potato chips, and which has a crisp texture and a potato flavor resembling that of potato chips. An important advantage of the potato snack is its capability of being manufactured in conventional equipment in a continuous mass production process at a relatively low cost.

Briefly, the potato snack is prepared by mixing cooked potato solids from either dehydrated or raw potatoes with water and ungelatinized starch to form a dough having between 40 and 50% solids by weight. The dough is formed into pieces which are then fried immediately in cooking oil to produce an expanded potato product.

The potato dough at the time of frying contains a combination of ungelatinized starch, preferably raw potato starch, potato solids, including a quantity of intact potato cells, and a quantity of free available gelatinized starch solids. Best results are obtained when the ungelatinized starch is present in the range between 30 to 70% by weight of the total solids present in the dough. The amount of free available gelatinized starch in the dough is controlled so that the dough pieces expand at least about 1.6 times their original dimension upon frying to form a snack product having a cellular internal structure encased in a dense exterior layer of substantially reduced porosity.

The quantity of dehydrated potatoes chosen for the process, and the inert starch, such as ungelatinized potato starch, salt and seasoning as desired are mixed with an appropriate amount of water to yield a solids content between 42 and 48%. Stirring for one minute in a standard Hobart mixer fitted with a paddle at 60 rpm is satisfactory for complete blending of these ingredients. Following this, a portion of the mixture is placed in an extruder, extruded and, at substantially the original moisture content, dropped direct into cooking fat and fried about 90 seconds.

The potato based dough formed is normally friable and free-flowing, as mixed, and somewhat putty-like, but not excessively sticky after compression, and can be formed or shaped in many types of standard food shaping equipment. Breakage of potato cells during extrusion, and the resulting release of gelatinized starch, alter the texture and expansion of the fried product, which, if not controlled, could cause excessive puffing.

A piston type extruder is one preferred method of forming. Roller sheeting equipment commonly used for macaroni products can be used if care is exercised that excessive cell damage does not occur during extrusion of the dough through the roller apertures. The use of this type extruder permits the continuous mixing of dry ingredients, water and seasonings in one single step along with the extrusion, thereby providing considerable economy of operation.

Raw potatoes are washed, peeled, trimmed and cut into appropriate sizes in a conventional manner prior to cooking. Generally, it is sufficient to slice the potatoes to uniform thickness and cook the slices in atmospheric steam for 25 to 35 minutes, depending on the variety of potatoes and the solids content. The cooked potatoes are mashed by ricing them through conventional equipment using apertures of 1/16 inch to 1/8 inch diameter, by forcing the cooked potatoes through round bars spaced 1/8 inch apart, or by passing them between rotating rollers maintained at a distance of 50 to 75 mils.

In any case, the mashed potatoes are allowed to cool to a temperature below the gelatinization point of potato starch, namely, below 140°F. If desired, the cooling is effected by passing cooling water through the mashing rolls, by blowing cold air on the potatoes or by other means known to the art. The cooled, mashed potatoes are mixed with the required amount of standard ungelatinized potato starch and, if desired, additional quantities of pregelatinized starch.

The cooled, mashed potatoes and dry ingredients are blended to form a dough in a suitable planetary mixer or continuous ribbon blender of standard design. At this point the mixed dough is friable, but can be forced into any desired shape by hand manipulation. The dough is extruded and then fried in the same manner as described above in connection with dehydrated potatoes.

The finished product has a full, rich potato flavor and has a thickness approximately 1.6 to 3.0 times the thickness of the extruded dough. The texture can be varied by adjusting the height of the extruder slot, base potato ingredients, and the solids content of the extruded dough to produce products either firmer or more tender than standard potato chips or corn chips. Savory ingredients such as dehydrated onion powder or garlic, barbecue spices and other standard flavoring ingredients such as MSG, salt, etc., can be applied either internally by mixing into the dough prior to extrusion or by dusting on the finished products after frying.

The finished product has a relatively porous internal structure encased in a continuous relatively dense exterior surface layer of fried potato solids. The structure of the outer surface layer of the finished product is very similar to the structure of a fresh potato chip. Thus, the product closely resembles two overlying thin potato chips joined by a porous internal structure of expanded potato solids. The exterior layer of the product shatters when chewed to provide a crunchy sensation.

The release of potato flavor from the snack when chewed is similar to that of fresh potato chips because of the similarity between potato chips and the outer layer of this snack. The inner porous structure can be controlled to modify the texture of the product. For example, a completely dense product (produced by a solids content outside the 40 to 50% range) is hard and horny, and its interior is characterized by overbrowning. Conversely, the dense outer layer of the snack product separates slightly when fried, and entraps water vapor which produces the porous inner structure which does not become overcooked by the hot cooking oil. Thus, overbrowning does not occur and the snack maintains the desired fresh potato chip flavor.

Example: The following ingredients were combined and blended in a five quart Hobart mixer using a paddle, turning at low speed for one minute.

	Grams
Standard potato flakes made from Idaho Russet potatoes having a screen analysis of 1.5% on 4 mesh (U.S. Standard); 34% on 10; 41.8% on 40; and 8.4% through 40 mesh	150
Potato starch, standard, unmodified, ungelatinized	150
Salt	7

During an additional one minute of mixing, 347 ml of water at room temperature was added. The mixing was continued on the same low speed for a third additional minute to insure uniform moistening of all components. This mixture contained approximately 42.8% solids, and in this state was friable, but could be shaped into a desired shape by application of pressure such as by squeezing into the shape of a ball with the hand.

The mixture was then introduced into the cylinder of a piston extruder. By the application of force from a screw, the piston forced the potato mixture through a die opening one inch wide and 36 mils thick. The extruded dough was smooth and uniform and was cut with a knife into pieces approximately two inches long.

The pieces fell into a standard laboratory fryer, containing hydrogenated vegetable oil maintained at 340°F where they were fried with gentle agitation for about 90 seconds. At this time they were removed, salted, and found to have a pleasing potato flavor resembling potato chips and a desirable crisp but not hard or brittle texture. The pieces had a slightly curled, attractive appearance and were fully strong enough for dipping in typical flavored dip mixes.

Ten such pieces were broken along a straight edge and when measured were found to have an average thickness of 75 mils giving a ratio of thickness to the original extrusion thickness of 2:1. This is the method of determining expansion ratio. The potato flakes used in this test were examined microscopically and found to have 21% broken cells. The quantity of free gelatinized starch contributed by the potato flakes was calculated by multiplying the dry weight of flakes by 0.21 (the percentage of broken cells) and by 0.72 (the percentage of starch in the flakes).

This quantity of free gelatinized starch, 20.8 g, represented 7.6% of the total dry solids in the dough. This calculation assumes all of the starch in a broken cell as available starch for binding purposes. The amount of ungelatinized potato starch in the dough is about 47% by weight based on the total dry solids present.

Preparation Using α-Amylase

In the process described by *C. Kortschot and P.F. Adams; U.S. Patent 3,840,673; October 8, 1974; assigned to Corporate Foods Limited, Canada* α-amylase is incorporated into a batter of potato solids from which a snack food is produced. The α-amylase partially hydrolyzes the starch molecules of the potato solids thereby increasing the solids content and reducing the viscosity of the batter. The potato snack produced has a lower oil content than normal. The product involves mixing a foodstuff containing potato solids with an α-amylase enzyme to form a premix. This premix is dispersed in water at a temperature at which the enzyme has good activity. The mixture is then heated until the enzyme is deactivated. The resulting mixture is shaped to the described thickness and then dried to a moisture content so the dried shaped mixture will produce a golden color when cooked. The product when cooked rapidly by immersion in hot oil or shortening or by baking or toasting results in a chip with an oil content that is reduced by at least 50%.

A preferred variation of the process involves following deactivation by aeration. The objective of this step is to create a number of very small air bubbles in the mixture. Although this aeration is not essential and a chip with good eating qualities can be made without its use, aeration seems to improve drying rates and by means of this step it is possible to more accurately control the tenderness of the chip. Aeration alters the fragility of the product by creating thinner layers of solids in the product.

In other processes used to make snack products similar to potato chips, where a dough containing potato solids is rolled, sliced or extruded it cannot be expected that a continuous surface film is formed as is the case in this process where a mixture with a batter consistency is cast onto a flat surface and dried and a continuous surface film is formed. It is believed that the treatment with an α-amylase enzyme results in the formation of dextrin and this improves the ability of the material to form these surface films.

The process produces chips with an oil content that is reduced by at least 50% as has been indicated above. The reduced oil content is accompanied by a lower viscosity which is probably caused by increased porosity in the interior of the chip which in part is increased due to penetration of the oil or shortening used in the cooking step. When the oil or density of the product or process is compared with regular chips it is found that there is a reduction of at least 20%.

When the reduction in oil, the reduction in density and the addition of some nonnutritive additive is combined in the process, a suitable method by which to produce a chip with a 50% reduction in calories per serving, if the serving is measured by volume rather than weight, is provided.

Example: A premix was prepared by blending together the following dry ingredients: 75 parts potato flour; 25 parts rice flour; and 0.05 part amylase enzyme. 150 parts by water were heated to 80°C. The dry premix was added to the hot water and because the premix was at ambient temperature, the temperature of the mix dropped to the 60°C range where the enzyme has good activity. The addition of the premix was regulated so that the viscosity of the mixture remained low enough to allow the proper agitation. The addition took three to four minutes.

After the addition of the premix was completed the temperature of the mix was raised to 80°C and this temperature was maintained for ten minutes to completely deactivate the enzyme. The next step was to aerate the material. The resulting aerated, hot suspension of potato and rice flours was then cast into a sheet with a thickness of about 45 mils. The resulting film was dried to a moisture content of about 30% and flash-fried in oil (or shortening) at about 375°F for a period of 10 to 15 seconds. Alternatively the film can be preserved by drying to lower moisture or by freezing and kept as a nonperishable semifabricated product.

Using Variable Potato Stock Made into Dough

According to the process described by *L.W. Wisdom and B.W. Hilton; U.S. Patent 3,835,222; September 10, 1974; assigned to Frito-Lay, Inc.* potatoes of different varieties, sizes and compositions may be used as starting materials. Potatoes generally contain from 70 to 85% by weight of moisture. The raw potatoes are peeled and blemishes are graded out. The potatoes are then sliced into potato pieces and washed.

The potato pieces should be treated so as to prevent enzymatic darkening. This is preferably accomplished by blanching the pieces in hot water or with steam for a time sufficient to gel a substantial portion of the starch contained therein, e.g., at 180° to 212°F for 1 to 10 minutes. The potato pieces are then removed from the blanch water and rinsed with a water spray to cool them and to remove excess free starch from the surfaces thereof.

After rinsing, the potato pieces are dried to reduce the moisture content thereof to 35 to 45% by weight. The potato pieces may be dried at ambient temperatures, or, preferably, by heating in an oven at 175° to 225°F. The dried potato pieces are then formed into a dough. This may be accomplished by grinding them in a food grinder which is fitted with a grinding plate having hole sizes one-fourth inch or less in diameter.

If the raw potatoes used have a reducing sugar content in excess of 0.2% by weight, it is preferred to treat the potatoes to lower the sugar content. This may be accomplished by adding 0.1 to 1.0% by weight of yeast, based on the total solids content, to the dried potato pieces before they are ground into a dough. The yeast may be added to the potato pieces in the form of an aqueous slurry. It is preferred that the potato pieces to which the yeast is added have a moisture content within the range of 50 to 60% by weight.

The yeast-treated pieces are preferably formed into a dough at 80° to 115°F. The dough is then allowed to ferment at 75° to 100°F for from one to four hours. By controlling the reducing sugar content of the dough, the extent of browning of the final product may also be controlled. Since heat browning does not occur unless reducing sugars are present, browning may be controlled by removal of a portion of this constituent. If the reducing sugar content of the raw potatoes is below about 1.2%, yeast treatment is not necessary.

Before the potato dough is formed into shaped bodies, it may be admixed with other starch containing materials such as rice flour, tapioca flour, potato starch, potato flour, wheat flour, etc. It is preferred that not more than about 40% by weight of the total solids in the dough be other starch containing material. If other starch containing material is mixed with the potato dough, the moisture content of the resultant dough should still be between 35 to 45% by weight, before it is formed into shaped bodies.

In forming the dough into shaped bodies, it is preferred to extrude the dough into a ribbon, to air dry the ribbon in order to case harden it so that the surfaces thereof are not adherent, and then to cut the ribbon into shaped bodies. A suitable extrusion apparatus is one which is capable of generating high pressures and elevated temperatures and which exerts a high degree of shear force on the dough. It is preferred to employ an extruder fitted with a tapered auger which will raise the temperature of the dough to 175° to 215°F when it emerges from the extrusion orifice. The extruded ribbon, which preferably has a thickness between 0.015 and 0.045 inch may be cut into shaped bodies by conventional means such as with a die. While the process is being run in a continuous manner, it is preferred to recycle any excess dough from the ribbon to the extruder to be mixed with fresh dough.

The shaped bodies are then dried to a moisture content of 8 to 16% by weight. This drying may be accomplished by placing them in a hot air oven which is heated to 120° to 140°F for 40 to 80 minutes. The resultant dried potato pellets may be fried immediately or they may be shipped in moisture tight containers and/or stored for an indefinite period of time.

Chips made by this process have a moisture content below about 3.5% by weight and an oil content of 30 to 36% by weight. The products are characterized by uniformity of color, flavor, texture, oil content, size, etc., both within each individual chip and between all of the chips. They are crisp and have an elegant flavor. Moreover, they are sufficiently rigid to withstand breakage during packaging and shipping and during use with dips.

Example 1: Raw potatoes (100 lb) having a moisture content of approximately 80% and a sugar content of less than 0.2% are peeled, trimmed to grade out blemishes and washed leaving about 94 lb of potatoes. The potatoes are then sliced into French cut shapes about ⅜ inch in thickness. These slices are blanched by contacting them with steam in a chamber maintained at atmospheric pressure for 2⅓ minutes. The steam is introduced to the chamber at a pressure of 15 psi and the temperature in the chamber is thereby raised to 198°F. The blanched potato slices are removed from the chamber, excess free starch is rinsed from the surfaces of the pieces and the pieces are cooled by a water spray.

Excess water is drained from the potato pieces and they are then passed through a hot air drying oven. The oven is operated at 200°F and an air velocity of 200 feet per minute. The dried potato pieces have a moisture content of 40% and weigh 30 lb. The dried potato pieces are ground in a meat grinder fitted with a grinding plate having orifices one-sixteenth inch in diameter to produce a uniformly mixed potato dough. This dough is fed into an extruder fitted with a tapered auger. In the extruder, the potato dough is subjected to a high degree of shear force. The dough emerges from the extruder at about 200°F in a strip or ribbon 10 inches wide and 0.020 to 0.025 inch in thickness.

The extruded ribbon, which is in a uniform, amorphous form, is then cooled and the surface is air dried to case harden and render it nonsticky. The ribbon is then cut by means of a die into pellets which are dried to a moisture content of 12% by passing them through a hot air dryer at 130°F for 50 minutes. The pellets are then fried by submerging them for 13 to 15 seconds in frying oil heated to 370°F. During frying, the pellets expand and form chips having a crisp, friable texture, a golden color and good potato chip flavor. The fried chips contain about 35% oil. The chips are then salted and packaged. About 26 to 28 lb of fried chips are produced from the original 100 lb of raw potatoes.

Example 2: Raw potatoes (100 lb) having a moisture content of 80% and a reducing sugar content of 1.0% are peeled, trimmed and sliced as described in Example 1. They are then blanched by immersion in boiling water for 1½ minutes and washed to remove free starch. The potato pieces are then dried to a moisture content of 52.5% and a weight of 38 lb. A yeast slurry is then blended with the dried potato pieces in an amount sufficient to give 0.3% of yeast based on the total solids content of the mixture. This requires 0.054 lb of active dry granulated yeast for the approximately 38 lb of dried potatoes. The yeast slurry is prepared by suspending the 0.054 lb of active dry granulated yeast in 6.3 lb of water. The potato pieces having the yeast coated on the surfaces thereof are ground in a meat grinder fitted with a grinding plate having orifices $1/16$ inch in diameter and having a cooling jacket to maintain a dough temperature of 96°F.

The resultant potato dough is allowed to ferment for $2\frac{1}{2}$ hours in a high humidity environment at a temperature of 85°F. After fermentation, the dough is extruded into pieces one-fourth inch in diameter and one inch long. These pieces are dried to a moisture content of 40% and are fed into an extruder, extruded into a ribbon, cut into pellets, dried and the dried pellets fried as described in Example 1. The resultant chips have good color and flavor. By contrast, chips made by conventional techniques from potatoes having the same sugar content as those used in this example have a very dark, burned appearance.

Two Stage Frying Process

P.H. Sijbring; U.S. Patent 3,812,775; May 28, 1974; assigned to Instituent Voor Bewaring En Verwerking Van Landbouxprodukten, Netherlands describes a process for the preparation of a fried edible product in two stages. In the process the edible product bodies are fried in the first stage in oil to a moisture content of 5 to 20% by weight, after which the prefried bodies are further fried in the second stage under reduced pressure and at a temperature not exceeding 100°C until the product has a moisture content not exceeding 2.5% by weight.

When the starting material is a potato derivative product, it already contains some sugars so that it is not essential to add an additional sugar. When the starting material consists wholly of starches some sugars must be included. In this latter connection it is to be observed that in the absence of sugars, the problem of considerable discoloration in frying does not normally occur. The starches may be used both in the gelatinized and the ungelatinized state.

In order to be able to shape the starting materials as required for frying, in slices or sticks, the starting materials may, if desired, be mixed with water or other suitable liquid such as milk, to form a stiff paste. In order to aid in obtaining a stiff paste condition, binding agents may be added, e.g. methylcellulose, polygalactomannan gum (guar gum), locust bean gum, and waxy maize starch. In order to improve the rheological properties of the mass, monoglycerides may be added. Flavoring may be added as required. The shaped bodies for the frying operation may conveniently be produced from such stiff paste products by a molding or extrusion process.

A final product with an attractive color can be obtained when the prefried product bodies are fried in the second stage in oil at a temperature not exceeding 100°C and under reduced pressure. In the process the frying in the first stage is effected at a temperature between 110° and 190°C until the desired attractively colored or golden brown product is obtained yielding product bodies with a moisture content of 5 to 20% by weight. During the after-frying in the second stage, the color of the product hardly changes, if at all.

In the second stage the frying preferably takes place at a temperature of 60° to 95°C. At a frying temperature below 60°C the frying takes a considerable time to attain the desired low moisture content. It is essential that, for the after-frying, the pressure does not exceed 500 mm of mercury absolute, while preferably it is from 50 to 100 mm of mercury absolute. In order to obtain a palatable and crisp product it is necessary to effect the frying in the second stage in oil.

A suitable oven for carrying out the second stage fully (described in the patent) consists of a closed housing, supply and discharge sluices, suction means for drawing off water vapor and to keep the pressure below atmospheric, conveyor means for moving the edible product toward the discharge outlet and means for removing the fried edible product from the oil before such product reaches the discharge sluice.

It is a great advantage of the process that the duration of the after-frying need not be accurately controlled. Since during the after-frying the color hardly changes any further and it is very difficult to obtain a moisture content below about 1.5% by weight, the risk that the frying time selected for the second stage be too long, is in practice almost excluded. A frying time of 5 to 10 minutes is in general sufficient, but a longer frying time is not detrimental. The risk of obtaining a quantity of fried product which is a failure is therefore substantially eliminated.

It is a further advantage of the process that the fried product bodies, such as chips, are homogeneous in color, i.e., that they all have practically the same color. If the product is potatoes, the latter are first prepared by peeling, removing the eyes and the discolored and unsound parts, and cutting them in the desired form, such as slices (for chips) or sticks. Subsequently the cuttings are washed with cold water so as to remove the starch that has been liberated from the cells during cutting.

The prefrying process is carried out as above, usually in a continuous cooker. After this, it is possible to introduce the prefried product, in a metal basket, into oil at a temperature not exceeding 100°C after which the pressure is reduced to the desired value and the frying is continued until the product has a moisture content not exceeding 2.5% by weight.

By means of a few simple trial tests it can easily be determined how long the frying must be continued at a given temperature of the oil and a given moisture content of the prefried product. After the termination of the second stage of the frying process, the product must first be removed out of the oil before the pressure is raised to 1 atmosphere again. In this way an excessive fat content of the finished product is prevented.

For the evaluation of the color of the fried product essentially visual methods are applied, use being made of standard samples. The evaluation of the color is expressed in a scale from 1 to 10, in which 10 refers to a very light-colored product, while 1 indicates a brown-black product. A color 5.5 is just permissible from the viewpoint of salability. A color 8 may be considered the optimum; in this case the product has an attractive color as well as a pleasant flavor. Products with a color value above 8 have too little flavor. At a color value below 8 and in particular below 5 to 6, the flavor is also less good. The flavor is judged by a number of trained test persons.

The frying of prefried product bodies, such as potato cuttings, in oil under reduced pressure can take place in an oven consisting according to the process of a closed housing with at least one supply sluice and at least one discharge sluice for the supply of the cuttings to and their discharge from the oven, a suction pipe for sucking off mainly water vapor from the oven and maintaining reduced pressure in the oven, conveyor means for moving the product bodies in the direction of the discharge sluice and for pushing the product bodies into the oil, means for taking the product out of the oil before it enters the discharge sluice and means for the supply, discharge and circulation of the oil.

Since in the second phase oil is used as the heating medium, it is mainly water vapor which has to be aspirated off in order to maintain a reduced pressure in the oven. The quantity of this water vapor is relatively small, so that in contrast to the use of air as the heating medium a small power consumption is necessary for the maintenance of the desired reduced pressures. Oil has the advantage that it can absorb many calories per unit of volume while no oxidation of the oil in the product bodies takes place.

The power consumption for the maintenance of reduced pressure in the oven will be low in particular if the aforementioned suction pipe is connected to a condenser, condensed water occupying a considerably smaller volume than water vapor. There are preferably separate means for the circulation of oil in the direction of movement of the product bodies and separate means for the circulation of oil transversely to the direction of movement of the product bodies. Thus a uniform distribution of the supplied heat is achieved, while the longitudinal circulation at the same time causes a uniform movement of the product bodies. The process further provides an efficient construction of the oven sluices, which does not involve any risk of the pulverization of the product bodies during the opening and closing of the sluice lids.

Example: Potatoes of the Bintje variety with a reducing sugar content of 1.20% by weight, calculated on solids, were peeled, the eyes and discolored parts were removed, and then the potatoes were cut into slices each having a thickness of 1.20 mm. The slices were washed in cold water for two minutes. 170 parts by weight of these slices were fried at 170°C in 7,000 parts by weight of peanut oil until they had acquired a color 8. This was the case after 72 seconds. The moisture content of the product was then 17.2% by weight.

The prefried product was put into a metal wire basket which was then immersed in an oil bath having a temperature of 90°C contained in a vacuum tank which was brought under a pressure of 60 mm of mercury absolute. The reduced pressure was maintained for six minutes. The basket with the fried product was then lifted from the oil bath. The oil was allowed to drip off for some time, after which the pressure was raised to 1 atmosphere again and the tank was then opened. The color of the product appeared to be unchanged, viz 8, the moisture content was 1.8% by weight and the fat content 42.6% by weight.

For the sake of comparison, 170 parts by weight of the aforesaid washed slices were fried in one stage at 170°C in 1,700 parts by weight of peanut oil until they had a moisture content of 1.8% by weight. The color of this fried product was 3. From the viewpoint of color and flavor the product was unfit for sale.

Use of Low Grade Potato Material

D.R. D'Arnaud Gerkens; U.S. Patent 3,753,735; August 21, 1973; assigned to Nibb-It Products Association Ltd., Switzerland has found that if potato flour or other potato sources having a high reducing sugar content (above 3% on the dry basis before water-blanching) are mixed with dried gelatinized starch which is produced in large quantities and can readily be purchased on the open market in the approximate weight ratio of 20 to 50% starch to 80 to 50% potato powder having a high reducing sugar content, and extruded and dried, a half product may be produced which contains reducing sugar in the right amount which will produce, upon frying in hot fat, a crispy, expanded product which will have the desired color, taste and bite characteristics. These raw materials are much cheaper than when premium grade potatoes are used.

The dried gelatinized starch having no reducing sugar content and no potato taste and having no cell walls gives an almost resistless bite when processed and in fact melts or dissolves in the mouth and, therefore, cannot be used alone to produce the snack food product, but when mixed in the above stated ratio with the potato flour it produces a half product which, when fried, has the desired potato taste, the desired puffiness and the desired color, as described below.

In addition the dried gelatinized starch has a high swelling power and when mixed with the potato flour it influences the swelling power of the mixture in a favorable manner. This enables the use of poor grade potato flour having a low swelling power or, more advantageously, the replacement of some of the potato flour having a reducing sugar content above 2% and a good swelling power by low grade potato powder.

The low grade potato flour used to dilute the water-binding or swelling power during frying and to a lesser degree also the reducing sugar content is well known. This low grade potato flour would have a swelling power as measured by the modified rehydration factor of less than 7. Examples of suitable low grade potato flour are instant potato products, potato flakes and potato flour which are off grade and do not come up to the standards required for making an expanded potato product.

Instant potato products and potato flakes of good quality always have a low modified rehydration factor, since starch not enclosed in the cell walls makes the product sticky. These products can be used as an admixture in this process, even if the amount of free starch is too high to make them acceptable as an instant potato product. Also, dried potatoes which have been stored for a long time and which have a relatively high degree of retrograded starch and a low modified rehydration factor may be processed to potato flour and utilized.

An accurate measure of the suitability of the dried potato powder mixture with respect to its water-binding property for producing the desired puffed end product can be obtained by determining the rehydration factor of the dried powder mixture. This is the quantity of water, which a certain quantity of dried powder can bind, divided by the weight of the powder used in the test.

Good potato powder mixtures for producing puffed products can have a rehydration factor of 12 to 15 but the ideal rehydration factor for producing the best puffed product is 8 to 11. Therefore, it is possible to mix various potato powders in the desired proportions to produce a mixture having a rehydration factor of 8.5 to 11 and to extrude, dry and fry to produce the best type of puffed end product. The swelling power of the half material in the hot oil can be accurately measured beforehand by measuring the rehydration factor of the ground potato powder mixtures.

From the dried potato or other powder to be investigated, a portion is sieved and the portion which passes through a 70 mesh sieve and is retained on a 100 mesh sieve is used. 2 g of this sieved powder are put into a calibrated measuring cylinder with an inner diameter of 1 inch. 40 ml of tap water of room temperature (20° to 25°C) are added, and the mass is stirred with a glass rod, care being taken that no lumps remain. The cylinder is now left quiet for two hours and the swollen potato meniscus is read. This reading, divided by two, is the modified rehydration factor (mrf).

From the Bintje variety of Dutch potato (a yellow fleshed potato), several batches of the puffed end product were made by the prior art process, varying only the cut, the blanching-time and temperature and the drying conditions in order to vary the modified rehydration factor of the potato flour; all other conditions were kept constant (e.g., salt content 4.5% on half material with 9% moisture). The results are shown below.

Batch	Modified Rehydration Factor	Weight to Volume Ratio of Puffed Final Product
1	2	≈1
2	6	0.31
3	9	0.18
4	12	0.16
5	13	0.14
6	17	0.12
7	20	0.10

Although it may seem advantageous to make a product with very low weight to volume ratio which means a highly puffed product, the practical limitation is that the more the product is puffed, the thinner and thus the more brittle are the material walls. In handling, there is too much breakage and pulverization so that a balance between puffiness and breakability must be maintained.

In marketing, the puffed product is packed in bags by weight. The weight of the contents of a bag is indicated on the bag. Variations in the weight to volume ratio of the product will result in half filled bags up to overfilled bags with broken contents, and a highly puffed, weak product will result in breakage in the bags producing fine crumbled pieces which the customer will reject.

For these reasons, a weight-to-volume ratio near 0.18 is preferred. This means that potato powder mixes having an mrf near 9.5 should be used as the starting material. The process readily enables the adjustment of the potato powder mixtures to within the desired reducing sugars content of from 1 to 2%, based on the dry weight of the powder, and a swelling power as determined by the modified rehydration factor between 8.5 and 17.

The potato flour used as one ingredient of the potato powder mixture may be produced from full raw potatoes which may be ground into a slurry and dried to a powder on a drum dryer or other scraped heated surface, or from cut, blanched

Potato and Other Snack Foods

and dried potatoes or may be low grade mashed potato powder, granules or flakes having a high reducing sugar content (above 2% on the dry basis).

When this potato flour is mixed with dried, gelatinized (tasteless) starch of commerce, in the right proportions and extruded into pieces and dried, the half product has the desired potato taste, the starch imparts additional puffiness to the fried product and the reducing sugar content of the dried half product can be adjusted to give the desired color to the fried product.

The weight ratio of dried, gelatinized starch to dried potato product or flour can vary from 20 to 50% starch to 80 to 50% potato product, depending upon the color, puffiness, bite characteristics and weight to volume ratio desired in the final fried product, and the process can, therefore, be used with a wide variety of potato products having a reducing sugar content above 2% on the dry basis and still be adjusted by means of the starch:potato ratio to give a half material having a reducing sugar content between 1 to 2%, which on frying will produce a fried, puffed, crispy product of substantially uniform characteristics regardless of variations in the potato raw materials available for use in the process.

Example: Second quality field crop potatoes of the Bintje variety containing 22% solids content and 3.2% reducing sugar based on the solids content were washed and lye peeled. The peeled potatoes were then ground in a hammer mill to obtain a thin slurry of finely divided potatoes and sufficient sodium bisulfite was added thereto to obtain an SO_2 content of about 50 ppm. The slurry was dried on a drum dryer (or scraped surface heat exchanger), then ground to a size whereby 100% was –40 mesh, at least 70% was –50 mesh and at least 50% was –70 mesh.

The powdered flour had a reducing sugar content of 2.9%, a modified rehydration factor of 8 and a moisture content of about 8%. 300 kilos of the potato flour were admixed with 300 kilos of gelatinized raw potato starch having an mrf of 17 to provide a reducing sugar content between 1 and 2% and an mrf of 12.5 in the mixture.

100 kilos of the mixture was then made into a dough by the addition of 5 kilos of salt and 35 kilos of water, to produce an extrudable mass having a moisture content of 28 to 35%. Other flavoring materials may be added to the extrudable mass. This mass was extruded under pressure into coherent bands and the bands were cut into pieces of about 30 mm and dried to a moisture content of 8%. This intermediate product or half product may be fried immediately or shipped to a frying point and then fried into the final crispy expanded food product. When the pieces are fried for about 15 seconds in fat at 180°C, a crispy expanded food product having a pleasing light brown color, a weight-to-volume ratio of 0.15, and an agreeable taste and bite is produced.

Use of Potato Flakes in Flour Matrix

The process described by *C.F. Glasgow; U.S. Patent 3,698,915; October 17, 1972; assigned to Pate Foods, Inc.* relates to a method for producing a chip-type fried food product containing as a major portion thereof potato flakes which are in particulate form distributed throughout a farinaceous flour matrix. The method comprises the following steps. A homogeneous mixture comprising 100 parts by weight water-rehydratable dried potato flakes, 40 to 70 parts by weight wheat flour, and 80 to 140 parts by weight water at 40° to 80°F are blended to provide an opaque nongelatinous crumbly structurally-discontinuous amorphous dough-blend having a temperature of 40° to 80°F wherein the potato flakes are in undissolved particulate form within the amorphous dough-blend. A finite-volume batch of the amorphous dough-blend is loaded into a hollow dough compression apparatus, the elongate annular side-wall of the apparatus surrounding a longitudinal-axis and defining an elongate internal chamber having a regular cross-sectional area representing a fixed-areal-quantity.

The finite-volume batch of the amorphous dough-blend along the longitudinal axis of the apparatus is compressed to attain a reduced-volume deaerated dough-log form that represents less than about 85% of the finite-volume to provide a relatively abrasive-resistant opaque nongelatinous dough-log having a temperature of 45° to 85°F and having the regular cross-sectional fixed-areal-quantity. The potato flakes are in undissolved particulate form within the self-sustaining dough-log.

The dough-log is extruded to provide a self-sustaining dough-ribbon having a regular cross-sectional area representing less than 10% of the fixed-areal-quantity. The dough-ribbon is cut into relatively short length dough-pieces which are then cooked in an oleaginous medium having a temperature above 330°F for a time period of 30 to 90 seconds to provide a golden brown chip-type food product. The food product has a regular cross-sectional area less than 20% of the fixed-areal-quantity to provide a nonpuff chip-type food product wherein the potato flakes are present in particulate undissolved form. The patent describes in great detail by means of accompanying diagrams the mechanical means for carrying out this process.

STARCH-BASED SNACKS

Chip Fracturing from Fried Ribbon

G.M. Campbell and S.G. Liedman; U.S. Patent 3,937,848; February 10, 1976 and V.E. Weiss, G.M. Campbell and G.L. Wilson; U.S. Patent 3,935,322; Jan. 27, 1976; both assigned to General Mills, Inc. describe not only the method but also suitable apparatus for the preparation of a dough material, sheeting and cutting the dough material into a ribbon of dough pieces, frying the ribbon of dough pieces to produce a ribbon of chips and then severing the fried, shaped ribbon into individual chips.

The dough may be prepared from any of various particulate starchy food materials such as potato granules, potato flakes, wheat flour, rice flour, corn grits and the like. The dough, when preparing fabricated potato chips, may be prepared from a mixture of potato flakes and potato granules. Alternatively the dough may be prepared solely from either potato flakes or potato granules. The The dough may have various other added ingredients.

The total moisture content is such that the dough has satisfactory handling characteristics. In other words, the dough has sufficient cohesiveness to stick together as a sheet and not so much adhesiveness to stick to equipment. Water is added to the particular material in an amount sufficient to form a dough. The total moisture content of the dough may vary somewhat depending on the particular starchy food material being used but will typically be in the range of 25 to 45% by weight unless otherwise indicated. The preferred moisture level is about 40%.

The dough is sheeted to any desired thickness. The preferred dough sheet thickness is about 0.015 to 0.06 inch. The dough sheet may be cut into any desired shape of pieces (i.e., unfried chips) such as round or oval. The pieces remain connected by a narrow portion thereby providing a continuous ribbon of pieces. The connecting portion is large enough to permit processing of the ribbon through the fryer and shaper without separation or breakage of the ribbon. The connecting portion is small enough to permit easy separation of the chips after removal from the fryer by fracturing the connecting portion. The connecting portion, for example, may be about one-eighth to three-eighths inch in width and the chips may be about 1 to 2 inches in diameter.

The ribbon is transported through a bath of hot oil to fry the ribbon. The moisture content during frying is reduced, for example, to less than 5%. Any type of frying oil may be used such as cottonseed oil, coconut oil, peanut oil and the like. The temperature of the frying oil is sufficient to fry the dough pieces to form fried chips but not so high as to burn the oil (i.e., below the smoke point of the oil).

During frying the dough is puffed or expanded and flavor is developed. The dough typically will expand about 100% in thickness during frying. In other words, the final thickness of the puffed chip may be about twice that of the unpuffed dough. The amount of expansion may be increased or decreased, if desired, such as by confining the dough during frying. The frying oil may be at a temperature of about 350°F. The frying time will be preferably 8 to 20 seconds.

The fried ribbon is pliable immediately upon leaving the fryer and becomes brittle or friable after about 5 to 10 seconds. Although the exact mechanism is not fully known, it is believed that the change from the pliable state to the friable state is a result of two factors, namely, cooling and dehydration. The change appears to be irreversible in the absence of the addition of major amounts of water.

The friable chips are then separated into individual chips by applying tension (e.g., bending force) to the ribbon causing a fracture across the connecting portion. In other words, one chip is held while a moment of force is applied to the adjacent chip sufficient to cause a fracture across the connecting portion.

Wetting Dough Surface Prior to Frying to Eliminate Blistering

Dough flats for eventual deep fat frying to produce snacks of the potato chip type are normally produced in the moisture range of 20 to 50%, although if a predrying step is employed, the moisture can be as low as 10 to 12% prior to frying. The process described by *M.A. Shatila; U.S. Patent 3,883,671; May 13, 1975; assigned to American Potato Company* relates to an added processing step conducted on such a flat immediately before the deep fat frying step. If water is applied to thoroughly wet the surfaces and then the wetted flat piece is introduced into the hot fat before the added surface moisture has had an opportunity to penetrate appreciably into the flat, the surface is apparently made more porous and the steam formed within the piece during deep fat frying is released uniformly and blister formation does not occur. With most doughs of this type, the optimum time of application with water prior to frying is only 1 to 5 seconds as it is necessary only to wet all surfaces; however, if the flat is allowed to stand with moistened surfaces for more than 1 minute before deep fat frying, moisture penetration into the interior of the flat affects finished texture adversely, producing an undesirably flinty texture.

A brief draining step of a few seconds duration can be employed if desired to remove free surplus surface water prior to frying. Excess water can also be removed by blowing it from the surfaces with an air jet. This draining step reduces spattering which occurs when free water is added to hot fat. The manner in which water is applied to the flat surfaces is not critical. Spraying or dipping in water as well as exposing to steam have been found equally effective.

Example: A dough of about 32% moisture was produced, the solids of which comprised about 98.5% of potato granules possessing high cold water absorption characteristics and 1.5% by weight salt. The dough was sheeted 0.03 to 0.045 inch and cut into flats roughly the size of conventional potato chips. The flats were divided into two test groups.

Test 1-A was immediately deep fat fried at 350°F for about 15 seconds. Test 1-B was dipped in water for about 2 seconds; allowed to drain for about 2 seconds and then immediately deep fat fried as above. The snacks of Test 1-A were good in flavor but had a soft-type texture and an unattractive appearance due to some surface blistering. The snacks of Test 1-B were free from surface blisters and were excellent in texture and flavor.

Shaping Fried Dough Product After Frying

In the method described by *J.E. Hunter and A.L. Liepa; U.S. Patent 3,864,505; February 4, 1975; assigned to The Procter & Gamble Company* snack foods prepared from farinaceous doughs are shaped into any desired shape after complete frying and removal from the frying medium during a fleeting moment of flexibility before the dough becomes rigid.

It has not been heretofore recognized that completely fried farinaceous dough material is flexible for a fleeting moment after frying. In particular, for a brief few seconds, generally for about 20 seconds after complete frying, the chip material is flexible. The precise time of flexibility is dependent upon the degree of hydration of the dough during frying and the moisture content.

Longer fry times remove more dough moisture and necessitate faster shaping. For fry times up to 30 seconds, shaping can be accomplished as long as 15 to 20 seconds after frying. However for longer fry times such as above 40 seconds, shaping should be within 5 seconds of frying. This period of flexibility can be taken advantage of in order to shape the fried farinaceous material into any specifically desired geometric shape.

Complete frying is determined by measuring the moisture level of the farinaceous fried material. Farinaceous dough material, as explained hereinafter, generally contains from 20 to 70% by weight of moisture. During frying, since the temperature is above the boiling point of water, the water is evaporated away from the farinaceous material. Thus, measuring the amount of water in the fried product is in fact a measure of the completeness of frying. The higher the moisture level, the more incomplete the frying; or, stated in the reverse, the lower the moisture level, the more complete the frying process. Complete frying designates products having a moisture content of 12% or less, and generally within the range of 1 to 5% by weight. Products fried for times sufficient to provide less than 1% moisture are difficult to shape. In addition to the moisture specified herein, a completely fried snack product is characterized by complete cooking and, at least after the period of flexibility, product rigidity and crispness.

The process is further explained with regard to potato chips made from dehydrated potato dough. Dehydrated potatoes and water are mixed to provide a coherent workable dough mixture suitable for frying to provide snack chips. The moisture level ranges from 20 to 60% by weight of the total dough mixture in order to provide a coherent workable dough mixture having the consistency approximately of bread dough.

Next, the moisture-adjusted coherent dough mix is sheeted. While sheeting can conceivably be accomplished by extruding, slicing, and stamping, it is usually accomplished by a roll milling operation. In this process the coherent dough mixture having a proper moisture content is fed into a roller mill and passed therethrough to provide a coherent workable dough sheet.

Where the proper moisture content is employed, one pass through a roller mill is sufficient to provide a coherent workable dough sheet. While additional roller milling at times may be necessary to form a good dough sheet, it has been found preferable to employ only the minimum number of roller mill passes. This is so because it has been found that the more work input put into the dough sheet, the greater will be the potential for flavor loss.

Sheet thickness is a matter of practical importance. Generally, very thin sheets will give a less intense potato flavor because the increased work input necessary to form thin sheets causes some cellular impairment; conversely, the thicker the sheet, the more intense is the potato flavor. However, very thick sheets result in a fried chip of poor eating quality because uneven frying often occurs resulting in chips burned at the edges and raw in the center. Preferred sheet thicknesses are from 0.014 to 0.030 inch.

After sheeting is accomplished, the sheet may be cut into any desired shape, size portioned, and fried in hot frying fat to provide a snack food chip. If frying is conducted without constraining during frying, and without subsequent shaping in accord with the process of this method, the product will be a random shaped product. On the other hand, if frying is controlled carefully by constraining sized pieces of dough sheet between mating molds, the final shape of the product will be rigidly controlled.

Generally, frying in hot vegetable oil is conducted above 212°F with the specific temperature and time employed dependent upon the farinaceous material from which the original dough is made. For example, with production of potato chips from dehydrated potatoes frying in hot vegetable oil is conducted at 300° to 375°F for 7 to 15 seconds. Frying times within this preferred range are quite short because short fry times destroy less of the naturally present potato reducing sugar content which therefore results in a chip with a slightly sweeter flavor note. Frying for times within the above specified ranges at temperatures as specified above will generally provide a product having a moisture content of 3% or less, and in nearly all instances will provide a product having a moisture content of 12% or less. In other words, the product will be completely fried.

After complete frying to a moisture content of 3% or less, the fried farinaceous material is ready for the final step. The final step is shaping the fried farinaceous dough material before the dough becomes rigid. Typically, this means within about 20 seconds after completion of frying, and preferably within about 10 seconds after completion of frying. Of course, the precise time period available for shaping will depend to a certain extent upon the precise farinaceous material utilized, the frying time, and the starch content of that material. However, the important factor is that shaping after complete frying must be done as quickly as possible before rigidity of the fried dough, believed to be caused by hydrogen bonding of amylose molecules, occurs.

There is no criticality with regard to the shaping, other than the time in which it is completed; accordingly, the precise method of shaping after frying can vary endlessly. For example, an entire farinaceous material dough sheet can be fried, the sheet can be cut into sized portions and shaped, all after complete frying but before the fried dough becomes rigid; the dough material can be formed into portion pieces; the portion pieces can be stacked; the stacked pieces can be fried, and after complete frying but before the stacked pieces become rigid, a compressing force created by oppositely disposed mating molds positioned at the top and the bottom of the stack can compress the fried portions into a uniform shape conforming to the shape of the molds. As shown in the example below, this method has worked well to provide uniform saddle-shaped potato chips.

Example: A snack food potato chip was prepared from a potato dough, which is a farinaceous dough, having the following formulation:

Ingredient	Percentage
Potato flour	59.6
Monoglyceride	0.8
Water	39.6

In mixing the formulation in order to provide a farinaceous potato dough, the monoglyceride was melted and added to the water. This mixture was heated to about 180°F and the potato flour was blended in after which the entire formulation was mixed thoroughly in a small Hobart mixer.

Thereafter a dough sheet was prepared by rapidly passing the dough through a 2-roll mill to provide a coherent workable dough sheet having a thickness of 0.016 inch. The roller mill was operating at a front roll temperature of 150°F and a back roll temperature of 190°F.

The rolled sheet was cut into flat oval shaped pieces which were then placed in 340°F frying oil and allowed to fry freely without constraint. Approximately halfway through the frying cycle the chips were turned to insure relatively even frying.

Attempts to shape the fried chips immediately after completion of frying were made at intervals specified in the table below. The chips were conformed into a uniform saddle shape by applying oppositely disposed mating molds to opposing lateral faces of the chips.

Time Lapse After Complete Frying and Before Shaping

Frying Time, sec	Moisture Level After Frying and Cooling, %	5 Seconds After Removal	10 Seconds After Removal	20 Seconds After Removal
10	4.7	yes*	yes	yes
20	4.1	yes	yes	no
30	2.9	yes	no	–
40	1.9	no	–	–

*yes indicates satisfactory shaping to conform to the shaping mold without breakage.

In yet another run a dough of the formulation of this example was fried at 340°F until it reached a moisture content of 9.5% and was tested and found to be shapeable 9 seconds after frying.

Low Density Puffed Product Using Protein Gel

In the process described by *E. Epstein; U.S. Patent 3,851,081; November 26, 1974; assigned to Beatrice Foods* puffed foods of lower densities and greater tenderness are provided by puffing foods, such as cereal snack foods, with a moisture containing protein gel.

The basis of the process is the discovery that certain protein gels in divided form may be dispersed in a food composition for subsequent increased puffing. Although the gel is in a solid, relatively dry and nonsticky form it contains sufficient water bound therein that during the heating step of a forming or cooking operation, moisture from the gel is uniformly liberated and promotes efficient puffing, lower densities and greater tenderness of the puffed food. Also, as can be easily appreciated, the addition of a protein gel substantially upgrades the nutritional value of the resulting puffed food.

While protein has been added to foods in the past to, among other things, upgrade the nutritional value of the food, these additions have always depressed the expansion properties of the food rather than increased them and, accordingly, have been unacceptable for puffing composition. Thus, as a commercial operation, proteins have not been successfully incorporated into puffed foods.

The success of this process resides in that the protein utilized is a protein gel which contains specific amounts of bound water. A protein gel is defined as a coagulated colloidal system having a three-dimensional network of protein structure and the interstices of the structure having water dispersed therein. It should also be noted that the softening or melting point of the protein gel is inversely proportional to its moisture content. Of course, the precise melting point of a gel will also depend on the particular protein used to form the gel. For purposes of the process, however, the gel should have a melting temperature between 250° and 550°F.

The protein gel may be made from any animal or vegetable protein which is capable of absorbing and retaining additional water and thereby forming a gel of the present nature. For example, animal protein such as conventional gelatin, or vegetable protein, such as acid soy protein, or milk protein, such as acid casein or sodium caseinate, may be used. Also, egg protein, such as lactalbumin, may be used. The protein may be placed in the gel state by absorbing water into colloidal protein. Thus, a dilute solution of colloidal dispersion of the protein is dried to the correct moisture content or water in intimate contact with the protein may be mechanically worked and absorbed into the protein. In any case, after the water is absorbed by the protein, the mixture must be allowed to dry at a rate sufficiently slow as to allow time for the protein molecules and colloidal particles to be arranged in a gel structure. Thus, rapid drying methods cannot be used to make the gel. Gel formation can be determined since the dried gel composition will be brittle and vitreous or glass-like in appearance and somewhat translucent, e.g., will have an appearance resembling a translucent plastic solid.

The temperature of gel formations is not critical so long as it is consistent with preventing denaturing of the protein and allowing the water to be in the liquid state. However, temperatures between 60° and 120°F are preferred. Any convenient mixing and drying apparatus may be used as long as the drying time and temperature are consistent with allowing sufficient opportunity for the protein to form a gel structure.

The extent of drying must be controlled so that the resulting protein gel has a moisture content between 9 and 12% by weight. These amounts of water in the gel will provide the above described properties of the gel and also allow proper puffing of the food. While the protein gel can be used for puffing any food, it is particularly useful in puffing snack foods and the like made from a grain or cereal such as wheat, oats, barley, rye or corn. A convenient material is simply cornmeal, since this is the carbohydrate normally used in the industry for producing snack foods.

The protein gel is ground to a powder by any conventional means, such as a rod mill, to an average particle size equivalent to approximately a 16 U.S. screen sieve or smaller. The gel and the cornmeal are mixed to form a uniform mixture. The amount of protein gel which can be added to the cornmeal (or other grain or cereal) can be from as little as 1% by weight up to any content desired.

Of course, the amount of protein gel and the amount of bound water in the gel will have a direct effect on the amount of moisture liberated during a subsequent heating step and, consequently, the amount of puffing performed. Of course, when additional water is used to make a dough or the like of a grain or cereal for shaping and cooking purposes, the water used in forming the dough will contribute to the puffing, although that water will be far less efficient in puffing than the water of the protein gel. Nevertheless, generally, on a weight basis, the protein gel will be contained in the composition to be puffed in amounts between 9 and 12%.

If desired, although not required, water may be added to the cornmeal and protein gel to form a dough, e.g., between 10 and 17% of water based on the total weight of the mixture of cornmeal, protein gel and water. The cornmeal mixture may also be shaped in any desired manner. Thus, the shaping may be by conventional food molding, extruding, etc. However, if the shaping step does not raise the temperature of the cornmeal mixture sufficiently high to cook the cornmeal and puff the cooked product, then a subsequent cooking and puffing step will be required.

For these reasons, it is preferred to extrude the cornmeal mixture at elevated temperatures wherein the cornmeal is shaped, cooked, or at least partially cooked, and puffed in the single extrusion step. Thus, as a preferred embodiment, the cornmeal mixture is extruded in the conventional extruder with a barrel temperature of at least 250°F and up to 500°F and with a die temperature of at least 275° to 450°F. Preferably, the mixture should not dwell in the extruder for an extended length of time and should be masticated, extruded and cooled preferably within less than 15 seconds.

The extrudate is then cooled by ambient air, or if desired, a blast of air may be used and the extrudate is then chopped with rotating knives to form the desired length of collette. The collette, as extruded, may have more moisture than desired, e.g., up to about 5 to 7% moisture, and if so, the collette may be dried in an oven or the like to a moisture content of about 2% or less. The collette is then flavored with any desired flavor such as a cheese flavor and the like by conventional methods such as tumbling, dusting, oil slurry, and so forth. The collette is then ready for packaging and consumption.

Example: Production of a Gel — Casein is dispersed in water to form a suspension of about 75% by weight. The suspension is slowly stirred with heating at about 150°F until a gel is formed. The gel is passed through a conventional food grinder to further incorporate water into the gel, and then broken in small pieces and slowly dried at temperatures not in excess of 150°F until a moisture content of about 10% by weight is reached. The dried brittle protein gel is then ground in a rod mill until the average particle size corresponds to about a 25 U.S. screen sieve.

Production of Snack Food — Ground casein gel of about 10% by weight moisture is added to cornmeal to produce a dry mixture having 20% by weight of the protein gel. Water is added to the mixture until the total mixture contains 11 to 15% moisture including that in this protein gel. A dough is produced by mixing and extruded in an Adams extruder with a barrel and die temperature of about 320°F. The emerging collettes are cut in 1 inch lengths and dried to a moisture content of 2% by weight. The collettes are flavored with an oil slurry of cheese solids by tumbling. The collettes had a density of about 2.4 to 2.8 pounds per cubic foot and were of exceptional tenderness. This procedure was repeated with differing amounts of casein gel and the corresponding bulk density is shown in the following table.

Percent by Weight of Casein Gel	Bulk Density, lb/ft
0	5.4
1	4.4
2	3.9
5	3.6
10	3.3
20	2.4 - 2.8
30	1.9

Using Starch with Specified Abrasion Rating

V.D. Harms, E.R. Jensen and R.E. Langan; U.S. Patent 3,753,729; August 21, 1973; assigned to CPC International Inc. describe a method for preparing snack food compositions. The process comprises preparing a mixture made up of a particulate starch material having an abrasion rating of less than about 30% and containing a minor amount of moisture, and a minor proportion of an oleaginous material. This mixture is forced under pressure by means of a screw-type extruder through a relatively small orifice. The product is dried, and then may be treated with flavoring ingredients as desired. Alternatively, flavoring ingredients may be incorporated into the mixture prior to extrusion through the orifice. The product is ready-to-eat, has a good texture and is free of the usual corn flavor normally associated with this type of food snack.

The particulate starch material used as the raw material in this process may be of any type providing it has an abrasion rating of less than about 30%. It may be a root or root-type starch or a cereal starch. Because of its ready availability, corn starch is preferred. The starch material may be an acid-modified starch, a chlorinated starch, dextrins, acid-hydrolyzed starch, enzyme-hydrolyzed starch, etc.

The oleaginous material ordinarily is a fatty glyceride such as olive oil or peanut oil. Vegetable oils are a preferred class because of their ready availability and low price. Olefinically unsaturated fatty glycerides are very suitable. The presence of the oil with the starch material serves to prevent localized overheating in the extruder and thereby diminishes the possibility that the product will be charred. It also results in smoother operation of the extruder and virtually eliminates the necessity for frequent shutdown for purposes of cleaning. It also diminishes dusting.

As much as 1% based on the weight of the starch material is effective to serve these purposes and an increase in the advantages resulting from its use is observed with an increase in the concentration of the fatty glyceride up to a level of about 10%. Beyond that, the effect does not appear to be increased; furthermore, more than this maximum proportion of oleaginous material diminishes friction to the point where too little heat is generated to cook the starch material. The preferred level of concentration is about 2%.

The process involves merely adding the mixture of starch material and fatty glyceride through a hopper into a housing containing a screw which receives the mixture and forces it through the housing and out through a small orifice. The screw speed in the extruder is preferably 300 to 450 rpm. The screw, or auger, is 5 to 10 inches long; it compresses the starch and oleaginous material and the combination of this developed pressure and shearing action causes the temperature of the starch-oil mixture within the housing to rise above 100°C.

The developed pressure is believed to be of the order of 350 to 500 psi. The residence time of the starch-fatty glyceride is but a matter of seconds and as it emerges from the orifice it is immediately puffed to several times its previous volume. The extruded material may be cut into relatively short lengths by a rotating knife. The extruded or expelled starchy product is fully cooked and readily digestible.

A particularly preferred material, however, is an acid-modified starch. Particularly preferred starch materials are those having abrasion ratings less than 20%. The abrasion rating of a starch material is determined by placing a 200-gram sample in a 100-mesh sieve and shaking it for 5 minutes, then weighing the material in the pan, i.e., that which has passed through the sieve, and designating it original dust. The remaining material on the sieve is placed in a two-quart Mason jar and the jar is rotated at 75 rpm for 60 minutes; this material then is

Potato and Other Snack Foods

shaken through the 100-mesh sieve for 5 minutes and the material in the pan is designated abrasion dust. The percent abrasion is determined as follows:

% Abrasion = (Abrasion dust, g x 100)/(200 g − Original dust, g)

A particularly suitable starch material is one which has been acid-modified to a Scott viscosity of about 15 g/44 sec, then spray dried (or flash dried) to a moisture content of about 12%. This dried material is compacted by passing through heavy rolls from which it emerges in the form of a sheet; this sheet is powdered in a hammer mill. Other known methods of preparing starch having these characteristics may, of course, be used.

The starch material ordinarily contains about 10 to 15% moisture which is effective in the overall process to cause the extrudate to expand to several times its volume prior to extrusion. As the material is extruded, there is an immediate pressure drop and the moisture entrapped within the extrudate causes it to puff out to as much as 1200% of its previous volume. The particle size of the starch material should be such that it passes through a 4-mesh sieve (U.S. Standard) having 0.187 inch openings. No more than 50% should pass through a 140-mesh sieve having 0.041 inch openings.

As the starch-oleaginous material mixture emerges from the extruder it contains some moisture and this may be substantially removed by passing the extrudate through a drier. In most instances, it is desirable to have a moisture content in the final ready-to-eat material, of about 1 to 3%. The extrudate generally contains about 5 to 10% moisture. Additional fatty glyceride may be applied to the extrudate, e.g., by spraying, so as to comprise up to 20% by weight of the ready-to-eat snack material. It enhances the flavor and also serves as a vehicle for additional flavoring ingredients and coloring agents.

Example 1: A homogeneous mixture of 98 parts of an acid-modified cornstarch having a Scott viscosity of 15 g/44 sec and 2 parts of a hydrogenated vegetable oil are fed into the hopper of a housing containing a 6-inch horizontal screw having a 3-inch diameter and 1-inch pitch. The acid-modified starch has an abrasion rating of 15%, a moisture content of 12%, and a particle size such that all of it passes through a 4-mesh sieve (U.S. Standard) having 0.187 inch openings and no more than 7% passes through a 28-mesh sieve (Tyler) having 0.0232 inch openings.

The screw is operated at 400 rpm, and the starch-oil is fed into the hopper at such a rate as to produce extrudate at the rate of 300 lb/hr. The extrudate contains 8.5% moisture which is decreased to 3% by drying on trays in an oven at 150°F. The dried material then is sprayed with hydrogenated vegetable oil and a cheese flavoring agent added.

Example 2: Several starches of varying abrasion ratings are each homogeneously mixed with 1 to 2 parts of vegetable oil. The premixed blends are extruded in the manner described in Example 1. Each of the starch samples contained 11.0 to 12.5% water. In some samples, additional water is added with no apparent effect on the results or the operation of the extruder. The characteristics of each of the starches in the tests are set forth in the table on the following page. The granulated starch used in Trials 1 and 2 has a Scott viscosity of 15 grams/40 to 48 seconds. The starches used in Trials 3 through 6 have a Scott viscosity of 12 grams/70 seconds. The particle size of the starches used in Trials

1 through 4 is such that all of it passes through a 4-mesh sieve (U.S. Standard) having 0.187 inch openings and no more than 7% passes through a 28-mesh sieve (Tyler) having 0.0232 inch openings. The particle size of the starch used in Trials 5 and 6 is such that substantially all of it passes through a 10-mesh sieve (U.S. Standard) having 0.787 inch openings and more than 50% passes through a 140-mesh sieve having 0.0041 inch openings.

Trial	Type of Starch	Premix Additives Oil Added, %	Premix Additives H_2O Added, %	Abrasion Rating, %
1	Acid thinned granulated cornstarch	1	2	8.5
2	Acid thinned granulated cornstarch	2	0	8.5
3	Granulated unmodified cornstarch	1	2	28.8
4	Granulated unmodified cornstarch	1	0	28.8
5	Unmodified non-granulated cornstarch	1	2	38.1
6	Unmodified non-granulated cornstarch	1	2	38.1

Trials 1 and 2 produced an excellent extrudate with no feeding or extruding problems. The product is a ready-to-eat bland food which can be modified by drying and spraying with hydrogenated vegetable oil and a flavoring agent. In Trials 3 and 4, minor feeding problems were encountered due to the higher abrasion rating of the starch. In Trials 5 and 6, wherein the percent abrasion ratings of the starch averaged 38.1%, the starch could not be extruded because the product bridged in the opening of the extruder causing a feeding stoppage.

It is apparent from the above comparative tests, that the abrasion rating and particle size of the starch are critical to the successful extrusion of the starch. Therefore, it is essential that the granulated starch material have an abrasion rating less than 30%, however, better results are obtainable with granulated starches having an abrasion rating less than 20% and the particle size of the granulated starch material being such that less than 50% will pass through a sieve screen having 0.0041 inch openings.

The mixture of starch material and fatty glyceride used in the process may contain substantial proportions of corn grits, i.e., dehulled and degerminated corn. In these instances, the abrasive character of the starch material is not so critical and the abrasion rating of a starch material in such a mixture may be somewhat higher than otherwise, although it still should be less than about 30, however, an abrasion rating of less than about 50 can be tolerated when 50% or more of the mixture contains corn grits. An illustrative mixture of this sort contains 40 parts of starch, 56 parts of corn grits and 4 parts of hydrogenated vegetable oil.

Extruded Item Requiring No Further Cooking

R.W. La Warre, Sr.; U.S. Patent 3,711,296; January 16, 1973; assigned to Beatrice Foods Co. describes a method and apparatus for extruding a cereal composition into a shaped snack food. The particular cereal composition is liquefied in the extruder and fully cooked in a short time. The extruded and chopped shape requires no further cooking and has a pleasing appearance and taste.

Briefly stated, the method depends on the use of a special composition of cereal meals which may be heated and pressurized to a liquid state and accomplishes a complete cooking of the meal in the shaping process, with no subsequent cooking being required. The composition is cooked and shaped by a particular extrusion process and the shaping die and chopper are of a particular configuration for use with the process, which provides a uniformly shaped product.

Any cereal meal may be used. Corn meal is preferred. Little or no additional oil is added to the composition. The natural oil of the cereal grain is generally quite sufficient, but up to 5% by weight, especially up to ½% by weight of an oil, may be used. The oil may be any vegetable oil. The water content is low; on a bone dry basis it should not be greater than 25% by weight of the meal.

For many uses no water at all is added to the composition. Furthermore, the coloring and flavoring agents may be added prior to rather than after extrusion. Hence the composition comprises a cereal meal, up to 5% of a vegetable oil, up to 25% by weight of the meal of water, coloring and flavor agents. Of course, if desired, preservatives, etc., and salt may be added to the composition. Generally, flavoring agents are contained in the composition up to 5% by weight of the meal and as low as 0.01% by weight. The color agents may be any of the certified food grade color agents and are chosen strictly as desired.

In the extrusion process, the composition must have at least 5% of water therein, based on the bone dry meal. The amount of water may be contained in the meal itself as the natural water associated with the grain. The exact amount of water in the grain meal will vary depending on the particular grain, the locality of growing of the grain, the growing conditions, etc. However, if an analysis shows less than 5% water in the meal additional water must be added to the meal prior to extrusion to result in a meal having at least 5% by weight of water.

With additional amounts of water the degree of puffing or expansion of the extruded product increases and if a highly puffed product is desired additional water, up to 25% by weight of the meal, is added prior to extrusion. However, no more than 25% of water by weight of the meal may be added since above this upper limitation a rubbery, tough, poor textured extrudant which is difficult to chop is produced and results in an unacceptable product.

The particular extruding device is not critical but it must be capable of grinding the meal to a fine powder. The powder must then be subjected to elevated temperatures and pressures sufficient to cause the powdered meal to go to a gel state and subsequent temperatures and pressures must be sufficient to cause the gel state material to then go to a liquid state. Hence the screw or screws of the extruder must have, in order, a feeding section, a grinding section, a first compression section, a second compression section and a pumping section. In connection with the above it must clearly be understood that the term liquid state means that the flow conditions of the meal are those of a liquid, not a solid or a gel, as is well understood in the art. The first, and preferably the second, compression zones must also provide a gas relief mechanism or the screw must be designed to allow back venting of gases from the compression zones through the feed zone and to the atmosphere.

When the product passes into the liquid state, the time for cooking of the cereal becomes exceedingly short. Depending on the pressures utilized, the liquefying temperatures (and hence the cooking temperature) may be between 200° to 450°F and the cooking time will be between 20 and 5 seconds. For example, complete cooking will take place with corn meal in the liquid state between 375° and 400°F in less than 10 seconds.

Since the exact cooking time and temperature are not narrowly critical, some overcooking and undercooking can be easily tolerated. However, for best results, the cooking time at any one temperature is slowly decreased (by increasing the throughput of the extruder) from about 50 seconds or more (60 to 80 seconds) until an optimum cooking time is obtained as determined by crispness, tenderness and taste of the extruded product, usually about 10 seconds or less.

The extruder die may be of any conventional design. Of course, if an onion ring, for example, is to be made, the die must be capable of forming a tubular shape which may be chopped to form rings. The die temperature may be from 375° to 400°F.

The knife blades of the chopper must be quite hard and sharp and are suitably made of tool steel which has been heat treated to eliminate distortion in the blades when operating at elevated temperatures. The knife body for holding the blades should also be heat treated to eliminate temperature distortions. The blades must not cut with contact against the die face, but must have a clearance between it and the die face.

At operating temperatures, at least 10 mils clearance between the blades and die plate is required, with at least 30 mils clearance being preferred. The clearance may be as high as 100 mils, but a clearance of less than 60 mils is preferred. Preferably the knife body and knife blades are adjustable both with respect to the clearance between the knife blades and the die plate and with regard to the position of the knife body which should also be perpendicular to the center line of the die plate. The thickness of the chopped shapes depends on the rate of extrusion, the speed of rotation of the knife blades and the number of knife blades.

Acylated High Amylose Starch as Expansion Prevention Agent

E.E. Bretch; U.S. Patent 3,703,378; November 21, 1972; assigned to Borden, Inc. describes the production of snack food products which expand upon baking or frying by heating a mix of a starch component and acylated high amylose starch as an expansion prevention agent to gelatinize the starch, cooling the mix to below gelatinization temperature and promptly thereafter shaping the mix into units of the shape desired.

The starch component can be a starch of any botanical origin, unmodified or modified by any chemical or physical modification. The preferred starch is any which has first been crosslinked with a polyfunctional etherification or esterification reagent followed by acylation, as with acetic or propionic anhydride. In this group of preferred starches, the modified waxy maize starches have performed admirably.

The edible expansion prevention agent is selected from high amylose starches, and more specifically, acylated high amylose cornstarches. This can be any product resulting from fractionation of whole starch to obtain the predominantly amylose component that is acylated and includes acylated whole starches composed of at least about 50% by weight of amylose. It is preferred to use the high amylose cornstarches which have been acylated as set forth in U.S. Patent 2,461,139. Such starches set in less than one minute, and more specifically, in a matter of seconds.

The above noted starch and agent comprise the important and essential components of the product which must be present in the paste before it is partially or completely gelatinized, formed, dried, and fried or baked. Depending upon the flavoring of the product desired, other starch materials, such as potato flour and tapioca, can also be incorporated into the starch component.

In addition to the starch component and expansion prevention agent of the mix, flavor and coloring ingredients are also added, depending upon the final product desired. Thus, for example, onion powder, dried apple, fruit flavoring and coloring, chicken flavoring, bacon pieces, barbecue flavoring and the like can be incorporated into the mix in the amount required to give the desired flavoring. The types and amounts of coloring and flavoring ingredients will, of course, vary depending upon individual taste.

As to proportions, parts by weight of the starch component to the expansion prevention agent may vary from 3:1 to 1:3, with the preferred range being 3:2. Effectiveness of the expansion prevention agent is lost if more than 3 parts of the starch component is used per 1 part of the agent. On the other hand, the final fried product is too hard for human consumption if more than 3 parts of the expansion prevention agent is used for every part of the starch component.

The steps in making the product are critical in order to have a continuous process and to obtain products having the smooth, nonblistering appearance required for saleability of the products. A paste is formed by mixing the dry ingredients with the water in a continuous mixer, as in a ribbon blender. The paste is one preferably of 65% solids. The paste is then continuously forwarded into a vessel adapted so that the paste can be heated to gelatinize the starches as it passes therethrough to the discharge end of the vessel.

A standard continuous cooker can be used for this purpose and the heating is ordinarily to a temperature of about 160° to 200°F. The partially or completely gelatinized paste, as it is removed from the cooker, is in the form of a continuous ribbon and is cooled to a temperature below that of gelatinization of the starch, i.e., below 100°F, although it can be held at the same temperature as the cooking temperature.

This is best accomplished by simply forwarding the ribbon of paste to an extruder on a conveyor exposed to the atmosphere. The continuously moving ribbon is then placed into an extrusion die of a configuration such that, as the ribbon is passed therethrough, it will impart the desired shape to the ribbon as it is being extruded. As the partially or completely gelatinized paste is extruded, it is cut into the size desired. Alternatively, extrusion may be eliminated and the product die-cut into the shape desired after it has been gelatinized and cooled simply by forming the paste into sheets of desired thickness.

The shaped partially or completely gelatinized paste is then dried to a moisture content of 8 to 12%. This can be accomplished by the use of ovens or by air drying. The drying is carried out in such a manner so as to avoid evaporation of water from the product since in preparing puffed products it is known that rapid removal of water by the use of high temperatures lessens the ability of the product to puff when fried or baked. However, drying temperatures of up to 185°F can be used resulting in rapid drying without expansion of the half-product.

In the preferred embodiment, the drying is carried out in two stages wherein after initial drying under atmospheric conditions or in an oven to a moisture content of 12 to 15%, the product is dried to a moisture content of 8 to 10% by being placed into revolving pans and hot air blown thereover. This acts to case-harden the exterior of the product by rapid removal of moisture from the outermost layers of the product and is preferably carried out just prior to frying or baking of the product. Also, the second stage of case-hardening can be accomplished in drying ovens, just before frying.

The case-hardening gives a smooth exterior surface to the product since it enables the drying air to be passed uniformly over all the surfaces of the product. In addition, and most importantly, case-hardening limits the amount of oil absorbed by the product if it is to be fried. The products can absorb as little as 10% oil.

The half-product at this stage is suitable for shipment in commerce since it is hard enough to withstand the severe agitation incurred in shipment of goods without breaking or crumbling. This is a significant economic advantage since these products, which require only frying or baking to be consumed, may be made in one central location and shipped great distances to be fried or baked, thus insuring a fresher product to the consumer and eliminating the need for many processing plants.

As noted, the half-product is puffed or cooked either by being baked or being placed in a fryer in the usual manner for puffing. After cooking, it is preferred for many products that additional seasoning be placed on the exterior of the product by tumbling the product with the seasoning desired as is conventionally done with other snack foods. The product is then packaged.

Example: A ring shaped onion flavored starch puff half-product was made from the following formula:

	Percent by Weight
Crosslinked modified waxy maize starch	35.55
Tapioca starch	31.12
Acylated high amylose starch	22.22
Potato flour	4.44
Coconut oil	4.44
Onion powder	2.22
Brown color	0.01

The components of the formula were admixed in water to give a 65% solids aqueous paste. The paste was heated in a continuous cooker to gelatinize the starch and, as removed from the cooker (in the form of a ribbon), was placed onto a cooling conveyor and carried directly into an extruder. The moisture content of the paste, as it left the cooker, was 25%.

The extruder extruded the gelled paste at a head plate in the form of a tube. Slicing means located at the extruder plate immediately cut the tube into individual rings about 0.075 inch thick. The rings were then conveyed through a drying oven maintained at a temperature of 184°F where the moisture was lowered to 15% H_2O in about 51 minutes.

The partially dried product was then further dried by hot air passed thereover in a revolving pan or drying oven to a moisture content of 8% and the product fried in cottonseed oil at a temperature of 360°F. After the frying the rings were tumbled with additional seasoning so that the final puffed product had the following formula:

	Percent by Weight
Crosslinked modified waxy maize starch	27.36
Tapioca starch	23.94
Acylated high amylose starch	17.10
Cottonseed oil	11.64
Onion seasoning	10.50
Potato flour	3.42
Coconut oil	3.42
Onion powder	1.71
Water	0.90
Brown color	0.01

Process for Aerating Batter and Casting into Thin Film

C. Kortschot and P.F. Adams; U.S. Patent 3,698,914; October 17, 1972; assigned to Corporate Foods Limited, Canada describe a process for the preparation of crisp snack foods wherein the food is made into a batter which is aerated or foamed and cast in a thin film prior to cooking. The combination of the aeration step, together with the step of forming a film allows storage of the uncooked food for prolonged periods and rapid cooking to produce a uniform product of good quality.

The process comprises the steps of dispersing the foodstuff with suitable edible additives in water to form a fluid batter, aerating the batter, casting the aerated batter into a film, and drying the film to a moisture content between 10 and 30%. While the resulting uncooked foodstuff may be stored for long periods in an uncooked state, in order to convert it into a crisp ready-to-eat snack food the dried film is cooked rapidly to a final moisture content of between 1 and 10%. This cooking step can be effected immediately by submerging in hot oil or by toasting at about 350°F.

The batter should be fluid enough to allow pumping and to allow handling in continuous mixers. It can be deaerated or aerated with close control, and the number and size of the entrained air bubbles can be regulated. In this aeration step the fluidity of the batter provides an advantage over prior processes.

A large number of factors affect the texture and eating quality of the finished product. Some of these factors are: total volume of entrained air, average size and uniformity of air bubbles, thickness of cell walls, solids content of the liquid phase and the structure of the foam after drying. The difference between an open and a closed cell foam is primarily in the rate of oil absorption during frying, this in turn affecting the appearance of the product. An open cell foam structure will result in a higher oil content and a more translucent chip.

Whipping agents such as egg or soy proteins and surfactants such as fatty esters can be incorporated to control foaming characteristics, plasticizers such as sorbitol and propylene glycol can be used to change the brittleness of the solid phase in the finished product. In the process of whipping the batter, adjustments can be made in the whipping time, gas pressure and the energy input to create a wide range of specifications.

In one embodiment, a satisfactory potato chip can be made when a batter containing potato and rice solids is whipped in a Hobart mixer using the wire whip. Whipping is continued until a foam density of 0.88 to 0.89 is reached. If this mixture is whipped to a density of 0.65 the walls of the foam tend to fracture during drying resulting in an open celled foam that after frying produces a very tender but rather translucent chip with a high oil content. Tenderness can be reduced by increasing the solids content of the batter and the translucency and oil content can be reduced by incorporating a colloidal material with good film-forming properties in the batter. This would result in more closed cells in the foam.

Another advantage of this process is that a simple casting of the fluid mixture on a solid sheet which may be a continuous belt is sufficient and the thickness can be controlled as desired. Towards the end of the dryer the product can be cooled and is then doctored off the belt as a continuous sheet. After die cutting the chips from the sheets, the final step of the process is a rapid cooking that may be accomplished by submersion in hot oil or by toasting in an oven. The regulation of the moisture content at the end of the dehydration step will result in proper development of color in the final cooking step.

Higher moisture will require longer frying or cooking resulting in more color development. Frying time in oil of 375°F is about 10 seconds for a potato chip formulation that contains 25 to 30% moisture after drying. Viscosity is controlled in this step. In the second step the batter is aerated and a foam with the right characteristics is prepared. In the third step the foam is dried to a certain moisture content and in the fourth step the product is cooked in oil or toasted. Each step can therefore be regulated independently as required and it becomes possible to adjust the process conditions and the material composition as necessary to produce both potato or corn chips and banana or apple chips.

Virtually any raw material is suitable for this process. Flours and starches have been mentioned already. Meat or fish in combination with fillers such as flours or starches can be made into attractive and nutritious products that are suitable for eating as a snack or can become an ingredient in dishes such as dehydrated casseroles. The formula would in the latter case be adjusted to provide the desired texture after rehydration. Soybean concentrates have been formulated into textured products and although these materials would normally result in very tough products, proper adjustment of the aeration can produce tender and friable products.

A variation of the process is to omit the final cooking step. After dehydration the products are stable when the moisture content is low enough. They can be stored at ambient temperatures for extended periods. One product possibility in this class would be a bacon slice that requires no refrigeration and can be fried into its final crisp texture in only 10 seconds. The bacon may be a natural composition or it could be made from a soybean composition with added flavors.

Another possibility is to produce dehydrated chips in a central plant and distribute these to institutional users or franchise holders. The chips would be fried for immediate consumption or fried and packaged for local distribution. This same procedure can be utilized when there is a fluctuating demand for the product. The dryer can operate continuously and dried chips can be stored until demand increases. In this manner only the fryers and packaging equipment will have to be large enough to handle peak demands. This represents a distinct advantage over current procedures resulting in a more scheduled operation and lower production costs.

Example: Potato flour and rice flour are dispersed in water to give a composition that contains 16.03% potato flour, 6.87% rice flour and 77.1% water. The batter is aerated to a density of between 0.88 and 0.89 in a Hobart mixer using the wire whip. The film was cast on the belt of a microflake dryer in a thickness of 60 mils and dried in about 4 minutes to a moisture content of 25%. The film at this moisture content is pliable and can be handled easily. The film is die cut into oblong shapes of approximately 1½" x 2" and the pieces are cooked by immersing them in oil at 375°F for 10 seconds.

Granular Modified Starch Binder for Dough Forming

C.W. Cremer, J.E. Eastman and R.V. Schanefelt; U.S. Patent 3,966,990; June 29, 1976; assigned to A.E. Staley Manufacturing Company provide a modified, granular starch dough binder which is especially useful in preforming bakeable half products which require only a single cooking step to produce a final, puffed crispy food product having good texture and mouthfeel. The preferred starch derivative is an acid thinned, waxy maize starch which has an alkali fluidity ranging from 17 to 61 ml, 2.5 g sample, 0.37 N NaOH, and has a hydroxypropyl degree of substitution of from 0.3 to 0.5.

About 30 to 70% by weight of the above granular modified starch derivative is blended with 0.5 to 10% shortening; 0 to 2% salt; 0 to 30% other food ingredients including meat, soy protein, dried cheese, sugar, corn syrup solids, powdered dry milk, dried whey, colorings, flavorings and emulsifiers; and 10 to 40% water. A dough mixture of excellent consistency is formed by blending the above ingredients at typical ambient temperatures of about 32° to 100°F without auxiliary heating to avoid gelatinizing the starch derivative.

The dough is easily preformed into half products by cold extrusion sheeting or other similar forming procedures. The half product can then be stored without deterioration for periods up to about 6 months prior to final baking, or it may be fried or baked immediately to produce a crispy, puffed product of good texture and mouthfeel characteristics. When the half product is to be stored, it is desirable to add about 0.1% by weight calcium propionate, or other similar preservative to retard spoilage, and the product should be suitably packaged to avoid contact with air. Refrigeration or freezing also insures half product freshness.

The storage period can be extended up to and beyond 6 months when the half product is held in a frozen condition, and airtight packaging tends to extend the period for which the refrigerated half product may be stored.

There is no requirement that the half product be made up ahead of the time of use, and all the advantages of formability and dough consistency apply equally well even when the baking or cooking of the product takes place immediately after forming.

The half product described here differs somewhat from the half products described heretofore in the snack food industry. The term has been used to refer to a shaped, gelatinized preformed product which has not yet been subjected to sufficient heat to cause the product to puff. Half product as used here refers to the shaped and cut dough pieces prior to any gelatinization step. By eliminating the pregelatinization step known in the prior art, the granular starch derivative greatly improves the handling and forming properties of the dough used to make the half product.

The preferred base starch is waxy maize starch. The granules of the cold-water-swelling starch derivatives of this process exhibit birefringence under a polarizing microscope. When water is added, the granules swell and lose their birefringence. This cold-water-swelling characteristic is believed to enhance uniform water absorption by the blended dough mixture.

RICE-FLOUR-BASED SNACKS

Rice Starch Snack Food

S. Abe; U.S. Patent 3,925,567; December 9, 1975 describes a process for preparing snack-foods from glutinous type starch, which is characterized in that a cake material prepared by kneading with steam glutinous type starch containing 20% or more of rice flour and/or other cereal flour, is immediately cooled and solidified, then cut to a desired shape, dried and baked into the desired snack foods with improved quality.

Glutinous type starch mixed with 20% or more of rice flour and/or other cereal flour can be used as the raw starch material. The glutinous type starch such as glutinous rice starch, waxy corn starch, glutinous millet starch may be used by mixing with rice flour (either glutinous or nonglutinous rice flour) and/or other cereal flour. The mixing ratios of rice flour and/or other cereal flour to the raw starch material is selected to be 20% or more in accordance with desired products.

The glutinous starch material containing 20% or more of rice flour and/or other cereal flour is kneaded with steam, with addition of water, for about 8 to 10 minutes to give a homogeneous cake material. After kneading, if necessary, steam may be discharged from a steam kneader so as to remove a bad smell of the starch material and obtain snack foods of good taste. It is desirable to prepare a fine and homogeneous cake material by satisfactorily kneading with steam. Since unhomogeneous cake material is easy to break in a drying step and undergoes bad effects on the swelling in a baking step, sufficiently swelled products cannot be obtained from unhomogeneous cake material. Therefore, the step of kneading with steam has to be carried out carefully in order to produce a fine and homogeneous cake material.

The homogeneous cake material is immediately transferred to a cooling step where it is essential to cool the cake material itself to a lower temperature as quickly as possible. That is, the cake material is preferably cooled to about 5°C within at least six hours after preparation thereof. The cooling is then further continued to give a solidified material of a satisfactory hardness for the next cutting step. The more quickly the cake material is cooled, the more favorable the taste and texture of snack foods become. Freezing of the cake material should be avoided since it adversely affects the quality of the product. The cooling has to be carried out under the above conditions, otherwise there cannot be obtained a satisfactorily swelled product with soft texture.

The rapid cooling and solidifying of the cake material is effectively carried out in such a way that the cake material is extruded into a sheet of 1.0 to 1.5 cm in thickness by a kneading and extruding machine and the sheet material is taken out on a plate spread with a flour, then immediately put into a refrigerator at 1° to 5°C and allowed to stand for 12 to 18 hours therein.

When the thickness of the material is more than 1.5 cm, a special high power refrigerator should be used. Thus, by means of the rapid cooling and solidifying of the cake material a satisfactorily swelled snack food of good taste and soft texture can be obtained. Moreover, even if the temperature of the cake material itself falls to less than 5°C by the rapid cooling, the cake material does not become too hard to be cut.

The cooled and solidified material is cut to a desired shape of 1.0 to 2.5 mm in thickness and then dried. When the thickness is more than 2.5 mm it is difficult to efficiently dry the shaped material, and the swelling of the material is disturbed in the baking step. It is desirable that the temperature of the solidified material be kept low for cutting thereof. The cutting is preferably carried out at a room temperature of 2° to 15°C within 2 hours. Subsequently, the cut and shaped material is effectively dried with ventilation at a lower temperature, for example, by a ventilating drier at 25° to 50°C within six hours.

The drying of the shaped material should be performed as rapidly as possible for preventing the retrogradation of the material. A conventional drier for nonglutinous rice crackers at 60° to 80°C may be also used in the drying step, thereby giving a product of improved quality. However, compared with the drying by a ventilating drier at a lower temperature, the shaped material is unhomogeneously dried and the quality of the product is apt to deteriorate.

After drying, the dried material is allowed to stand for 8 to 24 hours (aging) for the purpose of adjusting the water content thereof to definite level and obtaining homogeneously baked products. The aging is carried out preferably at 5° to 15°C because a higher temperature accelerates the retrogradation of the material. In the next baking step, the material is preferably baked a little at a time so as to produce a favorably swelled product of improved quality. Further, in the seasoning step after baking, the baked material is spread with a desired liquid relish when the temperature of the material is about 30° to 50°C, since the seasoning at a lower or higher temperature except 35° to 50°C cannot give the satisfactorily glazed product. As described above, snack-foods of improved quality having soft texture and good taste such as crackers, pellets, and the like can be obtained from the raw starch material containing 20% or more of rice flour and/or other cereal flour according to the process.

Example: 80 kg of a mixture of commercially available waxy cornstarch and nonglutinous rice flour (mixing ratio 7:3) was put into a steam kneader. After adding 50 kg of water thereto, the mixture was kneaded with steam under the steam pressure of 0.5 kg/cm^2 for 9 minutes to prepare a cake material. At the end of kneading the cover of the steam kneader was taken off and steam was discharged so as to remove a bad smell. Thus prepared cake material was further passed through a kneader in order to make a homogeneous cake material.

The homogeneous cake material was extruded into a sheet of 1.0 cm in thickness by a kneading and extruding machine and taken out on a plate spread with a flour. The sheet material was at once put into a refrigerator at 2° to 5°C and left for 14 hours so as to be cooled and solidified. The solidified material was cut into pieces (10 mm x 45 mm x 1.2 mm) and dried in a ventilating drier at 30° to 35°C until the water content was reduced to about 20%. The dried material was allowed to stand overnight at a room temperature in an air-tight container, then baked at 280°C, 1 kg at a time, in a baking oven. Thus baked material was spread with salad oil in the amount of 10% based on the material by a rotating drum-type glazing machine and seasoned with salt, thereby obtaining a fried snack food of improved quality.

Rice Flour Expanded Snack

V. Prakash; U.S. Patent 3,922,370; November 25, 1975; assigned to Societe d'Assistance Technique pour Produits Nestle SA, Switzerland describe a process for preparing a snack product which comprises forming a dough from a dry mix comprising at least 70% by weight of rice flour, and water, shaping the dough into separate pieces, subjecting the shaped dough pieces to a heat treatment to gelatinize the starch present, the water content of the dough pieces during the gelatinization treatment being maintained above 27% by weight, drying the gelatinized pieces to a water content below 15% by weight and optionally deep-frying the dried pieces.

It should be noted that the deep-frying need not be carried out immediately after drying, as the dried pieces are per se a stable intermediate product that may be stored, although, of course, the product is fried prior to consumption. The intermediate product is in the form of shaped pieces comprising at least 70% by weight gelatinized rice, 0 to 10% by weight cold swelling starch, 7 to 15% by weight of flavorings and/or colorings and 0 to 15% by weight of water, the rice having been gelatinized after shaping.

The process also provides a crisp snack product, in the form of pieces puffed by deep frying, containing 25 to 40% by weight of fat, 50 to 75% by weight of gelatinized rice and 0 to 10% by weight of flavorings and/or coloring and having a density between 50 and 90 grams per liter.

The starting material for the process is a rice flour, preferably having an average particle size of about 300 microns. Particularly preferred is a rice flour of which 75% by weight passes through a screen with 439 micron apertures and all remains on a screen with 180 micron apertures. In general, the starch of the rice flour is not gelatinized but, in a variant of the process, a mixture comprising ungelatinized flour and pregelatinized rice flour may be used, with the major proportion of the total rice flour being ungelatinized.

Before forming the dough the rice flour may be dry blended with different flavorings and/or colorings, such as spices and salt, these constituents normally representing 7 to 15% by weight of the blend. The flavorings and coloring may alternatively be added to the deep-fried product. The mixture may also comprise small amounts, preferably 1 to 10% by weight, for example 5% by weight, of modified cold swelling starch.

The rice flour, to which have optionally been added flavorings, spices and modified starch, is mixed with water in sufficient quantity to obtain an extrudable dough. The water content of the dough is preferably 30 to 38%. The resulting dough is then shaped, for example, by extrusion, to provide pieces having any desired shape, and preferably a thickness of 0.5 to 1.5 mm. If extrusion is used, the pressure may be between 20 and 80 kg/cm^2 and the temperature of the extruded product is generally not above 40°C. Extrusion produces a continuous ribbon or tube which is cut into pieces, and, according to the die used, the pieces may have the shape of shells, twists, gnocchis, tubes and the like.

After shaping, the pieces are subjected to the gelatinization treatment. In a preferred embodiment of the process, the product is placed on perforated trays and the treatment is carried out in a chamber or tunnel supplied with saturated or superheated steam. The operation may be performed at a pressure close to atmospheric and generally takes between 2 and 15 minutes, preferably 8 to 12 minutes at around 100°C.

During the gelatinization treatment the water content of the product should be at least 27% by weight and the temperature is desirably maintained above 97°C. The minimum duration of the treatment depends on these two factors but may be prolonged beyond the maximum times indicated above without affecting the quality of the final product.

As the gelatinized pieces are soft and tend to stick together, their separation without damage is facilitated by predrying, preferably at temperatures about 40° to 50°C. The predrying may advantageously be performed in a recirculating air drier, the product remaining on the trays used for gelatinization, and the duration of the operation is selected having regard to the air temperature. It is generally between 5 and 30 minutes, whereby the water content of the pieces should desirably be reduced to below 32% by weight.

The predried product is then subjected to a final drying step. This operation may be carried out in a continuous drier comprising a conveyor band on which the predried gelatinized pieces are placed. During the final drying step, the water content of the product is lowered to below 15% by weight, preferably 7 to 9%. The drying may normally be performed at any temperature between 20° and 90°C but, preferably, the temperature is maintained relatively low, between 40° and 50°C. The duration of the operation is related to the temperature; for the values indicated above, it is between about three and four hours. The dried pieces are a useful intermediate product, and they may be stored in appropriate air-tight containers.

The final snack product is obtained by deep-frying the dried pieces. The frying is preferably carried out by immersing the pieces in a bath of oil or fat which is held at between 180° and 230°C, for 4 to 14 seconds. Good results are obtained by deep-frying in fat heated to 200° to 210°C, the contact time of the shapes with the fat being limited to 5 to 7 seconds.

The fried product is in the form of attractive puffed pieces having a volume which is 4 to 7 times that of the unfried product. The pieces have a crisp texture and a very pleasant flavor. They are very light, their density lying between 50 and 90 grams per liter, as compared with 250 to 300 grams per liter for the dried intermediate product.

The low density is attained despite adsorption of fat during frying, which may represent 25 to 40% by weight of the finished product, and is directly attributable to the excellent puffing properties of rice flour. One particular feature of the product is its stability, in that if packed in appropriate containers, it retains its properties after prolonged storage at ambient temperature. In the following illustrative example, the percentages are by weight.

Screen (size of apertures in microns)	Product Retained (%)
560	0.5
535	1.0
439	5.0
320	31.5
225	24.0
180	18.0
125	4.5
105	7.5
fines	8.0

8.5 kg of rice flour, 0.5 kg of modified cold swelling starch, and 1.0 kg of an onion flavor composition are dry blended in a mixer. 3.6 liters of water at 20°C are then added to the dry blend (moisture content 10%). The mix is stirred for about one minute to form a coarse dough containing about 34% of water. The dough is fed into a screw extruder for pasta products which has a head provided with 10 annular dies 0.7 mm in thickness. The extrusion pressure is 55 kg/cm^2 and the dies shape the product into gnocchis, which are joined end to end and severed at the exit of the head with a rotating knife.

The dough shapes are placed on perforated trays which are fed into a tunnel supplied with saturated steam. The product is treated at atmospheric pressure for 12 minutes, at about 100°C, to obtain gelatinization of the starch. The steam passes from below and because of the large number of openings in the trays, the gnocchis are in contact with steam over most of their surface. During the whole length of the treatment, the water content of the product is around 32%.

The trays of gelatinized product are loaded into a recirculating air drier where the moisture content of the shapes is lowered to about 23 to 25%. The predrying is carried out at a temperature of 45°C for about 20 minutes. The predried product may then be removed from the trays without damage and fed directly to a continuous drier. The final drying is carried out at 45°C for three hours and 50 minutes. At the end of this operation, the moisture content of the product is reduced to 7 to 8%.

The pieces of gelatinized and dried dough are then deep-fried by immersion for about four seconds in fat heated to 207°C. The fried pieces have a fat content of 29%. The product has a very attractive appearance (shape, color) and the gnocchi-shaped pieces have a smooth uniform surface. The density of the product is 65 grams per liter, the texture is firm and crisp and the flavor very pleasant. Suitably packed, the product retains its properties after a storage period of more than three months at ambient temperature.

NUTRITIONALLY ENHANCED PRODUCTS

Protein Snack Food

H.J. Huelskamp, J.J. Collins and J.E. Devero; U.S. Patent 3,911,142; October 7, 1975 describe a ready-to-eat snack food product which is high in protein content and contains soy protein, whey and potato flakes. The product results from a critical sequence of processing steps.

The product utilizes soy protein, whey, dry milk, wheat flour, potato flakes, sodium bicarbonate, sodium potassium tartrate, vitamin concentrates and water. These dry ingredients are thoroughly mixed before adding water to bind the mass. This mixture is blended with part of the water and permitted to rest for a period of time sufficient for hydration of the mass through to the interior. The remaining water is added subsequently and as rapidly as possible. The formulation may be expressed in broad terms as follows:

	Range, %
Soy protein (at least 70% protein)	15 - 50
Whey powder	10 - 17
Nonfat dry milk	10 - 50
Wheat flour	7 - 15
Potato flakes	7 - 15
Flavoring	1 - 3
Sodium bicarbonate	0.2 - 0.3
Sodium potassium tartrate	0.2 - 0.3
Water	20 - 30
Vitamin concentrate	plus

The initial step of the mixing process comprises dry blending of the soy, whey, nonfat dry milk, flour, potato flakes, sodium bicarbonate, sodium potassium tartrate and vitamin concentrate for 10 minutes. Since the soy, whey, milk, flour and potato would not form a homogeneous hydrated mass if water were added without the particles of each material being thoroughly separated from the others it is necessary that the mode in which such separation is accomplished and the time, become a critical factor. This preblending of the dry ingredients is so critical that an acceptable product is impossible without it.

Following blending of the dry ingredients 75% of the water is added and incorporated into the mass. This composite is left to stand for 20 minutes to permit hydration through and through. If this is not done the mass will continue to hydrate in the forming and cooking processes with consequent failure to produce an acceptable product. After it has been determined that the first addition of water has penetrated the entire mass, the remaining 25% is added, which brings the mass to a condition of uniform stability. The remaining water is added rapidly, e.g., 30 seconds, since prolonged mixing at this point of time will render the mass sticky and unmachinable. Forming of the product to the desired shape and character may be accomplished by sheeting or extrusion. Imparting stability for transportation and consumption may be accomplished by air dehydration and frying. Analyses of the final product from a baking or air dehydration process is given below.

	Percent
Carbohydrate	52.75
Protein	35.50
Fiber	5.00
Moisture	4.00
Minerals	2.00
Fat	0.75
Vitamins	plus

Analysis of a final product achieved by frying follows.

	Percent
Carbohydrate	42.06
Protein	28.44
Fiber	4.00
Moisture	3.00
Minerals	1.75
Fat	20.75
Vitamins	plus

High Protein Expanded Food

A.V. Brown, Jr. and E.V. Oborsh; U.S. Patent 3,852,492; December 3, 1974; assigned to Ralston Purina Company describe a process of producing a high protein food product from oilseed meal, fish meal, meat meal, poultry by-product meal, and microbial protein, by mixing into the proteinaceous material having a controlled moisture content, a special reagent of edible water-soluble ammonium or substituted ammonium compound, and extruding such water-soluble compound under elevated temperature and pressure conditions to cause physical and chemical changes, and discharging such into a zone of substantially lower pressure, such steps resulting in the conversion of the particulate moist material into an expanded, water stable, readily hydratable, chewy product having a reticulated network of interconnected fibers or cell walls.

The process employs materials that are relatively high in protein content, and low in fat or oil content. They may be generally divided into two different classes of materials, the first including meat meal, fish meal, poultry by-product meal and oilseed meal, and the second being microorganism proteins such as brewer's yeast or equivalent microorganism protein from other sources.

The materials may assume a variety of sizes and configurations such as flakes, granules, etc., resulting from oil extraction processes. Solvent (usually hexane) extracted oilseed meal should be used because the residual oil, i.e., fat content is relatively small, usually about 0.5%.

Vegetable oilseed meals useful for this process basically comprise those edible substances resulting from the oil extraction of soybeans, cottonseeds and peanuts.

Such meals are relatively high in protein, usually 40 to 50% by weight, and low in carbohydrates. This protein content can vary as low as 35% up to 70% or more, and can be fortified by protein isolates or concentrates up to about 75% or so if desired. The carbohydrate content of the material should also be relatively low. That normal amount present in oil extracted materials can be tolerated. Specifically, added carbohydrate content should normally be less than about 25% by weight of the meal in the case of 44% soybean meal for example.

The moisture content of the material, normally about 12% by weight, is raised by adding moisture, usually water, to provide a moisture content within the range necessary for the process. Specifically, the moisture level is preferably raised to 27 to 33% by weight of the meal.

The special additives are also added at this stage of the process, usually dissolved in part of the added water. Dissolution in the water enables uniform distribution of the additive throughout the material. Broadly, the additive comprises an edible, water-soluble ammonium substance, specifically ammonium hydroxide and basic or acidic ammonium salts, or an edible, water-soluble substitute ammonium substance such as amines or amides, e.g., urea, or the like which leave no toxic residues in the resulting product.

Only relatively small amounts of the special additive reagent need actually be added. About 0.5 to 5 parts per thousand of the material, by weight, are effective, with usual amounts added being about 1 to 2 parts per thousand, i.e., about 0.1 to 0.2% by weight.

Particularly good results were obtained when using a combination of ammonium hydroxide (i.e., a solution of ammonia gas) and ammonium sulfate. Typically these would be present in an amount of about 0.1% by weight of the former (usually a 28% NH_3 solution in water) and 0.1% of the latter. The ammonium ions from both probably produce some free reactive ammonia under the elevated temperatures of the process, and although this would largely be retained in solution due to the elevated pressures, a certain degree of gaseous mobility would exist at the phase equilibrium at these conditions, so that this reactive group would not be strictly limited to liquid mobility, to thereby aid in the conversion.

Further, the sulfate radical may react with the protein also. This seems to be substantiated by the fact that a combination of these two reagents effects better results than either reagent taken alone.

A factor affecting the nature of the product, particularly the product produced from oilseed meal, is the pH of the treated meal. Normally the pH will be kept between 6.2 and 8 which ranges are above the isoelectric point of the protein or point of minimum solubility. Since these special additives are usually slightly basic in nature, and since the pH of stored soybean meal, for example, usually declines from an initial 6.7 to 6.9 down to about 6.1 to 6.4, the addition of the additive raises the pH to a desirable value of about 6.7 to 7, particularly if NH_4OH is used.

After the water and additive have been mixed thoroughly through the material, the mixture is fed into the inlet of an elongated extruder which has an elongated, rotatably driven, helical flight screw inside a tubular barrel. The screw has its helical flights around a central shaft, with the outer periphery of the flights being closely adjacent the barrel inner periphery surface. Preferably the barrel inner periphery has elongated grooves in it. Also, preferably the root diameter of the screw shaft increases toward the discharge end of the extruder. The discharge end has a die with restricted orifice outlet means.

The moist material fed into the inlet end is forcibly advanced by the helical flights of the rotating screw toward the discharge end, creating an elevated pressure in the unit as the material is forced to flow out the restricted outlet. Friction occurring between the material particles themselves and between the material and the extruder components causes the temperature to rise as the material approaches the discharge. Frequently, no further heat need be added to boost this temperature near the discharge end to the desired range.

This, however, can vary with the screw speed, the screw design, the extruder length, and other such factors so that sometimes it may be desirable to add heat to the outside of the barrel as by one or more conventional peripheral steam or hot water jackets along the length of the extruder barrel. Sometimes it may be desirable to pass cooling water through one or more of these jackets while steam, hot water, cool water, or nothing, is passed through one or more of the other jackets, to elevate the temperature at controlled zones up within the necessary range but prevent it from going too high before the material leaves the extruder.

Normally, the retention time of the material in the extruder is somewhat less than one minute, but can vary between about 25 to 150 seconds or so. It should be long enough for complete conversion of the material at the temperature and pressure present, but not long enough to cause objectionable scorching of the product. Scorching seems to be related to both time and temperature.

The elevated temperature in the extruder specifically must be above 212°F, and should usually be above 220°F. It should not be above 410°F, and should usually be below 375°F. The most preferred range is 240° to 320°F. Variation of the temperature enables some product variation without changing its basic nature.

The pressures within the extruder are relatively high, usually being somewhere between 200 to 1000 psi or so. The exact pressure does not appear to be critical but must be elevated to the extent that the back pressure prevents the material from passing through the extruder without complete conversion. Reasonable control of the pressure can be had by varying the added heat, the screw speed, the discharge die orifice size and the like.

In operation, therefore, the material has moisture added to bring the moisture content to 27 to 33%, and has the small amount of special ammonium or substituted ammonium reagent added, in water solution form. The material, moisture and additive are thoroughly mixed along with optional coloring or flavoring agents, and the mixture is fed into and forced through an extruder under elevated pressures and in the elevated temperature range of 225° to 375°F.

The product is then suddenly released through restricted orifice means into a zone of substantially lower pressure and temperature, normally ambient, to cause flash off of superheated moisture, partial dehydration of the protein structure, and expansion of the chemically and physically altered protein base material into a cellular or fibrous reticulated product. The product may be cut into chunks and is normally dried to a stable moisture content of 8 to 12%. It may have the capacity to be rehydrated rapidly, usually in about 20 to 50 seconds, simply by adding water, to constitute a resilient, elastic, porous, chewy but chewable, reticulated network of thin, integrally interconnected, soft, pliable fibers or membranes forming cell walls. These combined characteristics afford chewing and mouthfeel properties approaching those of meat.

The products from the meals constitute a combination of integrated reticulated fibers and membranes. The product from brewer's yeast is largely fiber-like in nature and in fact resembles chicken or turkey very closely. Various further processing can be practiced on the extruded product such as addition of flavoring agents and dyes, to render the food most effective for the market intended. The extruded product is highly nutritious. It has a bland flavor susceptible to alteration by additives.

Example: Soybean meal from which the oil had been hexane extracted to a residual level of 0.5% by weight and which had 44% protein content was increased in moisture level by adding water until the moisture was 30% by weight. A portion of the water added had ammonium hydroxide (28% NH_3 by weight) and ammonium sulfate dissolved therein in the amounts of 0.1% by weight of each to the meal. This solution and the rest of the water were thoroughly mixed into the meal with a paddle mixer.

This mixture was then continuously passed into and through an extruder, reaching a temperature approaching 300°F near the discharge end of the extruder under elevated pressures, followed by discharge out the extruder restricted orifice into the atmosphere. Upon material discharge from this orifice, a portion of the superheated moisture flashed off, causing partial dehydration, partial cooling, and expansion of the integral substance into a lattice type, water stable, integral, expanded rope of cellular texture.

The expanded product was several times the size of the restricted opening and constituted a reticulated network of integrally interconnected thin membranes. It dried readily and when rehydrated by adding an excess of water, constituted a resilient, elastic, porous network of thin, integrally interconnected, soft pliable membranes. The product was completely stable against disintegration in the water, and exhibited a chewy but chewable texture approaching that of meat.

Protein Fortified Snack

P.A. Blagdon, W.R. Malzahn and H.K. Fujiwara; U.S. Patent 3,849,582; Nov. 19, 1974; assigned to Ralston Purina Company describe a process for producing a nutritious protein-fortified low calorie snack food. Briefly, the process involves fortifying carbohydrate materials such as substantially gelatinized starch with a protein material which has not been substantially heat gelled. The fortified carbohydrate material can then be formed into a variety of snack food products, such as snack chips, which exhibit an increased shelf life, improved organoleptic properties, reduced calorie content, and improved nutritional value.

A modified starch source, such as an acid modified waxy maize starch, may be used in the process. It is preferred that the starch material be substantially pregelatinized before being used. If a modified starch is used, it may be added in proportions up to about 15% by weight. Typical modified starch materials are the acid modified, esterified and enzyme modified starches.

The protein source may be any high purity protein, for example, milk, egg, or oilseed proteins. The protein material should not have been substantially heat set or gelled prior to being used in the process, however. A functional isolated soy protein having a protein content of at least 90 to 95% by weight on a dry basis is preferred.

The starch modifying and complexing agent may be a saturated monoglyceride material which will react to mask the hydrophilic sites on the starch molecule to prevent the hydration of the starch molecule by water. A preferred saturated monoglyceride material for masking the hydrophilic sites on the starch molecule is glyceryl monostearate.

The process involves preparing a mix of the starch source, the protein source, the starch complexing agent, and water. The water is added in smaller proportions than would normally be required without the starch modifying agent. The mix is then formed into the shape of a snack food product such as a snack chip. The forming is preferably performed on an extruder. The dough should be extruded under conditions that do not heat gel the protein present in the dough mix in order to preserve the heat gelling characteristics of the protein until the fat frying step.

In forming the dough mix the starch source is added at a level of between 41 and 49% by weight of the mix and the protein source is added at a level of between 16 and 25% by weight of the mix. Between 0.25 and 4% by weight of the starch modifying reagent is added to the mix and between 30 and 48% by weight water. The mix is worked to form a free-flowing mixture, usually between 5 and 25 minutes. A conventional dough mixer may be used, such as a commercial ribbon blender.

It is believed that the starch complexing agent acts to align the starch and protein molecules of the mix and to lubricate the molecules so that intermolecular slippage is possible at a much lower moisture content than in a dough made without the added reagent. The starch complexing agent is a polar structure which is hydrophilic at one end of the molecule and lipophilic on the other end. The hydrophilic end of the starch complexing molecule attaches itself at the sites of the starch molecule which would normally be occupied by water, particularly the sites in the amylose fraction of the starch molecule.

The lipophilic portion of the starch modifying reagent resists hydration by water and acts to lubricate the spaces between the molecules. The resulting dough is thus able to develop the proper viscosity or elasticity for working at a lower moisture content. The starch modifying reagent also is believed to operate on the protein source in a similar fashion, though the water resisting effect may be somewhat less than that occurring with starch.

Due to the blockage of the water accepting sites on the starch and possibly the protein molecules there is less total water present in the dough and in the intermediate product formed from the dough. As a result, there is less water to boil off during the frying operation to be replaced by fat from the frying bath.

The forming of the dough into the intermediate product by extrusion is performed by passing the dough through the barrel of the extruder where the dough is mixed and worked by the action of the extruder screw. The screw flights tend to advance the dough faster than it can be expelled from the extruder causing backmixing and a great deal of internal friction in the dough. The friction develops heat in the mix and care must be taken to prevent the buildup of heat in the product to the point where the protein source is prematurely heat set or gelatinized. Preferably, the extrusion is performed in an extruder which is equipped with cooling jackets along the length of the barrel. Heat can also be added along the extruder barrel to maintain the temperature at a desired level, if necessary.

Preferably, the extruder is operated to maintain the product at a temperature between 155° and 185°F as the product leaves the extruder. The optimum temperature of the product leaving the extruder is about 170°F. The product leaving the extruder passes through a restricted outlet or die which forms the dough mix into a flattened sheet or ribbon. To form a desirable, crisp snack product when fried, the sheet or ribbon will be between 0.018 and 0.050 inch thick as it leaves the die. After the sheet or ribbon leaves the die, it passes over rolls onto a belt. The rolls and belt are preferably operated at a speed which will stretch the dough sheet or ribbon.

By imparting a stretch to give the dough an elongation of 25 to 100% or more, the cooking characteristics of the dough are improved. The stretched ribbon exhibits much better texture on frying; the fried product has fewer large, fragile bubbles, is denser and has greater strength than an unstretched product.

The unstretched product tends to form large, hollow, balloon-like structures when fried which are not suitable for snack chip products. The large bubbles break during handling, packaging, and transporting and produce a crumbled, unsatisfactory product. The large balloon structures also do not have the strength required of a snack chip product and fracture when used as a dip cracker. However, the hollow structures could be satisfactorily used for containers for filled type products such as egg rolls or ravioli.

The desirable elasticity in the dough mix is believed to be developed by the use of the starch modifying material during the mixing of ingredients prior to extrusion. The starch chains and possibly the protein chains are believed to be longitudinally aligned due to the action of the starch modifying material with the intermolecular spaces lubricated so that intermolecular slippage is possible. The alignment and slippage are believed to give the mix the resilience and elasticity needed for a good stretch prior to frying.

The ribbon or sheet is then cut to form strips by a conventional means such as a rotating cutter or a similar device. A finished cooked snack food product would preferably be in the form of a thin rectangular strip of approximately 1¼" x 2½" x ⅛" dimensions. The snack food intermediate strip leaving the extruder will contain 41 to 49% starch, 16 to 25% protein, 30 to 48% water, and 0.25 to 4% of the starch modifying reagent. The cut strips may then be transferred to a fat frying bath. During the transfer operation the strips may lose between 2 and 4% moisture. The moisture content of the strips placed in the frying bath will typically be between 30 and 46% water by weight.

The strips are fried in a fat fry bath for 15 to 60 seconds at 350° to 425°F to develop the palatable taste expected in a snack product. The material should have a pleasant golden color when removed from the fry bath, should have friable texture in the mouth, and be free of any raw spots. Excessive browning should be avoided in the product to prevent a dark color in the product which is not appealing to the consumer and to prevent deterioration of the nutritional quality of the product due to the browning reaction of the protein. The pleasing taste which develops in the product is due in part to the controlled development of flavor by the browning reaction and in part by the adsorption of fat. The presence of fat in the product is essential for proper palatability; however, excess adsorption is not desirable since the energy content or caloric value of the resulting product is increased and the tendency of the product to develop fat oxidative rancidity is increased.

Due to the low moisture content of the material entering the frying bath, the excessive pickup of fat during the frying operation is prevented. During frying, the heat from the frying oil causes the water in the fried product to boil, resulting in a dehydrating action on the fried material. The water which leaves the product is replaced by fat from the frying bath resulting in a fried product which is lower in water and higher in fat than the original starting material. By controlling the amount of water present in the starting material, a finished fried product can be produced which has a controlled fat content.

The frying operation also heat gels the protein material to a crisp submatrix which resists readsorption of water by the finished product. The gelled protein submatrix and the starch matrix which has been modified to resist water adsorbtion combine to produce a product which remains crisp for a long period of time even at relatively high moisture content.

Example: A protein fortified potato snack chip was prepared from 920 parts by weight pregelatinized potato flakes; 300 parts by weight isolated soy protein; 60 parts by weight salt; 20 parts by weight glyceryl monostearate; and 720 parts by weight water by mixing the water, salt, and glyceryl monostearate in a blender and by mixing dry ingredients in a mixer. When blended, the wet ingredients were added to the dry ingredients and mixing was continued until the mass was free-flowing.

The mixture was then extruded on a press using a 0.050 by 1 inch ribbon die. Water at 165°F was circulated in the extruder jacket; the extruded ribbon was stretched from 40 to 60% as it left the die. The ribbon was cut into 2 to 3 inch lengths and fried at 375°F for about 45 seconds. The fried product had a light golden color and a highly pleasing taste with a very crisp mouthfeel and fiber texture.

Protein Coated Potato Chips

R.H. Waitman, M.H. Kelly and F. Hollis, Jr.; U.S. Patent 3,754,931; August 28, 1973; assigned to General Foods Corporation describe a method for making high protein potato snacks. In practice, a thin potato slice is the preferred structure to which the coating of proteinaceous material is applied prior to deep-fat frying. Potato slices of a thickness used for the manufacture of potato chips are ideally suited because the potato slice is fully cooked at about the same time as the coating of proteinaceous material when the deep-fat frying takes place in a conventional batch and continuous equipment under frying conditions normally used for potato chip manufacture.

In addition to affording a product quite similar to the desirable crisp texture of potato chips, thin potato slices are also preferred because of their large surface area per unit weight which is conducive to adhering a significant amount of proteinaceous material in a relatively thin, uniformly distributed coating to achieve a high-protein-containing potato snack product.

Potato slices having a thickness of 0.030 to 0.060 inch are most suitable. As with conventional potato chip manufacture, the raw potato slices are optionally subjected to a sulfite solution dip to inhibit surface darkening prior to deep-fat frying. The sulfited slices are then surface dried of excess water and immersed in an aqueous mixture of heat coagulable protein.

A dilute aqueous solution of egg white has been found to be the preferred heat coagulable protein material for applying to the potato slices to effect excellent adherence of the majority of coatings employed. Fresh egg white or reconstituted dry egg white to which is added about 1 to 9 parts of water has been determined to produce the most preferred binding medium. This degree of dilution of the egg white assures a uniformly thin, tacky coating when applied to the potato slice; the coating permits the steam to escape from the potato as it is being cooked and yet tightly binds the proteinaceous food supplement to the potato surface.

Also, the use of the above range of dilution of egg white limits the amount of egg white which is applied to the potato surface to the extent the egg white flavor is not a predominant factor in the overall taste of the finished product. With the use of some proteinaceous coating materials, notably with fish, it has been discovered that the coating material inherently contains sufficient amounts of heat coagulable protein to satisfactorily adhere the supplemental protein coating to the potato slice without the use of egg white or any other binding material.

The coatings of supplemental proteinaceous material which can be applied to the potato slice can be selected from many sources. The critical factor, with all types of coating, is the capability of being adhered to the potato slice with a heat coagulable protein medium and that this adherence should be satisfactorily effective both before and after the heat coagulable protein is coagulated. Coatings of such materials as shredded fish, chicken, bacon, and ham have been successfully applied to potato slices by employing this method. In the case of fish, it has been found to be unnecessary to employ any binding medium.

The most desirable appearing and most effective adherence of the coating occurs when the coating is in a shredded form. A shred size ranging from 8 to 20 mesh is preferred. The coating is applied to the potato slice by any one of a number of conventional methods. The coating may be cascaded over the potato slices or the slices dredged in a body of the coating material. Preferably, a coating of 5 to 40% by weight of the deep-fat fried product is applied. The amount of protein added to the potato slice will, of course, depend upon the protein content of the coating material. In general, however, the protein added to the potato slice will range from 10 to 25%.

The coated potato slices can be deep-fat fried in conventional equipment of either the batch or continuous type, and using the standard operating procedures employed for the deep-fat frying of potato chips. With potato slices of a thickness of 0.030 to 0.060 inch coated with 5 to 40% proteinaceous material, deep-fat frying of 60 to 35 seconds at 350° to 450°F has been determined to yield excellent, flavorful well-cooked products.

Example 1: Peeled raw potatoes were sliced to chips having a thickness ranging from 0.035 to 0.045 inch. The chips were surface-washed in cold water, drained and then dredged in shredded, dry, salted codfish. The coated chips were then deep-fat fried in a commercial frying oil at 350°F until substantially all of the water in the chips was removed, as evidenced by near cessation of bubbling in the fat. The cooked, fish-coated chips were removed from the fat, drained and cooled and then packaged. The finished chips had a tightly adhering coating of codfish shreds which provided a desirable delicate fish flavoring. Analysis showed a protein content of approximately 20% on a product weight basis.

Example 2: Raw potato slices prepared as in Example 1 were dipped in a 1:1, by weight, aqueous dilution of raw egg white and then allowed to drain. The egg white coated chips were then dredged in coarsely ground, well-fried bacon shreds. The bacon-coated chips were then deep-fat fried as in Example 1 resulting in chips having a unique, tightly adhering bacon shred coating which imparted a desirable bacon flavor to the product. Analysis showed the bacon coated chips to have a protein content of about 15%.

CONVENIENCE POTATO AND GRAIN PRODUCTS

"INSTANT" POTATO PROCESSES

Ambient Temperature Storage-Stable Item

Prepeeled potatoes have heretofore been treated with minor concentrations of sulfite salt solutions to prolong their storage life under refrigeration. However, when significant concentrations of sulfur dioxide or its salts are used on raw prepared potato pieces, substantial potato cell destruction occurs, resulting in considerable fluid loss from the cells. As a consequence, commercially available potato pieces are either canned, refrigerated, frozen or dehydrated.

The prior art does not disclose or suggest means for producing high moisture potato products in the class of convenience foods which can be stored at ambient temperatures and which can be simply and quickly utilized to make a variety of potato dishes.

Frozen french fried potatoes are by far the biggest volume frozen food item sold in the United States. Over 2 billion pounds were sold in 1959. Such commercially available parfried products must be kept frozen throughout the distribution channels up to final heating prior to consumption. The inherent high cost is accepted since no other means has heretofore been developed for keeping the product microbially stable without such refrigeration. Prepeeled french fries are likewise sold in tremendous quantities. Such products must be held under refrigeration and even then have a limited storage life.

M.A. Shatila; U.S. Patents 3,959,501; May 25, 1976 and 3,895,122; July 15, 1975; both assigned to American Potato Company has found that uniform dispersion of sulfur dioxide in a critically controlled concentration throughout such potato pieces results in a product which can be packaged and stored at room temperature without microbial growth and without adverse effects on appearance and taste.

Ultimate consumer use involves either no preparation or merely heating and/or completion of cooking. The sulfur dioxide-containing potato pieces can be readily stored at ambient temperatures for periods in excess of six months.

It has been found that the process is useful even though the treated potato pieces have a high residual moisture content resulting in water activity far above 0.85. This level of water activity has been thought to be the maximum at which microbial stability can be attained by conventional methods of suppression of water activity, such as is employed to preserve intermediate moisture food products. The water activity of the gelatinized treated pieces of this process is 1.0. Thus the product is actually in equilibrium (at 100% relative humidity) with the surrounding environment.

Particularly advantageous results have been obtained where the ultimate concentration of sulfur dioxide in the treated product is at least about 200 parts per million (0.02%) with 500 to 700 parts per million being especially preferred. These concentrations of sulfur dioxide are intended to include both absorbed and free sulfur dioxide.

When the process is employed with an impervious container in order to exclude contaminating bacteria, it has been found that storage of the sulfur dioxide-containing potato pieces can be further enhanced by packaging them in an inert environment, that is, either in a substantially oxygen-free gas such as nitrogen, carbon dioxide, nitrogen-containing mixtures, or in at least a partial vacuum.

Special advantages have been obtained where absorption of the sulfur dioxide by the potato pieces is accomplished in a sealed container filled with a gaseous environment composed essentially of sulfur dioxide and nitrogen. The package is also preferably impermeable to moisture vapor and oxygen, thus maintaining both the desired moisture level and absence of oxygen.

It has also been found that rate of absorption of gaseous sulfur dioxide by the potato pieces is directly related to their temperature during treatment with sulfur dioxide. Thus the rate of absorption is sharply reduced when the potato pieces are subjected to a temperature reduction near freezing.

The product can be formed by treatment with sulfur dioxide both in the gaseous form and as a sulfurous acid solution. In order to insure that the interior of parfried potato pieces will be completely protected from the growth of microorganisms, it is necessary not only to employ a sufficient amount of sulfur dioxide, but to allow it to be absorbed generally uniformly throughout the piece by contacting all surfaces of the potato piece with sulfur dioxide. When a solution is employed, the sulfur dioxide absorption is accomplished by dipping the gelatinized or cooked pieces into the solution for a brief time such as a few minutes.

Generally speaking, when sulfur dioxide is introduced as a gas, the process can involve either the addition of sulfur dioxide to the ultimate package or the pieces can be tumbled in sulfur dioxide environment (such as would be provided in an air-tight rotatable drum) for a time sufficient to enable the pieces to absorb the prerequisite amount of sulfur dioxide gas after which the pieces are transferred to a package which is swept free of oxygen by flushing with inert gas before sealing. Absorption of the quantities of sulfur dioxide set forth herein to produce prolonged product microbial stability at ambient temperature decreases the pH of the potato pieces from 5.7 - 6.3 to 5.1 - 5.3.

It has been found that when potatoes are parfried, potatoes with sugars as high as 3% can be utilized without any sugar reduction treatment. By including a blanching step in the process, potatoes with sugar contents as high as 5% can be preserved successfully by reducing their sugar level to about 3.0%.

When potato pieces are prepared by parfrying, the amount of oil retained by the parfried pieces can be varied widely although generally the conventional level is from 5 to 15% by total weight.

For the reason that sulfur dioxide has a bleaching effect on the deep fat fried potato pieces, it is most desirable to provide additional coloring for the pieces following parfrying through the application of a heated coloring oil such as Vegetone, a natural color extract. The most desirable coloring has been attained when a coloring pigment such as Vegetone Popcorn Color, in an amount of 0.025 to 0.050% by weight was suspensed in Task oil (an animal-vegetable fat) and the oil suspension heated to about 100° to 250°F.

The following examples illustrate the process. All testing was performed at room temperature (about 75°F) and a barometric pressure of about 672 mm mercury. To determine concentrations of SO_2 at standard conditions, the following volume amounts would have to be modified by a factor of about 0.813.

Example 1: Fresh potatoes were washed, peeled, trimmed and cut into french fry strips about ⅜" x ⅜" in cross-section. The odd sized pieces were removed and the remaining properly sized strips washed to remove any free starch. The strips were blanced in 180°F water for 5 minutes and drained. The strips were then parfried by submerging in Task oil at 320°F for 4 minutes.

The parfried pieces were dipped in 200°F Task oil containing 0.05% Vegetone, drained and cooled near freezing after which one pound portions were added to impermeable flexible bags. Air was removed from the bags by displacement (sweeping) with nitrogen gas after which the bags were heat sealed. 0.290 gram (1 milliliter) of sulfur dioxide was injected into each bag which was then resealed.

The bags were stored at room temperature and examined periodically over a period of 6 months for microbial growth, appearance and aroma. Measurable sulfur dioxide concentration was found to be about 500 parts per million at time of packaging. The products were found to be stable in all instances. At periodic intervals, strips were removed from the bags and were oven heated at 450°F for 15 minutes. Large consumer panels judged them to be comparable to those made directly from fresh potatoes and markedly superior to those made from other commercially available potato products.

Example 2: Whole, unpeeled potatoes were washed and scrubbed to remove dirt and loose corky material; then cooked in Task oil at 250°F for 40 minutes. The cooked potatoes were then cooled at room temperature, packaged in the impermeable flexible bags and flushed with N_2 gas and sealed. 105 ml SO_2 per pound of cooked potatoes was injected into the bags which were then resealed and stored at room temperature. 105 ml equals 0.244 gram.

After prolonged storage, the product was found to be microbially stable and of excellent quality. The product needs only be heated for a baked potato.

Preformed Potato Pieces

M.L. Weaver, E. Hautala and M. Nonaka; U.S. Patents 3,946,116; March 23, 1976 and 3,812,274; May 21, 1974; both assigned to U.S. Secretary of Agriculture describe the product produced in a process by which potatoes are converted into convenience food products using techniques which provide advantages over customary operations which involves, in the case of French fried potatoes, washing, peeling and cutting potatoes into strips.

The potato strips are then washed with cold water to remove surface starch, leached in hot (about 150° to 180°F) water to remove reducing sugars, drained, and then fried in edible oil. The fried products may be utilized directly, or frozen for future use. When the products are to be consumed, the frozen strips are heated in the oven, or given a short (finish) fry in hot edible oil. Although the production of fried potato products is a relatively simple process, various problems confront the manufacturer. These problems are outlined as follows.

The necessity for peeling the potatoes involves substantial losses of valuable potato flesh. In the usual peeling operations, the losses average about 15 to 25% of the raw stock. Also, the peeling of potatoes requires the installation of complex equipment and procedures, and the use of corrosive chemicals such as caustic soda. Another factor is that conventional peeling systems yield enormous volumes of water containing organic matter, the disposal of which is a serious problem from a pollutional standpoint.

The cutting operation invariably yields a substantial proportion of irregular and/or undersized pieces. Such substandard pieces cannot be processed in the regular way and must be diverted into other channels which do not provide a full return.

The conventional step of washing the strips results in the release of both soluble and insoluble components from the cut cells into the wash water. Thus, there is a net loss of valuable potato material. Additionally, the wash water presents a disposal problem because of its content of organic matter. The conventional step of leaching the strips with hot water entails similar problems of loss of nutrients and disposal of the waste water. Another problem is the difficulty of producing products of acceptable and uniform color. This problem is brought about by variations in the chemical composition of the raw potatoes.

These and other such problems are eliminated by using the procedure of this process in which raw potatoes are cooked and mashed, the feature being that the cooking may be applied to unpeeled potatoes, whereby the peels become loosened during the cooking operation and can be readily separated as an incident to mashing.

In this way, the usual cumbersome peeling steps, requiring the application of lye or other corrosive substances, are completely eliminated. Moreover, by first applying cooking and then removing the peels, the procedure is not only simplified but losses of potato material are reduced. For example, peeling losses are generally 3.5 to 8% of fresh weight in contrast to losses of 15 to 25% in conventional peeling operations. The potato mash is shaped by extrusion, into strips or other desired forms. This technique completely eliminates the raw material losses and waste disposal problems which invariably accompany the usual procedure of cutting the tubers into pieces.

Substantially all the potato flesh is utilized. Moreover, since the pieces are from potato mash rather than by cutting from the whole tuber, it is not necessary to start with large tubers—potatoes of any size can be used. The problems of nonuniformity within the individual tubers is also eliminated.

The shaped pieces of potato mash are treated—as by applying a hot-air or hot-air plus steam treatment—in order to form a thin crust or case-hardened layer on the surfaces of the pieces. This crust improves the mechanical properties of the pieces. It renders them capable of further handling without danger of breakage, and it also ensures that the final product will have a desirable crisp exterior. It also protects the interior portions so that these portions retain their desirable mealy texture. In sum, the formation of a crust or case-hardened layer is a critical part of the process as it ensures that the final product will have the desirable qualities of a good quality conventional fried product, namely, a crisp exterior and a mealy interior.

Following the formation of these shaped pieces of mash enveloped in a case-hardened shell of potato tissue, various procedures may be used to advantage. A typical one is to fry the pieces and freeze them for future use. For ultimate consumption the frozen product merely needs to be heated in an oven to make it table-ready. A feature is that fried products produced in this process do not become limp as they cool; they retain their rigidity even when they cool to room temperature.

In addition, the products are of completely acceptable color even when the raw stock is potatoes which have been held in cold storage and which by conventional operations would yield unacceptable dark products. And since there is no need to wash and remove surface starch in this process, there is no loss of nutrients by any leaching effect and the disposal problems encountered in the usual systems which employ the water-contacting steps are avoided.

Another advantage of the process is that it yields products which have a higher solids content, i.e., more nutritive value, then conventional products. Moreover, the fried products contain a lesser proportion of fat than conventional products. In many conventional procedures, particularly where the products are sold in an intermediate stage for future frying or the like, it is necessary to incorporate preservatives such as sulfites to maintain color during storage. Another feature of the process is that no binders, preservatives, or other additives are required.

Another important factor is that the chilling does not cause the individual pieces to stick together; the pieces remain separate even where they are in close contact. This is a very useful attribute of the products—it permits the user to readily remove any desired portion from a package of the refrigerated pieces. It is further to be noted that the pieces retain their integrity; they do not crumble or break apart but are able to withstand the usual stresses encountered in packaging, shipping, and other handling operations.

In the following illustrative examples certain tests were carried out as described below.

Color Test: Color was gauged by comparison with a set of color standards used in the industry: USDA Color Standards for Frozen French Fried Potatoes, No. 64-1, Second Ed., 1966, Munsell Color Co., Inc., Baltimore, Maryland. The standard colors are numbered 0 to 4, with the higher numbers indicating darker color. Products generally regarded as acceptable in the trade are those which exhibit colors 1 and 2; products of color less than 1 are too light, those of color higher than 2 are too dark.

Deflection Test: Equipment was set up comprising a platform and clamping means so that a single potato strip could be held on the edge of the platform with 3.5 inches of its length projecting horizontally out into space. A protractor was arranged so that the angle of deflection (sag) of the strip could be measured. In this test, a small angle of deflection indicates a rigid strip, a large angle indicates one that is limp.

Example 1: The raw material used in these experiments was a lot of Russet Burbank potatoes (solids content 21 to 23%) which had been held in cold storage (40°F) for 4 months, and were used without applying any reconditioning treatment. It may be noted that these potatoes if used in conventional manner would produce French fries of undesirably dark color.

The potatoes were washed and cut transversely into 1-inch thick slabs which were cooked in steam at atmospheric pressure for 18 minutes. The cooked slabs were pressed through a screen, forming a mash, the peel fragments and defects being retained on the screen and discarded. The potato mash was extruded through a die to provide long rods of potato mash having a cross-section of ⅜" x ⅜". These rods were then cut transversely into pieces about 4" long.

The pieces of potato mash were then spread on Teflon-coated mesh trays and treated to case harden them. This involved contacting them for 3 minutes with a current of hot (250°F) air, then for 30 to 45 seconds with steam, and finally for 15 minutes with the current of hot (250°F) air. Weighing of samples before and after case hardening indicated that the pieces had a weight loss of 35%. The case-hardened pieces were then frozen in an air-blast freezer (air temperature, –36°C). The product was stored for several days under freezing conditions. It was noted that the pieces did not adhere to one another and they did not crumble or break apart.

A sample of the frozen product was fried in hot (365°F) oil for 1.5 minutes. Examination and testing of the fried product demonstrated that they had excellent flavor, a crisp exterior, and a mealy interior. Color of the product was No. 2 by the standard designated above. It was also observed that the product did not become limp. Initially—and even after standing until they had reached room temperature—the strips gave zero deflection when subjected to the test described above. In contrast, French fries prepared in conventional manner from the same of lot of tubers when tested after they had cooled to room temperature, gave deflections of 20° to 25°.

Example 2: The potatoes used in these runs were the same as those described

Convenience Potato and Grain Products

in Example 1. The potatoes were subjected to the same procedure when pieces of potato mash were spread on Teflon-coated mesh trays and treated to case-harden them, however different lots of the pieces were subjected to currents of hot air at either 200°F or 300°F for varying periods of time (as indicated below).

The case-hardened pieces were frozen in an air-blast freezer (-36°C) and held overnight at -10°C. The next day, the frozen pieces were fried in hot oil (365°F) for 1.5 minutes. The conditions used, and the results obtained are tabulated below.

	Run 1	Run 2	Run 3	Run 4
Case-hardening treatment:				
Air temp, °F	200	200	300	300
Time, min	20	30	15	20
Weight loss, %	31	36	31	42
Properties of fried product:				
Texture, exterior	Crisp	Crisp	Crisp	Crisp*
Texture, interior	Mealy	Mealy	Mealy	Mealy
Color, No.	2	2	2	2
Deflection:				
Directly after frying	0	0	0	0
After cooling to room temp	0	0	0	0
Total solids, %	43	46	n.d.**	n.d.
Fat/nonfat solids, %	16	16	n.d.	n.d.

*The product of Run 4 was crisper than the other three products.
**Not determined.

With regard to the data on total solids and the ratio of fat to nonfat solids, the following observations may be made. The products of the process are more nutritious than conventional French fries in that their total solids is over 40%, in contrast to an average of about 30 to 35% for most commercial French fries. Moreover, the products have a lower fat content—16% based on nonfat solids in contrast to 20% for most commercial French fries.

Reconstituted Rapid Drying Granules

E.R. Purves and C.O. Snively; U.S. Patent 3,917,866; November 4, 1975; assigned to The Proctor & Gamble Company describe a process for substantially increasing the available free starch in potato granules, whereby the level of retrograded starch is substantially decreased.

In addition, the rehydration rate of potato granules is significantly increased. In its broadest sense the process comprises mixing granules and hot water to provide a reconstituted mixture and rapidly drying that mixture. The reconstituted mixture preferably comprises a ratio of granules to hot water of from 1:1.5 to 1:5, and the hot water is preferably at a temperature of from 140° to 210°F. In a preferred embodiment the rapid drying is accomplished by a drum dryer.

In the first step of the process, conventional untreated potato granules prepared conventionally are mixed with hot water to provide a reconstituted mixture. It is essential if the retrograded starch level is to be decreased that the ratio of granules to water in the reconstituted mixture be at least 1:1.5. In the event that lower moisture levels are utilized, extreme difficulty in application to dryers occurs. Preferably, the granule to water ratio is 1:2 to 1:4. Where amounts of moisture in excess of the ratio 1:5 of granules to water are employed, the reconstituted mixture becomes too soupy and contains too much water for use; and, in addition, the process becomes extremely inefficient in that all of the excess water must be removed during the drying step.

The hot water employed in providing the reconstituted mixture should range from 180° to 210°F. If water at a temperature of less than 140°F is employed in preparing the reconstituted mixture, it has been found that the level of retrograded starch may not be significantly decreased by the process and the addition of heat input at later processing steps may be necessary as well as longer process times. On the other hand, the upper limit of 210°F is merely a practical one. No criticality exists with regard to the time of mixing of the reconstituted mixture, but preferably mixing should continue for at least 10 minutes.

In the final step of the process the reconstituted mixture is rapidly dried to yield a product having a decreased retrograded starch level and an increased rehydration rate when compared to conventional dehydrated potato granules. It is important to note that the final drying procedure is characterized as a rapid drying procedure.

While no precise criticality exists with regard to the specific drying technique employed, it is important that the reconstituted mixture not remain in the drying zone for long periods of time, for, if such occurs, the retrograded starch levels will substantially increase.

Preferably the residence time within the drying zone for any particular portion of the reconstituted mixture is from 10 seconds to 2 minutes. 10 seconds is the minimum time any known drying technique effects satisfactory final moisture contents. If any portion of the reconstituted mixture remains within the drying zone above 2 minutes, the retrograded starch level begins to increase and continues to increase rapidly with longer residence times in the drying zone.

The decrease in the retrogarded starch level and the increase in the rehydration rate is shown in the graph in Figure 3.1. The amount of retrograded starch which determines the amount of available free starch, as well as the rehydration rate of potato granules, has been found to correlate with viscosity measurements of certain slurries of the resulting potato granules. More particularly, if the amount of retrograded starch is low, the amount of available free starch is high.

The free starch when wetted becomes sticky and tacky, and the more free starch, the more viscous the slurry becomes. Consequently, a measure of the viscosity provides an indication of the amount of free starch and correspondingly the level of retrograded starch. These viscosity measurements which demonstrate the rehydration rate and the retrograded starch level are measured by an amylograph viscosity test. The resulting viscosity is measured in Brabender units, which is an arbitrary unit of viscosity measurement roughly corresponding to centipoises.

The amylograph is connected to a thermal regulator which allows the temperature to gradually rise from 25° to 55°C over a 20 minute period of time. The thermal regulator allows the temperature to be increased 1.5°C per minute. During this period of time the amylograph is constantly measuring the slurry viscosity.

As the viscosity measured in Brabender units increases, the material becomes more viscous because heating releases more free starch. A measure of the rehydration rate can be obtained by examining the slope of a curve which plots the viscosity against the run time in minutes as the temperature increases 1.5°C per minute.

In the graph, line **10** represents an amylograph run for ground potato granules which were not subjected to this process. Line **11** represents an amylograph run for a typical dehydrated potato flake. Line **12** represents a typical amylograph run for potato granules which have been subjected to this process.

FIGURE 3.1: RETROGRADED STARCH LEVEL vs REHYDRATION RATE

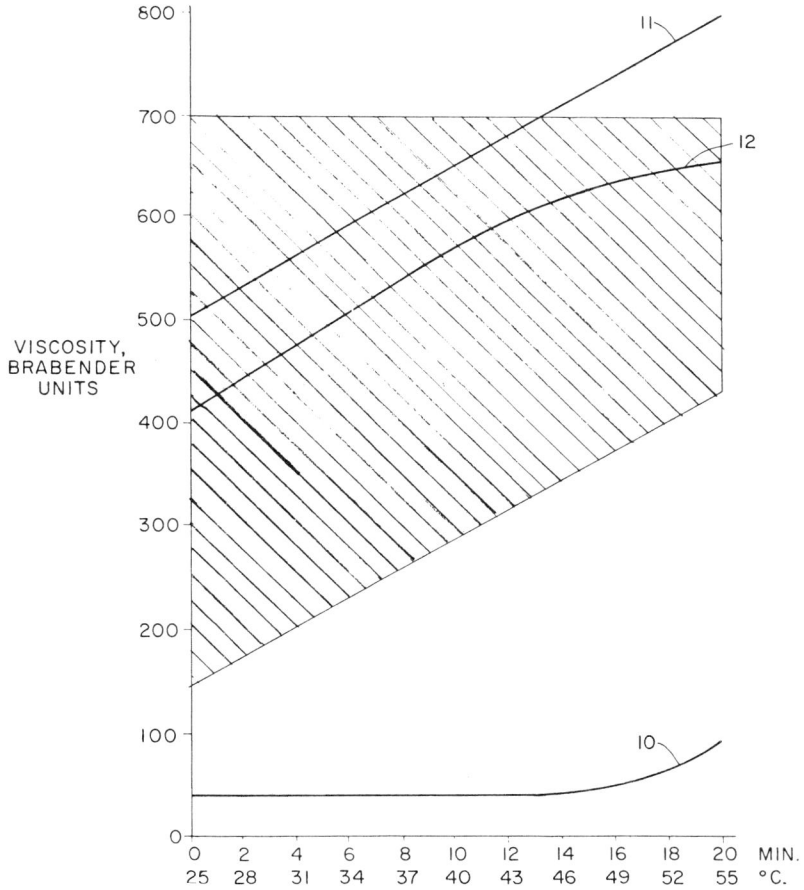

Source: U.S. Patent 3,917,866

Analysis of amylograms of potato granules which were not subjected to the process, amylograms of potato granules which were subjected to the process, and amylograms of potato flakes have lead to the following conclusions.

(1) No sample with an initial amylograph viscosity of less than 150 Brabender units can be utilized to successfully prepare a coherent workable dough sheet which is suitable for subsequent sizing and frying to produce a good quality snack chip product.

(2) All samples of conventional potato granules not treated by this process have an initial amylograph viscosity of less than 150 Brabender units.

(3) Subjection of potato granules to the reconstitution rapid drying procedure of this process will provide an initial amylograph viscosity between 150 and 700 Brabender units. In addition, the sample's amylograph will have a slope which is a measure of the rapidity of the rehydration rate, of at least 18 Brabender units per minute.

(4) All samples which have been subjected to this process to provide an initial viscosity of 700 Brabender units or greater, are capable of being utilized with success to form a coherent workable dough sheet which can be subsequently presized, shaped and fried as long as the amylograph curve slope is not negative.

All potato granules treated by this process at least have an amylograph viscosity curve falling wholly within or above the hatched area defined in the graph. These samples are especially suitable for use in preparing snack food chips because they have an initial viscosity of 150 Brabender units or greater and a rapid rehydration rate, i.e., a slope of at least 18 Brabender units per minute per 1.5°C temperature rise. In addition, samples having an initial viscosity of at least 700 Brabender units are all suitable for the purpose of this process provided they do not have a negative slope.

Further examination of the graph reveals that the retrograded starch level of a typical granule treated by this method can be brought to a level equal to that of a typical flake **11**, and that the retrograded starch level of ground granules which have not been subjected to the process are unsatisfactory as evidenced by line **10**. In addition, the slope of line **10** is substantially smaller than 18 Brabender units per minute per 1.5°C, indicating that granules not treated by this process have an unsatisfactory rehydration rate.

Example: 22 lb of conventionally processed potato granules having an amylograph corresponding to line **10** were reconstituted with 66 lb of hot tap water. The estimated temperature of the tap water was about 140°F and the ratio of granules to water in the reconstituted mixture was 1:3.

The reconstituted mixture was mixed for 15 minutes to provide a mash similar to that of whole cooked potatoes. The reconstituted mixture was then dried using a pilot plant drum dryer. The drum steam pressure was 40 psi and the drum was rotating at 2½ rpm. The dried flakes had a moisture content of about 8%, and the estimated time period for any portion of the reconstituted mixture within the drying zone was about 30 seconds.

Thereafter, the thus treated product was pulverized through a micropulverizer to an average particle size of 100 microns, and amylograph testing showed that the entire amylograph fell within or above the hatched area of Figure 3.1, indicating that the product was characterized by rapid rehydration and a low level of retrograded starch. Substantially similar results with those indicated above were obtained when a 20 lb sample of conventional granules was utilized with 60 lb of water at a temperature of 210°F and where the mixing time was 15 minutes.

The two treated dehydrated potato products previously mentioned in this Example, which had amylographs falling wholly within the hatched area of the graph shown in Figure 3.1, when mixed with 666.5 grams of treated dehydrated potato and 429 grams of water with respect to the former, and 605 grams of pulverized treated dehydrated potato granules and 390 grams of water with respect to the latter, formed excellent coherent workable dough sheets when passed through a roller mill. These sheets upon sizing and shaping and frying in vegetable oil at 340°F for about 15 seconds formed snack chips of excellent quality.

Method for Removing Peels for Dehydrated Flakes

The overall objective of the process disclosed by *J.D. Westover and E.M. Kiploks; U.S. Patent 3,862,345; January 21, 1974; assigned to The Pillsbury Company* is to provide a means for effectively removing the peel in preparing dehydrated potatoes.

In the process whole potatoes are first washed and sliced into pieces which can be cooked uniformly. This is accomplished by slicing them into slabs of uniform thickness. Pieces of any thickness can be used but from about one-quarter to one inch thick are preferred. These pieces are then inspected and undesirable pieces are removed. The sliced potatoes are then subjected to heat in the presence of moisture for a sufficient period of time to swell without gelatinizing (causing an outflow of starch from cells) the starch granules and without appreciably softening the potatoes.

In hot water at 165°F this can be accomplished in about 15 to 25 minutes with 20 minutes being preferred for pieces that are about five-eighths inch thick. It should be understood that at higher temperatures, the starch granules can be swelled in less time but if the temperature is too high, for example above 185°F, the starch cells on the outside of each piece may rupture before the starch granules in the interior of the piece are swollen. At lower temperatures, such as 150°F, swelling to the desired degree will require a longer period of time. Likewise, with thicker pieces, the blanching step will require more time.

To prevent starch gelatinization which if present will result in a pasty product, the pieces are preferably cooled to 70°F or less, and held at that temperature for a sufficient period of time to have a uniform temperature throughout. In a preferred form the pieces are cooled to 70°F and held for about 20 minutes to assure temperature equilibration.

The pieces are then cooked for just sufficient time to soften them to the point where they can be mashed (herein referred to as a mash consistency). This condition can be tested by placing a piece of potato between the fingers and applying pressure.

If the bonds between the potato cells are weakened sufficiently for the piece to be squashed without hard lumps being present, the mash consistency has been reached. If atmospheric steam is employed for cooking, about 15 to 25 minutes is required for pieces five-eighths inch thick. About 15 minutes is required for pieces one-half inch thick and about 25 minutes for pieces about three-fourths inch thick. In all cases, the uniform thickness of the slices assures the desired degree of cooking throughout each piece.

The potato should not be cooked past the mash consistency since to do so will cause the finished product to be pasty or glue-like. When potatoes are blanched with their skins on, the cortex portion of the potato becomes gray in color. Discoloration inhibiting chemicals can be used to prevent this color change. Sulfur dioxide is preferred, particularly with regard to cost and effectiveness. When sodium bisulfite is used to liberate sulfur dioxide, it is used in an amount that will maintain the SO_2 concentration at about 2,000 parts for each million parts of water.

In addition to sulfur dioxide, other materials can be used, such as sodium acid pyrophosphate (SAPP) and ethylenedinitrilo tetraacetic acid (EDTA) in the amount of about 0.066% by weight of the blanch water, and phosphoric acid in an amount necessary to bring the blanch water to a pH between about 4.0 and 4.5. These amounts would be capable of effectively preventing undesirable discoloration and the residual amounts remaining in the potato after processing would be edible in the quantities present (All quantities given are in parts by weight).

While the process is particularly useful in preparing a dehydrated potato product that can be reconstituted to provide a mashed potato product, it is also useful in preparing potato pieces for the manufacture of French fries and the like. In this application, the center portion of the potato is removed and sliced into pieces of the size desired for making French fries. The outer portion of the potato is then processed in the same manner.

The potatoes are next placed between a pair of perforated pressure drums which are rotated toward one another to force the cooked edible portion of the potato through either or both of the perforated elements and collect the peel on the perforated surfaces. The peel is removed from the surfaces of the drums and the edible portion of the potato is dried.

Example: Whole white potatoes are washed and sliced to five-eighths inch thick slabs, inspected for the removal of undesirable pieces and transferred to a blanching tank containing an aqueous color removal solution at 165°F composed of SO_2 in a concentration of 2,000 parts per million parts of water by weight and sodium acid pyrophosphate in the amount of 0.275% by weight. If continuous processing is used, enough sodium bisulfite and SAPP is added periodically to maintain the SO_2 and SAPP concentrations at the desired level.

The potatoes are held in the solution for 20 minutes to swell the starch granules without appreciably softening the potatoes. The potatoes are then removed from the tank, cooled to 65°F and held at this temperature for 15 minutes. They are then cooked by exposure to steam at atmospheric pressure for 20 minutes and passed between two rolls which are set with a clearance of 0.01 inch and run at a speed of about 12 rpm.

Half of the potato will transfer into one drum and half into the other drum. At this point, a solution of emulsifiers such as calcium stearyl-2 lactylate in the amount of 0.05% of the final product and distilled monoglycerides in the amount of 0.1% of the final product are introduced.

The resulting mashed potato is then transferred to a drying drum and dried to form flakes. The resulting dried potato when reconstituted had a taste, texture and color similar to that of freshly cooked potato and a protein content of about 7½%.

Vitamin Enriched Flakes

The process described by *D.C. Pedersen and P.M. Sautier; U.S. Patent 3,833,739; September 3, 1974; assigned to The Pillsbury Company* relates to a vitamin enriched, dehydrated potato flake product. Vitamin flakes are added to conventional potato flakes to obtain, preferably, the original nutritional level of raw potatoes.

The vitamin flakes are comprised of vitamins and minerals encapsulated in fat. The vitamin flakes are essentially nonsegregating in the potato flakes and substantially invisible to the eye. More specifically, dehydrated flaked potatoes are produced by several commercial processes.

The potato flakes have a packed density, i.e., bulk density after settling, ranging from 0.24 to 0.26 g/cc and, when white potatoes are used, the color is white to cream colored. There are generally no darkening effects due to the methods of processing.

Vitamin flakes are then added to the dehydrated potato flakes preferably to attain a nutritional value equal to freshly dug potatoes. The vitamin flakes have thicknesses ranging from 0.007 to 0.020 inch. The surface diameters of the vitamin flakes, like those of the potato flakes, are of irregular configuration and the size distribution of these flakes conforms to the normal bell-shaped distribution curve.

A majority (60%, preferably 80%) of the vitamin flakes have surface diameters ranging from one-sixteenth to one-quarter inch. The density of these flakes ranges from about 0.45 to 0.55 g/cc. Vitamin flakes meeting the above size criteria are essentially nonsegregating in the dehydrated potato product. This nonsegregating feature is essential and critical to this process to obtain proper distribution of vitamins and minerals in each portion of the reconstituted potato product.

In addition to the size criteria, the vitamin flakes must be free flowing at normal temperatures (below 95°F) to facilitate processing of the product. Additionally this temperature stability insures that the flakes can be transported and stored without lumping. Another temperature related requirement for these vitamin flakes is that the vitamin flakes must not grease the potato flakes in the final product. The encapsulating agent, therefore, is a very important component of the vitamin flakes.

The encapsulating agents used herein are water-insoluble substances, solid or semisolid at room temperature, consisting predominantly of glyceryl esters of fatty acids. This definition includes monoglycerides, diglycerides and triglycerides which, for convenience, will be called fats herein.

Fats used herein preferably are noncolored, that is, water white. This color is desirable because it is very similar to the color of the flaked potatoes, and therefore, the final vitamin flake is not readily discernible within the flaked potato.

The fat should also have a Wiley melting point ranging from 130° to 155°F. Wiley melting points are very difficult to obtain with monoglycerides because monoglycerides are soluble in alcohols. Therefore, the congeal point is used as the equivalent of the Wiley melting point. These melting characteristics of the fats are essential to insure that the vitamins and minerals are properly encapsulated while packaged and properly released during the final rehydration step.

If the melting point of the fat is too low, the vitamins and minerals may be exposed in the package and degraded with concomitant color and flavor changes of the flaked potato product. Additionally, the flakes may become greasy and adversely affect the rehydration characteristics of the potato flakes. If the melting point of the fat is too high, the vitamins and minerals may not be released from the vitamin flake during rehydration of the product and may contribute a waxy, grainy texture to the final product.

The fats as described above having these melting points must be predominantly comprised of saturated alkyl moieties containing preferably from 12 to 18 carbon atoms. The fats can be used singly or in combination to attain a melting point in the above range.

The vitamin flakes are comprised of 60 to 70% by weight fat. This amount of fat is sufficient to properly encapsulate the vitamins and minerals without loading the potato product with excess fat. The vitamins suitable for use are all nonreactive with the fat. Some oil-soluble vitamins, e.g., Vitamin A, can be used.

However, in most applications it is highly preferred that only water-soluble vitamins be utilized in these vitamin flakes because of the tendency of the fat-soluble vitamins to remain at the surface of the vitamin chip where they may be degraded or where they may cause color or flavor degradation of the potato product. The preferred water-soluble vitamins include Vitamins B_1, B_2, B_6, C, niacin, folacin, biotin and pantothenic acid. These vitamins can be used singly or in any combination within the vitamin flake.

The vitamins are utilized in granular form and generally have a particle size diameter of less than 0.018 inch. This size is required to obtain the proper thickness of vitamin flake without exposing the vitamins. Preferably, the vitamins are within a size range such that 70% of the particles are less than 0.003 inch.

From 10 to 50% of the vitamin flake is comprised of the above vitamins. If substantially more vitamins are utilized in the flakes, it is difficult to encapsulate the vitamins with the available amount of fat. If less vitamins are used in the flakes, the potato flakes carry an increased fat load and a substantial increase in calories.

From 0 to 40% of the vitamin flake is comprised of minerals. The minerals utilized herein are also nonreactive with the fat and with the potato product and preferably are not oil-soluble. Therefore, the minerals retain their integrity within the fat and are readily dispersed in the mashed potatoes during the preparatory step of rehydrating the potato flakes. The particle size of the minerals must also be less than 0.018 inch and preferably is such that 70% of the particles are less than 0.003 inch.

Specific minerals which may be added to the vitamin flakes include calcium, iodine, phosphorus, iron and magnesium. These minerals are added as food grade salts such as dicalcium phosphate, tricalcium phosphate, potassium iodide and ferric orthophosphate.

The vitamin flakes can be manufactured by any suitable method. Generally, the fat is melted and the vitamins and minerals are added with agitation thereto. The molten mass is then flaked by any of the well-known methods. Preferably, the molten fat mixture is fed to the nip of a two-roll, chill roll. One roll is chilled and the other roll is heated. The fat is solidified on the chilled roll and scraped therefrom with a doctor blade. The continuous sheet obtained from the chill roll is rubbed through a mesh screen or cut to give pieces with a surface diameter of about one-quarter inch.

The vitamin flakes are mixed with the potato flakes in amounts ranging from 0.1 to 5% by weight of the potato flakes. To obtain proper distribution of the vitamin flakes in the potato flake product, the vitamin flakes are added by a proportional feeder into a stream of potato flakes in a continuous mixer. In a preferred embodiment, from 0.5 to 1% vitamin flakes by weight of the potato flakes are incorporated into the potato product.

The vitamin enriched potato product has the same appearance as ordinary dehydrated flaked potatoes. The vitamin flakes are substantially the same color and shape as the potato flakes, are practically invisible to the eye and do not segregate in the package. There are no color or odor negatives associated with the incorportion of these flakes with dehydrated potato flakes.

Example: A distilled monoglyceride was added to a steam-jacketed kettle and heated to 180° to 185°F until the monoglyceride was completely melted. The monoglyceride was a hydrogenated vegetable oil having a congeal point of 158°F. Essentially all of the alkyl moieties were saturated. The alkyl chain length distribution was 0.02% C_{14}, 12.2% C_{16}, 85.6% C_{18}, 2.0% C_{20}.

A premix of vitamins and minerals was prepared containing:

	Percent
Vitamin C	86.6
Folacin	0.0482
Vitamin B_1	0.3564
Niacin	2.9490
Vitamin B_6	1.5380
Potassium iodide	0.0492
Vitamin B_2	0.0004
Dicalcium phosphate	8.4588

The mixture of vitamins and minerals had particle sizes within the following range: 96% through a 60-mesh screen, 70% through a 200-mesh screen, and 40% through a 325-mesh screen. The premix was added with stirring to the molten monoglyceride and then pumped to a two-roll chill roll. One of the rolls was 8 inches in diameter and heated with 5 psig steam. The other roll was 4 feet in diameter and cooled with city water at 70°F. Both rolls were 10 feet long and were rotated at the same peripheral speed. The gap between the rolls was adjusted to 0.01 inch. A doctor blade was utilized to scrape the solidified film from the cooled roll.

The continuous film was passed through a breaker bar which divided the solidified film into pieces having a surface diameter of about one-half inch. These flakes were held at room temperature for 24 hours and then conveyed to a Urschel cutter. Therein the pieces were cut into flakes; 60% of the flakes having a surface diameter between one-eighth and one-fourth inch.

The resultant vitamin flakes were fed continuously by a vibratory feeder into a conveyor line containing dehydrated potato flakes. The dehydrated potato flakes had a thickness from about 0.007 to 0.010 inch and a moisture content ranging from 5.5 to 6 weight percent. Over 60% of the surface diameters were within the range of one-eighth to one-fourth inch.

The potato flakes were conveyed at a rate of 99½ pounds per minute and the vitamin flakes were added to this conveyor and mixed with the potato flakes at the rate of one-half pound per minute. The bulk density of the resultant product ranged between 0.238 and 0.263 g/cc.

The vitamin flakes were not visible to the untrained eye within the flaked potato product and the nutritional level of the resultant product was substantially equal to the nutritional level of freshly dug potatoes. A storage test was conducted where an analysis was made of the following vitamins: Vitamin B_2, niacin, Vitamin B_1 and Vitamin C. In the table the initial vitamin content of the potato product is compared with potato flakes which were not fortified.

Vitamin	Vitamin Enriched mg/100 g	Natural mg/100 g
Vitamin B_2 (riboflavin)	0.139	0.090
Niacin	8.42	6.12
Vitamin B_1 (thiamine)	0.72	0.10
Vitamin C (ascorbic acid)	127	14.7

Storage tests were run at 6 weeks, 17 weeks and 30 weeks and in each case substantially all of the vitamins were available in nondegraded form. Test results showed that the encapsulated vitamins are not denatured over long periods of time even under rather severe storage conditions. In the product maintained at 100°F, the vitamin flakes did not grease out on the potato flakes and did not affect rehydration characteristics of the flakes.

Dehydrated Granular Product with High Cold Water Adsorption

M.A. Shatila and R.M. Terrell; U.S. Patent 3,968,260; July 6, 1976; assigned to American Potato Company strives to produce dehydrated potato granules without the use of addback and without the necessity for conditioning the starting materials. It is an object of this process to use whole potatoes without the necessity of precooking and cooling.

It is possible with this process to produce granules suitable for final drying within 45 minutes after the mashed potatoes are ready for granulation and drying. The product is low in additives and has unusually high cold water absorption characteristics.

The first stage of processing is to prepare the potatoes. Raw potatoes are lye peeled, washed and trimmed as usual. The potatoes are then dipped into a sodium bisulfite solution (½% as SO_2) to neutralize any residual lye prior to cooking. This results in a SO_2 content in the finished product which is far below the amount normally found in dehydrated instant mashed potato products.

The prepared potatoes are then cooked preferably with atmospheric steam. The cooked potato cells are separated and the separated cell surfaces are uniformly coated with a film of starch complexing emulsifier. This step is preferably accomplished by partially mashing the cooked potatoes as by ricing and immediately mixing with a starch complexing emulsifier, such as glyceryl monostearate at a temperature above its melting point.

During the mixing, which is necessary to accomplish complete cell separation, the emulsifier is uniformly distributed and the surfaces of the separated cells are uniformly coated with a thin film of the melted emulsifier. This coating accomplishes two functions. Starch complexing emulsifiers complex with the soluble amylose starch fraction that is at least partially responsible for the cohesiveness of freshly mashed potatoes. Such emulsifiers also appear to lubricate the potato cell surfaces so that they are not ruptured during subsequent moderate mixing and drying.

As one example the potatoes are mixed at about 190°F with Myverol 18-06 (a distilled glyceryl monostearate) at a concentration of 1.0% by weight based upon potato solids to coat the intact potato cells with a film of monoglyceride. The next stage of processing is granulating the cooked potatoes by mixing and drying them in the mixer-dryer and then airlifting the granulated particles out of the system for final treatment.

The time necessary to convert the hot mashed potato-emulsifier mix to a fine granulate ready for final drying is about 30 to 45 minutes. This is only a fraction of the time required in prior art potato granule processes. The brevity of the process inherently results not only in improved quality but in physical characteristics.

Due to the rapid completion of drying, natural flavor is retained and the soluble amylose fraction of the starch is not appreciably retrograded to its insoluble form prior to drying. By retention of amylose in its soluble form, the product rapidly absorbs appreciably more cold water than other commercial potato granules. The final stage of processing is final drying and dehydrating the granulated particles to a final moisture content of 7 to 8% by conventional means, such as a hot air fluid bed dryer.

The dried product has a particle size substantially passing a standard 40 mesh screen and about 70% by weight passing through a standard 60 mesh screen. The small plus 40 mesh fraction comprises fibers and other undesirable particles and is discarded. The dried product is made into mashed potatoes by rehydrating in 5 parts by weight of salted water-milk mixture heated to boiling.

The texture and appearance are excellent and the product is judged to have a more natural potato flavor than other commercial instant mashed potato products. This is attributed to such factors as lack of additives, short processing time and lower product temperature during processing.

This process, by eliminating the necessity of the precook-cool steps prior to cooking, is simplified and gives increased yields with less water usage. Additional research has shown that the cold water absorption and other physical characteristics of the dehydrated granules of this process can be varied by adjustment of feed rates and air temperatures. Of course, higher feed rates require hotter air to accomplish equivalent drying in a given piece of equipment.

As feed rate increases, the residence time within the mixer-dryer decreases and the cold water absorption of the resulting end product increases. When the feed rate is decreased, the time in the undried state is increased, apparently allowing retrogradation of soluble amylose to take place, resulting in an end product with reduced cold water absorption—closer to that of conventional potato granules.

Therefore, within limits, the process allows one to produce end products having different physical characteristics which cannot be duplicated by potato granules produced by prior art processes and which give this product utility in specialized applications in which potato granules are not satisfactory. Comparative analysis of this product with typical commercial potato granules and potato flakes are shown in the following table:

Procedure	Process Product	Commercial Potato Granules	Commercial Potato Flakes
Soluble starch:			
Hot extraction[1]	50.5	52.0	4.0
Cold extraction[2]	100.0	100.0	56.5
SO_2 (ppm)	0-80.0	380.0	375.5
BHT (antioxidant, ppm)[3]	0.0	7.0	14.2
Recipe rehydration ratio[4]	5.5:1	4.8:1	6.0:1
Cold water absorption[5]	4.85:1	3.2:1	5.75:1
Amylograph units:			
Cold[6]	2,300	545	3,300
Hot[7]	540	650	450
Flavor evaluation	Fresh potato	Bland	Starchy
Texture evaluation	Very good	Very good	Slightly sticky

[1] Percent transmission, 185°F extract, 0.1% solution with iodine added.
[2] Percent transmission, 70°F extract, 0.1% solution with iodine added.
[3] Butylated hydroxytoluene.
[4] Parts of boiling liquid per part of product required to make mashed potatoes.
[5] Parts of water at 70°F, absorbed by 1 part by weight product.
[6] 100 parts product, 400 parts water, 10 minutes at 0° to 4°C.
[7] Five parts product, 450 parts water, 45 min starting at 25°C and ending at 92.5°C.

The above data show that the product of the process is comparable to potato granules in soluble starch and far less than potato flakes. The sulfur dioxide value of the product is much lower than flakes and granules which are comparable. The product is far above potato granules and slightly below potato flakes in the ability to absorb hot liquid and above both in cold water absorption.

The product has a cold amylograph viscosity far higher than potato granules and slightly lower than potato flakes. The hot amylograph viscosity is higher than potato flakes and half way between flakes and potato granules. The product was judged to have superior flavor and texture when compared to potato flakes and a superior flavor to conventional potato granules.

FRIED POTATO PROCESSES

Water Leaching Prefried Potato Slices

The process described by *M.L. Weaver and M. Nonaka; U.S. Patent 3,934,046; January 20, 1976; assigned to U.S. Secretary of Agriculture* enables the production of fried potato products of greatly improved texture, flavor and color from raw stock that exhibits excessive browning tendencies and which would normally yield fried products of excessively dark color.

The process essentially involves the following steps. Pieces of raw potato are prefried, that is, fried for a short time in hot oil. Next, the prefried pieces are leached by contact with water. Following the application of these critical steps, the treated pieces may be subjected to any of various procedures, depending on the type of final product desired.

The critical item in the process is the combination of the steps of prefrying and water-leaching. The prefry insolubilizes starch and proteins, thereby maintaining flavor that would otherwise be lost in the leaching step. In addition, the prefry conditions the cells in such a way as to provide rapid removal of sugars in the subsequent water-leaching step. It is a special attribute of the process that such sugars are removed equally from the entire surface area of each potato piece. As a result, excessive browning, which would normally take place, is prevented or at least substantially lessened.

A particular advantage is that the color of the final product can be varied over a wide range. This is so because the final color is dependent upon the degree of sugar removal and this in turn is dependent upon the times and temperatures employed in the water-leaching step following the prefry. Thus, by adjusting these variables one can control color of the final product to meet specific consumer demands.

Another advantage is that the texture of the products is enhanced. For example, when French fries are prepared by this method, the combination of a prefry and a water-leach followed by a conventional par-fry increases the crispness of the exterior of the potato piece, but at the same time maintains a soft, mealy, baked potato interior. It is particularly important to note that use of a prefry creates a very crisp, rigid surface in the final product.

This is a unique feature of the process that cannot be duplicated by standard practices. Thus application of a prefry, a water-leach, and a par-fry provides a means for setting a crisp texture in the French fry and this texture is maintained on the consumer's plate. Without a prefry, French fries, prepared simply by leaching in water and par-frying in oil, shrivel on the consumer's plate and exhibit a rubbery exterior. Moreover, it is of no consequence whether these French fries are prepared for the table by baking in an oven or by finish frying in oil, the process fixes a crisp texture in the potato strip that is maintained equally well through either means of final preparation.

In the case of potato chips, the process maintains crispness and potato flavor, as well as yielding a desirable color. On the other hand, if raw potato slices are merely leached in water without a prior prefry, the chips have a tough, cardboard-like texture and very little flavor.

Another advantage in relation to potato chips can be explained as follows. Potato chips prepared by slicing peeled potatoes and frying the slices in oil often develop blisters where several layers of tissue separate from other tissue and assume a bubble-like form. Not only do these blisters detract from the appearance of the chips, but they can also trap oil thus raising the oil content and lowering the nutritional value of the chips. Potato chips prepared in accordance with the process are free from blisters.

Example 1: Potato Chips from High-Sugar Potatoes: Effect of Prefry and Leach Times — The potatoes used in this example were Kennebec variety, stored at 42° to 45°F for 6 to 8 months, containing 2.6% dwb (dry weight basis) reducing sugars. The potatoes were washed, peeled and sliced (about 0.060 inch thick).

Lots of the slices were prefried in oil at 365°F for different times (5, 10, 20, 30, and 45 seconds). The prefried slices were then leached in water at 104°F for 10 or 15 minutes. Finally all of the slices were finish-fried in hot oil (365°F) until frothing ceased (standard practice). A control was also prepared in which some of the potato slices were finish-fried without prefrying or leaching.

The chips were examined for color, texture, appearance (uniformity of color), and flavor. The color was gauged by comparison with a set of color standards used in the industry. The standard colors are numbered 0 to 10, with the higher number indicating darker color. Products generally regarded as acceptable in the trade are those which exhibit colors 3 to 5; products of color less than 3 are usually considered too light; those of color higher than 5 are usually considered too dark. The conditions applied and the results obtained are summarized in the following table.

Run	Time of Prefry, sec	Time of Leach, min	Color
1	4	15	4.5
2	10	15	4.0
3	20	10	4.5
4	20	15	3.5
5	30	10	4.5
6	30	15	4.0
Control	-	-	10

The products prepared by the process exhibited excellent flavor, texture, and color. The control chips were not only excessively dark, but also exhibited an undesirable charred-sugar taste.

French Fried Potatoes from Potato Dough

J.F. Harmon, R.D. Johnston, J.H. Lach, W.H. Von Der Lieth and T.L. Murphy; U.S. Patent 3,890,453; June 17, 1975; assigned to American Potato Company describe an apparatus suitable for combining a dry potato product with water to reconstitute it into a firm homogeneous potato dough suitable for shaping into French fry potato pieces. In the process a variable volume chamber is provided for constraining the contents of the chamber which has an outlet opening and a reciprocating piston within the chamber for consolidating the contents thereof. The outlet opening of the chamber is sealed with an externally mounted liquid impervious member. A predetermined quantity of dehydrated potato product and water is metered into the chamber in front of the piston through the inlet opening.

The contents are reconsolidated by moving the piston within the chamber toward the outlet end of the chamber thereby reducing the volume of the chamber to a predetermined volume bounded by the impervious member, the chamber and the piston so that the water substantially fills the available voids in and between the individual dry product particles without agitation to form a homogeneous dough suitable for forming into French-fry-cut potato pieces.

The process further comprises the step of latching the impervious member in the sealing position. Metering of the dry product and water into the chamber is performed simultaneously with moving the piston to the consolidation position.

The metering step includes pumping the water from a tank to the inlet opening through a conduit and draining the unused water in the conduit back to the tank and heating it to a predetermined temperature in readiness for subsequent metering steps to attain precise control of the water temperature at all times.

French-fry-cut potato pieces are then dispensed from the homogeneous dough which has been thus reconstituted. This involves moving the impervious member to an open position spaced from the outlet opening of the chamber, advancing the dough through the outlet opening to divide the dough into French-fry-cut potato widths and separating the protruding portions in synchronism with the advancing step so that the portions are separated into French-fry-cut potato bodies.

Simultaneously with advancing the dough to divide it into French fry potato widths, the dough advances through the spaces between a set of parallel spaced-apart wires fixedly spanning the outlet opening which subject the dough to only a slight pressure as it is advanced through the spaces between the wires.

During the separating step a pivotally mounted transverse wire cutter is swung in an arcuate path across all the spaces between the set of parallel wires spanning the outlet opening. The advancing and separating steps are continued until the chamber is substantially emptied of dough.

Further operation of the apparatus following initiation of the moving step is inhibited until the impervious member has reached the full open position to assure adequate clearance from the outlet end to accomplish the advancing and separating steps without interference from the impervious member.

The patent itself contains detailed operating instructions for the fully illustrated apparatus.

Unrefrigerated Shelf Stable French Fried Potatoes

The process described by *A.C. Capossela, Jr., J.F. Halligan and L.S. Makaron; U.S. Patent 3,881,028; April 29, 1975; assigned to General Foods Corporation* permits the formation of a French fried potato product that is dehydrated and may be stored on the shelf without a need for refrigeration. The product does not need any special wrapping materials, although a moisture-impermeable container is desired for extensive storage times to prevent water absorption from the atmosphere. When the product is to be used by the consumer, it is soaked in water to cause rehydration and warmed to heating temperature in an oven.

In the technique of this process, the starting whole potatoes are preferably peeled and cut to shape. Extremely thin pieces are avoided since, at frying, total penetration of the oil is not desirable and would change the product into a potato chip.

The cut potatoes are preferably blanched which comprises heat treatment either by water or steam. The heat treatment is sufficient only to blanch the potato without extensive cooking and gelatinization. The purpose of the blanching is to inactivate the enzyme content of the potato. After blanching, an optional step is a soaking of the potato in a salt solution such as sodium chloride. This soaking is not of absolute necessity, although it has been discovered that a higher quality product results if this soak is included.

A critical procedure in this process is subjecting the potato pieces to microwave heating for a period of time. Although minimal moisture reduction generally takes place during the heating, this step is not considered to be essentially for dehydration. The maximum moisture reduction from the microwave processing will be of the order of 2.5 to 3.0%.

After the microwave heating, the potato pieces are fried in a fat or oil. After deep-fat frying which causes penetration of the fat or oil through the outside as well as some inner layers of the potato without total penetration throughout the pieces, the potato pieces are dried to remove additional moisture. A suitable drying technique is by microwave heating, although generally conventional heating techniques are satisfactory.

The formed dehydrated product now has the capability of being stable for extensive time periods without the deterioration of the product. Since a moist atmosphere will cause surface absorption of water, the product is preferably stored in a moisture-impermeable material such as a pouch or can. In such a container, the product need not be refrigerated.

For consumption as a French fried potato, the product is removed from the container and rehydrated in water. The product is then heated in an oven at elevated temperature to produce a similar French fried potato product that has not undergone dehydration and extensive storage times.

Example: A Sebago potato is peeled, cut into a rectangular shape ¼" x ¼" x 2½", washed in cold water, and blanched for a 1-minute time period at 212°F. The blanched product is quenched in cold water and soaked in a 1.5% sodium chloride solution at 180°F and again washed with cold water. The potato pieces are placed in a microwave oven for about 45 seconds and then fried in a hydrogenated, coconut oil at 350°F for about 6 minutes. The product was then removed and placed in the microwave oven for about 75 seconds to dry. To prepare the dehydrated French fried potato product for serving, the potato pieces were soaked in tap water at a temperature of about 140°F for 10 minutes. The rehydrated product was heated in an oven at approximately 425°F for 7 minutes.

Frozen French Fried Potatoes Surface Coated with Atomized Fat Globules

According to the process proposed by *R.J. Kellermeier, J.T. Knight and B.E. Steljes; U.S. Patent 3,865,964; February 11, 1975; assigned to Ore-Ida Foods, Incorporated* partially prepared French fries or the like are produced and frozen in conventional manner. Thereafter, liquid or semiliquid oil or fat is applied to surfaces of the frozen fries, usually and advantageously by atomization spraying.

The applied oil or fat congeals on and adheres to the frozen potato surfaces as preferably a thin, superficial, substantially uniform coating of solidified oil or fat. Upon thawing and oven-heating these so-treated fries, the superficial coating of fat melts and provides an environment sufficiently similar to deep-fat frying to prevent the usual undesirable results of oven heating. The resulting product has more nearly the color, flavor and crispness of freshly deep fat fried French fries than has been previously possible without actually resorting to deep-fat frying for reconstitution purposes.

Although the method of the process is especially advantageous in connection with frozen, deep fat fried French fries or the like produced directly from freshly cut whole potatoes, it may also be applied to frozen fries extruded to shape from mashed potato mixes or the like.

Various edible oils and fats can be utilized, but it is preferred to use 100% soybean oil that has been partially hydrogenated. Heating of the oil or fat prior to introducing it into the spraying system will ensure atomizing fluidity. Temperature typically ranges between 100° to 250°F.

The addition of oil or fat in the amount of about 1.0% by weight of the frozen, deep fat fried French fries is satisfactory as a minimum. Up to about 6% by weight can be economically and usefully applied for the purpose, although in instances of larger cuts even a greater amount can be applied without waste. From 3.5 to 4.5% is preferred for regular French fries, somewhat more for crinkle cuts, and from 2.5 to 3.5% for shoestring cuts. The amount is generally determined on the basis of surface area of the individual potato pieces.

Application of the oil or fat by atomized sprays is the most effective way to achieve substantially uniform distribution of the relatively small amounts that are preferably utilized to effect the purposes of the process. The atomized globules or droplets adhere to the frozen surfaces of the individual fries as a thin, discontinuous but substantially uniformly distributed coating and provide the desired deep fat frying environment for each potato piece during oven reconstitution of the frozen product.

The individual solidified globules or droplets of oil or fat are preferably about 0.1 mm or less in diameter so as to, in effect, constitute a fog or mist of the oil or fat and to achieve most effective distribution thereof over the surfaces of the potato pieces within the preferred quantitative ranges. For accomplishing this, utilizing the preferred partially hydrogenated soybean oil, spraying pressures of 30 to 400 psig are normally employed depending upon the type of nozzles utilized and the type and temperature of the oil or fat. In any given instance the variables are so adjusted that the desired quantity of oil or fat is applied to the particular frozen deep fried potato pieces concerned.

The individual globules normally solidify within about 10 seconds after application to the frozen surfaces of the potato pieces. Some of the globules may inevitably coalesce before solidification. This is not detrimental.

French Fried Potatoes with Reduced Oil Content

M. Nonaka, E. Hautala and M.L. Weaver; U.S. Patents 3,846,572; November 5, 1974 and 3,729,323; April 24, 1973; both assigned to U.S. Secretary of Agriculture describe a process which not only improves the texture, rigidity and color of fried potato products but also reduces the oil content of the fried potato products by immersion in oil-free dichlorodifluoromethane. In the process potato strips are immersed in difluorodichloromethane at $-21.6°F$ for 11 seconds prior to being leached in water at $125°F$ for 20 minutes in order to effect maximum crispness and rigidity in the final product.

The strips are then parfried and subsequently immersed with agitation in oil-free difluorodichloromethane at $-21.6°F$ for 1 to 2 minutes, thereby freezing concomitantly with oil extraction. The nutritive properties of the fried potato strips are improved by the removal of excess oil by the extraction.

In typical practice, fried potatoes are prepared in conventional manner: raw potatoes are peeled, cut into strips, blanched, and fried in hot oil. The fried potatoes are then contacted with a fluorocarbon liquid whereby excess oil is removed therefrom. Usually, the contacting is achieved by feeding the fried potatoes into a pool of the fluorocarbon and applying agitation to enhance good contact of the liquid with all the surfaces of the material under treatment.

Other means of contacting can be used such as spraying or flooding the fluorocarbon over the material while it is supported on metal screening or the like. It is obvious that such factors as time of contact, degree of agitation, etc. may be varied to attain an oil reduction of desired degree. In general, an increase in such conditions will result in a greater degree of oil removal.

The fluorocarbons used are volatile substances. This means that when contact of the product therewith is terminated, any residual fluorocarbon on the product is quickly vaporized. In many cases no special provision needs to be taken to ensure removal of fluorocarbon from the product as the vaporization occurs almost instantaneously as the pieces of material are removed from the pool of fluorocarbon.

This is particularly the case where the fluorocarbon is one which has a boiling point below room temperature. Residual heat in the treated pieces may also be utilized to attain rapid removal of residual fluorocarbon. For example, fried products while still hot from the frying operation may be contacted with the

Convenience Potato and Grain Products

fluorocarbon. When the contact is terminated, residual heat in the product quickly vaporizes any residual fluorocarbon thereon. If desired, however, the treated products can be heated to ensure complete removal of the fluorocarbon. The heating may be at temperatures from room temperature up to 350°F, and may be effectuated in various ways, for example, by exposing the products to infrared ray lamps or other hot body, by contacting them with a current of warm air, or by heating in an oven.

Following contact with the fluorocarbon liquid and vaporization of any residual portion of such liquid from surfaces of the product, the treated product may be further handled in any conventional or desired manner. For example, it may be consumed directly, stored for future use, frozen for long periods of preservation, etc.

It has been noted that the fluorocarbon liquid applied to the fried food must be in an essentially oil-free condition. This is necessary so that the desired removal of oil from the food will take place. If, on the other hand, the oil is not removed from the fluorocarbon, an equilibrium condition will be attained whereby the oil content of the treated food will be the same as before contact with the fluorocarbon. In other words, accumulation of oil in the fluorocarbon is undesirable as it impedes the ability of the fluorocarbon to remove oil from the food product under treatment.

To secure the desired objective of maintaining the fluorocarbon in an essentially oil-free condition, an oil separation procedure is applied to the pool of fluorocarbon used for contacting the fried food. One technique of attaining the oil separation is based on the principle that the fluorocarbon is volatile whereas the oil is not.

An application of this technique may take the following form: the fluorocarbon after having contacted the fried food is subjected to evaporation. The fluorocarbon vapors are condensed and recycled for treating an additional quantity of fried food. The oil remaining as a residue from the evaporation step is recycled to be used for frying an additional quantity of food.

Example 1: Parfried potatoes were prepared by a standard commercial process. Potatoes were peeled, cut into strips, blanched for 15 minutes in water at 150°F, postblanched for 3 minutes in water at 180°F and finally fried for 1 minute in oil at 320°F. A portion of the fried product was removed and its oil content determined.

The remainder of the fried product while still warm was immersed for 1 minute in a bath of oil-free difluorodichloromethane at -21.6°F. The treated pieces were then removed from the bath and their oil content determined. The results are tabulated below.

Oil Content, %	Reduction in Oil Content, %
4.3 (before treatment)	--
2.5 (after treatment)	42

A portion of the product was prepared for the table by heating it in an oven at about 450°F. The product was found to have an excellent taste; no foreign taste or odor could be detected. Also, the product when handled did not leave any oil smears on the fingers.

Example 2: Potatoes were peeled, cut into strips, and the strips were given a surface freeze by immersing them for 11 seconds in difluorodichloromethane at −21.6°F. The strips were leached with warm (125°F) water for 20 minutes, then parfried for 1 minute in oil at 323°F.

A portion of the parfries was reserved for oil determination. The remainder was divided into four lots. Each of these lots was immersed in oil-free difluorodichloromethane at −21.6°F, with variation as to time of immersion and with or without agitation in the fluorocarbon liquid. After such treatment the products were tested for oil content. The conditions used and the results attained are tabulated below.

Sample	Treating Conditions		Oil Content, %	Reduction in Oil Content, %
	Time, min	Agitation		
Untreated	–	–	3.65	–
Lot 1	2	Yes	1.5	57
Lot 2	1	Yes	1.8	52
Lot 3	0.25	Yes	2.1	41
Lot 4	0.5	No	2.5	34

Portions of the product of Lots 1, 2, 3 and 4 were prepared for the table by heating in an oven at about 450°F. They were found to have excellent taste; no foreign odor or taste could be detected. Moreover, the products when handled did not leave any oily smears on the fingers.

EDTA Esters to Reduce Oil Darkening

Briefly stated, the process described by *E.R. Lowrey and V.E. Weis; U.S. Patent 3,846,457; November 5, 1974; assigned to The Procter & Gamble Company* relates to a process by which frying fats and oils that are resistant to darkening and foaming are produced. The process involves the addition of 1 to 1,000 parts per million by weight of alkyl di-, tri-, and tetra-esters of ethylenediaminetetraacetic acid, or mixtures thereof, to a frying fat or oil. These esters are of the formula

$$\begin{array}{c} \text{R-O-C-CH}_2 \\ \parallel \\ \text{O} \end{array} \begin{array}{c} \\ \\ \end{array} \begin{array}{c} \text{CH}_2\text{-C-O-R} \\ \parallel \\ \text{O} \end{array}$$
$$\text{N-CH}_2\text{-CH}_2\text{-N}$$
$$\begin{array}{c} \text{R-O-C-CH}_2 \\ \parallel \\ \text{O} \end{array} \begin{array}{c} \\ \\ \end{array} \begin{array}{c} \text{CH}_2\text{-C-O-R} \\ \parallel \\ \text{O} \end{array}$$

where R is hydrogen or an alkyl radical containing from 6 to 24 carbon atoms, but where at least two R groups must be such an alkyl radical. The preferred amount of such ester is from 10 to 200 parts per million by weight and the preferred ester is the dioctadecyl ester. Frying fats or oils made by this process exhibit longer fry life due to reduced darkening and foaming tendencies.

Example: 50 parts per million of the dioctadecyl ester of ethylenediaminetetraacetic acid was added to deodorized soybean oil with an iodine value of 107 which contained small amounts of phosphoric acid and Dow Corning 200 Fluid, dimethylpolysiloxane, which had a viscosity of 500 centipoises at 25°C. The EDTA ester-containing oil was fry-tested and its color compared with that of a fry-tested deodorized control oil which contained no EDTA esters, but did contain the same amounts of phosphoric acid and Dow Corning 200 fluid as the EDTA ester-containing oil contained, and a small amount of Cab-O-Sil, which is a fumed silica anticoloring agent.

Ten 200 gram lots of a frozen foodstuff were fried in each of the oils over a three day period. The oil temperature was carefully maintained at 350°F. The Lovibond Red color of the oils was determined after every second fry by using Red Lovibond color glasses as shown in *Bailey's Industrial Oil and Fat Products*, edited by Daniel Swern, published by Interscience Publishers, 3d edition, 1964, page 769. The following chart shows the results of these tests.

Lovibond Red Color of Frying Oil

Number of Frys	With the Diester	Without the Diester
0	0.8	0.8
2	2.0	2.5
4	3.6	6.0
6	7.1	14.3
8	12.3	23.4
10	19.6	38.0

After each of the frys, there is considerably less color (represented by a lower Lovibond Red color number) in the oil containing the EDTA ester additive than in the oil which did not contain the EDTA ester additive.

Freeze-Thaw Stable French Fry Potato Product

M.A. Shatila and R.G. Beck; U.S. Patent 3,968,265; July 6, 1976; assigned to American Potato Company have devised a method for preparing a freeze-thaw stable French fried potato. A successful parfried frozen potato must have several characteristics. Primarily, it must have the structural strength to maintain piece integrity during all the processing steps especially after thawing, prior to refrying, as well as during refrying; it must not be too oily after final frying and must be crisp and tender when consumed, even after holding under a heat lamp.

A dry uniform mix of solids of starting materials is prepared including by weight 85 to 95% essentially intact cooked potato cells such as potato flakes or potato granules, 0.5 to 5% of a binder such as guar gum, and 2 to 15% extracellular raw starch such as potato, wheat, rice, arrowroot, corn or tapioca.

Water at a temperature of 45° to 200°F is then added in an amount equal to 1.5 to 3.2 times the weight of the solid matter present and mixed to form a uniform potato dough. The final dough has a solids content in the range of 23 to 40% and a moisture content in the range of 60 to 77%. The dough can be produced continuously by adding the ingredients continuously to a mixer and collecting the discharge dough for continuous formation into French fry size pieces.

The preferred apparatus for forming the dough into pieces is described in detail in U.S. Patent 3,605,647. In brief, the dough is advanced in a container by a driving means through a grid of wires of either straight or crinkled configuration spaced apart by the width of the desired French fry which is usually in the range of one-fourth to three-eigth inch, but can be larger or smaller.

When the dough has advanced through the wires by the same distance as the grid spacing, the protruding portions, or dough slabs, are cut off by a second moving wire to produce a firm fabricated piece of dough formed with a square cross section and a length corresponding to the length of the openings in the wire grid, usually about 2 to 4 inches.

The fabricated pieces are then parfried in oil for about 20 to 120 seconds at an oil temperature of 300° to 370°F to produce a firm parfried piece of 40 to 65% moisture content and 5 to 20% oil content. The parfried pieces are allowed to cool and are then frozen. The latter two steps may be either separate or combined processing steps.

The frozen parfried pieces are then distributed in that form to eating establishments or to individual consumers who can prepare them for consumption directly, or after thawing, either by frying in deep fat for about 1 to 2 minutes at a temperature of about 340°F or by heating in an oven for 10 minutes at 400° to 450°F. The finished product has a moisture content of 35 to 50% and an oil content of 12 to 22%.

The potato solids used in producing the dough must be essentially cooked intact potato cells to duplicate the texture and mouth-feel of a natural potato piece which has essentially intact cells. The minor starch and binder constituents of the dough seem to function as a replacement for the binding between the intact cells of a piece of natural cooked potato.

The preferred process uses as the sources of intact cooked potato cells solely dehydrated instant mashed potatoes including potato granules, potato flakes and potato agglomerates. Freshly cooked potatoes as a prominent source of intact cells can also be used.

In the latter case, a debris-free, damage-free, cooked potato slurry of about 17% solids is produced by preparing potatoes by peeling and trimming, cooking the prepared potatoes, and then slurrying with water and removing the debris. The solids level is then best adjusted to the desired 23 to 40% range by the incorporation of dehydrated instant mashed potato products.

Guar gum, or equivalent binder, was found to be necessary to provide sufficient cohesiveness to allow formation of distinct pieces which would retain their piece integrity prior to, and during, the first part of parfrying. Successful formulations contained 0.5 to 5% gum in the solids.

The extracellular raw starch ingredient of the dough serves multiple functions and is an ingredient of primary importance for the production of products of optimum characteristics. In the production of the dough itself, the presence of starch serves a minor function since raw starch has very little cohesiveness or water holding ability. In the dough formation, the gum binder furnishes the cohesiveness required so that the dough can be divided into desired shapes without losing piece integrity. However, after dough formation and during the parfrying step, the extracellular raw starch swells and gelatinizes, thereby binding the water present into a firm gel which is not disturbed thereafter. Raw potato starch and corn starch are preferred.

Although the percentage of raw starch required varied with the source of potato solids and the intensity of dough mixing, successful product was made with as little as 2% of the dough solids as raw starch. There were no added advantages of using more than 15% starch.

Optional ingredients, such as salt, sucrose, dextrose, flavor enhancers, vitamins and coloring agents can also be incorporated into the dough to give the desired flavor and color. The percentages by weight of the solids of these optional ingredients are usually in the range of 0 to 3%.

The manner by which the pieces are formed has an effect on the final appearance and physical characteristics of the piece after frying. When forming is done exclusively by wire cutting, as described above, all four major surfaces of each piece have an uncompressed porous surface which allows ready escape of water vapor from within during frying, thereby allowing retention of the formed shape. When forming is done by extrusion, the inherent pressure seems to seal the surfaces, thereby impeding the escape of water vapor during frying, sometimes resulting in blistering or other piece deformation. Any such distortion detracts from a natural cut potato look.

Parfrying was found to be essential. The normal parfrying temperature of about $300°$ to $370°F$ is sufficient to increase the product temperature to a point where the extracellular raw starch present gelatinizes to form a matrix which binds water in the dough and forms, upon cooling, a firm undisturbed gel which imparts required structural rigidity after thawing.

The formation of an outer crust also results from parfrying and helps to provide structural strength, but in itself is not sufficient without the freshly gelatinized starch matrix. The parfry temperature, of course, must be high enough to increase the temperature of the piece center above the gelatinization point of the raw starch.

Also, during parfrying, some dehydration occurs due to moisture loss. If parfrying is terminated before the moisture content is reduced to about 65% or lower, the resulting piece has unacceptable fragility. If parfrying is continued until the moisture content is 45% or below, the resulting refry tends to be excessively tough and leathery.

The parfried pieces are substantially lower in moisture content then parfried natural potato pieces, thereby resulting in a much shorter required refrying time, as well as a much higher yield of finished product per weight unit of parfried pieces. Furthermore, excessive oiliness is avoided by the proper selection of dough ingredients and the extent of rehydration.

The freezing and storage of the parfried potato pieces is conventional. After draining, the parfried pices are further cooled and frozen by being exposed to a cold air blast for a short time interval, such as an air blast at $0°$ to $-20°F$ for about 10 to 15 minutes, followed by packaging and storage below 0°F. The product of the process can be refried from the frozen state, or allowed to thaw before refrying, without loss of piece integrity or quality of the finished fry.

Example 1: Deep Fat Fry Finish — A dry uniform mix of the following composition was prepared.

	Percentage by Weight
Potato granules (2.5% reducing sugars)	90.0
Raw potato starch	7.0
Guar gum	1.5
Salt	1.5

The above formulation was continuously metered into the inlet end of a horizontal mixer equipped with paddles around a horizontal shaft. Simultaneously 2.26 parts by weight of water at $140° \pm 2°F$ was metered with the dry material to form a uniform dough of about 71% moisture content. The discharged dough was advanced continuously downward by means of a helical screw in a vertical container, the bottom of which was open and spanned by parallel wires spaced five-sixteenth inch apart.

The protruding slabs formed by the dough passing through the wire grid contacted a sensing element which activated a wire which moved transversely to the path of the dough and severed the protrusions into French fry shapes of square cross section and about 4 inches in length.

The formed pieces discharged into a continuous deep fat fryer operated at 340°F and with a residence time of about 35 seconds. The parfried pieces had a moisture content of 56.0% and an oil content of 6.0%. The pieces were then discharged on an inclined draining belt which in turn discharged the drained pieces in a single layer depth into a blast freezer at an air temperature of $-10°F$ and a residence time of 15 minutes.

The individual frozen pieces were packaged in wax coated cartons at 4 lb/carton. Six cartons were combined in a shipping container and stored at $0°$ to $-10°F$. After about 24 hours frozen storage, a representative frozen sample was allowed to thaw and stand at room temperature for 6 hours. A second frozen sample was refrigerated at 40°F for 7 days (this sample thawed after a short time). Twenty pieces of each sample were then tumbled for 10 minutes in a rotating container, after which treatment the number of unbroken intact pieces remaining was 19 from the thawed room temperature sample, and 15 from the refrigerated sample.

In another series of tests the oil content was measured against a prior art product. Two samples of each were finish fried, one directly after frozen storage and, the other after storage for 1 week at a temperature between 35° and 40°F. The oil content of this product fried directly from frozen storage was 12.0% and for the refrigerated sample 13.2%.

In the case of the standard commercial French fries, the oil content of the sample finish fried direct from the frozen state was 11.0% and for the refrigerated sample, 27.6%. The higher oil content for commercial French fries is significant because many food establishments have only refrigerated storage, and an oil content in excess of 20% is generally considered completely unacceptable.

Another portion of the frozen parfries was finish fried in oil at 350°F for 60 seconds. The yield of finished product was found to be 88% of the parfried weight. The moisture of the finished product was 45%, and the oil content was 13.0%. In contrast, conventional frozen French fries usually yield only about 65 to 75% of the parfry weight and have an oil content of about 10 to 15%.

The product was golden brown in color with a crisp bite and excellent texture and flavor. A portion of the finished product was held under a standard restaurant heat lamp for 15 minutes. The held product was still crisp in contrast to a sample of conventional frozen French fries which became decidedly limp and soggy after only 5 minutes under the heat lamp. If a more tender product is desired, the amount of reconstitution water can be increased.

Example 2: Oven Bake Finish — A dry uniform mix of the following composition was prepared:

	Percentage by Weight
Potato granules (2.5% reducing sugar)	92.5
Potato starch	5.0
Guar gum	1.0
Salt	1.5

Using the above procedure, a uniform dough of 73% moisture content was produced using 2.4 parts by weight of water at 145°F to 1 part by weight of the above dry mix. Dough pieces were formed as before and parfried in deep fat at 330°F for 100 seconds. The parfried pieces had a moisture content of 48% and an oil content of 16%.

The pieces were drained, frozen, packaged and stored as before at 0° to -10°F. The stored pieces were prepared for consumption by placing in an oven preheated to 450°F for 10 minutes. The yield after baking was 81%. The finished product had a moisture content of 38% and contained 18% oil.

RICE AND GRAIN PROCESSES

Frozen Cooked Rice

H.W. Zukerman; U.S. Patent 3,961,087; June 1, 1976; assigned to American Frozen Foods Corporation describes a process for the preparation of a cooked rice which has its grains joined together and a portion of its amylose and amylopectin modified by utilizing starch-complexing agents which impart freeze-thaw stability.

In a detailed description of the process dry rice in the form of mixtures of whole grain, broken grain, and rice particles can be received and temporarily stored together. Specific varieties of rice are stored separately. The rice mixtures, separated into whole grains, broken grains and rice particles are then cleaned. All foreign material and all defective rice is removed and discarded.

Off-color, broken grain, and rice particles are not considered to be defective rice. They are an excellent raw material providing they are of wholesome quality and have a good taste and odor.

The clean dry rice should be first preheated to about 160°F. A single or double screw conveyor that is equipped with a steam-jacket and/or hollow flight screws is an excellent preheater. The heat from the steam in the conveyor's jacket or flights warms the clean dry rice as it moves to the rice-cooking equipment.

Vents, located on the conveyor's cover, help remove excessive steam evolving from the heated rice. The dry rice preheating step assures that the temperature of the cooking water for the rice will not be lowered because of the cold rice. This is desirable since most of the starch-complexing chemicals are insoluble or only very slightly soluble in cold water. They become much more soluble in hot water. To assure an efficient starch-complexing reaction, the water for cooking rice should have a steady temperature maintained at 190°F to 210°F.

The preparation of the cooking water for the rice may be accomplished in a steam-jacketed kettle equipped with mixers that create good turbulent agitation. The water is heated to 190°F. The complexing chemicals, if dry, can be premixed with the powdered flavoring ingredients, such as salt, monosodium glutamate, and powdered onion and slowly poured into the heated and agitated water. When the starch complexing chemicals are in solution, the oil and oil containing flavors such as cheese and the larger flavoring particles such as onions are added. A chelating agent such as sodium acid pyrophosphate should be added to the solution if the heavy metal content of the rice is high.

A variety of tests were conducted in which the chelating agent was dissolved in a starch solution and the starch solution then topically coated onto the shaped rice units. The starches tested were high amylose, high amylopectin, and modified starches of rice, potato, tapioca and wheat. These tests indicated that the topically applied solutions produced about the same surface color, physical properties, and textural crust as was obtained when the chelating agent was merely put into the water that cooks the rice. The extra step did not make the units more structurally stable, or improve their taste or textural properties, or eliminate the heating step which is essential to the formation or setting of the crust.

The preheated rice particles or grains are moved to the cookers at a rate of about 1 pound of dry rice for every 2.5 to 4.0 pounds of hot water solution. The dry rice and the hot water solution both enter and become mixed together in the cooker. The water solution which contains the starch complexing chemicals is heated to about 190° to 210°F in the cooker as the rice is gently agitated. Within about 20 minutes, the rice absorbs most of the water and its starch has been reacted with the starch complexing chemicals. Then it is discharged from the cooker before the rice grains become joined or bonded together.

The cooked rice grains become joined to each other without added gelling agents or vegetable gums or polymeric carbohydrates such as sodium alginate or low methoxyl pectin which gel when water-soluble calcium salts are added. These gelling agents can be used to assist in the production of special textural effects in the rice product, but the same or similar texture can be obtained with the modified starch technique. Because these added gelling agents add a foreign taste to the rice product, they are usually avoided. The hot, moist rice grains continue to absorb surface moisture. Cooked rice with about 55% moisture may require gentle compression to bond or join the rice grains together while rice with about 70 to 80% moisture usually becomes joined without compression. Rice that cannot be joined is improperly prepared.

Rice can be cooked at temperatures greater than 212°F in pressure cookers. This cooking increases the rate of moisture absorption and of the starch modification reaction. It may also afford a better starch complex for those starch-complexing chemicals that only react at the elevated temperatures.

Example: 100 pounds of broken grain rice was preheated to 150°F and then added to a cooking kettle that contained 375 pounds of water, 2.5 pounds of vegetable oil, 1.0 pound of pure distilled glyceryl monostearate, 4.2 pounds of salt, 1.25 pounds of monosodium glutamate, 0.4375 pound of dextrose and 0.020 pound of sodium acid pyrophosphate.

The rice slowly absorbed the water while it was simmering at a temperature of 190° to 210°F for about 20 minutes. During this period of heating, the rice grains were gently agitated so that the grains would uniformly absorb the water and monoglyceride with a minimum of rice-cell breakage. The fully cooked rice was usually discharged from the heating apparatus before the grains become joined and difficult to transfer. Subsequently, the fully cooked and water swollen grains became joined to each other.

Quick-Cooking Brown Rice

D. McCabe; U.S. Patent 3,959,515; May 25, 1976 describes a method by which brown rice is so processed that it is quick-cooking, that is, requires only 5 minutes of boiling before being eaten, whereas unprocessed brown rice requires 30 to 40 minutes of such boiling. This improvement in a commercially processed food is accomplished by an unusual process consisting of the following sequence of operations: soaking, baking, a second soaking and a second baking. In the operations of soaking and baking, the sequence itself and the times and temperatures are the essence of the process.

Step 1: Soak in room-temperature water for 2 to 3 hours in order to saturate the brown rice with water. The time can be reduced somewhat by using warm water, but hot water causes undesirable stickiness and mushiness.

Step 2: Bake for about 40 minutes at a temperature of 300 to 350°F to dry the brown rice and impart to it a light brown color. Note: Step 1 can be eliminated if Step 2 is performed for about 20 minutes at a temperature of about 450°F, but this modification in the process has the disadvantage that extreme caution is required to avoid scorching, which detracts from the optimum odor, taste and palatability of the finished article of manufacture.

Step 3: Soak a second time in room-temperature water for 2 to 3 hours. This operation causes the brown rice to swell to double its original size with the completion of the operation being indicated by the fact that no further swelling occurs. The time can be reduced somewhat by using warm water, but hot water is undesirable as it causes stickiness and mushiness.

Step 4: Bake a second time for about 40 minutes at a temperature of 300° to 350°F to dry the brown rice and impart to it a medium brown color. Note: The time and temperature factors described above for the two baking operations are based upon the use of an oven which does not have forced air circulation and which does not vent moist air; in the case of ovens having forced air circulation and/or venting of moist air, practical experience indicates the optimum time and temperature, both of which, but particularly the time, will be somewhat less than as described above.

The size or capacity of the oven to be used for the baking operations is determined by the commercial quantity desired; in the case of relatively small quantities, the tray-type cabinet ovens, for example, which are commercially available presently in the food processing industry are suitable, while in the case of larger quantities the continuous-flow rotary-type cylindrical ovens, for example, which are presently commercially available in the food processing industry are suitable.

The product does not stick to the pan when boiled and therefore stirring by the cook is unnecessary, while, in addition, the pan is very easy to clean. It has an appetizing cooking odor and a delicious taste which is somewhat nut-like, both the odor and taste appreciably excelling in quality the mild and more subdued odor and taste of unprocessed brown rice, while white rice in its various forms is odorless and tasteless.

Quick-Cooking Whole Grain Rice

J.P. Cox and J.M. Cox; U.S. Patent 3,879,566; April 22, 1975; assigned to Martin, Robertson & Bain Limited, Canada set out to provide a quick-cooking rice having whole grains which are strong and not fractured or mutilated, having good color both before and after cooking and having no objectionable odor or taste.

In preparing quick-cooking rice according to this method, the rice grains are not subjected to mechanical action to modify their physical structure. Neither is reliance placed on bloating the rice grains followed by drying them in a manner to retain their expanded condition so as to facilitate subsequent water imbibation during final cooking.

Instead, the process relies on molecular or internal structural modification of the rice grain chemical components accomplished by the use of chemicals and heat treatment to facilitate penetration of water into the rice grains and to expedite imbibation of the water during preparation of the quick-cooking rice and also during its final cooking to palatable condition.

It is believed that the internal structure of a rice grain may include an integumental web formed by the protein component which sequesters the starch to deter imbibation of water by the starch to gelatinize it. Such theory could be responsible for the long time ordinarily required to cook rice in boiling water.

According to this process heat treatment of the rice with aqueous chemical apparently modifies the protein component and/or the starch component to facilitate penetration of water into the interior of the rice grains and to expedite imbibation of such water by the starch during gelatinization.

The heat treatment can be effected either by the rice being processed in hot, preferably boiling, water at atmospheric or higher pressure, or by the rice being steamed at atmospheric pressure or superatmospheric pressure, or by torrefaction of the rice in an autoclave in the presence of a small amount of water, or the rice can be subjected to a plurality of such heat treatment steps, either of the same type or of different types, in succession.

If the rice has been milled before being subjected to the process, it is desirable to rinse the rice initially in warm water, i.e., 85° to 95°F, to remove talc, glucose and free starch from its surface. The rinse water preferably is a mildly alkaline solution, such as 0.002% of sodium bicarbonate having a pH of 7 to 8. Rinse water having a pH range of 5 to 9 can, however, be used.

Rinse water having a pH of less than 6.8 will tend to produce a white product, whereas considerably higher pH will produce a yellow or greenish yellow tint. Rinse water having higher pH, such as above 7.5, will increase the hydrophilic character of the rice. Successive rinse waters can be used until the rinse water is clear.

The rinsing preferably should not be continued for more than 3 to 5 minutes if the rice is to be subjected to dry steam heat treatment subsequently. Otherwise the rice may remain in the rinse water for a considerable period of time, such as 10 to 30 minutes, to increase the depth and uniformity of penetration of the water into the rice kernels.

Such penetration reduces the tendency of the rice kernels to disintegrate or to become mutilated from the action of internal osmotic pressure acting to burst the rice grains during subsequent boiling, which results in starch being lost to the cooking water. A brief after-rinse in calcium chloride brine deters adhesion between grains which would cause mutilation if the grains were forced apart.

Heat treatment of the rice is effected in the presence of the aqueous chemical or chemical solution. An aqueous solution can be used which initially is either cold or hot. Such chemical may be alkali metal phosphate, i.e., phosphate of sodium or potassium including orthophosphates, pyrophosphates and metaphosphates.

It is believed that alkali metal phosphates act principally to modify the starch of the rice for increasing its hydrophilic character, but may also modify the protein of the rice to reduce its protection of the starch from water absorption. Trisodium phosphate, is undesirable because of its adverse crosslinking characteristics which may actually deter absorption of water by the rice and prevent its gelatinization.

Chemicals believed to act principally to modify the protein structure of the rice by attenuation, disruption and/or disintegration are citrates, including magnesium citrate, sodium citrate, and calcium citrate. Such citrates are not sufficiently effective alone to produce a desirable quick-cooking rice product in conjunction with heat treatment.

Such a citrate should be used either with alkali metal phosphate as specified above or with calcium chloride. Calcium chloride and alkali metal phosphate should not be used together in the heat treatment aqueous chemical, however, because they react with each other to prevent effective action of either to modify the rice protein. A beneficial effect of the calcium chloride is to reduce the temperature of heat treatment required in preparing the quick-cooking rice product.

Calcium chloride provides the further benefit of serving as a desiccant to deter loss of moisture from rice grains and thus reduce weight loss of the rice during storage. For this purpose the calcium chloride can be supplied to rice grain either during a rinsing operation or a precooking operation or, by addition of rice grain which has not been treated to reduce its final cooking time, by mixing the calcium chloride with glucose and talc for coating the rice grains during the milling process.

Auxiliary chemicals having beneficial effects are fatty acid glycerides and silicones which deter adhesion, and primary calcium phosphate, or secondary calcium phosphate, which facilitates absorption of water by the starch and enhances the whiteness of the rice product. Any or all of such auxiliary chemicals can be used in combination with alkali metal phosphate as specified above, or with an alkali metal phosphate and citrate combination, or with a citrate and calcium chloride combination.

The proportions by weight of the various chemicals as compared to the dry rice to be treated, usable in a rice-treating solution in which rice may be heated or which can be sprayed on rice to be heated, or which can be mixed with the rice, are as follows:

Chemical	Range, %	
	Possible	Preferred
Alkali metal phosphate	0.001 - 7	0.3 - 1.5
Citrate	0.001 - 7	0.2 - 1.5
Calcium chloride	0.001 - 7	0.3 - 1.5
Fatty acid glyceride	0.05 - 9	0.5 - 1
Silicones	0.001 - 5	0.3 - 1.5
Calcium phosphate	0.001 - 5	0.1 - 0.8

Heat treatment is required for reaction between the chemicals and the rice to produce quick-cooking rice. The rice can be heated in an abundance of water containing the desired chemicals in solution for a period of 3 to 60 minutes, depending upon the chemicals used and the concentration of the solution of the various chemicals. The treatment time should be increased if the rice is placed in cold water which must be brought to a boil. The processing time can be shortened by increasing the temperature of the water in the range of 212° to 280°F by maintaining the heat-treating vessel under pressure.

An alternative type of heat treatment can be effected by subjecting the rice to steam. In such process ample chemical solution of the type described above is sprayed onto or mixed with the rice intermittently during the steaming process. The rice is then subjected to live steam at a temperature of 212° to 280°F for from 5 to 45 minutes.

Again the time of heat treatment is dependent upon the amount of chemical solution used, the temperature of the steam, the concentration of the chemical solution, the duration of presoaking and the type of rice. A longer treatment time is required where the steam is at a lower temperature and/or the solutions are less concentrated.

A third type of treatment is torrefaction. For such treatment the rice is sprayed or mixed with a chemical solution of the type described above in the amount of 5 pounds to 50 pounds of solution per 100 pounds of rice or mixed with an equivalent amount of dry chemical powder. Such heating may be accomplished in an autoclave within a temperature range of 212° to 285°F and under a pressure of 1 lb/in^2 to 40 lb/in^2.

Following the heat treatment the rice is rinsed to remove excess chemical solution and exudates and to eliminate clumping. The rinsing may be effected in calcium chloride brine for this purpose. The rice is then dried, such as by a steady current of warm air not exceeding about 160°F or by intermittent blasts of hotter air.

The resulting product will be ready to be packaged for sale as quick-cooking rice. The grains of such product will be unmutilated and strong. The rice will be approximately as white as the rice was before being subjected to the treatment, and the grains will be of generally the same size as the grains of the initial rice.

Example: This example will serve as a specific method of conduct for this process. The initial rinsing is optional. An aqueous chemical treating solution is made up of 0.75% by weight of the dry rice of monosodium phosphate and 0.5% by weight of the dry rice of calcium citrate.

The rice is cooked in ample chemical solution under atmospheric or higher pressure at a temperature of 185° to 280°F until the rice has been substantially completely cooked. The time required is 1 to 50 minutes. At boiling the usual time required is about 17 minutes. The rice is rinsed in water to remove chemical residue and separate the grains. The rice is air-dried to a moisture content of 13 to 17%. The quick-cooking rice product can be cooked finally to a palatable state by boiling in water at atmospheric pressure for a period of 4 to 8 minutes.

Prefried Grain Product

C.C. Huxsoll and D.N. Homnick; U.S. Patent 3,745,019; July 10, 1973; assigned to U.S. Secretary of Agriculture describe a process by which prefried food products are prepared from grains such as rice, wheat, oats, barley, corn and the like.

Basically, the process involves the following operations: (1) Raw rice is hydrated to a moisture content of about 30% by soaking in excess water and, then, gelatinized and partially cooked by the application of steam. Repetition of these processes serves to further hydrate (to a moisture level of about 65%), gelatinize, and cook the rice.

At this point, the twice-hydrated rice is mixed with additional water; and protein supplements such as soy flour, etc., are added to increase the nutritional value of the product. The incorporation of such material helps to improve the protein to carbohydrate ratio. The mixture is then further cooked by the use of steam. Finally, additional ingredients such as spices, seasonings, and other food materials are added, and the resulting conglomeration is held to aid flavor development and intermittently steamed to maintain the high temperature and to finish the cooking process. Alternately, the second hydration, rather than being a distinct step, can be included in the step which involves mixing and cooking the rice with a protein supplement and other ingredients. It is important to note, however, that the initial hydration must be conducted separately so that the rice in the final product will have the proper texture. Since the rice is very bland, the mixture can be effectively flavored and seasoned. In addition, the spicy flavors can be used to mask any undesirable taste resulting from the protein supplement.

By-products from the production of other food products such as meat, fish, poultry, etc., can be used to supplement the flavor of the rice material, thereby enhancing its value as a dish for breakfast, lunch, or dinner. For example, the filling for a chili-flavored prefried rice product is prepared as follows: onion, garlic, bell pepper, ginger, chili powder, bits of beef, tomato paste, salt, monosodium glutamate, and pinto bean powder are incorporated with precooked rice and further cooked to increase the flavor and texture of the whole. It is important to note that the texture of the cooked rice mixture must be such that the final product exhibits a soft, but not mushy, inner core. By application of the above steps, the proper texture can be attained.

(2) The cooked material, either hot or warm, is extruded such that uniform, dispensable pieces are obtained (the shape is unimportant).

(3) Next, a thin layer of flour is applied to the surface of the pieces. The layer is set by blanching with steam which partially cooks the flour and insures the formation of a crisp crust. This cooking operation is essential to the production of a crust which will adhere to the product during subsequent frying operations.

The flour for the crust may be selected from a wide variety of sources such as potatoes, beans, wheat, etc. The important criterion is that a crust of desirable color, flavor, and texture is produced. The flour may be flavored with various spices and seasonings before application to the preformed rice product.

One advantage of the crust is that its crispness provides an effective and desirable contrast to the soft inner core. Also, control of the type of crust produced will insure that the prefried and frozen material will yield a desirable product upon oven-warming by the consumer. Another advantage of the crusts is that oil, used in subsequent frying operations, is prevented from moving to the interior of the pieces.

Thus, the oil content of the finished product will be maintained on the surface and at a minimal level. A further advantage is that the crust shields the kernels of rice during frying operations so that they remain moist and soft. Small amounts of special film-forming starches may be added to the crust mix to enhance its functional character. Above all, the steps of coating with flour and blanching can be repeated until a crust of a desirable thickness is achieved.

(4) Finally, the so-formed pieces are parfried in an edible oil to develop the proper flavor, color, and texture, and to slightly reduce the moisture level of the whole. Alternately, the pieces may be first exposed to infrared heat or hot air to partially cook the crust. The former is preferred because it produces a better quality crust.

However, treatment with hot air is a much simpler operation and might be the method of choice for larger operations. Obviously, prior treatment with radiant heat or hot air will reduce the length of the aforementioned parfry. In addition, the predeveloped crust will prevent the uptake of excess oil during the shortened parfry.

The primary advantage of the process is the production of prefried food products which serve as an alternate to prefried potato products. Thus, as with potato chips, the products can be used as snack items. On the other hand, the products can be served as part of a meal in much the same way as French fried potatoes, hash-brown potatoes, and the like.

Example: Beef-Flavored Prefried Rice Product — Rice, 1 kg (about 87% solids) content), was soaked in 1 kg of water at 70°F for 30 minutes, separated from excess water, and steamed in a conventional manner for 12 minutes at 212°F. At this point the rice had absorbed 250 grams of water (about 30% moisture level).

This partially cooked rice was soaked in 1 kg of water at 190°F for 5 minutes. The excess water was separated, and the rice was steamed for 15 minutes at 212°F. The absorbed water now totalled 1,480 grams (or about 65% moisture).

The steamed rice was lightly blended with 120 grams of soy flour, 100 grams of pinto bean powder, and 500 ml of water and steamed for 10 to 15 minutes. Other ingredients, the amounts of which are given below, were added. The mixture was allowed to stand for 5 to 10 minutes to allow the flavor components to diffuse throughout. During this period the temperature was maintained at 160° to 170°F by intermittent heating with steam.

Ingredient	Weight (grams)
Onion, dehydrated, minced	25
Vegetable hydrolyzate	30
Garlic powder	0.75
Salt	50
Monosodium glutamate	2.0
Black pepper, ground 30 mesh	1.25
Ginger, ground	0.4
Emulsifier	4.0

The hot material was extruded in a conventional apparatus and cut into pieces 2" x ¾" in diameter. Potato flakes were ground into a powder and placed in a vibrating trough. The so-formed pieces of rice product were directed through the potato flour so that a thin coating was applied to the surface. The pieces were then blanched with steam at 212°F for 2 minutes. After cooling, the pieces were again conveyed through the flour and blanched with steam at 212°F for 2 minutes.

Following this operation, the pieces were heated with infrared heat for 2 minutes while being slowly rotated. Finally, the so-heated pieces were fried in an edible oil at 350°F for 2 minutes, cooled, and frozen in a blast freezer at -34°F.

For taste judgements, the frozen pieces were warmed in an oven at 450°F for 10 minutes. Approximately 40 persons tasted and rated the products, which were judged to have an excellent flavor, a crisp exterior, and a soft, but not mushy interior.

Quick-Cooking Rice Prepared by Preliminary Frying Process

R.C. Tolson, Sr. and R.C Tolson Jr.; U.S. Patent 3,706,573; December 19, 1972; assigned to G.T. Products, Incorporated have devised a process in which the raw rice is fried at a relatively high temperature for a short period of time to produce a product which is simply and easily cooked to yield flavorable, separate, attractive rice kernels for serving at a meal.

In general, the process comprises placing raw rice kernels into a hot oil bath and frying the rice kernels therein for a very short period of time. The fried rice kernels are quickly removed from the hot oil bath, the excess surface oil clinging to the kernels is removed and the kernels are permitted to cool to room temperature. The cool kernels are then packaged for ultimate sale to the consumer.

The rice produced by this process is not completely cooked or fried in the usual sense, since it is necessary to subject the rice product to further cooking with water just prior to consumption; however, the fried product is definitely altered in appearance and edibility from raw rice. It is quite milky and opaque in appearance as opposed to raw rice which is shiny and translucent. Further the rice kernels are rather crunchy and have a flavor somewhat reminiscent of popcorn although when cooked in water as described hereafter, the product has a true rice flavor.

In addition, the fried rice product can be stored for long periods of time without deterioration or the development of rancidity. When desired, the product is very quickly and simply cooked with water to produce a completely edible and attractively flavored rice.

In greater detail, raw milled white rice having a water content of some 15% or less is placed into a feeder unit. The feeder unit is disposed above a hot oil bath such that the rice grains are fed directly thereinto. In any event the raw rice grains are fed into an oil bath where the temperature of the oil is maintained at 350° to 420°F, although under ideal conditions the oil temperature should be 385°F, or as close thereto as possible.

After being introduced into the hot oil the rice grains are fried therein for 7 to 14 seconds, after which the grains are immediately removed from the hot oil and conveyed away from the bath for cooling and draining of the excess oil therefrom. After the excess oil is drained from the rice and it has cooled to room temperature, it is placed into suitable containers which are thereafter sealed and stocked for later shipment. Although the rice may be fried by a bath process, it is desirable to prepare the product in a continuous processing apparatus since large quantities of rice can thereby be prepared in a short period of time.

One such apparatus consists of a raw rice feeder, for instance, a vibratory hopper, disposed over a shallow hot oil bath. A rice conveyer mechanism is submerged a few inches below the surface of the hot oil and leads to an exit funnel emerging from the oil bath. An auger mechanism passes through the funnel which has screen walls to permit drainage of excess oil from the processed rice. The auger passes to a cooling table, from where a second conveyer passes to the packaging area.

Raw rice is dropped from the hopper directly into the hot oil which is continually circulated through the shallow bath at the temperature previously noted. The frying rice is conveyed through the hot oil and into the exit auger all within a period of a few seconds, e.g., 7 to 14. The total frying time is controlled by regulating the speed of the conveyer, but in any event, at the temperature contemplated herein, a frying time of from 7 to 14 seconds is sufficient to prepare the desired product.

The hot fried rice is then augered up from the hot oil bath through the screen funnel section where the centrifugal force developed in the auger section helps in separating the excess liquid oil from the fried rice grains. The excess drains through the screened section back into the bath section where it is eventually reused.

The rice, now essentially free of excess oil is then conveyed to the cooling table where it is permitted to return to room temperature, after which it is reconveyed to the package filling section, where it is packed into suitable containers. The oil used for frying the rice may be selected from any number of edible oils. It is only necessary that the oil be edible and reasonably resistant to oxidation at the temperature utilized in the process.

The rice produced by the process loses approximately 5% by weight of its initial moisture content during the frying process. On the other hand the rice picks up oil about 8% of its initial weight, whereby the rice gains weight by several percent during the process. As noted previously, the rice assumes a chalky white appearance after the frying process and under magnification presents a rather porous aspect. The rice remains in individual kernels and increases in volume by some 50 to 60% over the raw untreated rice.

The temperature of the oil in the frying bath is quite critical since too high a temperature will result in the explosive emission of moisture from the rice causing the kernels to crack and shatter and thus yield an undesirable product. Further, too high an oil temperature tends to brown the rice and change the flavor. On the other hand, too low an oil temperature results in incomplete frying of the rice kernels or necessitates an excessively long cooking time with concurrent decrease in the production rate.

The rice product has a shelf life in the package commensurate with raw milled rice. Prior to actual consumption, the rice product must be further cooked with water to provide a thoroughly cooked, palatable rice dish. Preferably the rice product may be prepared for consumption as follows.

The desired measured quantity of rice is removed from the package and is placed into an equal quantity of rapidly boiling water. Boiling of rice and water is continued for about 2 minutes, after which the heat is removed and the rice is permitted to stand while covered, for about 10 additional minutes. The rice is now ready to serve.

It is quite similar to correctly cooked milled rice, in that the rice separates cleanly and uniformly into individual grains and there is no starchiness or stickiness. The flavor is also quite similar to plain cooked milled rice, with perhaps a slightly nuttier flavor. Of course, as in the case of plain cooked rice, spices and/or condiments may be added to the cooked rice as desired.

SYNTHETIC FOOD PROCESSES

HIGH PROTEIN ITEMS RESEMBLING MEAT PRODUCT

Quick Cooking Foodstuff

A. Spiel; U.S. Patent 3,912,824; October 14, 1975 describes the preparation of an edible, bland, high protein composition derived from proteinaceous plant materials, such as soybeans, peanuts, and other legumes and nuts, which is a textured or meat-like material and bland when hydrated.

In the process plant protein material such as, solvent-extracted soybean meal or flakes, or peanuts, sesame seeds, cotton seeds, lentil beans, etc. containing some moisture is subjected to a pressure of at least 1,800 pounds per square inch for a time and at a temperature sufficient to convert the moisture into steam. As a result, the plant protein material is rendered partially or substantially bland, e.g., disembittered, toasted without scorching, and compacted into a hard and substantially fused mass which is textured or meat-like when hydrated.

The mass is fragmented into chunks which are preferably graded. The chunks are heated in hot or boiling water for a period of time selected in accordance with the mean size of the chunks and sufficient in length to substantially hydrate the chunks and to dissolve out some of the soluble constituents whereby the chunks are softened to a chewable consistency. The chunks are separated from the hot or boiling water. At this point, the chunks can be rinsed and after drying are cohesive, porous, bland, storable, appetizing in appearance and quick and easy to cook or prepare for consumption. When subsequently hydrated in boiling water for a few minutes or in hot water, the chunks are chewable, bland, light colored, meat-like in texture and palatable. The resultant food is extremely high in protein content.

The several varieties of soybeans are useful. The soybeans are usually processed to prepare soybean meal. The resultant textured vegetable protein food has a higher protein content than most textured vegetable protein foods. Even more importantly, the various heating steps in the process greatly increase the relative

Synthetic Food Processes

protein efficiency of the resultant textured food over the initial starting material and destroy certain growth inhibitors in the soybean or other proteinaceous feed material.

The product does not have to use chemically treated flours, nor does the pH used in treating the chunks with hot or boiling water have to be adjusted by the use of any pH adjusting agent.

The dry and hydrated products are cohesive, meat-like in texture chunks which do not require a binder. The chunks are not fibrous in taste or chew, although they are a textured vegetable protein resembling the fibrous structure of natural meats. The hydrated chunks are therefore able to and do have a texture similar to natural meat. The meat-like texture of the chunks is aided by the fact that it is not (but can be) coated or impregnated by an edible oleaginous material after the drying step.

The dried chunks can be used to produce products which simulate beef, veal, liver, mutton, ham, turkey and chicken as dehydrated, canned or frozen materials. The dehydrated product is usually supplied in multiwall bags or fiber drums and hydrated products are usually supplied in cans or frozen packages. As a general guideline, the dry product requires rehydration on the customers part and additional processing for finished products by commercial facilities.

The rehydration product in a frozen form is ready to use upon thawing and is especially recommended for institutional use. The rehydrated product in a canned form is ready to use and is recommended for institutions with limited kitchen facilities. All of the meat-like products normally use a simple rehydration step to place them in shape for consumption. This step can be done by the consumer, or the step can be achieved before the consumer receives the end product.

A very important feature is that the dried processed chunks or the rehydrated chunks can withstand the usual retorting conditions for canned products (i.e., 250°F, for one hour). Unless otherwise stated in the following example, all percentages, parts and portions are expressed on a weight basis, based upon total compositions. The following example illustrates the process.

Example: The starting material is flakes of dehulled, solvent-extracted, soybean having a moisture content of 7.5% and a protein solubility range expressed in NSI or PDI, respectively, Nitrogen Solubility Index and Protein Dispersability Index (AOCS Test BA 10-65) of about 50%. The soybean flakes are processed in a modified Anderson expeller.

The soybean flakes are preheated to about 180°F in the preconditioning chamber. The retention time in the preconditioning chamber is 1 minute, and steam having a pressure of 65 psig is used in the steam jacket. The soybean flakes have a moisture content of 6.8% upon exiting from the preconditioning chamber and are passed through the vertical force feeder into the main horizontal pressing chamber. The processing retention time (time during which the pressure is applied) is 2 minutes; the pressure applied is 2,000 psi and the thickness of the cake is about three-eighths inch. The cake during the pressing has a temperature of 305°F. The exiting cake has a moisture content of 5.5%, is allowed to cool and is fragmented by means of chopping blades into chunks. The chunks have a light yellowish brown or buff color and are not porous in appearance.

The chunks are separated by screens to give retained chunks having a chunk size that pass through a one inch screen and stay on a one-half inch screen. The feed chunks (compacted chunks) have an analysis (weight percent on a dry basis) as follows:

TABLE 1

	Compacted Chunks	Final Chunks
Protein (N x 6.25)	53.5	61.5
Fat	1.2	3.3
Fiber	4.0	3.0
Ash	6.7	5.2
Carbohydrate (difference)	34.6	27.0

The calculation basis for total protein is N x 6.25, N being the value obtained by analysis for protein nitrogen by Kjeldahl Test, 6.25 being the standard factor for soy. The amino acid profile for the compacted soybean chunks is:

Amino Acid	Percent	Amino Acid	Percent
Lysine	4.798	Glycine	3.293
Available lysine	4.421	Alanine	3.546
Histidine	2.016	Cystine, half	Trace
Arginine	5.664	Valine	3.038
Aspartic Acid	9.142	Methionine	1.281
Threonine	2.882	Isoleucine	2.732
Serine	3.977	Leucine	4.858
Glutamic acid	14.230	Tyrosine	2.455
Proline	3.996	Phenylalanine	3.614

The following is the vitamin analysis for the compacted soybean chunks:

Vitamins	Amounts, mg/lb
Thiamin	3.49
Riboflavin	2.18
Niacin	8.17
Vitamin B_6	2.27
Vitamin B_{12}	None detected

The Protein Efficiency Ratio of the compacted chunks is 87% of that for casein. The following is the mineral analysis for the compacted soybean chunks:

Mineral	Amount
Calcium	0.216 percent
Phosphorus	0.660 percent
Potassium	0.230 percent
Magnesium	0.280 percent
Iron	90.5 ppm
Copper	15.0 ppm
Manganese	20.0 ppm
Zinc	81.0 ppm
Sodium chloride	0.222 percent
Cobalt	0.033 ppm
Iodine	<0.14 ppm

Synthetic Food Processes

225 pounds of water (pH is 6.8) are placed in a steam jacketed Groen tilting kettle and the water is brought up to a temperature of 212°F (vigorously boiling). Twenty-five pounds of the above mentioned feed chunks are placed in boiling water and the chunks are cooked at that temperature (vigorously boiling) for 1.5 hour. The cooked chunks are drained by tilting the kettle and dumping the cooked chunks on a one-eighth inch opening screen. The cooked chunks on the screen are washed with warm water (150°F). Approximately 300 pounds of warm water are used to wash the cooked chunks over a period of 15 minutes. The cooked chunks are drained and have a moisture content of 75% by weight.

The cooked chunks are then placed on a one-eighth inch openings screens in a cabinet dryer. The bed depths are about one inch, and the dryer screen area is 4.28 square feet. Air, having a temperature of 200°F and a relative humidity of 30%, is used to dry the chunks to a final moisture of 5% by passing the air upwardly through the cooked chunks for 2½ hours at a velocity of 500 feet per minute. The average yield of solids for the entire process after drying is 75%. The final chunks have an analysis (weight percent on a dry basis) as given above in Table 1.

Comparison of this analysis of the dry chunks with the analysis for the feed chunks (compacted chunks) shows that the chunks made according to this process possess a protein content which is 8% higher (based on the protein content of the feed chunks) than the feed chunks. The following is the vitamin analysis for the dried processed chunks.

	Amount, mg/lb
Thiamin	2.62
Riboflavin	1.07
Niacin	7.19
Vitamin B_6	0.62
Vitamin B_{12}	None detected

This shows that a very high percentage of vitamins is retained. A mineral analysis of the dried processed chunks shows 0.25% magnesium. This shows that a very high percentage of minerals is retained.

One part of chunks is placed in 2 parts of boiling water for 11 minutes. (The chunks can absorb from 1 to 3 times their weight of water). The resultant hydrated chunks are bland, light-colored, meat-like in texture and palatable. They do not contain any noticeable bitter beany flavor and taste. Further, there is no objectional odor when any storage package is opened, during the rehydration or at any time thereafter. The rehydrated chunks are very high in protein content.

Food Flavor Pellets

E.G. Huessy; U.S. Patent 3,851,072; November 26, 1974; assigned to Peavey Company describes a method and formulation for preparing edible food cubes or pellets having a meat-like texture, primarily for incorporation in dry food systems as a substitute or supplement for meat wherein the edible cubes or pellets have a wheat flour, soy flour, and vegetable protein or tow base. The method includes the preparation of a homogeneous mixture of the selected formulation, and thereafter passing the mixture through a product agitating zone which holds the material at elevated temperature and pressure over a rather substantial holding or retention time. The material is thereafter extruded from the agitating zone in the form of a continuously extruded product which is cut at intervals into the desired product size and length.

The edible food flavoring cubes or pellets find their primary utility in combination with dry food systems or mixes, such as soup mixes, salads, omelet and casserole mixes, and the like.

As indicated, the compositions are based upon wheat flour, soy flour, and vegetable protein solids. Vegetable oil is also used in order to provide the fatty component necessary for certain texturing features of the product. Vegetable oil also provides a mechanical advantage in lubrication of extruder during the processing operation.

The compositions also contain a quantity of a hydrocolloid, preferably xanthan gum. Xanthan gum is a high molecular weight linear polysaccharide which functions as a hydrophilic colloid to stabilize the high sugar content formulations. Essentially, xanthan gum is classified as a carbohydrate, being a complex polysaccharide with a molecular weight of more than one million.

The incorporation of xanthan gum in the dry formulation further assists in the later extrusion operation, the xanthan gum functioning as a lubricating agent for lubricating the mechanism while in combination with water. Xanthan gum also retains water while the adverse conditions of elevated temperatures are being encountered in the processing. It has been found that modified hydrocolloids may also be employed, however, xanthan gum is specifically preferred.

The wheat flour component is utilized primarily as a bulking agent, and also provides for limited gelatinization. The soy flour component, in addition to performing as a bulking agent, has been found to provide texturing for the product. The vegetable protein solids utilized in the mixture provides texture for the product. With this variety of components present in the product, it is possible to extrude the homogeneously mixed material into cubes or pellets.

The edible food cubes or pellets have a relatively long shelf life and normally will not deteriorate or adversely modify their characteristics by becoming soft, sticky, or runny while retained under normal modern packaging techniques. The food flavoring cubes or pellets have good shelf life and retain their characteristic texture and flavor over extended periods of time, and will not deteriorate under normal environmental conditions.

Essentially, a formulation is initially prepared having a relatively high wheat and soy flour content, such as a content in excess of about 40%. The formulations are prepared, mixed homogeneously, and maintained with only a low or modest water content. Following formulation, the mixture is passed through a product agitating zone where it is held under conditions of elevated temperature and pressure until it is ultimately extruded from the agitating chamber.

Example: To prepare the formulation for processing, the following dry bulk ingredients are thoroughly mixed together so as to provide a homogeneous mass. The fat phase is then added and the components again thoroughly mixed until homogeneous. The water phase together with the flavor and color added thereto is then added to the mix and the total mass is then continued to be mixed until

Synthetic Food Processes

homogeneous. Conventional mixing chambers and vessels may be employed for this treatment.

Dry Bulk Ingredient	Percentage
Wheat flour	33.70
Hydrogenated vegetable oils	13.48
Soy flour	13.48
Vegetable protein	10.11
Sugar	8.42
Salt	6.74
Water	4.46
Hydrogenated plant protein	3.37
Sorbitol	1.49
Glycerin	1.49
Lactic acid	1.19
Artificial flavorings	1.04
Beet powder	0.59
Monosodium glutamate	0.15
Sodium citrate	0.15
Res-oleum black pepper	0.05
Oleoresin carrot	0.05
Xanthan gum	0.05
Res-oleum thyme	0.02

The semiheavy dry mix is then placed into the auger chamber of an extruder, with the die being provided with a cut-off blade. The auger chamber is heated to between 180° and 200°F, however if higher temperature ranges are utilized, care must be taken to control the water content of the finished product, since a certain quantity may be flashed off at the die.

The viscosity of the product while in the extruder chamber assures elevated pressures within the auger chamber such as in the range of about 500 psi. A heated auger may be employed in order to achieve the desired temperature range during mixing, heated chambers of this type being, of course, commercially available. Steam is normally employed as the heating medium. If desired, a conventional tumbler can be utilized to form an agglomeration of the raw material to form the cube or pellet. Such agglomeration tumblers are also, of course, commercially available. After the individual cubes or pellets are cut from the extruder die, they are permitted to cool and are available for use.

In the composition of the example, the function of the individual ingredients has been partially described hereinabove, with the wheat flour being a bulking and gelatinization agent, and with the soy flour being a texturing and bulking agent. The vegetable protein provides the texture for the meat substitute product. The hydrogenated vegetable oil is the fatty ingredient also needed for texturizing, and to give the material a meat-like consistency. The vegetable oil also functions as a lubricating medium. Salt provides a conventional flavoring for the material, and glycerin functions as a humectant.

The flavoring ingredients, lactic acid, beet powder, and artificial flavor are all utilized for flavoring purposes. The flavoring employed is an imitation ham flavor. The xanthan gum is a humectant and water-retaining component and its function has been described in some detail hereinabove.

The product can be utilized for its textural characteristics in either a wet or dry medium. The extruded product contains a substantial quantity of modified starch with a high fat content. Furthermore, the material substantially retains its configuration and flavor after extended exposure to cooking environments, including exposure to boiling water. This composition and formulation provides an artificial ham nugget on a substantially dry basis.

In order to prepare similar products for imitation meat, such as ham, the following table suggests a range of ingredients which may be employed:

Ingredient	Percentage Range
Wheat flour	30 - 35
Hydrogenated vegetable oils	12 - 15
Soy flour	12 - 15
Vegetable protein	8 - 12
Sugar	7 - 9
Salt	4 - 8
Water	3 - 5
Hydrogenated plant protein	3 - 5
Sorbitol	1 - 2
Glycerin	1 - 2
Lactic acid	1 - 2
Artificial flavorings	0.8 - 1.2
Beet powder	0.5 - 0.7
Monosodium glutamate	0.1 - 0.2
Sodium citrate	0.1 - 0.2
Res-oleum black pepper	0.03 - 0.06
Oleoresin carrot	0.03 - 0.06
Xanthan gum	0.03 - 0.06
Res-oleum thyme	0.01 - 0.03

Textured Expanded Food

S.F. Loepiktie and R.J. Flier; U.S. Patent 3,759,715; September 18, 1973; assigned to Ralston Purina Company have determined that a meat-like structure can be obtained with the use of inexpensive equipment by cooking a dough of a secondary protein material such as vegetable protein or microbial protein, if the dough is controllably expanded substantially along the longitudinal axis of the dough. This may be accomplished by rolling or shaping the dough into a cylindrical or rod-like shape, followed by confinement of the major surfacial portion of the dough, with the ends of the shaped dough or smaller surfacial portions of the dough being essentially unconfined. This permits expansion of the dough along the longitudinal axis or the axis of the unconfined surfacial portions of the dough. When such expansion occurs, then the protein product formed has a fibrous structure similar to that of meat and is characterized by excellent rehydration characteristics.

If the dough is subjected to various mechanical working steps such as rolling, folding or stretching in combination with unidirectional or controlled expansion of the mixtures, an expanded food product is produced which remarkably resembles meat in structure and it is produced with inexpensive and readily available equipment. The product may be characterized as an expanded, irreversible proteinaceous structure having excellent physical properties, including texture, moisture stability and tensile strength, which properties make it particularly suitable for various food uses. The product has excellent tensile strength not only when wet but also when dry, and in addition retains these excellent physical properties even after being subjected to extreme heat and moisture conditions such as by cooking.

The desired product is best achieved by mixing together secondary protein source materials such as a vegetable protein source material containing at least about 30% protein and an aqueous liquid to form a dough type material. Water alone is the preferred liquid, but mixtures of various other liquids with water could be employed.

Also various vegetable protein materials, especially oleaginous materials, can be employed preferably in defatted condition, including isolated soy protein, soy flour, defatted soy flakes, cottonseed meals, sesame seed meals, peanut meals, and the like.

Although it is preferred that substantially unheated protein materials be employed, it is understood that partially toasted or partially hydrolyzed protein materials may also be employed where the degree of heating or hydrolysis is only such that the proteinaceous mixture still expands to form the product.

Any of the protein-containing materials employed as starting materials should have water dispersible properties, such properties being especially useful in making the protein available to form the expanded structure. It has also been found that the product must contain at least about 30% by weight protein in order to obtain the desired physical properties such as the desired texture, degree of expansion, tensile strength, etc.

The most favorable results are obtained when the aqueous liquid is added to the portion-containing material to form the dough in an amount from 40 to 50% by weight of the dough.

After mixing together the oleaginous seed material and the aqueous liquid to form the dough, it may be necessary to adjust the pH of the mixture to provide the necessary conditions for expanding the product. It has been found that the best results are obtained where the mixture has a final pH of 5.5 to 9.5. When the pH is below 5, it has been found that the product gels and discolors to form a crumbly product and does not have desirable water absorption properties. When the pH is above 10, it has been found that the resulting product has poor color and undesirable, unappealing physical characteristics. Where it is necessary to adjust the pH to a value within the above described range, the pH may be adjusted by the use of suitable known, food grade chemical compositions such as sodium hydroxide, ammonium hydroxide, ammonium carbonate, etc.

The aqueous protein mixture or dough so formed is preferably then subjected to a tempering operation to impart desired physical properties to the mixture and to the final product. The tempering operation improves the resilient, chewy, and meat-like properties of the material. A rolling step is particularly advantageous in imparting the desired meat-like characteristics in the final expanded product.

The tempering operation and the texture of the final product are greatly influenced by the presence of various humectant and preservative solvent materials in the aqueous proteinaceous mix. Typical preservative organic solvent and humectant materials are glycerol, 1,2-propanediol, and mixtures thereof. By adding from 10 to 50% by weight of the aqueous liquid of organic solvent material to the aqueous liquid, tempering, and expanding the proteinaceous mix into an irreversible structure, a product is formed which will remain stable and resistant to bacterial and mycotic contamination and which will have a pleasing soft, plasticized texture after prolonged storage under room temperature conditions.

Other reagents may also be added to the proteinaceous mix to influence the tempering operation or to impart other properties such as fiber toughness or rehydration characteristics which are important to the protein product. Sulfur, salt, sodium sulfite, sodium bicarbonate, calcium carbonate, hydrogen peroxide, cysteine, sodium hypophosphite, or other food grade reagents may also be added to the proteinaceous mix to modify the properties of the protein product. Cysteine may be particularly useful because it supplements the amino acid content of the proteinaceous source.

The tempered dough is then subjected to controlled expansion and preferably, substantially, unidirectional expansion to form a fibrous meat-like structure in the product and causing the product to have the resilient chewy characteristics of natural meat.

Unidirectional or controlled directional expansion of the partially confined dough may be accomplished in a variety of ways but may preferably and easily be carried out if the dough after tempering is rolled or shaped into an elongated or rod-like mass. This dough is then placed in an elongated container such as a pipe or tube or other container which may be rectangular as well as cylindrical, and which confines the major surfacial portion of the dough and with the ends or smaller surfacial portions of the dough being unconfined. This permits controlled or unidirectional expansion of the dough along the axis of these unconfined portions or in the direction of the unconfined portion and therefore, forms an expanded food product resembling meat.

The tempered roll or piece of dough in the container is then subjected to an elevated temperature and pressure sufficient to heat set the protein and form an irreversible heat stable structure of the protein material. Accordingly, when the pressure is released or reduced, moisture present in the dough will be released or volatilized and therefore, cause expansion of the dough along the axis of the unconfined surfacial portions or along the longitudinal axis of the dough. The water which is part of the protein aqueous liquid mixture or dough is believed to be rendered highly volatilizable by being exposed to the condition of high temperature and pressure and is therefore able to be quickly volatilized by a rapid pressure reduction causing the material to expand. However, because of the manner in which the dough is confined, controlled expansion results along the axis of the unconfined surfaces of the dough which is normally along the longitudinal axis of the dough so as to impart a fibrous structure to the product.

Generally the temperature will in the cooking vessel or chamber thereof vary between 300° to 500°F, with lower temperatures than these being insufficient to cause sufficient expansion and higher temperatures being conducive to burning or scorching of the protein material. The pressure within the chamber or cooking vessel in combination with the aforementioned temperature range will vary between 80 to 120 lb/in^2.

The time during which the tempered protein aqueous liquid mixture is subjected to the aforementioned temperature and pressure will vary depending on the specific combination of temperature and pressure which is employed, but most generally will vary between 1 to 5 minutes.

The pressure release time may be from 10 to 20 seconds. This pressure release time in combination with the conditions of temperature and pressure enhances controlled and unidirectional expansion, thus imparting a stretching effect to the material and producing a fibrous structure having the chewiness and resiliency of natural meat. The following example will illustrate the process.

Example : 110 grams of solvent extracted soybean meal having a protein content of approximately 50% by weight was mixed with about 90 grams of water and 0.1 gram of sulfur in a food mixer for about five minutes to form a generally homogeneous dough. The dough was then separated into individual chunks of 60 grams and rolled or formed into cylindrical rods of ½" diameter and 4" in length. These were then placed in a Teflon-coated aluminum tube of 1" diameter and about 8" long with the ends of the tube being open.

The tube containing the rod of dough was placed into a container to which pressurized steam could be added and an elevated temperature and pressure maintained for a predetermined period of time. Pressurized steam was added to the container with the tube therein until a pressure of 100 psi and a chamber temperature of 338° to 340°F was attained in the container for about two minutes. The pressure was rapidly released within 15 to 20 seconds. The product removed from the aluminum tube was a cylindrical-shaped, puffed and expanded product with a tough resilient fiber structure.

Expansion had occurred substantially unidirectionally along the longitudinal axis of the dough or along the axis of the unconfined surfaces of the dough or ends of the tube in an amount of about 4¾". On the other hand, expansion had taken place in the opposite direction or in the direction of the confined surfacial portions of the dough of only about ½" or so. The product was sliced and the internal structure was observed to be cellular and the material had a chewy resistance with the resiliency and textural characteristics of meat.

PUFFING PROCEDURES

Moist Food Puffing Using Inert Noncondensible Gas

The process described by *C.J. Merriam; U.S. Patent 3,958,032; May 18, 1976; assigned to The Griffith Laboratories, Inc.* relates to the controlled puffing of moist, puffable food products, usually proteinaceous, in such a way as to avoid the significant rupturing or disruptive puffing characteristics associated with so-called explosion-puffed extrudates.

The method, referred to herein as balloon-puffing, involves producing a major or substantial part of the expansion by vaporizing water contained in the viscous proteinaceous plastic mass or melt below its applicable boiling point in the deliberate presence of residual air in sufficient quantity to produce gradual or controlled puffing by reason of the air adding its partial pressure to that of the vaporized moisture. Small bubbles present or so generated within the advancing mass generally develop and grow along the path or direction of flow and against the positive confining pressure exerted by an elongated die.

When various proteinaceous food materials are subjected to this method, the puffed food products are textured to provide enhanced bite characteristics in the mouth.

The preferred edible fibrous proteinaceous extrudate made using this method has meat-like structure and organized balloon-puffed cells and is characterized by having good water absorption properties and by retaining its structural integrity under retorting conditions. The balloon-puffed cells preferably are arranged in substantially coaxially defined, laminar layers. The structured or textured extrudate may have a specific density of at least about 25 or 30 lb/ft^3.

The method includes the step of vaporizing available water in the advancing hot, moist proteinaceous mass or melt at a temperature below its boiling point in the presence of small bubbles of air (macroscopic and/or microscopic in size) distributed within the mass, to produce controlled expansion and balloon-puffing of the product. The water vapor is formed without requiring that the water boil, and contributes substantially to the increase in size of the air bubbles.

The moist proteinaceous feed mix or protein mix may be converted to a viscous, glassy plastic melt under substantial physical pressure at temperatures of about 180°F or more, as required. The inclusion of small air bubbles within the melt permits water vapor to be formed within the confined mass without requiring that any substantial amount of water be boiled and such generated water vapor substantially or significantly increases the size of the air bubbles.

The incorporation of air in the form of bubbles distributed in the advancing melt or extrudate permits puffing, namely, balloon-puffing, to occur in a gradual or controlled manner so that controlled expansion occurs without significantly rupturing or disrupting the mass or walls and at a temperature below that at which water boils at the prevailing pressure.

In the absence of air in the confined, advancing viscous mass, water vapor would not be formed at such prevailing temperature-pressure conditions, and hence puffing would not occur or result; the contained or incorporated air serves as a gas phase into which water can evaporate or volatize without substantial boiling, thus tending to increase the size of the air bubbles within the advancing mass by reason of the additive pressure of the water vapor, without the undesired and detrimental effects of explosion-puffing. Accordingly, the air bubbles initially formed provide nuclei for forming larger, balloon-puffed cells or bubbles within the extrudate.

The method contemplates, for example, that at least about ½ or ⅔ the size of the enlarged bubbles be due to the vapor pressure of water vapor contained therein. Furthermore, the vapor pressure of water vapor contained within the proteinaceous mass during extrusion may be, for example, from about 9 to 14 psi. Puffing may thus be conducted at somewhat lower extrusion temperatures, thereby providing, among other things, means of avoiding any burnt taste which might otherwise be present with some proteinaceous materials.

Synthetic Food Processes

The proteinaceous source material used in the protein mix or feedstock may include edible protein-containing material of a desired size or form as vegetable of cereal grain protein materials (e.g., wheat gluten or rice gluten) or defatted or solvent-extracted vegetable oil seed, oleaginous, or cotyledon seed materials (e.g., solvent-extracted soybean protein meal), or combinations thereof, having a protein content (dry weight basis) of about 30% or more, preferably 40%, 50%, or more. Soy protein concentrates having about 70% protein (dry weight basis) may be used, for example, and such concentrates may have a low or high nitrogen solubility index (NSI). Furthermore, if desired, soy protein isolate having a protein content of about 90% or more on a dry weight basis, or commercial casein may be used.

The protein mix should be in a substantially uniform, moist state and have an effective amount of water and occluded air (e.g., microvoids) when or as it is subjected to effective mechanical pressure, heat and shearing action to convert it to a melt (e.g., a substantially homogeneous, moist, viscous plastic melt).

The nature or composition of the feedstock and melt (as well as apparatus and processing conditions) at least in part determine the particular temperatures and/or pressure conditions applied to the die assembly and confined, advancing mass or melt.

When one uses, for example, appropriate amounts of proteinaceous material such as defatted soy protein (e.g., flakes or flour) in the feedstock and the feedstock is at least in part moistened with or includes water (e.g., moist, crumbly or nonfluid protein mix), a viscous but pressure flowable hot melt may be produced or formed, for example, at product temperatures of well above 212°F (e.g., under initially great pressure).

However, if one uses appropriate amounts of proteinaceous material such as casein or defatted soy protein isolate in the feedstock and feedstock is moistened with water, a viscous but pressure flowable hot melt may be produced at product temperatures below 212°F (e.g., at 180°F, or more).

The amount of water present in the feedstock during the application of mechanical pressure and working (shearing) and heat sufficient to convert the feedstock to a hot viscous mass (plastic melt), and nature of the feedstock material and other desired, added materials which may be blended therewith, and the conditions of temperature-pressure control, pH, mechanical pressure, shearing action, forming, and flow rate, and the nature of the particular type of equipment and processing conditions used, are all interrelated and should be coordinated. The amount of available water generally should be within the range of 20 to 35% by weight, based on the weight of the total moist feedstock or moist protein mix.

The proteinaceous product, as extruded, has a glassy skin and a three-dimensional network structure characterized by disulfide bonding and remaining significantly intact following retorting. The network structure preferably has sufficient crosslinking for the product to be considered as having a polymeric network akin to a vulcanized product.

A variety of injection molding machines and thermoplastic extrusion and compression molding machines or related equipment may be used, at least in part, in preparing, forming and extruding the hot melt or matrix.

The above described process represents an extension of and an improvement in the following four prior processes describing the production of simulated meat products from vegetable protein material whereby significant rupturing of the puffed product is avoided.

R.R. Reinhart and L. Sair; U.S. Patent 3,925,566; December 9, 1975; assigned to The Quaker Oats Company and Griffith Laboratories, Inc. describes a process for preparing a puffed food product which simulates meat. The process comprises admixing an oil seed vegetable protein material or casein or a caseinate salt having specified protein concentrations with specified amounts of water, subjecting the mixture to an elevated pressure and temperature, extruding the mixture in an annular shape without puffing it, placing the extrudate in a confined space, subjecting the extrudate to a water-boiling temperature for a specified time at a specified pressure, and instantly releasing the pressure on the extrudate causing it to puff and resemble simulated meat.

The process disclosed by *R.R. Reinhart and G.M. Smith, Jr.; U.S. Patent 3,925,565; December 9, 1975; assigned to The Quaker Oats Company* for preparing a puffed food product which simulates meat comprises admixing a proteinaceous mixture of a protein material comprising a member selected from the group consisting of gelatin, microbiological protein, egg white, muscle protein, keratins, lactalbumin, and blood having protein concentrations of at least 30% by weight with water in an amount sufficient to provide a final moisture content of 25 to 40% by weight. The mixture is subjected to an elevated pressure and temperature. The mixture is extruded in an annular shape without puffing it. The extrudate is placed in a confined space and subjected to a water-boiling temperature for a specified time at a specified pressure. The pressure on the extrudate is instantly released causing it to puff and resemble simulated meat.

The process disclosed by *C.C. Harwood and D.W. Quass; U.S. Patent 3,917,876; November 4, 1975; assigned to The Quaker Oats Company* for preparing a puffed food product comprises admixing a proteinaceous mixture of a protein material comprising a member selected from the group consisting of oil seed vegetable protein, casein, caseinate salts, gelatin, microbiological protein, egg white, muscle protein, keratins, lactalbumin, and blood having a protein concentration of at least about 30% with water in an amount sufficient to provide a final moisture content of from about 15 tc 40% by weight and about ½ to 3% by weight of a lubricating substance comprising a member selected from the group edible fats and oils, edible fatty acids, edible stearates, and edible polylactic acid esters of fatty acids. The mixture is subjected to increased shear and extruded without puffing. The extrudate is placed in a confined space and subjected to a water-boiling temperature for a specified time at a specified pressure. The pressure is instantly released on the extrudate causing it to puff and resemble simulated meat.

The process disclosed by *C.C. Harwood and G.M. Smith, Jr.; U.S. Patent 3,904,775; September 9, 1975; assigned to The Quaker Oats Company* for preparing a puffed food product which simulates meat comprises admixing a proteinaceous material with an amount of water sufficient to provide a final moisture content of 15 to 40% by weight. The mixture is subjected to conditions sufficient to convert it to a flowable substance such as increased shear, and extruded by forming it into an annular or cylindrical shape and cooling both the inside and outside of the cylinder with the extrusion not causing puffing of the product.

The extrudate is placed in a confined space and subjected to water-boiling temperatures and superatmospheric pressure. The pressure is suddenly released on the extrudate to cause it to puff and resemble simulated meat.

Gaseous Conveyor Heating

R. Toei, T. Aonuma, H. Watanabe and T. Yuasa; U.S. Patent 3,754,930; Aug. 28, 1973; assigned to Kikkoman Shoyu Co., Ltd., Japan describe a method of continuously producing an expanded foodstuff by entraining a material foodstuff in a pressurized heated gas stream in a suspended condition thereby heating and conveying the material which is then discharged into a gas atmosphere at a lower pressure, whereby it is expanded.

The process relates to both the method and an apparatus for continuously uniformly expanding materials such as: polished rice, glutinous rice, etc. which are readily gelatinized by heat, which tend to adhere to and harden on the walls of heating equipment in which they are heated or tend to form an agglomerate with the particles thereof bonded with each other; vegetables, fruits, fish and shellfish which are sensitive to heat; and those of uneven grain size (wide grain size distribution) in particular.

The primary object of this process is to heat these foodstuffs uniformly thereby expanding them efficiently in a short period of time. In the process a pressurizing and heating gas, i.e., a pressurized (3 to 15 kg/cm^2 gauge) superheated steam (100° to 300°C) is passed through a heating conduit. A foodstuff material is mixed with the gas by continuously introducing it into the gas stream whereby the material is heated in a very short period of time (within 10 seconds) while being entrained in the gas stream. The material is thereafter collected by a cyclone or the like and discharged continuously and abruptly into a gas atmosphere maintained at a lower pressure thereby expanding the material.

The operation of a suitable apparatus for conducting this operation is fully explained in the patent. Some examples of the expanding operation using the apparatus and method of this process are illustrated below.

Example 1:

Material:
    Polished rice (with or without rice-bran)
    Bulk density: 1,000 kg/m^3
    Water content: 14.5 to 15%

Heating medium:
    Superheated steam
    Pressure: 6 kg/cm^2 gauge
    Temperature (heating conduit inlet): 250°C
    Temperature (heating conduit outlet): 200°C
    Velocity: 25 m/sec

Material treating capacity
    (on a continuous basis): 1,000 kg/hr
Treating time (retention time): 6 sec
Properties of the product:
    Water content: 8%
    Bulk density: 100 kg/m^3
    Conversion to a starch: 98%

Example 2:

Material:
    Wheat

    Bulk density: 780 kg/m^3
    Water content: 13.5 to 14.5%

Heating medium:
    Superheated steam

    Pressure: 7 kg/cm^2 gauge
    Temperature: (heating conduit inlet): 280°C
    Temperature (heating conduit outlet): 220°C
    Velocity: 20 m/sec

Treating capacity: 1,000 kg/hr
Treating time: 8 sec
Properties of product:
    Water content: 10%
    Bulk density (expansion ratio: about 5 times): 150 kg/m^3
    Conversion to a starch: 99%

Example 3:

Material:
    Defatted soybean

    Bulk density: 450 kg/m^2
    Water content: 9.5 to 10.5%
    Particle size distribution:
        68.5%   4 mesh or larger
        18.9%   4 to 8 mesh
        12.6%   8 to 32 mesh

Heating medium:
    Superheated steam

    Pressure: 5 kg/cm^2 gauge
    Temperature (heating conduit inlet): 250°C
    Temperature (heating conduit outlet): 220°C
    Velocity: 18 m/sec

Treating capacity (on a continuous basis):   500 kg/hr
Treating time: 5 sec
Properties of product: Water content: 4%

Note: The protein can be completely denaturated.

OTHER SIMULATED FOOD PRODUCTS

Meat, Fish or Dairy Item from Fermented Vegetable Product

J.J. Liggett; U.S. Patent 3,885,048; May 20, 1975 describes a method of preparation of high protein food products which have the flavor, texture and appearance of meat, fish and dairy products.

In the process the basic unhulled vegetable ingredients including sesame seeds are cooked by boiling in water so that the vegetables pieces become saturated with water. With some vegetables, such as wheat, barley, corn and soybeans, it is desirable to soak the product in water for a few hours prior to cooking. Also, with the harder vegetables such as soy and other dried beans and grains, shorter cooking times and a better final texture is provided by initially splitting or slicing the vegetable before cooking. Soybeans, for example, when split will absorb from about 1½ to 2 times their weight in water during such cooking. An aqueous culture of *Rhizopus oligosporous* or similar organism is then inoculated into the cooked vegetable pieces and desired flavorings such as cumin, garlic, and onion and colorings may be added at that time. It is important that salt or other minerals which will kill or retard the growth of the mold organisms not be added at this time.

The inoculated vegetables may then be placed in thin layers of about ½" to 1" thick on trays or in small mold cavities and incubated at about 30° to 40°C for 1 to 3 days until the interspaces between the vegetable pieces are completely filled with the fibrous mycelia of the mold culture. This can readily be determined by inspection of the product during incubation since the mycelia of the mold has a different appearance than the vegetable pieces. When the vegetable pieces have been thoroughly knit together by the mycelia of the mold organisms, the cultured or fermented product is removed from the culture trays or mold cavities, sterilized, packaged and refrigerated.

Rather than seasoning and coloring the product prior to or during culturing it is preferable for certain simulated food items to prepare the cultured vegetable product without using any seasonings or coloring. In this manner, a cultured or fermented base is produced which can be broken or ground up and mixed with other ingredients to prepare a wide variety of different simulated meat, fish and dairy products.

It is believed that the meaty flavor results from a synergistic action of the methionine in the sesame seeds with the mold organisms. It was found that the combination of wheat, soybeans and sesame seeds gives a meat flavored, palatable product rich in methionine and lycine without yeasty flavor generally associated with cultured soybean products.

Example 1: Cultured Base Product with Sesame — A mixture of 50% split soybeans, 25% flaked sesame meal and 25% bulgur wheat is soaked in tap water at 25°C for about 2 hours and then boiled at atmospheric pressure in water for 30 minutes or at 5 psi for 20 minutes. The mixture is then drained, inoculated with an aqueous solution of *Rhizopus oligosporous* and spread out in thin layers about ½" thick in sterilized trays and incubated in a humid atmosphere at a temperature of 37°C for one day, at which time the fibrous mycelia of the mold will completely fill the interspaces between the vegetable pieces. The cultured product is then broken up and immediately sterilized to kill the mold or is mixed with seasonings, extruded to desired shape and size and then sterilized to stop the mold growth.

In the mixture, sesame isolate may be substituted for the flaked sesame meal. The resulting cultured product will be extremely high in methionine and have a strong meaty flavor which may be diluted with suitable seasonings.

Example 2: Simulated Meat Base — The following ingredients were thoroughly mixed together and extruded into strips ½" thick and 3" wide. The resulting product was fried and had the appearance, texture, and flavor of meat.

Ingredient	Amount, g
Cultured base product of Example 1	1,000
Hydrolyzed vegetable protein	25
Garlic powder	2
Onion	1
Monosodium glutamate	1
Disodium 5-inosinate (and/or disodium 5-guanylate)	0.1
Salt	20
Sugar or equivalent amount of artificial sweetener	5

Example 3: Simulated Canadian Bacon — The following ingredients, except for the fat, were blended together dry and the melted vegetable fat was then added. 750 grams of water in which 0.2% potassium sorbate was dissolved as a preservative was then added and the product was thoroughly blended until smooth. It was then stuffed into edible casings, tied off and pasteurized. After pasteurization, it was permitted to cool and then refrigerated. The product had the appearance, taste and texture of Canadian bacon.

Ingredient	Amount, g
Cultured base product of Example 1	1,000
Air classified 2 to 300 mesh hard spring wheat flour	100
Tapioca, pregelatinized	200
Fumaric acid, dry	1
Hydrolyzed vegetable protein	70
Egg white, powdered	100
Salt	30
Garlic	1
All spice	5
Sugar	10
Vegetable fat, melted	100
Liquid smoke	10
Coloring as desired	

Example 4: Simulated Shrimp — The following ingredients except for the cultured base were mixed to form a solution and the cultured base, formed into bite-size, shrimp-shaped pieces, was immersed therein and permitted to soak for ten minutes. The pieces of the cultured base were than removed, drained and the excess water was squeezed out. The pieces were then packaged and frozen. After defrosting, the pieces were dipped in an egg batter, french-fried and eaten. In flavor and texture they closely resembled natural shrimp.

Ingredient	Amount, g
Cultured base product of Example 1	1,000
Imitation shrimp flavor	20
Monosodium glutamate	10
Disodium inosinate	0.5
Disodium guanylate	0.5
Protein nuggets (70% protein)	2
Coloring, red and yellow as desired	
Water	500

Example 5: Soy Milk — The cultured base product of Example 1 is used in this example to formulate a soy milk product. The cultured base and water are mixed well and the liquid is then separated by centrifuging, filtering or squeezing. The other ingredients are then dissolved in the extracted liquor and the solution is homogenized at 2,500 psi and pasteurized at a temperature of 160°F for 30 min. After pasteurization the product may be packaged in liquid form or concentrated and spray dried before packaging as powdered milk. Soy milk prepared in this way has the nutritional value of cow's milk and also has the appearance, taste and mouth feel of cow's milk.

Ingredient	Amount
Cultured base product of Example 1	1 lb
Water	3 lb
Vegetable fat, melted (hydrogenated coconut oil, 92°F MP)	25 g
Dicalcium phosphate	5 g
Maltose or glucose	18 g

Artificial Caviar

The protein-containing food product obtainable according to the method described by *G.L. Slonimsky, V.B. Tolstoguzov, V.A. Ershova and D.B. Izjumov; U.S. Patent 3,717,469; February 20, 1973; assigned to Ordena Lenina Institut Elementoorganischeskikt Soedineny, USSR* has granules whose consistency, shape, color and luster closely resemble the natural caviar of sturgeon or salmon fish. The individual granules of the synthetic caviar are in fact homogeneous in size and color, semitransparent or opaque granules of a mixed gel of the proteinaceous (gelatin) and polysaccharide (calcium alginate or pectinate) nature, contained in an elastic digestible membrane or pellicle. The granules are not liable to melt when heated up to 50°C and above. The consistency of the finished product ranges from glutinous or sticky to high-quality friable or grainy. The product is recommended to be stored at a temperature of from -2° to +5°C.

Used as the initial valuable proteins, protein-containing food products or the substances of proteinaceous nature are pure proteins such as casein, albumin, proteins of soybean, fish, yeast, seaweeds, protein hydrolyzates, dispersed protein matter, proteins of milk, green leaves, of oilcakes and oil-bearing crops, and concentrated decoctions of foodstuffs.

For the preparation of 1 kg of the finished protein-containing product resembling the natural caviar, it is necessary to combine the following components (in grams), water not being taken into account:

Ingredient	Amount	Ingredient	Amount
Protein	50 - 300	Lecithin	0 - 10
Gelatin	30 - 100	Sorbic acid	0.1 - 2.0
Carbohydrate	0 - 100	Ascorbic acid	0.1 - 2.0
Polysaccharides capable of forming ionotropic gels	2 - 50	Tannides	0.1 - 15
		Monosodium glutamate	0 - 20
Salt of bivalent alkaline earth metals	2 - 50	Sodium inosinate	0 - 20
		Herring juice	0 - 50
Vegetable oil	30 - 300	Food dyes (ferric salts of edible acids, enolic and annatto dyes	
Common salt	20 - 100		
Cod-liver oil	10 - 30		0.1 - 2.0

The process for manufacturing the product will be more fully explained by the following examples.

Example 1: For the preparation of 1 kg of the finished product resembling the natural caviar of sturgeon, 150 to 200 grams of casein are dissolved in 100 ml of 0.1 N solution of NaOH at 50° to 60°C with continuous stirring for a period of 1.5 to 2 hours until completely dissolved. Then to the obtained protein solution are added 35 to 50 grams of gelatin and 10 to 20 grams of pectin at an ester value of about 25%, the solution being continuously stirred and heated up to 40° to 50°C. The obtained warm solution is then subject to shaping into drops in corn oil. The upper layer of the oil is constantly heated up to 20° to 40°C while the lower layer is continuously cooled down to 0° to 12°C.

Under such conditions the drops of the product are urged to move downwards to the cooled corn oil, thus assuming a regular spherical shape, and to congeal. As fast as the congealed granules appear they are extracted from the oil, washed out by water at a temperature of from 0° to 15°C and placed in a fixing solution where they are kept for 2 to 15 minutes at 0° to 10°C with continuous stirring.

The fixing solution is essentially a 4% solution of calcium acetate acidified with acetic acid to pH 2.8. The jelly-like granules treated with the fixing solution are then maintained during 20 to 30 minutes at 0° to 10°C in an aqueous extract of vegetable tannins under continuous stirring. The tanning extract is prepared by infusing or decocting 10 grams of tea leaf in 200 ml of water.

The membrane-covered granules of a mixed gel containing dispersed casein are then washed with cold water and treated with a 0.1 to 0.5% solution of ferric chloride during 0.5 to 2 minutes until obtaining the color imitating that of the caviar of sturgeon. The dyed granules are washed with water to make them free from the residues of the ferric salt solution. Thereupon to the granules obtained are added 30 to 60 grams of common salt, 2 to 5 grams of monosodium glutamate, 0.01 to 1 gram of sodium inosinate and 40 to 100 grams of cottonseed oil, the product being under continuous stirring.

Prior to its addition, to the cottonseed oil, cod-liver oil or herring juice are added at a rate of 0.5 to 2 grams and 0.5 to 15 grams per 100 to 200 grams of oil, respectively, these components imparting a distinctive flavor to the product. To prevent premature deterioration of the product preservatives of an antiseptic nature may be added.

Example 2: For the preparation of 1 kg of a granular protein-containing food product resembling the natural caviar of salmon fish, 100 to 150 grams of casein and 50 to 100 grams cornstarch are dissolved in 100 ml of 0.1 N solution of NaOH at 50° to 60°C with continuous stirring until complete dissolution.

To the obtained protein solution are added 20 to 40 grams of gelatin and 2 to 20 grams of sodium alginate, the solution being continuously stirred and heated up to 40° to 50°C. The warm solution prepared is subject to shaping into drops in cottonseed oil. The upper layer of the oil is continuously heated up to 20° to 40°C while the lower layer thereof is continuously cooled down to 0° to 12°C. Under these conditions the drops of the product are urged to move downwards to the cooled cottonseed oil, thus assuming a regular spherical shape, and to congeal. As fast as the congealed granules are formed they are extracted from the oil, washed with water at a temperature of 15° to 20°C and placed in a fixing solution (a 10% solution of calcium chloride) where the granules are to be kept for 5 to 30 minutes at 2° to 20°C with continuous stirring.

The jelly-like granules treated with the fixing solution are then maintained for 20 to 30 minutes in an aqueous extract of tannides at 0° to 10°C with continuous stirring. The membrane-covered granules are treated with enolic dyes to impart to them the color imitating that of the caviar of salmon fish.

Added to the dyed granules are 20 to 60 grams of common salt, 2 to 5 grams of monosodium glutamate, 0.01 to 1 gram of sodium inosinate and 10 to 80 grams of a 1:5 mixture of olive and corn oils, the product being under continuous stirring. Prior to adding the above oil mixture there are added to it cod-liver oil or herring juice at a rate of 0.5 to 2 grams and 0.5 to 15 grams per 100 to 200 grams of oil mixture, respectively. Permissible antiseptic preservatives may also be added to the finished product.

SIMULATED NUTMEAT PRODUCTS

Process Using Vacuum Treatment

The process described by *J.R. Durst and W.L. Ganske; U.S. Patent 3,872,229; March 18, 1975; assigned to The Pillsbury Company* relates to the production of foods having crunchy nut-like chewing characteristics and is particularly useful in preparing simulated nutmeats.

Such simulated nutmeat products and other products having a nut-like texture are prepared by forming a homogeneous dispersion composed of minute droplets of fat or oil suspended in a continuous phase composed of a hydrophilic film-former such as an aqueous protein suspension and mixing the dispersion under conditions which exclude gas such as vacuum treatment of at least 10 inches of mercury or mixing in a closed vessel filled with the dispersion. The pieces are thereafter dried in air to bring the final moisture content to between 1 and 3.5%.

The starting materials are preferably formed into a liquid dispersion composed of an edible film-former as a continuous phase and a discontinuous phase comprising an edible oleaginous substance such as a fat which is liquid at the time the dispersion is made or an oil. Edible food particles such as flour, sugar or starch in powdered form may be dispersed in the oil, distributed between the encapsulated fat droplets or, if desired, suspended in the film-former. In any event, as a first step in forming the composition, an oleaginous substance is dispersed homogeneously in a continuous phase composed of a polar material; viz, the edible film-former under conditions which exclude air. The product is then extruded as a ribbon or band having a defined shape or molded.

Water that is present in the continuous phase of the dispersion is removed from the product by drying. Since the moisture is present in the continuous phase, the suspended oil droplets are suspended in the hydrophilic film-former and upon drying, the oil droplets remain enclosed in the hydrophilic film-former.

The edible oleaginous substance may consist of any type vegetable or animal oil or fat or mixture thereof. The oleaginous fraction can be from 10 to 80%

by weight of the composition with the remaining fraction comprising the film-former on a dry weight basis exclusive of fillers and extenders. To produce different types of nuts, the ratio of oil to other dry constituents can be varied from 30:70 to 75:25. Water should be present in the finished product in an amount preferably less than 5% by weight for adequate preservation.

The film-former may consist of any edible substance that will form a film around an edible oil using any known process. Examples are nonfat milk solids, sodium caseinate, soy protein, egg albumen, egg yolk, wheat germ, gelatin, etc.

Minor amounts of modifiers can be added to the film-former if desired. Among such modifiers are salts, polysaccharides, polyhydric alcohols, and other edible food substances, such as starch and the like.

When wheat germ is used in synthetic nuts there are sometimes off flavors due to the enzymes in the wheat germ when the dispersion is dried at lower temperatures such as 140°F or lower. These lower temperatures are used to prevent the volatilization of added flavors during the drying period. The enzymes can be inactivated if the dispersions are dried at temperatures between 170° to 190°F but many of the added flavors are lost. The enzymes are inactivated at these temperatures because of the intitial water present before drying.

If the dispersion with added volatile flavors is initially heat treated at 180°F for about 20 to 60 minutes (depending on thickness of the piece) and then the temperature is dropped to 140°F for final drying, the enzyme activity is destroyed and many flavors that previously volatilized away can be kept in the synthetic nut.

Drying can be accomplished immediately or if desired the pieces can be allowed to stand for a time before drying is carried out. If elevated temperatures are used for drying, it is preferred to use temperatures between 100° and 200°F. In cases in which flavor development warrants it, the dispersion, after extrusion, is held at 180°F for 30 minutes to destroy enzymes followed by drying at a lower temperature to prevent volatilization of heat flavors. However, at the higher end of this scale some degree of roasting of the nut may take place which would be undesirable for some applications. Other forms of drying can be used, such as microwave drying. Generally, if the pieces are subjected to conditions of temperature above the boiling point of water, the pieces will puff and, therefore, no longer resemble nutmeats.

Drying converts the product to hard, dry crunchy pieces that have the desired crunch followed by a smearing sensation of real nutmeats and simulate almost precisely the texture and chewing characteristics of nuts.

Dispersing the oil component throughout the continuous phase of hydrated film former results in a gel-like mass which slowly dries with the oil globules in situ whereby the hydrated film former is gradually dehydrated without displacing any of the oil. If steam or oil vapor pressure is created through the application of too high a temperature during drying, the cellular structure will rupture and the oil particles will coalesce and bleed from the product. Hence, the drying is conducted over a relatively greater period of time, e.g., up to 20 hours. If the ingredients are selectively employed, the finished product may be roasted to simulate nutmeats and even particular varieties of nutmeats.

Example 1: Comparative Example —

Ingredients	Amount, %
Stabilized soybean oil	39.7
Dried egg albumin	4.6
Dried ground wheat germ	23.2
Sucrose	6.0
Black walnut flavoring	0.23
Water	26.27

The dried ingredients were placed in a Hobart mixing bowl and the oil added. The slurry was mixed at No. 2 speed using a paddle mixing blade until oil coated all the dry ingredients and the slurry was smooth. All the water (with the flavoring dissolved therein) was added and mixing continued for one minute. The sides of the bowl were scraped down and the mixer set at its highest speed. Mixing was continued for 5 minutes during which a stable dispersion formed. Again the mixer was stopped and the bowl scraped down. Mixing was continued for an additional 5 minutes.

This product was then placed on a polyethylene sheet and spread to ⅛ inch thickness and then placed in an air circulating oven set at 180°F for 45 minutes. This set up the stable dispersion and denatured any enzymes that may be present in the wheat germ. The product was then removed from the oven and cut into pieces ⅞" by ½" by ⅛" and air dried on stainless steel screens at 140°F for 18 hours in the air circulating oven. This allows incorporation of flavors which would volatize at 180°F.

The resulting product was nut-like and crunchy with the flavor of black walnuts but tended to break at air pockets after initial bite leaving small sandy particles in the back of one's throat.

Example 2: Process — The same dried ingredients as used in Example 1 were placed in a stainless steel Readco mixer equipped with a sigma mixing blade and the oil added. The slurry was mixed at low speed until smooth. At this time the mixer was stopped and all the water (with flavoring dissolved therein) was added. The top of the mixer was then placed on the mixer and a vacuum of 28 inches gauge pressure was pulled and the product mixed at high speed for 15 minutes. A stable dispersion formed during mixing which had a slightly darker appearance due to the removal of the air.

This product was then placed on a polyethylene sheet and spread to ⅛" thickness and then placed in an air circulating oven set at 180°F for 45 minutes. This set up the stable dispersion and denatured any enzymes present in the wheat germ. The product was then removed from the oven and cut into pieces ⅞" by ½" by ⅛" and air dried on stainless steel screens for 18 hours at 140°F in the air circulating oven. This allows incorporation of flavors which would volatize at 180°F.

The resulting product was nut-like and had the bite and flavor of a black walnut. Its bite and smear characteristics were the same as for a natural black walnut.

Compositions prepared in which air or other gas is allowed to contact the dispersion during its formation tend to be nut-like in character but when they were chewed, they often had a tendency to form small pieces that catch in the back of the throat when swallowed. However, when a vacuum is applied during the formation of the dispersion or mixing is conducted without gas present as described herein, this problem is eliminated and the resulting simulated nutmeats are characterized by having a crunchy texture followed by the natural smearing characteristics of a real nutmeat.

The improved eating qualities of the simulated nutmeats prepared using this method are correlated with physical tests performed on the nutmeats. Thus, the eating qualities of a nut can be variously described as hard or soft, tough or tender, crunchy, smeary, chewy, flaccid and so on.

It was found that by compressing standard simulated nutmeat pieces in a uniform manner using a fixed rate of compression and a fixed rate of movement of the compression device, the resistance to compression can be recorded on a strip chart as a function of time or displacement. Results of such testing show that the internal strength is much greater in the case of vacuum-treated nutmeats than those prepared as in Example 1 and the nutmeats are thus more crunchy or chewy.

It was thus shown that this method provides a simulated nutmeat product which has greatly improved textural characteristics and eating qualities compared with similar products prepared in the presence of gas such as air. It should, however, be made clear that physical tests alone cannot characterize the simulated nuts because their texture varies greatly from one nut variety to another as from cashews which are soft to almonds which are much harder. The improved product can be obtained either by vacuum mixing or by mixing in the absence of added gas such as air. While gas can be excluded in numerous ways it is preferred to use a mixer which is filled completely with the material being mixed.

Particle Bonding Using Pressure

In another process described by *E.L. Galle, M.O. Mikkelson and J.F. Kolosky; U.S. Patent 3,719,497; March 6, 1973; assigned to The Pillsbury Company* for the production of simulated nutmeat products, they are also prepared by forming a homogeneous dispersion composed of minute droplets of fat or oil suspended in a continuous phase composed of a hydrophilic film-former such as an aqueous protein suspension. The dispersion is atomized and dried to provide particles composed of an oleaginous internal phase encapsulated within the protein film.

In this process, however, the particles are placed in a press and subjected to sufficient pressure to cause the particles to become bonded together at their points of contact and to exclude most of the air to form a self-supporting structure having the shape of natural nutmeat preferably. These pieces are then unified by exposure to moisture vapor for a period of time sufficient to increase the moisture level by 10 to 15%. The pieces are thereafter dried in air to bring the final moisture content to between 1 and 3.5%.

The process is illustrated by the following examples. The quantities of ingredients are expressed on a weight basis.

Example 1: After melting the shortening if required, the following components are placed in a kettle and thoroughly blended before adding 215 ml of water at 120°F.

Ingredients	Amount, Percent by Weight of Dry Ingredients
Hydrogenated vegetable shortening	61.47
Isolated soy protein	2.52
Carboxymethylcellulose	0.80
Sucrose	12.29
Gelatinized tapioca starch	15.37
Dried egg albumen	7.55

The mixer is operated for about 15 minutes to obtain a uniform dispersion while being heated to maintain temperature of 120°F. The mix is then pumped to a spray dryer where the particles are collected with a moisture content of 0.8 to 1.7% moisture. Dry flavor is added and uniformly intermixed with the particles which are then transferred to suitable press and tableted at a pressure of 500 psi.

The tablets are then unified at 100°F dry bulb and essentially 100% relative humidity for 2½ hours to obtain a moisture gain of 4½%. They are then dipped in a coloring solution to provide the color layer for 15 to 30 seconds and 80 grams is placed in a radar range and exposed to microwave energy for 15 seconds. The pieces are then placed in a drying oven at 192°F for 5 hours or until the moisture content has been reduced to about 3½%. The pieces are then sliced and coated with an edible shellac. The edible shellac coating is then dried.

Example 2: A simulated nut product is prepared as in Example 1 except that the following components are used:

Ingredients	Amount, Percent by Weight of Dry Ingredients
Hydrogenated vegetable oil	72.0
Isolated soy protein	2.5
Dried egg albumen	7.5
Sucrose	7.0
Gelatinized tapioca starch	11.0
Water	125 ml

The ingredients are dry blended and water then added with mixing to form a dispersion as in Example 1. From the mixing kettle the mixture is pumped through a homogenizer operating at a pressure differential of 1,500 psi to the spray dryer nozzle at a nozzle pressure of 3,000 psi and at a feed rate of about 60 gallons per hour. The product is then spray dried with an air inlet temperature of about 450°F to obtain a spray dried product having a final moisture content of less than 3%. Dry flavor is then added and the powder is transferred to a tableting machine and molded into pieces having the surface configuration of a nutmeat.

Finished pieces are then unified at 100°F dry bulb at 100% relative humidity for 5 hours to effect a moisture gain of 14%. Pieces are then sprayed with a coloring solution, sliced and dried in an air-drying oven for 16 hours at 140°F to bring the final moisture content to about 1.5%. The pieces are then deep fat fried at 300°F for 2 minutes. A coating of 5% by weight of calcium stearate is then applied by tumbling in a panner. The product is packaged in a moisture impervious sealed packaging film composed of polyvinylidene chloride laminated to aluminum foil with air at a relative humidity of less than 10%.

FILLED FOOD PRODUCTS

MEAT-CONTAINING CONVENIENCE ITEMS

Shelf Stable High Moisture Product

This process described by *J.W. Bernotavicz; U.S. Patent 3,922,353; Nov. 25, 1975; assigned to The Quaker Oats Company* relates to a shelf stable, filled food product. The outer portion of the food product is cereal based. The inner portion is a high moisture meat-containing filling. The filling has a moisture content greater than about 50% by weight but is stable against mold and bacterial growth.

The process comprises the following steps: A shelf stable filling material is prepared by cooking a proteinaceous meaty material which is admixed with an edible, nontoxic acid and an effective amount of antimycotic in an amount of about 1.7 to 3.8% by weight which is sufficient to cause the filling to have a pH of 3.9 to 5.5. A hot cooked cereal dough is extruded under puffing conditions through a first die thereby forming an expanded cereal extrudate.

The shelf stable filling is simultaneously extruded through a second die which is positioned within the orifice of the first die in such a manner that the extrudate from the first die completely surrounds the extrudate from the second die and in such a manner that the direction of flow of the second extrudate is the same as the direction of flow of the first extrudate, the shelf stable filling being heated as it is being extruded within the first die extrudate. The extrudate is subdivided into food shaped pieces which are then dried to decrease the moisture content of the expanded cereal outer extrudate.

Example 1: A quantity of beef liver was crushed and cooked in a pressure cooker. The beef liver was admixed with other ingredients to give the formula shown on the following page. A cereal mixture was also prepared by admixing the ingredients shown on the following page. The meaty filling and cereal covering were placed in an extruder. The product was extruded with the cereal slightly exppanded about the centerfilling upon extrusion. This product was crimped into pillow-shaped particles about ¾ to 1 inch long. The filling had a moisture content of approximately 53%, a protein content above 25%, and a fat content of approximately 13% by weight. The pH of the filling was approximately 4.45. The product was a highly acceptable food and was shelf stable against mold and bacterial growth.

Beef Liver Filling

Ingredients	Parts By Weight
Beef liver	90.00
Lard	4.0
Gelatinized corn flour	3.0
Adipic acid	2.0
Emulsifier (Atmos 300)	0.5
Ethoxyquin	0.2
Sodium benzoate	0.125
Calcium propionate	0.125
Additional antioxidant (Tenox 6)	0.05

Cereal Covering

Ingredients	Parts By Weight
Poultry meal	24.0
Whole yellow corn	17.8
Dehulled soybean meal	16.4
Oat groats	13.0
Wheat	12.5
Propylene glycol	5.0
Phosphoric acid	2.0
Water	1.0
Salt	0.8
Vitamins, minerals, color, flavoring	7.5

Meat Roll

V.L. Moegle; U.S. Patent 3,904,772; September 9, 1975 provides an article of food composed of a wafer-thin slice of meat, preferably fresh or corned beef, coated with oil, a bread crumb mixture, and flavoring material such as an onion-tomato mixture or sauerkraut and Swiss cheese, and tightly rolled up for cooking and serving. The meat is preferably about $1/32$ inch thick, although the slice can be up to $1/8$ inch thick. The slice is also about 6 inches long and 5 inches wide and weighs approximately $3/4$ ounce, although the length and width and shape of the slice can be varied.

The finished meat roll has a thickness or diameter from a minimum of ½ inch to a maximum of 1½ inches, although the diameter is preferably in the range of from about 1 inch to about 1¼ inches, and a grated cheese or cheese product can be used with the crumbs in the coating. Moreover, the meat roll may be broiled or deep fried, as desired, and because of the thin sliced meat very little time is required to cook the meat roll, thus making it practically suitable as a "convenience" food, or fast order item at restaurants and the like. In the meat roll, the crumbs serve as both a stuffing and a uniform coating on the meat roll. If it is desired to deep fry the meat roll, it is dipped in a suitable batter.

TOASTER SANDWICHES

Dielectric Sealing Method

F. Kleiner and H.P. Fogel; U.S. Patent 3,769,035; October 30, 1973; assigned to General Foods Corporation describe a process for sealing toaster sandwiches. The sandwich comprises two slices of fresh bread with a slice of frozen filling within. An edible sealing material is spread on the edge area of one or both bread slices.

Carbohydrates are preferred as the sealing material because of their ability to form a physical bond when acted upon by heat in the presence of moisture. In the process if the foodstuff is substantially moisture-free, a mixture of water and carbohydrate must be used. Where the foodstuff contains a substantial amount of moisture, the carbohydrate may also be applied in powder form.

In either of the preceding two cases the carbohydrate is spread around the areas of the foodstuff which are to be sealed and the areas are then subjected to a high frequency alternating electric field, sometimes referred to as a dielectric field. When the field is energized, water molecules, whether present in the mixture with the carbohydrate or within the foodstuff itself, will change orientation every time the electric field changes. As is well known, water molecules are essentially electrically negative at one end and positive at the other. This explains their response to changes in the electric field. If the frequency of change in the field is high enough, the water molecules will be so vigorously agitated as to generate the heat necessary to combine the carbohydrates with the water and form a pasty seal.

The process provides the advantage of quicker and more effective sealing, making it most adaptable to assembly line processes for making food products which comprise two or more pieces of sealed foodstuff.

Example: Regular bread is cut into crustless rectangular slices about ¼ inch thick. This is necessary since the sandwich must easily fit into a toaster. A viscous food filling of desired flavor such as bacon and egg, ham and cheese, or tuna fish, etc. is prepared and poured into a rectangular mold, the cross-sectional length and width of which are smaller than those of the bread slices. The filling is frozen in the mold so that no moisture will seep into the bread when the filling is in contact with it. Approximately $1/8$ inch thick slices of filling are cut from the frozen block. One slice of the bread is placed on the lower plate, which is connected to a radio frequency generator.

A small amount of a 6% aqueous suspension of modified hydrolyzed tapioca starch is spread around the edge area on the upper surface of the bread slice. A slice of the filling is placed on the bread. A second slice of bread is placed directly on top of the first slice and the filling so that the edges of the second slice are aligned with those of the first slice. The upper plate is brought down manually or mechanically over the sandwich with its edge areas in registration with the edge area of the sandwich.

The upper plate is brought to within ¼ inch to $1/3$ inch of the lower plate. This will mean that the bread slices are compressed slightly around the edge area. The generator is energized for five seconds, at a frequency of 27 megahertz with the plate in this position. The sandwich is removed and observed to be well sealed around the edges. In this particular case the upper part of the sandwich is compressed at the edges due to the convergence of the plates. The polar water molecules are heated by agitation in the electric field. Under this heat the water is readily absorbed by the hydrolyzed starch, yielding a pasty starch residue around the edge of the sandwich which acts as the seal.

In the process described by *F.A. Zobel; U.S. Patent 3,862,344; January 21, 1975; assigned to General Foods Corporation* for sealing toaster sandwiches, an improved dielectric sealing method is afforded by the sequential creation of a plurality of interrupted electrostatic fields affording sequential dielectric heating in the sealing perimeter of superposed bread slices bordering and in spaced relation to an intermediate filling shielded against dielectric heating, thereby providing a controllable activation of a sealing coating such as a starch solution accurately applied to one of the faces of the sandwich.

In further detail, a coating composition is ideally "printed" in a plurality of merged individual sealing moieties onto a bread slice so as to form a rectilinear pattern complementary to the border of one of the bread slices. A feature of the process is that this border defines a sealing perimeter which is essentially spaced from the free edge of a filling located therewithin so as to minimize the existence of stray electrostatic fields and occasion the generation of arcing and the manufacturing hazards that stem from use of dielectric heating. The sealing composition is typically a pregelatinized starch such as tapioca starch which possesses the ability to be of relatively consistent viscosity over sustained periods of hydration in a colloidal suspension or solution and which may be readily applied by an applicator.

To assure the existence of a relatively electrostatically insulated zone within the perimeter of the coated bread slice the bread is preferably coated with merged moieties of sealing composition which are destined to create a continuous or at least a semicontinuous sealing coating in a predictable manner. The coating solution per se should be of sufficient viscosity that it will overlie the bread slice and will not be absorbed thereby and should have a sufficient concentration of heat activatable solids operative to form the adhering bond between juxataposing faces of the bread slice perimeter. By the same token, the sealing composition, be it a starch suspension or otherwise, should not be so viscous as to permit ease of application in the form of discrete "printable" mergable moieties in the sealing perimeter defined.

The bread slice in the coated condition will be advanced in stepwise fashion to a succeeding station whereby a filling slice will be deposited within the geometric center thereof, care again being exercised to assure that the bread slice is advanced in a relatively undisturbed transfer to a fixed station where it will receive a filling slice within and spaced from the inner edge of the sealing coating thereon.

Thereafter, a second bread feeding station for the top slice is operative to deposit the bread slice on the lowermost slice and cause the bread faces to oppose one another with the intermediation of the coating. In this connection the slice thickness will be such in cooperation with the flexibility of the bread per se as to promote abutment. The dielectric sealing of the sandwich involves a plurality of dielectric heating zones, preferably defined by a series of spaced upper electrode plates each adapted to move downwardly normal to the sandwich plane and engage the sandwich intermediate its advancement in stepwise fashion by a conveyor means overlying a continuous lower electrode bar, the conveyor having a very low dielectric constant operative to provide an insulating effect.

The top electrode plate will likewise be constructed to have a nonconducting filling shield area such as provided by a relatively thick Teflon ply recessed within the perimeter of the electrode plate and in turn underlaid by a like abutting insulating Teflon ply which spans both the insulating ply insert and the perimeter of the electrode and is complementary to and overlies the bread slice perimeters. Preferably, the top electrode plate, both on its bread slice engaging face and its lateral extremities, is covered by an insulating material intended to provide a limitation in the migration of electrostatic energy and thus mitigate arcing.

The electrode conditions described will receive applied voltage and generate the alternating high frequency electrostatic energy in the zone of greatest dielectric constant intermediate the conveyor and the top electrode plate, which area will be defined by the ribbon of sealing colloid in association with moisture present at levels sufficient to provide the intended localized heat diffusion to the colloid. It is a distinct feature that the dielectric heating is applied sequentially such that the moisture in the vicinity of the sealing perimeter is gradually evaporated and does not cause sticking to the bread slice face-engaging electrode as the latter is caused to engage the sandwich and maintain sufficient pressure and compression to assure bonding. Generally, a large plurality of dielectric heating zones will be employed, say, in excess of five sealing cycles.

As each succeeding dielectric heating operation transpires, moisture will be progressively evaporated initially from the electrode-engaging surface and eventually from the abutting portions of the sandwich. But by reason of the generation of the dielectric heat, there will be substantially uniform evaporation of moisture throughout the sealing perimeter and there will not be undesirable accumulation of moisture on the electrode face. Thus, a substantial amount of moisture is allowed to escape intermediate each dielectric heating cycle to cause a gradual reduction in the moisture content and activation of the sealing material as the heating electrode is withdrawn.

Example: A square-sided substantially rectilinear bread slice having a thickness of 0.21 inch is deposited on a slice conveyor which advances the slice periodically with a start-stop movement. Two bread slices are designed to sandwich a filling slice having a thickness of approximately 0.50 inch and having a rheology such that the slice will be essentially shape-retaining as formed under any operating temperatures which are preferably in the order of 50°F or lower.

The bread slice has a moisture content of approximately 35%. The moisture content of the filling slice will vary with the filling composition but typically in the case of a cheese slice will be 35 to 55%. The bread will have a crust that is essentially shape-retaining and one dimension will be a $4^{3}/_{8}$ inch square, and overlie a filling slice $3^{3}/_{8}$ inch square centrally located with respect to the bread slice. The bread will have sufficient compressibility such that upon activation of the sealing perimeter the bread may be compressed at its border to bring the sealing coating intermediate the bread slices into close proximity, the bread slice being compressible from a gap thickness of 0.42 inch and being adapted to

Filled Food Products

be compressed to a thickness of approximately 5/16 inch for a brief period during sequential dielectric heating.

A cold water soluble starch solution is prepared by dispersing pregelatinized, modified tapioca starch in cold water to produce a 6½% starch solution. This solution is pumped through a metering and pattern-forming starch applicator head, the sealing perimeter of the initially coated lower bread slice being formed as a rectilinear ribbon approximately ¼ inch wide. The inner free edge of this border is centered with relatively controlled and precise application to leave an uncoated bread surface of about ¼ inch between the inboard perimeter of the sealing solution and the free edge of the filling.

After application of the coating, the filling slice is also centrally deposited relative to the geometry of the bottom slice so as to leave the coating relatively undisturbed and uncontacted by the deposited filling slice reposing on the bread slice. After the top-most bread slice is deposited and overlies the filling slice and bottom bread slice, it is in a position to abut the intermediate starch coating prior to entry into the dielectric sealing zone.

The ribbon of sealing solution will be composed of a plurality of merged discrete bodies of starch reposing substantially at the surface of the bottom bread slice surface with minimal migration to the interior thereof. To assure this condition, the starch solution has a viscosity of 14–16 cp/60 sec at 60°F measured on a Bostwick viscometer. The ribbon in the dimensions indicated will be applied at a weight of 15% starch solution by weight of the bottom bread slice.

The assembled composite is introduced to a series of dielectric sealing apparatus each of which comprises a top electrode plate for engagement with the top bread slice having a nonconductive shield beneath the top electrode and overlying and overlapping the centered filling slice by approximately 1/8 inch on all sides, the shield being a ¼ inch thick Teflon insert within the top electrode plate. The top electrode plate has an overall dimension approximtely 1/8 inch beyond the top bread slice. The top electrode plate and the Teflon shield insert herein will be overlied by a 1/16 inch thick Teflon sheet adapted to directly engage the top bread slice both for sanitation and controlled dielectric heat generation in the sealing perimeter of the sandwich composite. The lower electrode is stationarily mounted beneath and in positive engagement with a nonconductive, carbon-free conveyor which transports the sandwich for sequential intermittent heat sealing by 16 dielectric sealing zones.

In each of these zones the composite is positively engaged by the top electrode plate through the Teflon coating and pressed 1/8 inch at the sealing perimeter, a dielectric energy source is increased to sealing power, the top electrode plate withdrawn and the partially heated sealing perimeter advanced to a next succeeding zone where the heating operation is repeated. With each dwell of the top electrode plate energy is transmitted through the sealing perimeter defined by the butting faces of the bread slice border and the intermediate sealing coating therebetween. Dwell time during each dielectric energization was approximately 0.4 second at intervals of about ½ second.

Heating in the electrostatic field generated between the electrode was produced by an energy source of 25 kilowatts output employing a high frequency generator operating at a nominal frequency of twenty and an actual frequency of approximately 19 to 20 MHz employing an applied plate voltage of 6,000 volts to each of the dielectric zones. The dielectric heating is sufficiently protracted yet gradual in the sequential generation of heat and evaporation of moisture to assure substantially complete dehydration of the sealing coating in the sealing perimeter intermediate the compressed bread slice perimeters upon sequential release of each electrode.

The sandwich assembly thus sealed has a substantially planar appearance, the compressed portions of the bread in the vicinity of the sealing perimeter springing back to be barely visible to the unaided eye and thus having no evidence of compression. The sandwich can be inserted in a conventional home electric toaster and will not delaminate but rather will be characterized by a faithful containment of the thawed and thereafter melted filling intermediate the toasted slices.

Method of Preparation

The problem in preparing a sandwich for toaster use is that the sandwich should have a crisp texture and the cereal coating which is applied for the crisp texture must be united effectively so that it resists abrasion and protects the sandwich in the handling operations.

F.G. Wheeler and F.J. Pratl; U.S. Patent 3,767,823; October 23, 1973; assigned to Armour and Company have found that blanching or wetting the food-filled raw dough to render the dough adhesive and then coating the dough with a dry cereal, such as corn meal, farina, dry hominy grits, etc., and finally anchoring the cereal coating on the sandwich by a second blanching or wetting, and thereafter cooking the coated dough body provides this crispy coating. Preferably, the food-filled dough body is blanched in hot water and, after draining, is coated with dry cereal particles. The coated body is then blanched a second time in hot water to anchor the coating upon the body so that it may be effectively cooked with the cereal coating in place.

Alternatively, the dry cereal particles can be rendered adhesive by precooking, and the precooked cereal after drying is applied to the food-filled dough body which is wetted to receive the coating, and thereafter the coat is anchored in place by a second cold water dip so that the product can then be effectively cooked.

A further advantage is obtained by dissolving in the second blanch water or cold water a browning improvement agent which aids in adherence of the particles while also improving browning during the subsequent cooking step which may be by deep fat frying or baking in an oven, etc. In a more detailed description, a suitable food filling, such as meat, egg, cheese or fruit is encased in a raw dough sandwich body which may consist of flour, salt and water. Shortening can be used and it is preferable to have it as a part of the dough formula. For example, a typical formula may be: 64% flour, 8% lard, 2.5% salt and 25.5% water.

After the filling is encased in the dough, the resulting raw sandwich is blanched in boiling water for 5 to 8 seconds. When the sandwich is removed from the blanching water, it is allowed to drain, after which it is coated with a cereal meal. The cereal-coated sandwich is then blanched a second time for 15 to 30

Filled Food Products

seconds, the blanching being in boiling water. In both blanching steps the water is preferably 200 to 212°F. After the second blanch or cold water dip, the sandwhich may be cooked in any suitable manner, such as by deep fat frying or by oven baking, etc.

The application of the cereal coating followed by the water dip causes a tight adherence of the cereal particles to the sandwich products, and after the cooking operation the product has an attractive surface appearance similar to the surface appearance of pretzels with coarse salt. The improved crisp surface texture renders the product suitable for handling in toasters and for other uses and improves the eating quality of the product.

If desired, the filling which may consist of cheese, sausage pizza, cheese and ham, cheese and salami, cheese and beef, etc. may be enclosed between two thin sheets of dough and crimped around the edge. Further, if desired, the sandwich may by crimped once or twice through the body of the snack sandwich so as to make it possible to break the final product into two or three individual snacks, etc. While the product may be designed to be heated in a toaster, it may also be heated in an oven or on a grill, etc.

If it is desired to improve the browning characteristics of the sandwich, the second blanch water or the cold water used with the precooked cereal can be modified by the addition of one or more of the following: sodium bicarbonate, monosaccharides, milk or whey. A second blanch or cold water dip in which 48 parts of water, 0.5 part sodium bicarbonate, and 1 part dextrose (all parts by weight) are added is preferred.

Example: A cheese filling was encased between two raw sheets consisting of 64% flour, 8% lard, 2½% salt, and 25½% water, and the raw sandwich then blanched in boiling water for about 8 seconds. The sandwich was then removed from the blanching water and allowed to drain for about 10 seconds, after which it was coated with corn meal. The coated sandwich was then blanched a second time for 20 seconds in boiling water and then cooked by deep fat frying at about 370°F for 1 minute. The resulting product had a crisp, hard surface in which the cereal parts adhered firmly to the surface, very much like coarse salt adheres to pretzels.

COATING PREPARATIONS

STARCH BATTERS

Batters Suitable for Use on Frozen Food

C.O. Moore, H. Cheng and R.V. Schanefelt; U.S. Patent 3,956,515; May 11, 1976; assigned to A.E. Staley Manufacturing Company have found that significantly improved starch batters can be prepared from batter starches comprised of ungelatinized granular starches and granular, cold-water swelling starches which possess sufficient cold-water swelling properties to convert cold or warm aqueous starch batter systems to a nonbirefringent form. These starch batters are generally comprised of:

(a) 1 to 40 parts by weight of a cold-water swelling starch characterized as possessing a birefringent, granular character prior to dispersion in water and a loss of birefringency within 10 minutes after being dispersed in water (1% by weight dry starch) at a temperature within the range of 40° and 120°F;

(b) 200 parts by weight of starch granules which are characterized as maintaining a birefringent granular character when dispersed in water for 10 minutes at a concentration of 1% by weight starch solids and a temperature of 125°F; and

(c) water at a starch solids to water weight ratio of less than about 2:3.

These batter starches provide the food industry with a batter system which can be applied or coated upon the surface of a food piece, breaded and frozen, and subsequently deep-fat fried to provide a high-quality, deep-fat fried, breaded food piece.

The starch batters of this process are obtained by dispersing the batter starches in an aqueous medium. Any edible aqueous medium which will impart the appropriate viscosity characteristics to the desired starch batter may be used for this purpose. Water or any other suitable water containing food product (for example, milk, eggs, etc.) may be used as a dispersant for the batter starches. Dispersion of the batter starches in an aqueous medium provides a batter system containing unswollen starch granules uniformly dispersed within an adhesive matrix of highly-swollen, nonbirefringent, hydrated starch granules.

In order to maintain the granular integrity of the high temperature pasting starch, the temperature of the aqueous medium dispersant is maintained below the gelation point of the high pasting temperature starch component. For example, if it is desired to employ a cold-water swelling granular starch with a capacity to fully hydrate and lose its birefringency in aqueous medium at 35°F in conjunction with a high amylose starch, the temperature of the aqueous medium employed in dispersing and formulating the starch batter may range from about 35° to about 230°F. For unmodified corn starch, the starch batter formulating temperature will generally be maintained at less than about 145°F.

Granular starches of lower pasting temperature or cold-water swelling starches of a lesser cold-water swelling power will have a more narrow temperature range to fully hydrate the cold-water swelling starch without pasting the birefringent granular batter starch component.

The batter starches are particularly adapted for use in starch batter recipes which are formulated at aqueous medium dispersion temperatures of less than 120°F. The starch solids to water weight ratio in the starch batter may range from 1:9 to 9:11. Atypical of conventional batter starches, the combination of batter starches herein enables the food industry to effectively apply starch batters to food pieces at a lower starch solids level.

Conventionally, starch batters will usually contain a starch solids to water ratio between 0.85 to 1.3 parts starch for each part by weight water with a 1:1 weight ratio being most typical. The starch batters of this process possess excellent adhesion to the food piece substrate and frying properties without necessitating predusting, addition of ancillary thickening agents or precooking of the food piece. If desired, the batter flours containing proteinaceous or glutenous material and ungelatinized starch granules (e.g., cereal flours) may be used as a source for the granular, birefringent starch batter component. The cereal flours may serve as a partial or complete source of the high temperature gelling starch component. Since the gluten portion of most cereal flours will impart both a thickening effect and an adhesive character to the starch batter, a lesser amount of cold-water swelling starch may be used therewith.

Advantageously the starch batters contain about 1 to 2 parts by weight batter starch solids for each 4 parts by weight water. Conventional breading agents may be directly applied to starch batter coatings to provide excellent adhesion during the frying thereof. Preferably the starch batters are prepared at temperatures less than about 70°F. At a batter starch to water weight ratio of about 1:3, the breading and deep-fat frying characteristics of poultry products of these starch batters are superior.

Excessive contamination of the starch batter mix and starch batters with pregelled starches should be avoided. On a dry starch solids basis, it is particularly desirable that the resultant batter starch contain no more than 15% pregelled starch (total dry starch solids basis). In preparing the starch batters, high shear mixing conditions or thermal disintegration of the granular structure of the high temperature pasting starches should be avoided. Likewise the addition of pregelled starches is suitably avoided in the starch batter formulations. Improved starch batter functional attributes are achieved from starch batters which contain no more than 10% by weight and preferably less than 5% by weight gelatinized starch.

If desired, other conventional starch batter additives such as seasoning, spices, flavoring and coloring agents, salt, cream of tartar, foaming agents, egg yolks, sweeteners, preservatives, antioxidants, thickening agents (e.g., mucilaginous and/or proteinaceous materials such as milk and nonfat milk solids, caseinates, wheat gluten, egg albumin, carboxymethylcellulose, alginates, gum arabic, hydroxypropylcellulose, etc.) may be incorporated into the dry starch batter mixes and starch batters of this process. Since the cold-water swelling starches impart excellent adhesiveness and viscosity to the starch batter such thickening agents can be totally eliminated from the starch batters.

The viscosity of the starch batter as applied or employed in coating of the food piece can be tailored (e.g., by the amount of batter water and/or cold-swelling starch) to fit its particular end usage. For example, a low viscosity starch batter (e.g., Brookfield viscosity of 50 cp at 23°C) may be suitably used in providing thin, adhesive food piece coatings. Conversely, a thicker coating for starch battered products can be accomplished by employing a more viscous starch batter (e.g., 10,000 cp). For most coating applications, the starch batter viscosity will range from 2,000 to 2,500 cp.

The starch batters may be utilized to coat a wide variety of food pieces. Food pieces which are adapted to be fried in the presence of cooking oils or fats (e.g., oven, skillet and deep-fat fried food pieces) can be suitably coated therewith. Typical food pieces coated with the starch batters include fresh and frozen meats, synthetic meat products, snack and vegetable products such as fish sticks, fish fillets, shell fish, poultry, veal, pork, beef, eggplant and onion rings, fish and crab cakes, potato puffs, hors d'oeuvres, meat balls, textured vegetable protein products, fritters, croquettes, etc.

The batter starches can be directly applied to poultry pieces, breaded and deep-fat fried to provide a high quality fried product. The cold-water soluble batter starch component also provides the additional benefit in preparing high quality, fried products from prebattered and breaded, frozen poultry pieces.

Example: A batter starch dry mix was prepared by uniformly dry blending in a ribbon blender 6.95 parts by weight of a granular, cold-water swelling starch and 100 parts by weight unmodified granular starch. This granular cold-water swelling starch component when dispersed in mineral oil (at 1% by weight dry starch solids at 23°C with manual stirring) and examined under polarized light indicated approximately 96% of the starch granules as being birefringent (5,000 different starch granules are examined).

Microscopic examination of the cold-water swelling starch under polarized light after being dispersed in water (at 23°C and at a dry starch solids concentration of 1% and mixed in a standard household mixer for 4 minutes) at a low speed indicated substantially all of the starch granules had lost their birefringency (5,000 different starch granules examined). The Brookfield viscosity of the aforementioned cold-water swelling starch at a pH 6.5 and 5% solids after dispersion in water for 10 minutes and 24 hours was 9,500 cp.

The starch batter dry mix was reconstituted in tap water (60°F) by mixing in a Hobart mixer at a medium speed for 10 minutes at a starch solids to water weight ratio of 1:3. The Brookfield viscosity of the resultant starch batter at 23°C was approximately 2,250 cp (No. 3 spindle at 20 rpm). Microscopic examination of the resultant batter indicated that the cold-water swelling starch had converted to the nonbirefringent form. The cold-water swelling starch granules were in a highly hydrated and swollen form with the unmodified food starch granules being uniformly dispersed therein in essentially an unswollen, discrete, birefringent starch granular form.

The starch batter was then employed to coat chicken pieces (breast, wings, drumsticks, thighs, backbone, neck) by dipping the chicken pieces into the starch batter. The starch batter was uniformly coated on all of the chicken pieces with excellent adhesion thereto.

A commercial breading dry mix containing a dry blend of wheat flour, bread crumbs, salt, malted barley flour, spices and herbs, monosodium glutamate, natural hickory flavor and artificial color was placed in a plastic bag along with chicken pieces and shaken to provide a breaded chicken piece. On a chicken piece weight basis, the batter and breading pickup by the chicken piece was about 20% by weight. A greater or lesser pickup was achieved by lowering or elevating the amount of cold-water swelling starch in the formulation.

For comparative purposes, the amount of cold-water swelling starch in the starch batter was reduced to 6.5 parts by weight and increased in another starch batter to 7.5 parts by weight. Each of these comparative batters uniformly coated the pieces with excellent adhesive characteristics, but resulted in a batter and breading pickup of about 15% for the lower level and 25% for the elevated cold-water swelling starch formulation. The breading firmly adhered to each of the starch batter coatings without any evidence of flaking or separation of either the breading or the batter coating from the chicken pieces.

Some of the chicken pieces were deep-fat fried for approximately 16 minutes in the hydrogenated vegetable frying oil at 375°F. The resultant fried pieces exhibited excellent breaded, batter adhesion to the chicken pieces with no concomitant flaking or separation therefrom. Physical handling of the fried, breaded piece indicated that the starch batter coatings had excellent adhesion to both the cooked chicken piece and the breading. The chicken substrate possessed excellent juiciness, moistness and tenderness. The fried chicken pieces were of a golden brown color with a tender, but crispy texture without any concomitant evidence of excessive fat absorption and generally possessed the attributes of a high quality fried, battered product.

The remaining portion of the breaded, battered chicken pieces were frozen. Upon completion of the freezing of the chicken pieces, there was no evidence of any separation of flaking of either the batter or breading from the chicken pieces. The frozen, battered and breaded chicken pieces were stable against fluctuation of divergent freezer temperatures as well as possessing excellent freeze-thaw cycling stability. In the frozen form, these breaded, battered chicken pieces were capable of withstanding the normal physical abuses as encountered in the commercial shipment thereof.

The frozen pieces were fried for 18 minutes in the same manner as the freshly prepared breaded, battered chicken pieces above. The fried chicken from these frozen pieces was equivalent in overall quality to that prepared from the freshly breaded and fried chicken pieces. It was further observed, as in the case with the freshly battered and fried products above, that the adhesion and overall breaded character of the divergent breaded chicken pieces employed in this example were substantially equivalent to one another.

The frozen, breaded and battered chicken pieces prepared in accordance with this example can be subjected to pressurized deep-fat frying conditions without adversely affecting the functionality of the starch batter coatings.

Baked Coating Resembling Deep-Fat-Fried Coating

A process is provided by *C.R. Lee, D.M. King and E.E. Clausen; U.S. Patent 3,843,827; October 22, 1974; assigned to General Foods Corporation* for simulating the texture and appearance of deep-fat frying to foodstuffs without the need for deep-fat frying itself.

The foodstuff to be baked is first coated with a batter containing specific ingredients, particularly wheat flour. The batter-coated foodstuff is then coated with a dry mixture comprising cereal fines, starch, flour and fat. The foodstuff is then baked until done. The result is a foodstuff with the texture and appearance of a foodstuff which has been batter-coated and then deep-fat fried.

The types of foodstuffs to which this process can be applied are meat, fish or vegetables. The process may be particularly applied to meats such as chicken and pork. The batter is formed by combining approximately 80 to 100 grams of a dry mix comprising wheat flour, shortening, cornstarch, pregelatinized waxy maize starch and optional flavoring agents, such as sugar and spices, with raw egg and approximately 2½ to 3½ ounces of milk or water. The foodstuff is preferably cut up into easily handled sizes and is dipped into or coated with the batter.

The batter ingredients each function together in a critical way to produce a batter which will coat foodstuff uniformly and produce a crisp, fried-like texture base upon baking of the foodstuff. The flour is the basic coating ingredient, the shortening acts as a lubricant and flavoring agent, the starches act as thickeners and the egg helps to emulsify the batter for better coating. The preferred ranges for the dry mix batter ingredients based on the total weight of the dry mix are as follows: 60 to 75% wheat flour; 7 to 12% shortening; 7 to 12% cornstarch; 1.5 to 3% pregelatinized waxy maize starch and 0 to 20% flavoring agents.

After the foodstuff has been coated with the batter, it is further coated with a second dry mix comprising, by weight of the second mix, 35 to 50% cereal fines, 15 to 25% of a pregelatinized modified waxy maize starch, 3 to 15% shortening, 10 to 15% wheat flour, 0 to 15% flavoring agents and 0 to 1% coloring. Again the ingredients of this second dry mix function together critically to produce the desired results of a fat-fried texture to the baked foodstuff. The cereal fines, waxy maize starch and wheat flour all function together to produce the desired fat-fried texture, and, as before, the shortening acts as a lubricant and flavoring agent. Spices, flavoring agents and colors may be added as desired.

After this second coating step, the coated foodstuff is then placed in an oven and baked until done. A coated foodstuff with a thick, crisp fat-fried texture and appearance results.

Example: A batter is formed by combining one raw egg and one-third cup of milk with 87 grams of a dry mix consisting of the following by weight of the dry mix: 71.3% wheat flour; 9.7% shortening; 9.2% cornstarch; 5.4% sugar; and 4.4% spice blend. 2½ pounds of cut-up chicken pieces are coated evenly with the batter, and the chicken pieces are then further coated with 85 grams of a second dry mix consisting of the following by weight of the dry mix: 41.0% cereal fines; 20.1% pregelatinized waxy maize starch; 13.4% shortening, 13.4% wheat flour; 11.6% spice blend; and 0.5% coloring.

The coated chicken pieces are then baked in an oven preheated to 350°F and are baked at that temperature for approximately 60 minutes or until done. The resulting chicken pieces have the appearance, texture and flavor of deep-fat-fried chicken.

SPECIALTY COATINGS

Coating Suitable for Imparting Flavor to Snack Foods

L.R. Luft and D.G. Murray; U.S. Patent 3,830,941; August 20, 1974; assigned to Grain Processing Corporation describe the preparation of edible coatings for snacks and other foods which comprise oil-water emulsions and a starch hydrolyzate having a relatively low dextrose equivalent value.

The food coatings of this process comprise oil-water emulsions and as a bodying agent a starch hydrolyzate having a relatively low dextrose equivalent value (DE) in the range of about 8 to 28. Such low DE hydrolyzates are known in the art as hydrolyzed cereal solids or maltodextrins and it is known that they can be produced by the controlled hydrolysis of starch with acids and/or enzymes. The starch hydrolyzates increase the total solids content of the coating emulsions thereby reducing the moisture content. Accordingly, the hydrolyzates serve to increase the rate of drying of the coatings.

In general, low dextrose equivalent hydrolyzed cereal solids have a bland taste, contribute little sweetness, have low hygroscopicity and possess suitable solubility in water. The particular food application will govern the choice of hydrolyzed cereal solids to employ. The low dextrose equivalent materials, such as 9 to 12 DE materials, contribute less sweetness, are less soluble and contribute the most viscosity to aqueous solutions. Thus, for applying flavors such as butter, cheese, meat, vegetable, taco and the like which are not compatible with sweetness, the low dextrose equivalent materials are preferred.

On the other hand, the high dextrose equivalent materials, such as those having DE values of 18 to 28, are more soluble and contribute less viscosity to aqueous solutions but do contribute some slight sweetness to the food product. Thus, these higher dextrose equivalent materials can be employed to coat food products such as snack foods where some slight sweetness is permitted and the food is not sensitive to the more hygroscopic nature of the higher DE materials. Examples of flavors compatible with some slight sweetness are barbecue, pork and bean flavors. Hydrolyzed cereal solids having intermediate DE values, such as 13 to 17 DE, can be used advantageously where low sweetness and low viscosity formulations are desired.

Representative of the basic coating composition according to the present process is the following:

Component	Weight Percent
Oil	15 to 40
Water	20 to 40
Hydrolyzed cereal solids (DE, 8 to 28)	15 to 60
Emulsifying agent	0.1 to 3.0
Flavor	As desired
Food color	As desired
Protein	1 to 15

The oil employed in the coating composition is an edible food grade hydrogenated animal fat or hydrogenated vegetable oil. Any suitable oil-soluble or water-soluble food flavor or flavors can be employed as well as desired food colors.

The emulsifiers which are employed are known edible oil and water emulsifying agents such as, for example, mono- or diglycerides, polysorbates, sorbitan monostearates, natural gums and the like.

The protein materials are employed in the composition as stabilizers and/or flavors and such representative materials are sodium caseinate, calcium caseinate, soy isolate, soy concentrate, soy flour, nonfat dry milk, milk whey solids, dried cheese solids, buttermilk solids, vegetable proteins, cottonseed proteins and so forth.

In preparing the coating composition it is preferred to blend the oil and emulsifier together in a melted condition and if an oil-soluble flavor is employed to incorporate the flavor with this oil mix. The hydrolyzed cereal solids together with other components including water-soluble flavors are added to water and then blended with the oil mix.

The finished coating composition is preferably applied to snack foods at elevated temperatures such as 125° to 200°F in any conventional manner that insures uniform coating. Thus, the coating composition can be applied to snack food in a revolving coating pan, a screw conveyor, a fluidized bed contactor and similar equipment which will continuously expose the snack food to the coating to achieve uniform distribution of the coating over the surface thereof. The coating composition can be metered onto the snack food as a separate stream in a continuous process or a premeasured quantity thereof can be added to the snack food in a batch operation.

Example: Cheese Glazed Popcorn —

	Ingredients, Coating Formula	Pounds	Percent by Weight
(A)	Coconut oil (100°F melting point)	2 lb, 8 oz	25.0
	Mono- or diglycerides	(27 grams)	0.6
	Imitation cheddar cheese flavor (oil-soluble)	To suit	To suit

(continued)

Coating Preparations

Ingredients, Coating Formula	Pounds	Percent by Weight
(B) Hydrolyzed cereal solids (10 DE)	2 lb, 11 oz	26.9
Salt	4 oz	2.5
Water	3 lb	30.0
Dehydrated cheddar cheese	1 lb, 8 oz	15.0
Total	10 lb	100.0

Procedure — (A) ingredients are melted together. A tempering period is allowed for stabilization of flavors. A heated solution of hydrolyzed cereal solids, salt and water is prepared. (A) and (B) phases are blended together. Cheese powder is added and blended into the mixture until uniform.

For optimum handling, the temperature of the coating preparation is adjusted to 160°F and is sprayed onto the preheated popcorn while tumbling in a heated coating reel. The product is dried with heated air while tumbling (approximately 30 minutes).

The batch weight of popcorn in the finished product was 36%; of the coating, 64%. The weight of popcorn in the finished product, i.e., after drying, was 45%; of the coating, 55%.

Vitamins A and C Coating for Food Particles

The process described by *P.A. Hammes and M.J. Boroshok; U.S. Patent 3,767,825; October 23, 1973; assigned to Merck & Co., Inc.* relates to the preparation of a vitamin-containing composition and to a method for applying it to foods. The vitamins which are to be used are the water-soluble Vitamin C and the oil-soluble Vitamin A.

A food to which the coating is especially adaptable is potato flakes which are to be restored by the addition of water to a consumable form such as mashed potatoes. The composition can, however, be applied to potato chips, cereal flakes, popcorn, crackers and practically every dry food item which is more or less in bitesize.

To make it possible to apply the water-soluble Vitamin C and the water-insoluble Vitamin A to the selected food, the process involves the use of commercially obtainable Vitamin A beadlets and an especially coated Vitamin C. The Vitamin A beadlets are to be used in the form in which they are purchased. The commercial Vitamin C must be coated to be used. This may be accomplished by using a fatty acid of 12 to 20 carbons or by using a monoglyceride of one of them. A representative process is the following.

A 90% coated ascorbic acid was made by using commercial stearic acid in the following procedure. 125 ml chloroform are placed in a vessel and 60.0 grams of commercial stearic acid (Myverol 18-07) are added thereto. The mixture is then heated to 50°C and stirred until a clear solution results. 540.0 grams of USP ascorbic acid (med crystal 30–80 mesh) are placed in a small Hobart mixer. The prepared stearic acid-chloroform solution is poured in and mixed until uniformly wet. Mixing is continued until almost dry due to chloroform evaporation. The mass is passed through a stainless steel #8 to #100 gauge sieve and is then spread on paper and dried in an oven at 40°C to remove any residual chloroform. A white free-flowing dry material results.

Any of the other fatty acids or their monoglycerides or mixtures of them may be substituted in the above process. Also, the amount may range from 30 to 120 grams to get a thinner or thicker coating.

The coated ascorbic acid is blended with the Vitamin A beadlets in a ratio of 7 to 30 grams (preferably 15) of the coated ascorbic acid per gram of Vitamin A beadlets. An important physical property of this blend is that it does not tend to stratify or segregate during shipping and handling in its actual application to the foodstuff.

Example: Vitamin C-Vitamin A Dry Mix — Coated Vitamin C and Vitamin A pellets were blended in a ratio to give a potency of 1,000 actual Vitamin A units per 50 mg of actual Vitamin C content. 200 grams of coated ascorbic acid, 90% Vitamin C content and 14.39 grams Vitamin A palmitate, 250,000 units Vitamin A per gram (dry beadlets, Type 250-CW, cold water dispersible) were blended using a twin shell or ribbon or other conventional blender. A white free-flowing preparation resulted.

When this blend was applied to a glass slide and heated to around 50°C, the material adhered to the slide when cooled. This is because the coating on the ascorbic acid attaches to the slide and also binds the Vitamin A beadlets to it. As a result, the water-soluble Vitamin C and the oil-soluble Vitamin A become attached to the slide in the form of a substantially continuous coating.

The blend is a dry product which becomes tacky at 40° to 60°C depending on the exact melting point of the coating on the Vitamin C, but which maintains its discrete granular form. The blend is dusted on the food which is at the temperature at which the blend is tacky as this causes the blend to adhere to the food surface. The product can then be allowed to cool in the ambient air or cool air may be directed on it to hasten the attachment of the coating composition to the food.

The coating blend may be applied to potato flakes using the apparatus and process of U.S. Patent 2,034,599. A soft mashed potato sludge is placed in the trough between plates shown in Figure 2 of that patent. The sludge is picked up by and dried on drums and scraped off by blades. It falls, as flakes, in a conveyor trough and the vitamin blend is dusted onto the still warm flakes as they are agitated and moved along by the conveyor. The blend will adhere to the flakes and remain on them due to the cooling further along the conveyor.

The coating blend may be applied to potato chips by dusting the chips after they are taken out of the frying vat and are still hot with the blend in the same manner that salt is dusted on them. The coating blend may be applied to popcorn by dusting the popped corn with the vitamin blend in the same manner that salt is dusted on the popped corn.

The coating blend may also be applied to crackers. As the crackers come out of the baking oven, such as on a continuously moving conveyor belt, they are dusted with the dry vitamin blend. The relative amount of the blend which is applied to the particular food may vary within wide limits. It can be very minimal so that a continuous film on the food is not formed and so that it is scattered on the food surface much as if it were table salt. The maximal amount is about that at which a continuous or nearly continuous film is formed on the

Coating for Use on Dehydrated Foods

N.E. Harris; U.S. Patent 3,726,693; April 10, 1973; assigned to U.S. Secretary of the Army has found that the hardening phenomenon observed in dehydrated foods coated with an aqueous-oil-protein emulsion upon exposure to elevated temperatures can be eliminated if the coated food product is dehydrated to and held at a moisture level below 2% by weight. Above this moisture level, hardening will occur upon exposure to temperature above 85°F.

While dehydrated foods are normally dried to a moisture level of less than 5% to prevent spoilage or nonenzymatic browning and when long term stability is a requirement to moisture levels of less than 3%, moisture levels of 2% or less were not sought or even desired since the added effort to lower the moisture level below 3% is quite significant and produces no known advantage from a storage stability standpoint.

Example 1: A suitable coating to stabilize the structure of low moisture or dried compressed food products is formulated as follows.

	Percent by Weight
Edible vegetable oil (400 hr AOM stability)	9.7
Sodium caseinate	9.7
Glycerin	2.8
Gelatin (275 Bloom)	2.2
Water	75.6

The coating emulsion is prepared by adding one-half of the sodium caseinate to the oil which has been heated to a temperature within the range of 150° to 160°F. The remainder of the caseinate is added to the oil and mixed until all the dry particles are coated with oil. The gelatin is soaked in cold water and allowed to swell and is thereafter heated to 140° to 150°F. Glycerin is added to the heated gelatin solution and mixed.

About one-fifth of the gelatin-glycerin water solution is added to the oil-sodium caseinate mixture and blended and the remainder of the solution is added and blended at moderately high speed. Entrapped air is removed by heating the mixture in a water bath to a temperature of 190°F and slowly stirring for 5 minutes. The coating emulsion is maintained at a temperature of from 160° to 180°F for coating application. The emulsion is stable for several months if held at a temperature of 40°F.

Example 2: A cocoa flavored coating is formulated as follows.

	Percent by Weight
Edible vegetable oil (400 hr AOM stability)	35.0
Sodium caseinate	12.0
Glycerin	7.0
Gelatin (275 Bloom)	6.0
Sucrose	33.7
Cocoa	5.5

(continued)

	Percent by Weight
Vanilla	0.5
Citric acid	0.1
Parabens (3 parts methyl and 1 part propyl)	0.1
Potassium sorbate	0.1
Water, 65 ml/100 gram of coating formula	

The cocoa coating is prepared by heating the oil to 150°F and mixing the heated oil with sodium caseinate, sucrose and cocoa. The gelatin is allowed to swell in cold water and then heated to 150°F. Glycerin, vanilla, parabens and potassium sorbate are added to the oil slurry and mixed until a stable emulsion forms. The citric acid in 1 ml of water is added to the emulsion and mixed and a vacuum is drawn on the coating emulsion to eliminate any entrapped air. The emulsion is heated to and maintained at a temperature of 160° to 180°F for coating application.

Amylose Coating for Deep Fried Potatoes

The prime object of the process described by *D.G. Murray, N.G. Marotta and R.M. Boettger; U.S. Patent Reissue 27,531; December 12, 1972; assigned to National Starch and Chemical Corporation* is to provide a class of coating materials for application to potato chips, French fried potatoes and specialty potato products prior to their being deep-fried; the latter coating materials serving to enhance the appearance, texture and taste characteristics of the resulting deep-fried potato products.

Starch is composed of two fractions, the molecular arrangement of one being linear and the other being branched. The linear fraction of starch is known as amylose and the branched fraction as amylopectin. Methods for separating starch into these two components are known. Starches from different sources, e.g., potato, corn, tapioca and rice, etc., are characterized by different relative proportions of the amylose and amylopectin components. Some starches have been genetically developed which are characterized by a large preponderance of the one fraction over the other.

The terms "amylose" or "amylose product" when used here refer to the amylose resulting from the fractionation of whole starch into its respective amylose and amylopectin components, or to whole starch which is composed of at least 55%, by weight, of amylose. The amylose may be further treated with heat and/or acids or with oxidizing agents to form so-called thin boiling products. Or, the amylose may be chemically derivatized by means of an esterification reaction which would thus yield amylose esters such as the acetate, propionate and butyrate; or, by means of an etherification reaction which would thus yield amylose ethers such as the hydroxyethyl, hydroxypropyl, carboxymethyl or benzyl.

In conducting the process, the selected amylose product is first suspended in water in a concentration of from 1 to 15%, by weight. The aqueous amylose suspension is then heated at at least 180°F for from ½ to 60 minutes until the amylose product has been completely dispersed, i.e., gelatinized, so as to result in the formation of a colloidal dispersion. The precise combination of time and temperature which are required will, of course, vary according to the particular amylose product whose dispersal is desired.

Coating Preparations

Prior to the actual coating of the raw potato slices which are to be used, the slices are usually washed in order to remove excess starch as well as to prevent their adhering to one another during the subsequent deep-frying operation. Excess water may be removed with a sponge rubber roller or by subjecting the slices to a hot air blast. It is to be noted that, in all cases, the natural starch content of the potato slices or of the compressed, raw potato fragments which are used in the subject process will be completely ungelatinized prior to the time they are subjected to the deep-frying operation, i.e., the cooking in a hot, edible cooking oil.

The thickness of the slices used for preparing potato chips will, of course, be substantially less than the thickness of the slices used to prepare French fried potatoes wherein it is desirable that the finished product have a soft, pulpy interior. Thus, since potato chips are always prepared so as to have an essentially flat, sheet-like structure which is devoid of any massive bulk comprising a soft pulpy interior, the raw potato slices to be used in their preparation should have a thickness of no more than 0.02 to 0.2 of an inch.

The raw slices are then immersed in the amylose dispersion while the latter is being maintained at a temperature of 100° to 210°F. The concentration of amylose product in the dispersion is, as noted above, at about 1 to 15%, by weight. The immersion of the raw potato slices is best accomplished by either passing them through a dip tank, by mechanical means, or by spraying the slices from both above and below while they are being conveyed upon a mesh belt. The slices are then allowed to drain for about 1 second to 10 minutes.

In some cases, the coated slices may be subjected to either a warm air blast or to a cold water dip in order to remove excess amylose. The coated slices are then subjected to the conventional deep-frying process whereby they are immersed in an edible cooking oil such as cottonseed, corn, coconut, soy or any mixtures of the latter oils, and cooked for 1 to 5 minutes at a temperature of 300° to 400°F. Here again, the precise combination of time and temperature which is utilized for the deep frying operation will, of course, depend upon the particular deep-fried product which is being prepared as well as on the oil being utilized.

It should be noted that when French fried potatoes are being prepared, the raw potato slices may be given a calcium lactate blanch, or any other desired treatment, prior to their being coated in the hot amylose dispersion. However, the amylose coatings employed in the process do, of course, eliminate the need for blanching the slices in methylcellulose or in natural gums which are sometimes employed in a generally unsuccessful attempt to improve crispness. The deep-fried potato products resulting from the process will be coated with from 0.002 to 0.02% by weight of an amylose product as based upon the weight of the deep-fried potato product less the weight of the coating.

Example: Potatoes which had been stored at about 45°F in order to reduce the formation of reducing sugars were washed, peeled, trimmed and then cut into slices having the shape of rectangular solids whose average dimensions were about ½ x ½ x 3 inches. The slices were then washed to remove excess starch.

The slices were placed in a wire mesh basket which was then immersed for 1 minute in a vessel filled with a 6%, by weight, aqueous dispersion of amylose acetate which was at a temperature of 185°F. The latter amylose acetate had a DS, i.e., a degree of substitution, of 2.5 and had been prepared by the reaction of acetic anhydride with a sample of high amylose cornstarch having an amylose content of 55%, by weight.

After being removed from the hot, aqueous dispersion of amylose acetate, the coated slices were drained for 1 minute whereupon they were deep-fried, for about 2 minutes, in cottonseed oil which was at a temperature of 380°F. The thus fried potatoes were drained for 1½ minutes and were then quick frozen at a temperature of −30°F.

Upon being reheated, the French fried potatoes were found to have good flavor and were exceedingly crisp while displaying excellent strength without being tough. It was also noted that variations in color as well as in the amount of oil which had been absorbed were minimal.

French fries displaying comparable properties were prepared using the following amylose coatings in place of the above amylose acetate:

(1) A high amylose cornstarch having an amylose content of 55%, by weight.

(2) A high amylose cornstarch having an amylose content of 70%, by weight.

(3) Amylose derived from the fractionation of potato starch.

(4) An acetate ester of amylose having a DS of 2.0, as prepared by the reaction of acetic anhydride with a sample of amylose derived from the fractionation of potato starch.

(5) A hydroxypropyl ether of amylose having a DS of 1.5, as prepared by the reaction of propylene oxide with a sample of high amylose cornstarch having an amylose content of 70%, by weight.

(6) A thin boiling amylose product prepared by the treatment, with sodium hypochlorite, of a sample of high amylose cornstarch having an amylose content of 65%, by weight; the final product having been converted to a degree known in the trade as 70 fluidity.

SPECIFIC PURPOSE MEAT COATINGS

Coating for Texture Improvement

The process described by *N.E. Harris and F.H. Lee; U.S. Patent 3,794,742; February 26, 1974; assigned to U.S. Secretary of the Army* relates to compositions for application as coatings to meats and other solid foods which require cooking before being consumed, more particularly to rehydrated freeze-dried meats, prior to cooking thereof, whereby the moisture in the food is better retained through the cooking than when the food is cooked without being coated, or is coated only with flour, before cooking. The resulting cooked food has an improved texture over similar food which is cooked without being coated with this composition.

Coating Preparations

The dry, powdery composition is prepared by mixing in the dry state finely powdered hydroxypropyl methylcellulose, dextrose, low DE hydrolyzed cereal solids and a pregelatinized tapioca starch. The hydrolyzed cereal solids preferably have DE values from 9 to 13. The hydroxypropyl methylcellulose is characterized by having from 84 to 93% of the alkoxyl groups attached to the anhydroglucose rings in the form of methoxyl groups and the remaining alkoxyl groups attached to the anhydroglucose rings in the form of 2-hydroxypropoxyl groups (Methocel HG).

Dextrose is available in a dry, powdery state from numerous sources. It is used in the dry, powdery composition largely for the purpose of producing browning of the cooked food by reaction of its carbonyl group with amino groups of proteins contained in foodstuffs. It may be omitted from compositions used in coating vegetables in which browning may be undesirable.

A useful low DE hydrolyzed cereal solids product is Mor-Rex, which is used mainly as a spacing agent for the purpose of reducing agglomeration and improving wettability of the hydroxypropyl methylcellulose when the composition is dispersed in water. The hydroxypropyl methylcellulose in the dry powdery composition remains more easily dispersible in water while in storage in the dry state over long periods of time with hydrolyzed cereal solids present in the composition and the composition is readily dispersible in water to produce an aqueous dispersion which produces a uniform coating on the food so that when the coated food is cooked, moisture is well-retained and the texture of the cooked food is greatly improved over that of a similar food product cooked without prior application of such a coating.

Similarly, if the fresh food or reconstituted freeze-dried food is dredged in the dry, powdery composition, a relatively smooth coating is produced because of the presence of the hydrolyzed cereal solids in the dry, powdery composition. Thus the coating of the hydroxypropyl methylcellulose on the food is made more uniform and the moisture present in the fresh food or reconstituted food is held in during cooking thereof to such a degree that the texture of the cooked food is markedly improved. This is particularly evident in the case of meats.

Pregelatinized tapioca starch (Redisol 412) is a precooked tapioca starch used in connection with various food products as a thickener-stabilizer. The concentration of the hydroxypropyl methylcellulose in the dry, powdery composition may be varied from 1 to 50%. The limiting factors with respect to this are that there be enough of the hydrolyzed cereal solids and the pregelatinized tapioca starch present to cause production of a good dispersion of the hydroxypropyl methylcellulose in water and enough water present to produce a smooth, nonviscous and uniform coating of the hydroxypropyl methylcellulose over the entire exterior surface of the food prior to the cooking thereof and that there be enough dextrose present to produce the desired degree of browning of the cooked food under the cooking conditions to which the food is exposed.

In general, it has been found desirable to have approximately equal proportions of the dextrose, the hydrolyzed cereal solids and the pregelatinized tapioca in the remainder of the dry, powdery composition after the percentage of hydroxypropyl methylcellulose is selected.

The preferred dry, powdery composition is as follows:

Ingredient	Percent, by Weight
Hydroxypropyl methylcellulose	3.25
Dextrose	32.25
Hydrolyzed cereal solids, DE 9 to 13	32.25
Pregelatinized tapioca starch	32.25

When an aqueous dispersion of this is to be used for coating a food prior to cooking, it may be prepared in a wide range of concentrations—as low as 2% and as high as 25%. In fact, the composition may be applied to the food in the dry, powdery state by dredging the food in the dry, powdery composition in much the same manner as is employed with flour in conventional cooking practices.

Example: An aqueous dispersion of the above-described dry, powdery composition was made by mixing 2 grams thereof with 100 grams of water, thus producing a 1.96% dispersion on a weight basis. Slices of fresh lean top round beef were dipped in the dispersion, allowed to drain off excess dispersion and sautéed in a pan containing corn oil along with slices of fresh lean beef cut off the same part of the round, but which were not coated with the dispersion. The latter slices were used as controls.

All of the slices of beef were sautéed on both sides to as nearly the same degree as possible, the objective being a medium rare degree of doneness. The moisture loss by each slice was determined by the difference between the original weight and the final weight after cooking. Average moisture loss for the coated slices was 10.6%. Average moisture loss for the control slices was 18.6%.

Alternatively, slices of fresh lean top round beef were dredged in the described dry, powdery composition in substantially the same manner as is frequently employed with flour when a meat is to be sautéed. These coated slices were sautéed in a pan containing corn oil along with slices of fresh lean beef cut off the same part of the round, but which were not coated with the dry, powdery composition. The latter slices were used as controls.

All of the slices of beef were sautéed on both sides to as nearly the same degree as possible, the objective being a medium rare degree of doneness. The moisture loss by each slice was determined by the difference between the original weight and the final weight after cooking. Average moisture loss for the coated slices was 8.9%. Average moisture loss for the control slices was 16.1%.

Dry Powder Coating to Impart Glaze

R.J. Mangiere, C.J. Dwyer and M.A. Bressler; U.S. Patent 3,769,027; October 30, 1973 have developed a dry composition which acts as a coating, a seasoning and a glaze for food products. To use the composition the consumer merely applies it to the raw foodstuff, as by placing the composition and the foodstuff in a bag and shaking them together, and then baking the coated foodstuff in an oven for the requisite amount of time. Preferably the foodstuff is kept uncovered during the baking operation, and can be baked on a flat utensil such as a cookie sheet. Preferably, the foodstuff is turned once, about halfway through the baking operation. During the baking a lustrous, soft (not crisp or crust-like) film forms

Coating Preparations

over the entire surface of the foodstuff. The film gives to the foodstuff an extremely attractive glazed appearance and also acts as a barrier to keep the moisture contained in the foodstuff from escaping. Furthermore, because flavoring materials, and optionally edible coloring materials, are contained in the composition, it additionally imparts flavor and color to the cooked foodstuff.

The composition, referred to as a glaze powder, comprises a blend of the following dry ingredients. (All percentages are by weight, based on the total weight of the glaze powder, unless stated otherwise.)

(1) 30 to 60% of a water-soluble low DE, i.e., 5 to 25, starch hydrolysate;

(2) 4 to 10% fat;

(3) 0.25 to 1.5% algin;

(4) 0.1 to 0.95% of a food-grade phosphate;

(5) A sufficient amount of a food-grade source of calcium to provide between 0.01 and 0.015% available calcium (a derivative of milk, such as whey, is best suited for this purpose);

(6) 0 to 15% corn syrup solids;

(7) 0 to 1.0% of a food-grade emulsifier and water-binding agent, preferably lecithin; and

(8) The balance comprising a member selected from the group consisting of flavoring materials and mixtures of flavoring materials and coloring materials.

The following observations were made during the cooking of cut-up chicken parts coated with the glaze powder in a 400°F oven. Near the beginning of the cooking period a glaze, which had almost a crust-like appearance, formed on the top surface of the chicken parts. After 15 minutes baking time the chicken parts were turned over and baked an additional 15 minutes, then removed from the oven. The crust-like appearance was gone and a uniform, lustrous, extremely attractive glaze covered both sides of the chicken. The chicken had a delicious flavor and an extremely appetizing, moist texture. (The actual baking time depends upon the size of the chicken parts.)

Example: The following ingredients were blended together:

Ingredients	Parts by Weight
10 DE starch hydrolysate	56.00
Fat (spray dried vegetable fat)	6.00
Algin	0.75
Tetrasodium pyrophosphate	0.25
Edible casein (spray dried)	1.00
Corn syrup solids (42 DE)	8.00
Flavoring materials:	
Salt	6.00
Barbecue oil	0.12
Imitation smoke flavor	1.50
Seasoning powder	1.50
Worcestershire sauce	10.00

(continued)

Ingredients	Parts by Weight
Onion powder	4.00
Garlic powder	0.50
Monosodium glutamate	5.00
Mixture of disodium inosinate and disodium guanylate	0.12
Total flavoring materials	28.74
Total ingredients	100.74

All of the above listed ingredients were commercially available products. 2¾ ounces of the mixture were placed in a plastic bag, and 2½ pounds of moist, cut-up chicken parts were added. The bag was shaken until the chicken parts were evenly coated. The chicken parts were placed on a foil-lined, lightly-greased cookie sheet and baked in a 400°F oven for 15 minutes, after which the parts were turned and baked for an additional 15 minutes. The cooked chicken was completely covered with an attractive lustrous glaze. The chicken had a delicious barbecued flavor, and an extremely moist, appetizing texture.

APPARATUS

Continuous Application of Wet Batter and Dry Coating

C.N. Harkey; U.S. Patent 3,703,382; November 21, 1972; assigned to J.D. Jewell, Inc. describes a method and a machine for continuously applying a combination wet batter and dry breader coating to continuously moving individual pieces of food such as cut-up chicken parts, shrimp, etc. The machine has a batter unit and a breader unit. A batter unit infeed conveyor receives the individual food pieces to be battered and breaded and conveys them continuously through a wet batter bath which coats the individual food pieces with batter.

The individual pieces then travel on continuously under a blower to strip off excess batter and smooth the product surface before the continuously traveling product is automatically drop transferred to a breading machine unit top conveyor which receives the product from the batter unit conveyor by a drop transfer on to a bed of dry breader material created by a breader unit gravity flow hopper and spreader to coat the bottom of the product with dry breader. Next, the continuously traveling product travels under a hopper sifter-type conveyor to coat the top of the product with dry breader.

The breader unit has three conveyors comprising stainless steel wire mesh belts running in opposite direction to the preceding conveyor placed under each other. A top conveyor drop transfers to a second (middle) conveyor with proper height spacing to cause the product to turn over (change sides) during the transfer. The same is repeated from the second (middle) conveyor to a third (bottom) conveyor. From the bottom conveyor, the product is dropped and turned onto a stainless steel wire mesh belt carry-out conveyor. The product is carried out and transferred to a packout conveyor while the dry breader falls through the same conveyor and through the wire mesh belt into a continuously traveling sifter then into a hopper. The dry breader is then transferred through vacuum pipe from the receiving hopper at the bottom of the machine back to the starting hopper on the top of the machine which completes a dry breader cycle of the breader recirculating system. The apparatus is fully illustrated and its operation fully described in the patent.

MEAT AND DAIRY PRODUCTS

PRECOOKED BACON ITEMS

Process and Apparatus for Precooking Bacon

In a method described by *W.C. McKay; U.S. Patent 3,873,755; March 25, 1975; assigned to Haberstroh Farm Products, Inc.* bacon slices are cooked in an oven while retained between upper and lower flights of a conveyor directed horizontally through the cooking zone of the oven. The heating source for the oven comprises a fuel burner located remotely from the bacon-cooking zone. The temperature generated at the burner is utilized to heat a gaseous medium which is in turn conveyed to the bacon-cooking zone at a relatively high velocity.

Furthermore, the heated gaseous medium is directed with an extremely high degree of turbulence against the bacon from above and below. The high velocity and turbulence of the gaseous medium effect an extremely rapid rate of heat transfer to the bacon and simultaneously rid the bacon and conveyor belts of the rendered fat which would otherwise tend to act as an insulator and produce an unattractive appearance when packaged. The temperature of the bacon conveyor is maintained below the flash point of bacon grease. Suitable apparatus for carrying out this process is provided in the patent.

Precooked Shelf Stable Bacon Product

R.B. Tompkin and F.G. Connick; U.S. Patent 3,868,468; February 25, 1975; assigned to Swift & Company have discovered a process for producing a precooked sliced bacon product which is shelf stable yet which contains a sodium chloride level within the range of human palatability, i.e., below about 4% by weight sodium chloride content. The product can be marketed and stored at ambient temperatures without deterioration. Moreover, the product does not support the growth of spoilage or pathogenic microorganisms during storage and can easily be prepared for consumption by heating to a desirable serving temperature or serving as is.

In the process bacon slabs, i.e., pork bellies prepared and cured by any conventional manner, are sliced to a desired thickness. The bacon slices are cooked to a constant percent weight yield of between about 30 to 40%. A plurality of the cooked slices are packaged in a container in a manner that inhibits mold growth and will produce throughout the resultant containerized product a water activity of below about 0.86 maximum and a percent brine level of at least about 13%, and each of the bacon slices of the product has below about 4% sodium chloride, by weight.

The resultant product is shelf stable, i.e., does not support the growth of spoilage and/or pathogenic microorganisms when stored at ambient temperatures, and can conveniently be prepared for consumption by heating to a desired serving temperature or serving as is.

The method comprises cooking conventionally prepared and cured bacon slices to a constant yield of about 30 to 40% (60 to 70% shrink) by weight, selecting an equal plurality of cooked slices from each butt, center, center and flank quadrant of at least one bacon slab, and packaging the selected slices in a container in the absence of air. By following this critical sequence of steps, the resultant containerized bacon product will have a water activity of below about 0.86 maximum, a percent brine level of at least 13%, and a sodium chloride level below about 4%, by weight, throughout each individual slice of product.

It is well known that water is an essential requirement for the growth of all microorganisms. The availability of water for microbial growth is more closely related to its relative vapor pressure or water activity than to the percent water present. Water activity (A_w) is defined as the ratio of water vapor pressure of a system under consideration (P) to vapor pressure of pure water P_o at the same temperature, and is represented by the following formula: $A_w = P/P_o$. When the moisture concentration of the system is in equilibrium with the relative humidity of its environment, water activity is directly related to relative humidity expressed in percent, e.g., $A_w = RH/100$.

Research has shown that containerized food products having a water activity above about 0.86 are susceptible to microbial spoilage when stored at ambient temperatures. Accordingly, it is accepted by those skilled in the art that containerized products properly packaged and exhibiting a water activity below about 0.86 will not support the growth of spoilage and/or pathogenic microorganisms when stored at ambient temperatures.

It has been found that there is a direct relationship between water activity and percent brine level

$$\% \text{ brine} = \frac{\% \text{ NaCl}}{\% \text{ H}_2\text{O} + \% \text{ NaCl}}$$

in cooked bacon slices. This relationship is reciprocal, i.e., the lower the water activity of the product, the higher the percent brine level. Tests have shown that, in order to be shelf stable at ambient temperatures, a containerized precooked sliced bacon product must have a water activity of 0.86 or below and a corresponding percent brine level of at least 13%.

Example: Pork bellies, skinned and trimmed of excess fat and muscle were pumped to 115% green weight with a 100°F saturated brine pickle solution containing butylated hydroxyanisole, butylated hydroxytoluene and a trace of commercial liquid smoke for a 110 to 111% green weight retention. The pumped bellies were hung directly after pumping and placed into a smoke house. The bellies were cooked and smoked to about 128°F internal temperature and removed to refrigerated coolers. The cooked bellies were chilled to about 26°F, taking about 24 hours. The chilled bellies were then pressed into slabs and the slabs sliced to provide slices weighing about 0.25 ounce each by the use of conventional bacon pressing and slicing devices.

The slices were placed on a continuous conveyor of a conventional infrared cooking apparatus. The slices were cooked for a time period sufficient to produce a constant percent weight shrink of 65% (35% yield). An equal number of cooked slices from each butt, center, center and flank quadrant of the bacon slabs were selected, placed on silicone treated paper and packaged in a metal container while still in a heated condition. The metal container was immediately sealed under maximum vacuum.

After holding for a period of about 12 hours, the containerized product was opened and analyzed for water activity, percent brine level and percent sodium chloride. Upon analysis, the resultant precooked bacon product had an average water activity of 0.834, a percent brine level of 13.9% and a sodium chloride level of 3.2%, by weight. No individual slice from the containerized product that was analyzed exhibited a water activity above 0.86, a percent brine level below 13.0% and a salt level above 4%, by weight.

PORK SNACK PRODUCTS

Puffed Unfried Pork Rind

The prior art disadvantage of the hair normally associated with commercially available pork rinds may be largely obviated by the process disclosed by *R.H. Bundus and P.P. Noznick; U.S. Patent 3,793,467; February 19, 1974; assigned to Beatrice Foods Co.* The process may be practiced with either pork bellies or pork rinds. Briefly stated, it has been discovered that the remaining hair on the pork rinds can be substantially removed by comminuting the pork rinds to a relatively small particle size, suspending and slurrying the comminuted pork in a liquid medium, and vigorously agitating the slurry for a sufficient length of time to substantially dislodge the hair associated therewith.

Subsequently, the hair is separated from the pork rinds by any convenient method such as with a conventional centrifuge or with a conventional floating process, e.g., with an air-foam, flotation-skimming tank. However, centrifuging is preferred.

The process also obviates the necessity of deep fat frying. After the pork rinds are removed from the liquid medium, the pork rinds are dried to a moisture content below 20% by weight and then extruded by a conventional food screw extruder in a gelatinized state through a heated die which cooks and puffs the gelatinizing extrudate while passing through the extruder die. Hence, the gelatinized pork rinds may be cooked and puffed by the extruder die and the cooked and puffed extrudate may be comminuted to any desired length. As can be appreciated, this extrusion process does not require that the rinds be first rendered, since this automatically happens in the drying process, and for efficiency hot fat rendering/drying in hot air may be combined. In this latter regard, the die of the extruder may not be heated and the extruded gelatinized mass may be cooked and puffed by the traditional method of deep fat frying, which alternative method still obviates the need of first rendering the pork rinds, although it does not mitigate entirely the problems associated with deep fat frying.

In summary, the process provides methods of removing substantial proportions of hair left on commercial pork rinds and allows the use of the product from the dehairing step to be used directly to produce puffed pork rinds without the conventional rendering step. Further, the preferred method of the process allows the production of puffed pork rinds without the necessity of utilizing deep fat frying.

Example: Raw pork rinds are comminuted to an average particle size of approximately $1/32$ of an inch in a conventional slicing mill. The comminuted pork rinds are then slurried in a 3% aqueous solution of sodium chloride and vigorously agitated in a cylindrical tank with a dished bottom, by means of a propeller mixer suspended from the top of the tank with the propeller disposed about $1/3$ of the distance from the bottom of the tank. The propeller operates at about 1,800 revolutions per minute and accomplishes vigorous agitation of the slurry of cut pork rinds.

The temperature of the slurry is ambient temperature, i.e., about 70°F. The agitation is continued for approximately 30 minutes, at which time a substantial portion of the hair originally on the raw pork rinds has been displaced by the agitation of the slurry of comminuted particles. Through a bottom draw-off of the tank, the slurry is passed, in a batch manner, to a centrifuge which centrifuges the slurry and deposits the aqueous solution and hair as an effluent of the centrifuge.

The dehaired pork rinds are removed from the centrifuge and placed in a conventional rotary tumble dryer. The pork rind particles are heated for approximately one hour at 200°F with hot smoke to a moisture content of approximately 10% by weight. The dried pork rinds are fed in a continuous manner to a conventional extruder and gelatinized in the screw portion of the extruder with additional heat being applied to the barrel of the extruder.

The barrel of the extruder has a maximum temperature of 300°F. The die of the extruder is a simple plate die with 18 holes of $3/16$ inch diameter. The die plate is heated to a temperature of 410°F. The extruder is operated at a rate of 160 lb/hr of the dried pork rinds. A cooperating knife blade adjacent the face of the die chops the extrudate to a length of 1 inch as it passed from the extruder die.

The cooked and puffed pork rinds are then tumbled in a conventional tumbling machine wherein the pork rinds are colored with a yellow food color and to which salt and a preservative, BHT, are added. The pork rinds are then packaged. The product has a very pleasant taste, is crisp and uniform in texture and has the general appearance of conventional puffed pork rinds.

Puffed Pork Skin Pellets

R.R. Rydeski and R.F. Conway; U.S. Patent 3,725,084; April 3, 1973 provide a method for preparing puffable food pellets which are low in fats and which have a uniform moisture content throughout the pellet to afford increased volume by expansion during a subsequent puffing process. The method contemplates introducing and uniformly distributing the moisture in the pellets by forcing the moisture into the spaces in the molecular structure of the protein or carbohydrate during a cooking cycle using steam under predetermined temperature and pressure conditions.

After the food product is subjected to steam in the cooking cycle, the food product is rinsed to remove the melted fats. The food product is then subjected to a drying cycle using a flow of heated air circulated by a blower around the pellets. The drying step entraps the moisture by the formation of a crust or shell around each microscopic deposit of moisture. The drying cycle removes surface moisture but not the moisture contained and distributed throughout the pellet.

The uniform interspersion of moisture in pork skins using this method increases the expansion ratio upon puffing to a 20:1 to a 25:1 ratio, whereas, the expansion ratio of pork skins prepared by prior methods may be 6:1 or 7:1. Moreover, the uniform distribution of moisture causes uniform puffing so that the ultimate food product is uniformly crisp without any undesirable or inedible portions.

Crispy Fried Pork Product

E.E. Davis; U.S. Patent 3,709,698; January 9, 1973 describes a method of preparing crispy snouts, tripe, pig ears, pig skins, and the like.

The two main tendons from the forehead to the tip of the nose of the snouts are cut out. In all products excess fat is trimmed and all lean meat is cut out. The product or products are covered with water in a pot and boiled for 30 minutes. They are then seasoned with a mixture of salt, red pepper, and garlic powder, and while being kept under water are boiled for another 2 hours. The water is drained off and the product is fried in deep fat set at 375°F, a small increment at a time to insure floating, for 5 to 10 minutes until the snouts are firm enough to handle with tongs without tearing.

The snouts, etc., are lifted out individually with tongs, opened up and put in a deep fry basket with another basket over them to maintain spread and reduce curling. They are then replaced in a fryer and fried until crisp for 15 to 20 minutes. The crispy snouts are removed and put in barbecue sauce, and served.

A highly palatable and delicious crispy food item which is not hard is obtained from the described method. The crispy items may be eaten without the barbecue sauce. It is desirable that the prepared product be eaten while crisp. Hence, it is advisable to store the crispy items in plastic or wax bags, or the like, in a cool place until ready to serve.

STABLE FOOD ITEMS FROM "WASTE" PROTEIN SOURCES

Achieving Structural Integrity Without Use of Supplemental Binders in Shaped Food Items

P.J. Magnino, Jr., W.B. Burgess and R.R. Meyer; U.S. Patent 3,904,776; Sept. 9, 1975; assigned to Ralston Purina Company have found a method of producing edible protein food products using edible synthetic secondary protein fiber which does not require the addition of supplemental binders or adhesives. The food substances produced by this method are of an enhanced structural integrity and texture.

The great improvement in structure and texture achieved enables the utilization of a wide variety of protein sources to form structured foods. These protein sources are those which, though providing good quality protein and flavor, have heretofore been unacceptable due to their lack of sufficient texture. For example, many animal sources of protein are not fully utilized due to their lack of structure. Mechanically deboned flesh, i.e., fish, meat, poultry, provides a much higher yield in usable protein than other means of utilizing the flesh protein.

This is particularly true of portions of the carcass which are not readily saleable, such as chicken necks and backs. Many species of "waste" or "trash" fish are not utilized as food sources because their flesh doesn't have sufficient structural integrity to withstand normal preparation and retain their texture.

Texture and structural integrity is imparted to protein foods without using supplemental binders by using a heat setting and self-binding protein fiber in the food system. The food system is prepared by using fibers which are susceptible to producing a binding action in the presence of heat. The food product is first formed, using the heat setting fibers and then subjected to a heat treatment to set the protein fibers and other ingredients into a coherent structure.

It has been found that structured food products having great structural integrity can be prepared using supplemental protein sources which have been severely processed to the point that they have lost their adhesive and self-binding properties, e.g., mechanically deboned flesh, by using heat settable fibers. The supplemental protein source need not be completely homogenized to be used in a food system, but may still retain some of its natural fibrous characteristics.

Food products formed by this method preferably will incorporate from 5 to 60% by weight of the edible heat setting synthetic protein fibers. Typically, they will preferably contain 5 to 60% of the heat setting fibers, 30 to 90% by weight of an additional food source, e.g., mechanically deboned chicken, waste fish, or by-product meat, and 0 to 6% supplemental flavors, spices, vitamins, minerals, etc. The relative percentages of ingredients in the food product are not critical since they will be dependent on the flavor, texture, or appearance of the product.

The food products are formed by blending the heat setting fibers and other ingredients and then heat setting the fibers to weld the fibers and other ingredients into a coherent structure. The heat treatment sets the heat settable fibers to a coherent structure and binds the fibers to each other and to the other ingredients in the formulation. The exact temperature employed is not critical other than that the temperature must be sufficient to heat set the fibers. It has been found, for example, that internal temperatures of 120° to 250°F for 3 to 120 minutes are preferred to heat set the fibers to the desired structural integrity. Suitable internal temperatures can be achieved by heating in an environment at a sufficiently high temperature and for a time sufficient to transfer enough heat to the product. In general, and as an example, environment temperatures of up to about 400° to 450°F may be used. The heat setting operation may be a one step or multistep operation.

Example 1: A breaded fish stick containing 30% heat setting fiber and having a good texture and structural integrity was prepared from hake, a mechanically deboned trash fish, as follows:

>   350 grams raw hake
>   150 grams heat setting fibers prepared as described in Example 1 of U.S. Patent 3,662,672
>   10 grams salt

The heat setting fibers were chopped to about ¼ inch in length on a food chopper and the hake, chopped fibers, and salt were added to a food mixer and mixed until blended. The mixture was formed into blocks by freezing under 25 psi pressure at −10°F in a press pan. Fish sticks, ½ inch x ½ inch x 3 inches were sawed from the frozen blocks and breaded. The fish sticks prepared as above were deep fried at 375°F for 5 minutes to raise the product to temperature.

The product heat set during cooking into a coherent structure. The structure and texture of the fish sticks prepared as above were compared with a commercial product and with fish sticks prepared from hake only. The hake-only fish sticks were unacceptable in texture and structure. The product was mushy and had no structural integrity. The commercial product remained intact but was mushy and didn't have the good bite and chew of the product of the process.

Example 2: A structured product containing 35% heat setting fiber was prepared from mechanically deboned chicken meat (necks and backs) as follows:

>   126 grams deboned necks and backs
>   70 grams heat setting fibers
>   2 grams flavor
>   2 grams salt

The heat setting fibers were chopped and the ingredients mixed as described in Example 1. The mixture was molded around a rod, breaded, partially heat set in a 350°F oven for 10 minutes, and deep fried at 350°F for 5 minutes to form the final product. The product exhibited good texture, was structurally sound and resembled a chicken drumstick in organoleptic characteristics. Heat set mechanically deboned chicken necks and backs had almost no textural and structural integrity.

Use of Waste Fish Material in Edible Fish Stick

Considerable effort has been directed into the recovery and refining of waste fish protein to enable it to be used in the manufacture of human foodstuffs. By way of example, purified fish protein (otherwise known as fish flour or fish protein concentrate) can be obtained from fish waste by any of several methods.

R.P. Carpenter, R.B. Weddle and F.W. Wood; U.S. Patent 3,873,749; March 25, 1975; assigned to Lever Brothers Company describe the manufacture of a product that is beneficial in the utilization of protein material having a low functionality, i.e., protein material which has become substantially denatured due to treatment such as heating or protein concentration or extraction procedures. The process enables such substantially denatured protein to be reconstituted into foodstuffs suitable for human consumption.

The product is in the form of a thermostable gel containing a characterizing protein ingredient, particularly a fish protein which is obtained by admixing at a pH above 7 the protein ingredient and a propylene glycol ester of alginic acid so that a water-insoluble protein-alginate polymer is formed.

The expression "fish protein ingredient" is used to refer to any protein material derived from fish or from crustacea. Moreover, the process may be applied to the use of protein material derived from other animal sources, such as animal or poultry muscle, milk or eggs.

The protein ingredient need not necessarily be purified or refined, provided that it is safe for consumption. For example, alternative sources of fish protein ingredient can consist of coarsely or finely comminuted fish muscle which has not been subjected to any protein extraction technique.

Suitable propylene glycol esters of alginic acid are soluble esters which may conveniently be prepared by reacting a food-grade alginic acid with 1,2-propylene oxide. The propylene glycol alginic acid esters may still contain free carboxyl groups. It is, however, advantageous for economic reasons to use propylene glycol alginic acid esters wherein at least 50% of the carboxyl groups of the alginic acid are esterified.

Other ingredients, such as edible salts, flavoring agents, coloring matter and texturizing aids as desired may also be used. The product may be prepared by first making a mixture of the protein ingredients and the ester of alginic acid, ensuring that the pH of the mixture is greater than 7, sufficient water being added when necessary to facilitate mixing and to allow polymerization to proceed, provided that the quantity of water added is not so great that the mixture becomes so fluid that the formation of discrete structures by extrusion is impossible.

According to a particularly preferred formulation, the mixture contains from 17 to 25% by weight of dry powdered fish protein concentrate, 0.6 to 2.0% by weight of propylene glycol ester of alginic acid, the balance, apart from minor ingredients such as salts, coloring and flavoring matter and texturizing aids, being water; the pH is adjusted at the time the mixture is prepared to a value of from 7.5 to 9.5.

The mixture can be allowed to set to a thermostable gel without further treatment, or it can be used as a component of a food product by admixing with other ingredients before or after setting. Alternatively, before it sets the mixture can be shaped to a thermostable gel by extrusion.

Setting after extrusion can be facilitated by contacting the extruded mixture with an aqueous solution of an alkaline material, such as sodium carbonate, sodium hydroxide or mixtures thereof, the use of a sodium carbonate solution being preferred. The mixture can thereby be converted rapidly to a thermostable gel of the required shape, which may be in the form of filaments, fibers, hollow fibers, tubes, rods or strips.

After setting it may be necessary to reduce the pH of the gel foodstuff to a more appropriate level. Ideally the final pH of the gel foodstuff should be about 5 to 8, although the use of slightly higher pH may be acceptable. The pH of the gel foodstuff may be reduced by washing with a dilute aqueous solution of an acid such as acetic acid or hydrochloric acid, and then removing extraneous fluid by, for example, centrifuging. Generally the concentration of the acid in the aqueous solution will be from 0.5 to 5% w/v, but the concentration chosen may depend upon the strength of the particular acid used, and the degree of alkalinity of the gel foodstuff.

Ideally the gel foodstuff should contain a level of moisture comparable to that of fresh fish muscle, i.e., about 80% by weight in the case of white fish muscle. However, the gelled product may contain a moisture level of 90% by weight, or more, after extrusion. The moisture content will be reduced somewhat by any acid washing used to alter the pH, as described above.

Nevertheless, such acid washing may not be sufficient to reduce the moisture content to a desired level, or may not be required anyway for pH reasons. An alternative method of reducing the moisture content is to dip the gelled product after setting into dilute brine for a short period of time, generally not exceeding 5 minutes, and then removing extraneous fluid by, for example, centrifuging. A combination of these techniques may be used if required. Generally the brine should contain from 0.5 to 5% w/v salt.

A particular use of this process is in the manufacture of fish portions, such as fish fingers, fish steaks, fish cakes or fish pie filling, which are intended to be stored in the frozen state until purchased or prepared for consumption. It has been found that up to 15% or more, of cod muscle in these products can be replaced by the gel foodstuff process in fragmented form without detracting substantially from the appearance, texture and flavor of these products.

The fish protein products can thus find particular utility as foodstuff extenders, or they can be used as analog foodstuffs in their own right. They reduce the likelihood of syneresis in products containing them, even when thawed from the frozen state, and hence are suitable for use in many types of foodstuffs where water retention on thawing and, where appropriate, on cooking is desirable.

Example: This example illustrates the preparation of flake from fish protein concentrate, which is suitable for inclusion in fish fingers. An aqueous mixture comprising by weight 22.5% decolorized fish protein concentrate (prepared from cod waste), 1% propylene glycol ester of alginic acid (75 to 80% of the carboxyl groups esterified) and 76.5% water was prepared, acetic acid being added to adjust the pH to about 8.

The mix was deaerated under vacuum, extruded through a 0.75 mm x 7 mm aperture into a mixture comprising 0.5 M sodium carbonate and 0.2 M sodium hydroxide, the residence time in the solution being not more than 5 seconds, to yield firm ribbons. The ribbons were subsequently adjusted to pH 6 by washing with 1% w/v acetic acid, and finally centrifuged to remove residual surface moisture.

The ribbons were chopped into 0.5 to 1.5 cm lengths to simulate flaked fish muscle, and incorporated without further treatment at a level of 15% or 30% on a wet weight basis into a mix comprising sliced, filleted cod and sodium tripolyphosphate.

The mix was subsequently shaped, frozen and battered to provide fish fingers. The products were shown to be organoleptically indistinguishable from commercially obtainable fish fingers.

Thermoplastic Meat Patty

A.J. Ganz; U.S. Patent 3,769,029; October 30, 1973; assigned to Hercules Inc. provides a process for the manufacture of an improved food product in which an admixture of a thermoplastic hydroxypropylcellulose polymer having an MS of at least 2 and a solid food material, in a polymer to food material weight ratio based on the food product, of 0.01:1 to 1:1 are thermoplastically shaped.

MS herein means the average number of molecules of propylene oxide reactant combined with the hydroxypropylcellulose per anhydroglucose unit. Although the MS value is in all instances at least 2, it is more preferably within the range of 3.8 to 4.2, although higher values up to 10 are advantageously utilized in some instances, dependent upon the particular food material component. During the shaping, any water from the admixture initially present therein in excess of a predetermined proportion up to 15 weight percent is vaporized. The resulting shaped food product is then recovered.

Any suitable food material can be utilized with the polymer component to form a food product such as proteins, carbohydrates, starch, or food products which in their natural form already contain some structure such as meat, fruit, or vegetables. The food material component may also contain additional ingredients often added to modify the organoleptic and storage properties of food products such as corn syrup, fat, surfactants, salts, color, flavor, antioxidants, and nonthermoplastic gums. While the use of these additional ingredients is not essential, they can be utilized in accordance with the particular texture, taste, and storage proprties desired.

Further exemplary, and now preferred, food material components are sucrose, meats, vegetables, fruits, nuts, cereals, milk powder, protein concentrates, and mixtures thereof.

Some food components, per se, of the food product inherently exhibit good texture such as meats, poultry, fish, vegetables, fruits, and nuts, whereas others may have very little texture, such as milk powder, protein (soy), gluten, corn flour, and sugar. In all events, however, the food product exhibits texture characteristics improved over those of the food material component, per se.

In practice, water need not be directly added to the process system inasmuch as the polymer-food material admixture is itself thermoplastic. However, any water, initially present in the food material component, is inherently introduced into the polymer-food material admixture. Water content of the food product does not exceed about 15 weight percent inasmuch as at higher water content levels firmness, texture, and stability characteristics of the food product are generally unsatisfactory. In order to assure an optimum degree of those characteristics, it is often preferred that the water content range from 3 to 7%. Pressure conditions during the shaping step are advantageously adjusted to also regulate the rate of vaporization of water and to regulate, or eliminate, loss of volatile components from the polymer-food admixture during the shaping period, as desired.

In preferred practice, the polymer and food material component are admixed, preferably in finely divided particulate form, in any suitable manner, generally at an ambient temperature level below the softening point of the polymer. The resulting admixture is maintained under suitable temperature and pressure conditions for effecting the requisite thermoplastic shaping. At the end of the shaping period the resulting shaped admixture is cooled to below the softening point of the polymer component to form a resulting solid integral mass of thermoplastically shaped food product.

In general, the thermoplastic shaping is carried out at 100° to 250°C, selection of a minimum temperature being limited by the softening, or thermoforming point of the polymer, and maximum temperature being limited by the tendency of the polymer or food ingredients to darken excessively or undergo undesirable chemical change during the shaping period.

The food product of the process is readily formed into any desirable shape. Thus, products simulating spaghetti or macaroni, ground meat, breakfast cereals, candy bars, and shaped candies are advantageously prepared. Powdery materials such as milk solids, wheat flour, protein concentrates, and the like can be formed into larger particles for any desired use, for example, as meat supplements. They maintain their integrity through the cooking operation, thus imparting a more desirable texture and taste to the cooked product as compared with use of the powdered food materials, per se, as a directly added ingredient.

Example: Twenty grams of a hydroxypropylcellulose flake having an MS of 3.7, an intrinsic viscosity of 1.5 and a water solution viscosity (5%) of 140 cp, and 80 g of powdered nonfat milk solids having a water content less than 5%, were admixed under high speed agitation conditions in a blender for 2 minutes. The resulting admixture was introduced into, and extruded through, an extruder having a ¾ inch diameter screw.

The extruder system temperatures were 125°C in the feed zone, 150°C in the barrel, and 175°C in the die zone. The extrudate was formed in a slit die 1½ inches by 0.035 inch. The resulting brown extrudate sheet, after cooling to ambient temperature, was brittle and hard, and it maintained its body for a reasonable time upon chewing. It was moderately pliable in cold water.

Fifteen grams of the resulting extrudate product was mixed with 85 g of a ground beef mixture, the latter prepared by addition of 2 oz of water, with seasoning, to 1 lb of ground beef. The mixture was pan fried, and the resulting product was similar to an all beef patty, from the standpoint of flavor and texture.

In a comparable experiment wherein the above described milk powder was incorporated into a gound beef mixture, a compact, dense, and less flavorful pan fried patty was obtained.

An attempt to extrude the above described nonfat milk solids alone, i.e., in the absence of the hydroxypropylcellulose polymer component was unsuccessful. The milk solid particles would not extrude through the die and they became badly charred. An attempt to similarly extrude a hydroxypropylcellulose, alone, having an MS of 1.3 and a water solution viscosity of 250 cp (1% solution) was unsuccessful. The polymer could not be extruded through the die; it darkened and charred in the extruder barrel.

Simulated Meat Pieces from Expanded Meat and Vegetable Protein Source

B.M. Payne, J.R. Cloute, E.A. Johnson, A.V. Brown, Jr., and E.V. Oborsh; U.S. Patent 3,968,269; July 6, 1976; assigned to Ralston Purina Company describe a method of making a protein food product which has the desirable flavor of real meat, while retaining the economic and functional advantages of employing a vegetable protein source. This food piece comprises an extruded mixture of a meat source and a vegetable protein source such as oilseed meal, oilseed protein isolate or similar material.

The resultant product has a texture substantially identical to extruded soy products in which the flavor of the meat source is retained. The product may be used in foods such as stews and clam chowders since it is sufficiently stable to retain its integrity after retort processing. It can also be dried after extrusion, to provide a dry food product which upon rehydration with water, simulates the textural and masticatory properties of meat, but with the added advantage of having the flavor of a cooked meat piece.

More specifically, the process combines an oilseed material such as soybeans, cottonseed and peanuts in meal or isolate form with a meat source in proportions such that the meat source is present in an amount between 5 to 80% by weight and the mixture has a protein content on a dry basis of at least 25% by weight. The moisture content of such a combination is maintained below 50% by weight, and the fat is maintained below 12% by weight.

The described formulation is then extruded at temperatures exceeding 210°F, to achieve a flavorful plasticized dispersion of the meat source and the oilseed material, which is then expanded by exposure to atmospheric temperature and pressure, thereby forming a resilient, meat-like chunk having the flavor of a cooked piece of meat, while retaining the structural characteristics of an expanded oilseed material. The product has a high degree of palatability because of its natural meat flavor, with the economic advantages of an extruded oilseed product along with the functional characteristics of chewiness and structural stability in water.

Example: A solvent extracted soybean meal having a fat content of 0.5% and a protein content of 50% by weight was combined with fresh liver and five different 500 lb batch proteinaceous mixtures were formed as indicated in the table below. One mixture omitted any liver addition at all. All five formulations included 454 grams of iron oxide No. 20 and 227 grams of sulfur as an extrusion additive. The liver was frozen, and ground in a meat grinder so that it passed a ¼ inch plate. These ground meat pieces were then combined with the defatted soy meal to form the described mixtures, whereby each mass was placed in a preconditioner and the moisture levels raised to the indicated levels on all batches.

The dampened mass was then conveyed to an extruder whereby the screw was rotating at 125 rpm. The exit temperature of the extrudate was found to vary between 354° and 378°F with an average temperature of 370°F. After extrusion, the extrudate from each batch was cut with a series of four rotating blades attached to a common hub mounted on the extruder head. After extrusion, the cut extrudate in the form of small meat-like pieces was dried to about 10% moisture.

	Soy Meal, lb	Sulfur, g	Iron Oxide No. 20, g	Liver, lb
100% Soy	500	227	454	0
10% Liver	450	227	454	50
20% Liver	400	227	454	100
30% Liver	350	227	454	150
40% Liver	300	227	454	200

The extrudates from all batches were flexible, resilient formed pieces with the lowest moisture level formulation, showing the least expansion. The four batches containing liver, had the chewy texture of an expanded product derived from the extruded soybean meal, although as the percentage of liver increased, the density of the fiber increased as evidenced by an increase in bushel weight. The expanded product from those batches which contained the liver had an aroma substantially similar to that of liver itself with the resilient characteristics of the expanded product derived entirely from the extrusion of soybean meal.

MEAT PRODUCT ADJUVANTS

Barbecue Sauce with Tenderizer

A meat tenderizing barbecue sauce having a pH below 5 and containing the proteolytic enzyme papain substantially free of amylase is provided by *F.E. Metz, F.O. Boyce and J.L. Segmiller; U.S. Patent 3,930,030; December 30, 1975; assigned to H.J. Heinz Company.* The barbecue sauce for tenderizing and enhancing the flavor of protein-containing food comprises amylase-free papain in combination with tomato paste, sugar, gum-oil, salt, spices, garnishes, preservative agents, vinegar and water. The pH of this product is about 3.5 and is prepared as follows.

At ambient temperature, the various spices and preservatives are mixed in water and this starting mixture is heated to 160°F. After this temperature has been reached, tomato paste and a "barbecue mix" comprising sugar and salt, along with gum-oil are added to the starting mixture to form a first phase mixture having a pH of 4.0. This first phase mixture is then heated to between 175° and 190°F and held there for 15 minutes. The first phase mixture is then milled by conventional means, and the temperature drops to 180°F. The milled mixture is then deaerated, also by conventional means, and the temperature drops to 120°F.

In the second phase of the process, the mixture leaving the deaerator at 120°F is maintained at that temperature while vinegar, oils, garnishes and amylase-free papain are added with agitation to complete the sauce and to bring its pH down to 3.5. The sauce is once again deaerated, whereupon its temperature drops to 95°F and, finally, it is cooled to 80°F, at which temperature the sauce may be packaged in containers. The barbecue sauce comprises, on a weight basis, between 0.05-0.20% amylase-free papain in combination with 12-18% tomato paste, 21-26% sugar, 0.007-0.01% gum-oil, 3.75-5.0% salt, 2.0-2.5% spices, 0.5-2.0% garnishes, 0.1-0.15% preservative agents, 12.5-15% vinegar and 33-48% water. The pH of the finished sauce is 3.5.

Example: A barbecue sauce with tenderizer was prepared as follows. First, a barbecue mix was prepared by dissolving 950 lb of sugar with 87.5 lb of salt in 250 lb of water. A gum-oil mix was prepared by dispersing 17.5 lb of guar gum in 25 lb of vegetable oil and mixing until the dispersion was free of lumps. A preservative-spice slurry was prepared by dissolving 6.5 lb of preservatives in 250 lb of water and then adding 50 lb of spices and mixing until uniform. A garnish mix was prepared by adding 25 lb of minced, dehydrated onions to 225 lb of water and boiling for 1 minute. A papain solution was prepared by dissolving 3 lb of papain in 50 lb of water at 60°F. 4 lb of vegetable oil was used.

The sweetener mix, preservative-spice slurry and the gum-oil mix were pumped into a first phase cook kettle, and mixed with 100 lb of water and 625 lb of tomato paste. In deaerating the mixture, the temperature was adjusted to 120°F.

In the second phase of the batch process, 1.175 lb of the first phase mixture was delivered into a second phase cook kettle, followed by addition of 275 lb of 100-grain vinegar, 25 g of the oil mix and 250 lb of the garnish mix. This second phase mixture was then gauged to a volume of 1,775 lb by addition of water and the temperature was adjusted to below 130°F. The papain solution prepared previously was then added and the final gauging and consistency adjustments were made so that 200 gal of the barbecue sauce was obtained. The barbecue sauce product which was thus prepared was then deaerated and filled at between 90° to 95°F into suitable containers.

The papain activity of the barbecue sauce product with tenderizer was then analyzed by preparing several types of meat and meat products, both with and without the barbecue sauce containing tenderizer. Comparisons were made, including taste panel organoleptic evaluation and shear-press texture measurements, in order to determine the tenderness of the meat and meat products. The effectiveness of the barbecue sauce in tenderizing meat, or like protein-containing foods, was clearly observed.

Concentrated Meat Extract and Flavoring

A process which relates to the production of concentrated meat-like aromatics and aromatic compositions is described by *H. Huth and H. Schum; U.S. Patent 3,796,811; March 12, 1974; assigned to Dragoco Spezialfabrik Konz, Riech- und Aromostoffe Gerberding & Co. GmbH, Germany.*

In the process, animal body parts are comminuted, mixed with water to form a pasty mass, heated, cooled and the aqueous phase thereof is treated with a protein-splitting enzyme. Concentration of the aqueous liquid results in a concentrated aromatic product that can be added to foods, particularly for the making of so-called "convenience" foods.

More particularly, meat, meat pieces, meat trimmings, meat scraps, animal organs, etc., with or without bones, are comminuted and water is added thereto during or after the comminuting to form a mass of pasty-like consistency, that is a pasty material which can be pumped. This pasty-like mass is then heated in an autoclave, at a temperature between 95° to 128°C and subsequently cooled to 50° to 55°C. The fat and aqueous phase are then separated from the solid water-insoluble residue using a suitable separating apparatus and the fat and aqueous phase are treated with a protein-splitting enzyme or enzymes to partially decompose the gelatinizing proteins. The aqueous phase may then be separated from the fat, if desired, and the aqueous phase is then uperized, preferably at a temperature of 145° to 160°C and concentrated, for example in a vacuum concentrater at a low temperature to obtain a clear water-soluble concentrate which is stable at room temperature. The concentrate is prepared so as to obtain 74 to 78% of dry substance in order to obtain a concentrate which is microbiologically stable at room temperature.

For purposes of standardization it is advantageous to maintain the fat content of the mass prior to the initial heating between about 10 and 20% by weight.

All types of protein splitting enzymes can be used for the treatment of the aqueous phase, including all of the commercially available proteolytic active enzyme preparations of microbiological, animal and plant origin. These enzymes include pancreases, pepsins, etc. The treatment of the fat and aqueous phase with the protein splitting enzyme is carried out to effect the decomposition of the gelatinizing protein to such extent that the aqueous extract can be evaporated to a concentrate which is flowable at 20°C while containing preferably 74 to 78% of nonaqueous components.

The treatment of the fat and aqueous extract with the protein splitting enzyme is preferably carried out at 50° to 55°C. The duration of the enzyme treatment is, as indicated above, mainly measured by the result obtained, namely such that the concentration to 60 to 85% nonaqueous components is flowable at 20°C. In time measurement this generally requires about 40 minutes of enzyme treatment.

The water-soluble aromatics produced can be directly used as an aromatic composition, or the aqueous concentrate can first be combined with the separated fat portion, or the aqueous concentrate can be emulsified with the fat portion and the emulsion then subjected to a roasting process. Depending upon the selected temperature and the duration of heating the obtained aromatic has varying aroma characteristics.

Thus, the roasting character is taken on during the heating period with increasing temperature, whereby a marked roasting reaction sets in at a temperature above about 100°C, while at above about 150°C a burnt smelling and tasting product is obtained. Within this temperature range of 100° to 150°C, the duration of heating time varies inversely with the heating temperature, i.e., the higher the temperature, the shorter the duration of heating. For example, the following heating temperatures and heating times result in substantially similar aromatics.

Heating Temperatures, °C	Duration of Heating, min
110	50
120	30
130	20
140	10

Aromatic compositions of varying aromatic character can be produced by mixing or emulsifying the aqueous concentrate of meat aromatics together with fat, spice extract and vegetable extract, and subsequent heating. In this manner it is possible to produce roast meat aromas with seasoning characteristics. Additional aromatic nuances can be obtained by adding ethereal spice oils, spice extracts and other seasoning substances, for example, yeast extracts and protein hydrolysates. The adding of these aromatic nuances can be obtained in ways known to those skilled in the art.

Example 1: 1,000 kg of deep frozen chicken parts are comminuted into small pieces in a bone bucket and by the addition of about 700 kg of water worked up into a pumpable pasty mass. The fat content of the mass amounts to about 9.2% and is standardized to 12% by the addition of about 4.8 kg of fresh chicken fat. The mass is subsequently heated in an autoclave to 125°C and maintained at this temperature for 40 minutes after which it is cooled to about 50°C and the insoluble residue is pressed out by means of a packet press.

There is thus obtained 42.0 kg of residue and 128.0 kg of an oily-aqueous emulsion to which there is added, for the purpose of decomposing the gelatinizing protein, 0.08 kg of pancrease-proteinase. The mixture is treated for 1 hour at 40°C and the emulsion is then subjected to centrifuging to separate the fat phase from the water phase, as well as to remove remaining insoluble residue. There is thus obtained 19.5 kg of fat.

The aqueous phase is subsequently subjected to enzyme inactivation and sterilization in a flow-through heater continuously for about 2 seconds at about 145°C and then for several seconds cooled to about 60°C and then evaporated in a vacuum evaporator under a vacuum of about 42 torr and a vapor temperature of about 35°C to a nonaqueous (dry) substance of about 78%. The yield amounts to 4.70 kg. The obtained extract is soluble in water without substantial turbidity.

5 g of the aqueous, concentrated extract are mixed together with 20 g of the obtained fat in 1 liter of water at 70°C with 0.5% cooking salt. The preparation smells and tastes remarkably like chicken broth.

Example 2: 60 kg of the aqueous concentrate obtained according to Example 1 are emulsified together with 40 kg of the fat of Example 1 in a high pressure, homogenizing machine and divided into several parts which are separately introduced into an autoclave and heated at different temperatures for a constant time period of 30 minutes and then quickly cooled to room temperature. The selected temperatures were 110°, 120°, 130° and 140°C. 20 g of each of the obtained products were dissolved in 1 liter of 0.5% salt solution at 70°C and tested by means of the human senses. The following results were obtained.

Treatment Temperature, °C	Results
110	Stronger odor and taste impression than in the case of the unheated sample, typically like cooked chicken broth.
120	Typical odor and taste of roast chicken.
130	Strong roast chicken character.
140	Strong roast chicken character with burnt aftertaste.

READY-TO-EAT MEAT PRODUCT ENHANCEMENT PROCESSES

Inhibiting Gel Formation in Meat-in-Gravy Product

The process described by *S.H. Reesman; U.S. Patent 3,843,815; Oct. 22, 1974; assigned to General Foods Corporation* relates to meat products packed in liquid and more particularly to preparing meat-in-gravy products which remain easily pourable throughout their shelf-life.

By this process gel formation in meat-in-gravy products which are subjected to heat processing after packaging is effectively inhibited by incorporating an acid in the product prior to packaging and sealing.

The process is applicable to any meat product which is combined with a liquid or gravy and processed with heat prior to or after packaging. Examples of methods of preparing such products include providing whole raw meat chunks, packing them in a can with gravy, and cooking the meat in the can; using precooked meat chunks and completing the cooking step after the chunks are packed with the gravy; using cooked meat chunks with a subsequent sterilization step after packaging; using comminuted meat either fresh or frozen, cooked or precooked, emulsified, mixed with binders or used alone, then mixed with gravy, packaged, and treated with heat; or other obvious variations all concluding with some form of retorting step.

The process is equally applicable to aseptically packaged products prepared by heating and cooking the meat and gravy together, placing the heated product in a container, and sealing the container. Upon cooling, this type product will similarly exhibit the gel formation noticeable in retorted products as described above.

The meat products contemplated include meat products which are acceptable for human consumption as well as such items as meat trimmings which may be used in pet foods. Depending upon the end product desired, i.e., whether intended for animal or human consumption, the term "meat" may include beef, chicken, pork, liver, lamb, goat, horsemeat, fish, animal trimmings, animal by-products, combinations of these, and the like. The meat may be mixed with vitamins and mineral supplements if desired and also fats, cereals, flavorings, colorings, proteinaceous materials, and other conventional additives.

The gravies normally employed in such products are basically water with added thickeners such as gums, starches, and mixtures thereof, and coloring and flavoring agents may also be added. The gravy is normally prepared separately from the meat pieces and is usually formulated so as to result in a specific viscosity dependent on how it is to be used. Desirable thick gravies, which have a more pronounced tendency to gel and become rigid, may be more widely used with packaged meat products when treated in accordance with this process.

When such meat products and gravies as described above are heated together after packaging, the protein collagen tends to cook out. The collagen dissolves to yield gelatin in the presence of heat, supplied from the cooking or sterilization step, and moisture, supplied by the gravy. On cooling, the gravy sets up in a gel due to the presence of the gelatin making it difficult for the consumer to pour out the contents of the can or package.

The addition of acid to the product has been found to effectively inhibit the formation of a gel in the gravy thereby producing an easily pourable meat-in-gravy product even when thick gravies are employed.

The acid may be added either to the gravy itself prior to mixing the gravy with the meat pieces or to the meat pieces themselves. While either method is suitable in most cases, the latter method has been found to be particularly advantageous when gravies containing milk products are used since the addition of acid to such a gravy tends to cause the milk protein to flocculate and settle out. Therefore, addition of the acid to the gravy portion of the meat-in-gravy product or to the surface of the meat after it has been processed is preferable.

Generally, any acid or acid solutions may be used to inhibit the gel-formation associated with retorted meat-in-gravy products. However, strong acids such as hydrochloric, sulfuric, nitric, and the like, when used in concentrated form, have been found to have a detrimental effect on the meat pieces which come in contact with such acids, such effect being generally in the form of rendering the meat mushy and destroying the integrity of the formed meat pieces. Sufficient dilution of these acids, however, enables their effective use.

A typical measure of the strength of acids is their ionization constant which is indicative of the degree of dissociation of the acid. Strong acids generally have ionization constants greater than 10^{-2} and, therefore, the preferred acids are those having constants not greater than about 10^{-2}, that is, weak acids. Examples of such acids are phosphoric, citric, succinic, tartaric, fumaric, adipic, acetic, malic, lactic, and the like, and mixtures thereof.

The amount of acid needed to inhibit gel formation is dependent upon the thickness of the gravy to be employed in the product, the severity of the heat treatment to which the product is to be subjected, the collagen content of the meat used, and, of course, the type acid used. Weaker acids usually require addition in greater amounts but this factor must be balanced against the flavor thresholds of the acid, i.e., the levels at which the acid imparts its own characteristic flavor.

For example, use of phosphoric acid is dictated primarily by its strength, levels greater than 3.0% causing the meat pieces to become mushy. On the other hand, acetic acid, due to its weakness as an acid, may be used at relatively high levels but the off-flavors imparted by it necessitate its use at significantly lower levels.

As a general consideration, the level of acid employed should not be so great as to significantly reduce the pH of the meat-in-gravy product since high acidity of the final product may cause overall palatability problems. Thus, the amount of acid added should not be such that the pH of the gravy or meat-in-gravy product is reduced to below about 2.5. Preferably, the pH should not be reduced below about 4.5.

Acids such as phosphoric acid are preferably added at anywhere from 0.1% by weight of the gravy mixture to 2.0% while citric acid may be added at levels from 0.5 to 3.5% subject to the considerations of strength, flavor, and pH mentioned above.

Microbial Stabilization of a Meat, Vegetable and Gravy Product

M. Kaplow and J.J. Halik; U.S. Patent 3,769,042; October 30, 1973; assigned to General Foods Corporation describe a process that is concerned with the art of stabilizing such products as meat cuts and/or plant material like beef and/or vegetables, potatoes, carrots or peas which are rendered shelf stable for non-refrigerated distribution and yet are compatibly combined with an aqueous liquid having sauce or gravy constituents which impart to the liquid desirable fat and/or thickened flavor and aroma values.

The process involves infusion of a polyhydric alcohol within a food solid matrix in any one of a variety of degrees of subdivision and the formulation of distinct aqueous liquid also containing a polyhydric alcohol, the food solid and aqueous liquid having moisture contents usually less than 40% each and having a total concentration of water soluble compounds where the two dissimilar phases are anaerobically or aerobically stable depending upon the packaging techniques intended, it being a further feature that the water activities in the food solids and liquid phases are so related one to another that they equilibrate to one another during storage and retain their microorganic stability.

A beef stew is thus formulated to contain beef chunks and whole or subdivided carrots, peas and potatoes, each of which is respectively dehydrated to a moisture content less than 50% and more ideally less than 45% through the infusion therein of a stabilizing solute containing a polyhydric alcohol such as glycerol. A "gravy" is formulated as an aqueous liquid containing a suitably emulsified fat and thickening colloid together with flavorants, colorings, spices and the like, which gravy is also of a moisture content less than 45% but has, as plasticizing solute therein, a significant level of polyhydric alcohols like glycerol serving to provide a flowable plastic or at least semiplastic fluidity under the anticipated conditions of use be they of ambient temperate climates or arctic conditions.

The respective water activities of the dehydrated food solids phase and the liquid phase will be such that migration of aqueous fluids from one phase to the other will not result in a substantial change in the relative concentration of stabilizing solutes in the respective phases. Commonly the level of the soluble solids and moisture present in the solid phase and the liquid phase will substantially approximate one another such that any moisture migration that may occur incident to storage of the packaged foodstuff will be minimal and in any event will not adversely imbalance the concentration of stabilizing solutes in the food solid phase and the liquid phase.

Generally the food solid phase will be "dehydrated" to a moisture level between 20 and 45% whereat maximum organoleptic acceptability and food solid plasticity are provided. (The term dehydrated here applies to the comparative moisture level of the food solid relative to its hydrated condition in either the pristine or cooked state.) Food solids may also be converted to a semimoist stabilized condition typically from a freeze dried state and are adjusted upwardly to a moisture content in excess of 20% by infusing the product with an aqueous stabilizing solution containing a polyhydric alcohol whereby the moisture level of the product has ultimately a moisture content between 20 and 50% and is caused to contain a level of polyhydric alcohol generally in excess of 5% of the weight of total water-soluble solids present in the product.

The aqueous liquid, be it a gravy or sauce, depending upon the condiments added thereto and the flavor intended, will commonly have a significant level of fat and thickening colloids such as starch, dextrins or flour together with seasonings, coloring, spices and the like and will be formulated to be in an essentially flowable liquid state under ambient conditions.

This aqueous phase will also be essentially plastic and to a large extent flowable or spoonable. To formulate such a stable, aqueous liquid, a significant level of polyhydric alcohol, typical of which will be glycerol, as well as salt and/or sugar compatible with flavor will be placed in solutions in the aqueous media which will generally range in moisture content from 20 to 40% content and be less than 45% by weight of the total sauce or gravy in the composite of liquid and solids as packed in ration form.

Water activity of the food solids and liquid phases will be predetermined in order that the phases will provide requisite bacteriostatic and overall microorganic stability under the anticipated conditions of treatment preparatory to packaging, during packaging and during storage. Such stability determination will be made by formulating the respective solid and liquid phases so as to provide a desired A_w, i.e., the relative humidity of a headspace atmosphere in equilibrium with the food or liquid, A_w being customarily expressed as a decimal fraction of one and the atmosphere understood to be that sensed by a hygrometer in a substantially hermetically sealed chamber.

Thus, the A_w can be determined by inserting the specimen in an air-tight jar and after storage for a suitable period of 24 hours to assure equilibrium, the relative humidity of the air or head space in the jar will be measured using a hygrometer.

Pure water has an activity of 1.0 and the water activity of bacteriologically stabilized foods is less than 0.9 of that of pure water. The water activity is, in effect, a dimensionless number equal to the ratio of the vapor pressure of water above the food to the vapor pressure of pure water both taken at the same temperature.

For most applications contemplated herein, the respective solid and liquid phases will both have A_w's of 0.60 to 0.90, the specific A_w of use being dependent on the nature of the food and liquid phase primarily. Generally, it will be preferred to formulate such phases at an A_w above 0.75 inasmuch as most foods are more flavorful and organoleptically acceptable at the higher A_w. On the other hand, as one approaches the upper part of the range, it becomes more difficult to consistently preserve the particular solid and liquid phases, and so most products will have an A_w less than about 0.85.

The A_w's to which the respective solid and liquid phases are adjusted during formulation and infusion prior to packaging will be such that upon packaging any equilibration that may take place between the respective phases due to imbalance of A_w will not detract from organoleptic acceptability and stability.

The most preferred range of A_w for the respective food phases as packaged upon achieving equilibration will be 0.80 to 0.85 with care being exercised at the upper water activity factor against possible instability. The solid and liquid phases can be separately infused and formulated to achieve the desired pasteurization or sterilization as well as A_w rectification by solute infusion.

Briefly stated, meat particles in the form of cuts or chunks, and vegetable pieces, can be microorganically stabilized by infusion with solutes by immersion in a measured excess of an aqueous stabilizing solution and the excess of spent infusion solution can be retained after infusing the solids phase (pieces of meat and/or vegetables) to form a stabilized gravy or sauce mixed with and surrounding the solids phase provided the water activity of the infused solids phase is substantially the same as that of the resultant excess infusion solution (sauce or gravy) and both water activities are within the range of 0.6 to 0.9.

It has been found that if the water activities of the solids phase and liquid phase are substantially in equilibrium, there will be no adverse imbalance of stabilizing solutes during storage and the mixture, as a whole, will remain stable. Thus, it is possible to have any reasonable proportion of gravy with relation to amount of solids without the danger of excessive moisture transfer from the gravy to solids phase and the solids phase, therefore, will retain its desirable texture and will not become unduly soggy or mushy—in effect, both microorganic stability and physical stability are realized in both physical phases of the food product.

Essentially, the two phases will retain different total water contents when combined and will retain their respective textures brought about by their individual moisture levels if the water activities of the solids phase and the liquid phase are in substantial equilibrium.

The process is applicable to the formulation of such products as beef, lamb and meat, and vegetable stews generally as well as casserole preparations having meat and/or fish in admixture with vegetables and grains such as rice and/or pasta foods such as noodles and macaroni in various shapes.

Customarily, it is practical to pasteurize the food solids phase by infusion at an elevated temperature, in excess of 160°F, the pasteurization being carried out sufficiently to at least kill any pathogens or inactivate enzymes; a common range of immersion heating temperatures will be 180° to 210°F for 15 to 25 minutes depending upon desired product texture of the food solids phase.

As distinguished from canned stew and like preparations, these compositions are intended to be packaged without commercial sterilization and advantageously may be cooled to sub-pasteurization temperatures, i.e., below 180°F, prior to packaging, thereby allowing greater manufacturing flexibility and a less expensive substantially nonhermetic package. On the other hand, the process may be practiced to advantage by use of hermetic anaerobic packaging, the food solid and liquid phases being at sub-pasteurization temperatures and the composition being thereby preserved in an oxygen-free atmosphere whereby rancidity, color changes and light decomposition are avoided, or at least reduced.

In all of the foregoing packaging applications, by virtue of the built-in microbial stability, leaks, pinholes or minor imperfections in packaging material, such as may be caused in handling, will not give rise to spoilage. The ration, of course, will be of lighter weight, not only due to the concentration of the foods per se, but also due to use of lighter packaging materials such as polyethylene coated foil and the like.

Example: A room temperature shelf-stable intermediate moisture beef stew with gravy was prepared by this method by formulating the solids phase from the following individual constituents (before infusion).

Ingredient*	Grams
Lean chuck beef	150
Potatoes	200
Carrots	75
Peas	75

*Subdivided into bite-size pieces.

The liquid phase (before infusion) was formulated as follows.

Ingredient	Grams
Glycerol	150
Beef soup base*	50
Salt	20
Sugar	37.5
Potassium sorbate	2.2

*A blend of salt (37%); vegetable protein (24.5%); cottonseed oil (13%); sugar (11%) and about 15% of suitable beef flavoring and coloring ingredients.

The liquid phase ingredients were thoroughly blended together to form the infusing solution for the particulates. The particulates of meat and vegetables were then added to the liquid phase and the mixture was simmered in a double boiler cooking vessel for 30 minutes to cook and infuse the particulates. Upon cooling, the mixture was determined to comprise a stew and gravy of the following constituents (particulates infused with stabilizing solutes).

Ingredient	Grams	Weight Percent	Moisture
Lean chuck beef	104	15.4	40.0
Potatoes	231	34.2	40.0
Carrots	61	9.0	44.0
Peas	61	9.0	35.0
Gravy	220	32.4	49.0

The finished beef stew with gravy product was determined to have an A_w of 0.81—a value indicative of room temperature shelf stability and resistance to microbiological spoilage.

The stew with gravy is a spoonable plastic aggregation which can be stored as such under ambient room temperatures preparatory to packaging or may be packaged directly from the mixer using aerobic, sub-pasteurization temperatures. Preferably, the stew with gravy will be cold packed in a flexible pouch and heat-sealed in a gaseous nitrogen atmosphere. These package preparations offer a microbial stability for all of the anticipated ration requirements therefor.

This, and similar products, such as lamb stew, chicken a la king, etc., can be formulated to be eaten as is or with additional water. The preparations can be eaten cold as well as warm. The products can be eaten under a range of storage temperatures and will be admirably suited to consumption under arctic conditions as well as temperate climates. The compositions essentially withstand storage with no significant changes in their organoleptic values such as sauce or gravy stability or color or flavor changes in the food solids.

DAIRY PRODUCTS

Apparatus for Making Expanded Dairy Item

The simplest apparatuses for expanding by the dissolution of gas are pressurized containers of the aerosol bomb type, provided with a valve, and adapted to produce a whipped cream, for example. The pressures used are relatively low, of the order of 5 to 7 bars, and it is therefore preferred to use gases having a high solubility in water, such for example as N_2O, CO_2, or Freons. The expanded products obtained must then be promptly consumed, because a gas having a high solubility in water diffuses in air at atmospheric pressure, which results in contraction of the product within a few hours.

All the known devices which permit the dissolution of gases having a low solubility have the major disadvantage of being incapable of producing an expanded product of constant quality. The expansion ratio varies very rapidly within a broad range. In effect, it is impossible to determine exactly the quantity of gas to be introduced into the product, and experience shows that a large excess of gas does not produce the result theoretically expected, that is to say a stable expansion ratio.

The expansion ratio, which is defined as the ratio of the volume of the expanded product to the volume of the liquid product before expansion, depends on the temperature, on the pressure, and on the percentage of dissolution of gas in the liquid product. In the known expansion devices, it is not possible to readily control these different parameters to obtain a constant expansion ratio. The difficulty is increased by the fact that certain of the products used contain stabilizers which result in a large variation in viscosity in response to changes in temperature. The expansion ratio obtained also varies with this variation in viscosity since it depends on the pressure in the mixing chamber which is a function of the pressure drop.

The device described by *D. Carasso; U.S. Patent 3,896,716; July 29, 1975; assigned to Compagnie Gervais-Danone, France* makes it possible to overcome these disadvantages and obtain a product, the expansion ratio of which remains constant within 10% of a desired ratio, which may reach and even exceed 3 to 1, and which has good organoleptic properties, by utilizing an apparatus of simple construction and reliable operation. The apparatus also has the advantage of being very easy to clean and maintain under excellent hygienic conditions.

The apparatus for expansion by dissolving gas at high pressure comprises essentially in combination a hopper for introducing the product while warm, a high pressure, which preferably delivers metered quantities of material, a smooth tube of small diameter and substantial length, which may be cooled, and a pressure regulating valve automatically controlled by a pressure detector positioned upstream of a nozzle for injecting gas under pressure.

The gases used in the apparatus are gases having a very low solubility in water, preferably less than 20 cm^3/100 ml of water at $0°C$, so as to avoid contraction of the product at atmospheric pressure due to diffusion of gas into the air. Suitable gases are, for example, nitrogen, air, and argon. In order to obtain a consistent expansion ratio, it is first necessary to ensure that the proportion of gas injected into the liquid product is constant if the output of the product does not vary, as is the case if a metered-volume pump is used. In the apparatus the gas is injected at a pressure greater than the pressure in the liquid and at the output of the metered-volume pump. An essential characteristic of the apparatus consists of maintaining the pressure difference between the gas and the liquid constant by means of a pressure regulating valve at the output of the apparatus controlled by a detector positioned at the outlet of the metered-volume pump and upstream of the gas injection nozzle. In this manner the inevitable variations in temperature and viscosity inside the tube do not influence the expansion ratio of the product obtained at the output of the apparatus.

The dissolution of the gas at high pressure in the liquid product is obtained as the result of both a suitable time during which the product and the gas remain in the tube and a substantial agitation created by the turbulence of the two-phase flow. According to an important characteristic of the process, the length of the tube and the volume of flow of the metered-volume pump are such that the time during which the product remains in the tube is at least one second.

It is advantageous to use a tube of small diameter and serpentine shape positioned in a chamber constituting a heat exchanger. In a preferred embodiment, the product is introduced at high temperature which makes it possible to maintain excellent hygiene while decreasing its viscosity, which increases the turbulence.

It is nevertheless desirable to cool the product before the decrease in pressure which results in the expansion itself. In effect, if the product is not cooled, the texture obtained will be poor and it will have the appearance of a rigid gel. The cold expansion, on the contrary, makes it possible to obtain a creamy texture, which is not gellified. In this embodiment, water at low temperature is circulated in the heat exchanger so that the temperature of the product at its outlet may be at most 25°C and preferably less than 10°C.

In another embodiment, the serpentine tube extends through two successive heat exchangers, which makes it possible to provide supplementary heating to the pasteurization temperature in the upstream heat exchanger and cooling in the downstream heat exchanger. This makes it possible to pasteurize at the same time that the expansion is carried out. In order to obtain a creamy texture the cooling must be such that the temperature of the product at the outlet is not in excess of 25°C and preferably less than 10°C.

Example: The dairy product introduced through the metered-volume pump is a mixture containing 76 parts of a sterilized milk having a fat content of 113 grams per liter, 13.8 parts of saccharose, 7.1 parts of glucose, 1 part of starch, 0.05 part of a gum or hydrophilic colloidal stabilizer, 0.15 part of carraghenates, 0.3 part of gelatin, 1.2 part of liquid coffee extract, and 0.3 part of soluble powdered coffee extract.

The pressure of the dairy product at the outlet of the metered-volume pump is 80 bars. Nitrogen at a pressure of 95 bars is injected into the dairy product. The diameter of the tube in which the gas is dissolved is 10 mm and the total length of the developed serpentine is 80 meters. The rate of flow of the metered-volume pump is 400 liters per hour. The time the product and the gas remain in the serpentine is thus one minute.

The heat exchanger is divided into two parts. The first or upstream heat exchanger is cooled by water and the second or downstream heat exchanger is cooled by ice water. The temperature conditions are shown below.

	°C
Temperature produced:	
Entrance first heat exchanger	70
Outlet first heat exchanger	40
Inlet second heat exchanger	40
Outlet second heat exchanger	8
Water Temperature:	
Inlet first heat exchanger	20
Outlet first heat exchanger	35
Inlet second heat exchanger	1.5
Outlet second heat exchanger	6

The pressure of the product at the outlet of the second heat exchanger is 60 bars. The expansion ratio of the product is between 1.8 and 1.9 to 1. After the expansion, the product is received in the hopper of a treatment machine. The resulting product has a creamy texture and the expansion ratio is very stable. The product may be frozen and unfrozen several times without impairing its organoleptic properties or its initial structure, especially without contraction, without substantial syneresis, and without any formation of ice crystals of substantial size, but only a very fine crystallization. This product may also be stored without loss of these qualities for 8 to 10 days at a temperature of 4° to 8°C.

Snack Size Extruded Cheese Item

H.G. Foster, Jr. and C.D. Frederick; U.S. Patent 3,761,284; September 25, 1973; assigned to Swift & Company describe a method for the continuous preparation of a snack food item of cheese in a snack size form.

In the process a heated plastic cheese formulation is evenly cooled under a high pressure of 165 to 195 psig, with agitation, until the product is sufficiently self-sustaining throughout to maintain shape and form. The cooled mass is then extruded through an orifice of up to 2 inches in size, to form a solid compact bar of product having a corresponding cross section or diameter.

Finally, the bar of product is cut into snack size pieces which are consumable in one or a few bites. The resulting snack size pieces of product are of a compact, homogeneous composition and are cooled evenly throughout. Each piece exhibits a smooth, glossy surface which is neat to the touch.

A cheese product is initially prepared by heating it at a temperature somewhat below the boiling point of water to provide a plastic or semiplastic condition which can be pumped and extruded. Usually the cheese is initially heated to 155° to 165°F which has been generally recognized to be a temperature sufficient to effect the pasteurization thereof. However, the process can be performed by utilizing cheese which has been heated to a lesser temperature, so long as the heating is sufficient to provide a plastic condition to the product.

The initially heated plastic cheese is first rapidly and evenly cooled or chilled, with agitation, under a pressure of 165 to 195 psig to sufficiently solidify the mass throughout to a self-sustaining condition. In this self-sustaining condition, the cheese is sufficiently solid and evenly cooled throughout to maintain shape and form but is still sufficiently plastic to permit the extrusion. The desired self-sustaining condition can be provided by rapidly and evenly cooling the heated plastic mass under the above conditions until the product reaches 75° to 80°F. If the plastic cheese mass is cooled to a temperature above about 85°F it is not sufficiently self-sustaining and upon subsequent extrusion, the resultant product is undesirably mushy and exhibits a separation of butter fat from the protein of the mass. Similarly, if the product is cooled to a temperature below about 70°F, the resultant extruded product is undesirably grainy and does not have the desired compacted homogeneous texture.

It is most critical to rapidly and evenly cool the initially heated plastic cheese mass to the sufficiently solid self-sustaining condition under a high pressure of about 165 to 195 psig so as to obtain a product of satisfactory density and homogeneous texture. It has been found that if the plastic mass is cooled to the preferred temperature range while subjected to a pressure below 165 psig, it is most difficult to subsequently extrude the self-sustaining mass through an orifice having a size sufficiently small to provide a continuously solid bar of product which can be cut into bite size pieces. The resultant extruded product has a very low density, and it is most difficult to subsequently cut into individual snack size pieces without malformation thereof.

Furthermore, if the plastic cheese mass is cooled to within the preferred temperature range while subjected to a pressure above about 195 psig the product tends to be too compacted which in turn is very difficult to extrude. On the other hand, when the heated plastic cheese mass is rapidly and evenly cooled under the above described range of pressure, the self-sustaining mass can be extruded to form a thin bar of product having an even distribution of butterfat therethrough and is sufficiently compacted and evenly cooled throughout to withstand subsequent cutting and packaging without malformation.

It is also essential to simultaneously agitate the initially heated plastic cheese mass as it is being cooled under the above described pressure. The simultaneous agitation during cooling provides an even reduction of temperature throughout the entire mass of product so that when the product is further processed, there is no malformation thereof due to temperature variations within the product.

Moreover, the simultaneous agitation mixes the cheese formulation during cooling which retards or inhibits the separation of butterfat globules from the protein mass and reduces the processing time required to cool the heated plastic product evenly throughout to within the desired temperature range.

After the cheese product has been sufficiently cooled to provide a self-sustaining condition throughout it is extruded through an orifice to form a continuous compacted bar of product. The cheese product may be extruded through an orifice of any desired shape such as circular, square, etc. However, in order to produce the desired snack or bite size pieces it must be extruded through a small orifice of up to about 2 inches in size. This forms a bar of product having a corresponding cross section size which is sufficiently small to provide the snack or bite size pieces of product when cut. Preferably, the cheese mass is extruded through an orifice of ¼ to 1½ inches in size.

The extruded compacted bar of product is then cut to any desired length to form snack size pieces. Preferably, the bar of product is cut into bite size pieces which are small enough to be consumed in a few bites, for example, ½ to 1½ inches in length.

The individual snack size pieces can then be packaged in any known manner. In view of the size of each particular snack size piece of product, it is desirable to package a plurality of pieces in a single package, to provide convenience to the consumer. The snack size pieces of product are more easily packaged, either by hand or by machinery, if after the cutting operation the pieces are tempered to reduce their temperature.

As was pointed out hereinabove, the processed cheese product is preferably cooled to 70° to 85°F. The product will maintain its shape within this temperature range but is still somewhat soft and can be deformed by excessive handling. Hence, it is preferable to temper the product, such as by subjecting it to a blast of chilled air, to further reduce the temperature approximately 1° to 10°F prior to packaging.

Superior results can be obtained by pumping the initially heated plastic cheese product through appropriate conduits into a scraped-surface heat exchange device and extruding the cooled product through a valve-controlled orifice.

When a heated plastic cheese mass is pumped into such a scraped-surface heat exchange device it is rapidly cooled as it contacts the chilled inner surface of the inner tube. The axially rotating scraping means simultaneously scrapes the cooled product from the chilled inner surface and exposes more product thereto. This continuous mixing and agitation subjects the entire mass to the chilled inner surface which results in an even reduction of temperature throughout the product.

The use of such a scraped-surface heat exchange device in combination with a valve-controlled orifice provides the capability of rapidly and evenly cooling the plastic cheese mass to the desired temperature under controlled pressure. Moreover, it provides the capability of cooling and extruding the cheese product in a continuous manner at high rates and at a cost which is economically feasible.

Any type of cheese or any blend of a variety of cheeses which can be melted to a plastic or semiplastic condition sufficiently to be extruded can be utilized. However, a final product having superior texture and appearance characteristics is obtained by utilizing a cheese formulation which can be classified as either a pasteurized process cheese, pasteurized process cheese food or a pasteurized cheese spread. Preferably, a cheese formulation having an analysis of 40 to 44% moisture, 23 to 30% fat and a pH of about 5.0 to 6.2 is preferred.

Example: A process cheese food formulation was first prepared comprising the following ingredients and amounts:

Swiss cheese (mellow bodied)	130 lb
Low moisture cheddar cheese (firm bodied—barrel curd)	225 lb
Provolone cheese (mellow bodied)	120 lb
Whey powder	9 lb
Skim milk powder	9 lb

(continued)

Sodium citrate (emulsifying salt)	17 lb
Salt	9 lb
Water (moisture control)	45 lb
Marchall #3—annatto color (control color preference)	300 cc

The Swiss and provolone cheese curds were selected to give the blend elasticity to enable the formulation to be compacted while being subjected to pressure. The low moisture cheddar was added to give the blend firmness. The moisture content of the low moisture cheddar cheese was within the range of 36.0 to 37.0% and was less than one week old. The various cheese curds were ground and blended with the other ingredients, whey powder, emulsifier, salt, water, etc.

The mixture was charged into a steam jacketed kettle, heated to 160°F and held to effect the pasteurization thereof. The heated plastic cheese mass was then dumped into a hopper and pumped by means of a variable speed pump through appropriate conduits into a scraped-surface heat exchange device. As the plastic cheese formulation passed through the heat exchange device, it was rapidly and evenly cooled under a pressure of 185 psig to a self-sustaining condition throughout having a temperature of 78° to 80°F. While the plastic cheese product was being cooled to the desired self-sustaining condition, it was simultaneously agitated by an independently driven scraping means which rotated axially within the heat exchange device.

The cheese was then extruded through a valve-controlled orifice of ½ inch diameter at the rate of 250 lb per hour to form a continuous, compact bar of product having a corresponding cross section size. A rotating knife cut the elongated bar into individual snack size pieces of about 1½ inches in length.

The individual pieces of product had an internal and external temperature of 78° to 80°F. The pieces then passed through a blast chill unit, whereby the temperature of each was reduced approximately 5°F.

Finally, a plurality of pieces were stacked in a package and wrapped. Each individual snack size piece had a homogeneous, compacted texture and exhibited no signs of a separation of butterfat globules from the protein mass thereof. The pieces had a flavor substantially similar to cheddar cheese and had an average analysis of 42% moisture and 24% fat.

Shelf Stable Low-Fat Biologically Fermented Dairy Product

R.L. Pavey and P.E. Mone; U.S. Patent 3,969,534; July 13, 1976; assigned to Swift & Company describe a method of preparing biologically fermented dairy products which possess all of the essential natural characteristics of body, texture, flavor and color exhibited by biologically fermented dairy products as they are prepared by prior art natural fermentation processes, yet are susceptible to being containerized without curd and whey separation, at the same time exhibiting a nonrefrigerated shelf life of at least 6 months before the development of either appreciable syneresis or bacterial contamination. Such shelf-stable cultured dairy or low-fat dairy products include yoghurt, buttermilk, dairy dips, and dairy spreads.

In the process, a pasteurized, low-fat dairy base is biologically fermented, to which is added a stabilizer. Next a syneresis step is accomplished by heating at a temperature high enough to promote "wheying off," but low enough to be below the pasteurization temperature of the particular dairy product. A homogenization step follows. This combination of a syneresis step followed by a homogenization step prevents wheying off in the final product. The product is then pasteurized.

In further detail, the low-fat dairy base contains a butterfat level of 0 to 5% by weight. The dairy base can be prepared from reconstituted nonfat milk solids plus water, or nonfat milk solids plus water and cream (having about a 36% butterfat content), or whole milk (containing about 3.5% butterfat content) or whole milk plus cream.

The culture utilized to naturally ferment the dairy base is one that is commercially available and suitable for the type of nonfat dairy product to be formed. For example, one especially suitable for formation of a yoghurt-type product is a culture of concentrated selected strains of lactic acid producing dairy bacteria, wherein the active organisms are *Lactobacillus bulgaricus* and *Streptococcus thermophilus*. The amount of culture utilized is on the order of 1 ml of culture per 10 to 35 pounds of completed product.

The stabilizer can be an edible starch in the amount of 0.1 to 3.0% by weight of the dairy base being produced. The starch must be edible and suitable for use at a low pH. Found to be especially suitable are starches that are modified waxy maizes that are smooth, nongelling and of bland flavor. A preferred starch has a pH of 5.8, a midpoint gelatinization temperature of 155°F, and a moisture content of 10%. Also suitable are food starches refined from tapioca. One such starch has a pH of about 6.0 and a moisture content of about 13%. The starches should be resistant to relatively high temperatures and acid conditions. If too great a quantity of starch is utilized, the final product will exhibit an excessively heavy body. Also, such a product would tend to leave residual material in one's mouth after it is eaten.

In addition to the starch stabilizer, a gelatin stabilizer may optionally also be included in the dairy base in the approximate range of 0 to 1.5% by weight of the dairy base being produced. Should the amount of gelatin be too high, the final product will exhibit an undesirable consistency. For example, in the case of yoghurt, a product having too great a gelatin content will exhibit excessive shine and a set that is too rigid. A gelatin has large, randomly coiled molecules of about 18 different amino acids joined together by amide linkages in long molecular chains. A gelatin found to be particularly satisfactory is one that has a Bloom index of 275.

If the product is flavored, it can contain from 5 to 25% by weight of one or more of a flavoring base, a fruit, a fruit base, a sweetener, a coloring agent, or any other food component as desired and recognized as conventionally compatible with such product.

The low-fat dairy product is of the type that is produced by natural biological fermentation. The final product has substantially the characteristics of a cultured low-fat dairy product that is freshly produced and distributed under refrigeration. Body, color, flavor and texture characteristics of this product are very similar to those of the freshly produced, refrigeration-distributed product. The product has exceptional consistency of such physical attributes as body, texture, flavor and appearance. It has a butterfat content of not greater than about 0.5% by weight, an edible starch stabilizer content of 0.1 to 3.0% by weight, an optional additional stabilizer of gelatin from 0 to 1.5% by weight, optional additionally added flavoring agents of 0 to 25% by weight, a final pH of 4.5 or lower, and is packaged in hermetically sealed containers.

In the process, the low-fat (about 0 to 5% butterfat content) milk base, in a liquid state, is mixed through a conventional homogenizer, while being careful to insure that the temperature of the milk base at no time exceeds 185°F. The homogenized base is pasteurized, with mixing, in a conventional manner, the pasteurization being sufficient to remove all bacteria that would interfere with the subsequent culture development. A pasteurization temperature of 180° to 185°F for approximately 30 minutes should be adequate.

The milk base is cooled to the incubation temperature appropriate for the type of product being prepared and the culture being used. For example, when yoghurt is prepared with a conventional yoghurt culture, the inoculation temperature is 108° to 110°F. A culture is added to the cooled milk base and incubated at the incubation temperature until an acid level of approximately 0.85% is attained. This acid level should be reached during an incubation time of roughly 4 hours.

After the incubation period, the starch stabilizer is added. The starch can be added as a fluid slurry to achieve more uniform distribution of the starch and thus a more uniform end product. Such a slurry would contain roughly 1½ parts by weight of water or whole milk for each part by weight of starch.

The gelatin which may be added as an additional stabilizer may also be added in fluid form to enhance the uniformity of the product, and would be added as a gelatin solution containing roughly 1½ parts by weight of water or whole milk for each 0.3 part by weight of gelatin.

The cultured milk base and stabilizer or stabilizers are mixed for a short period of time on the order of 5 minutes to achieve a relatively uniform consistency. The mixture is then heated to a temperature range of 100° to 150°F. It is a critical feature that the temperature be low enough to avoid setting of the starch and pasteurization of the product at this time, while at the same time being high enough to achieve syneresis, or separation of curd and whey. The exact temperature will depend upon the type of product being prepared and the particular starch utilized. For example, when preparing a yoghurt base including a modified waxy maize starch, the preferred syneresis temperature is about 125°F.

After the syneresis step, the cultured milk base and stabilizer mixture is homogenized through a conventional homogenizer, the mixture being kept at a temperature approximating the syneresis temperature. The homogenizer should be run within the range of 500 to 2,000 psi, an especially acceptable setting getting about 1,000 psi. During this homogenization step, the product having "wheyed off" through the syneresis step, is restructured to a smooth consistency. Since the syneresis step is carried out at a temperature sufficient to cause extensive coagulation or curd and whey separation and the thus coagulated product is then restructured by homogenization, coagulation or curd and whey separation will not recur during the subsequent pasteurization of the final containerized product.

If desired, the suitable flavoring agents, may be added with mixing for 3 to

10 minutes. The acidity of the product is then determined. If the pH is found to be greater than about 4.5, then a weak acid such as citric acid or malic acid is added. The amount of acid, if any, needed to adequately lower the pH will vary with the product being made, particularly because most of the flavorings that might have been added would themselves be acidic. Should the pH be found to be too high at this stage, the addition of about 0.05 to 1.0% by weight of, say, citric acid should adjust the pH to 4.5 or lower.

At this point in the process, since the starch has not yet been set, the product is flowable and still pumpable through conventional container filling apparatus to hermetically package the product with such apparatus. A variety of conventional packaging apparatus and methods can be employed.

Example: A yoghurt base was first prepared. The following percentages are by weight and are based upon the total composition of the yoghurt base. Water (77.9%) was placed in a steam-heated, water-jacketed vat equipped with baffles and a variable speed agitator. With continuous mechanical mixing, 12.3% nonfat milk solids were added to the water and mixed until the nonfat milk solids were completely dissolved to form a liquid skim milk.

It was necessary to allow sufficient headspace in the vat for foam developed while reconstituting the nonfat milk solids. With continuous mixing of this skim milk, 3.0% cream (containing 36% butterfat) was added. The water in the jacket was heated until the temperature of the skim milk-cream mix reached between 130° to 150°F. The mix was pumped from the mixer through a homogenizer set for single stage at 1,000 psi and then pumped back into the vat until the entire volume had been homogenized.

During this homogenization process, the product temperature was kept at 185°F or lower. The homogenization time was approximately 30 minutes. The temperature of the product was maintained at 180° to 185°F for 30 minutes so as to accomplish sufficient pasteurization to remove all bacteria. During the pasteurization, the vat was kept covered. The pasteurized mix was then lowered to a temperature of about 108°F. During this cooling process, slow mixing was maintained and the vat was kept covered. The mixing speed was then increased, and 1 ml of yoghurt culture per 11 pounds of yoghurt product was slowly added and thoroughly distributed throughout the mix.

The active organisms in the culture were *Lactobacillus bulgaricus* and *Streptococcus thermophilus.* After the culture was added, mixing was discontinued, and the covered product was incubated at 108° to 110°F. After about 4 hours an acidity test was run, the acidity being 0.85%.

A slurry of 3.0% water and 2.0% modified waxy maize starch was prepared. Also prepared was a solution of 1.5% water and 0.3% gelatin. The incubated mix was uncovered and mechanically mixed at slow speed, while adding the starch slurry and the gelatin solution. Uniform distribution of the total mix was accomplished after a mixing time of approximately 5 minutes. During this mixing, heating to effect a temperature rise was begun. The mix was heated to approximately 125°F, until appreciable syneresis was observed. After syneresis, the yoghurt base was pumped through the homogenizer set for single stage at 1,000 psi. The yoghurt base thus prepared had a calculated butterfat level of 1.17%.

A plain yoghurt product was then prepared, utilizing the yoghurt base just prepared. The following percentages expressed in this example are by weight based on the total composition of the final yoghurt product. A quantity of 93.55% of the yoghurt base was mixed for about 5 minutes in a mixing vat with 6.25% sucrose and 0.20% citric acid to form a flowable plain yoghurt dairy mixture.

The mixture was pumped from the mixing vat into a vacuum chamber to deaerate in excess of 21 inches of mercury. The deaerated mixture was pumped to a conventional automatic filling machine. Six ounce, 208 x 208 containers were filled under a minimum vacuum of 15 inches of mercury, the residual vacuum in each container being about 10 inches of mercury. The thus sealed cans were processed in a water bath of about 180°F for at least 25 minutes. The heating time was sufficient to effect setting of the starch and pasteurization of each of the plain yoghurt products. The containers were cooled to at least 80°F to complete setting to accomplish the desired consistency of the yoghurt. The final containerized product was stored at room temperature and exhibited acceptable stability 6 months later.

FOOD BARS

NUTRITIONALLY ORIENTED FOOD BARS

Meat and Vegetable Sticks ("Junior" Food)

R.H. Maher and F.W. Billerbeck; U.S. Patent 3,903,313; September 2, 1975; assigned to Gerber Products Company describe a method by which a palatable meat and vegetable combination stick of a desirable consistency and stability is provided. In carrying out the process, the raw meat is ground to a desired size and consistency. If frozen meat is employed, the temperature is raised above freezing, dry ingredients added other than the vegetables, such as spices, emulsifiers, food supplements, antioxidants, and the like, and the mixture blended to obtain the desired homogeneity. The mixture is then minced, resulting in emulsification of the meat.

The emulsified meat composition is then combined, preferably in an amount of from 51 to 60 weight percent of total ingredients, with the dehydrated vegetables, preferably in an amount of from 8 to 15 weight percent of the total ingredients, the preferred amount of from 25 to 45 weight percent of the total ingredients of water added, and the mixture blended with or without a mild vacuum. The substantially homogeneous mixture is then stuffed into an inert tubular casing and smoked and cooked under controlled temperature and moisture conditions. After the desired degree of protein coagulation in smoking and cooking has occurred, the casing is removed and the tubular shaped composition cut or linked to the desired size, sterilized and packaged in a broth medium.

The particle size for the vegetables will generally range from about U.S.S. No. 5 to No. 50, more usually from about U.S.S. No. 6 to No. 40. That is, greater than 80 weight percent, more usually greater than about 90 weight percent of the vegetable particles will pass through the larger openings and be retained by the sieve having the smaller openings. The moisture content of the particles (Method C-1.41) will generally be less than 15 weight percent, preferably less than about 12 weight percent and usually greater than about 5 weight percent.

Example: The following ingredients were used in the process.

Ingredients	Amount, lb
Meat	
Beef	25.01
Pork	22.90
Turkey	6.00
Vegetables	
Potato granules	5.00
Carrot granules	2.50
Peas, crushed	2.00
Water	30.39
Salt	1.50
Calcium reduced dry skim milk	3.50
Hydrolyzed vegetable protein	1.00
Spices	0.20

The process was carried out as follows. The frozen meat was ground through 3/8 inch orifices. After grinding, the temperature was checked to insure that the meat was at least at 35°F and water added as required. The dry ingredients other than the vegetables were then added, and about 10 to 15 weight percent of the total water to be added introduced and the mixture blended for about 6 minutes. The comminuted meat composition was then transferred to a Mince Master and minced first through a 2.5 mm plate, followed by mincing through a 1.7 mm plate. During the process, the temperature is maintained below about 55°F.

The minced meat composition was then transferred to a blender, the potatoes, carrots, peas and balance of water added and the mixture mixed for 5 minutes under a 5 inch vacuum (vacuum may be omitted). The substantially homogeneous meat-vegetable composition was then stuffed into a conventional nonedible cellulose casing of about 15 to 17 mm diameter and 95 inches long.

A smokehouse equipped for liquid smoke use was preheated to 110°F with the dampers open. The meat links were introduced into the smokehouse, the dampers closed, and the liquid smoke atomized and held for 10 minutes. About 1.5 ounces of liquid smoke was employed per 100 pounds of product. The following heat and moisture schedule was then followed.

| Time, minutes | Temperature, °F | | Dampers |
	Dry Bulb	Wet Bulb	
5	120	–	Closed
20	130	110	Closed
30	140	120	3/4 open
10	155	130	3/4 open
5	170	150	1/4 open

After the cycle of heating was concluded, the links were cooled with water by showering to 90°F. After holding overnight at 30°F the casing was peeled and the tubes cut into 2 1/4 inch sticks. Seven sticks were packed in a jar and broth having 0.74 weight percent protein was introduced into the jar to allow for 10/32 inch head space. The jars were retorted for 40 minutes at 240°F, (internal temperature, 80° to 120°F). The resulting meat and vegetable sticks have desired uniform consistency and are highly palatable. The sticks provide a convenient source of a high protein food in edible form which can be desirably eaten by young children with their hands. The process provides easy processing and handling, retains the moisture content of the food, giving the sticks a desirable texture, and provides for completion of rehydration during the cooking of the meat and sterilization. Upon storage in water or broth, the meat sticks retain their consistency and structural integrity, so as to minimize or totally avoid the presence of an unsightly precipitate at the bottom of the container.

Granola Product

V.H. Ode; U.S. Patent 3,903,308; September 2, 1975 prepares a ready-to-eat food unit containing a major portion of coarse particles of toasted organically grown grain bound into a coherent unit by a binder consisting of a sweetened, low moisture whole milk product. The food unit is readily prepared by baking the granola-milk product and the finished unit is characterized by a chewy texture and a pleasing taste. The toasted grains may include minor portions of natural foods such as dates, coconut and the like. The food unit has an outstandingly good shelf life.

The toasted cereal product is a granola cereal product comprising whole grains or coarse particles of toasted grains such as oats, wheat, barley, rye, rice, corn and millet. These cereals, which are used alone or in a variety of combinations, are prepared by toasting or roasting the grains in an edible unsaturated oil such as soy oil. The cereal used is characterized as whole grains or coarse particles of whole grain cereal which retain their natural texture. Other natural foods such as flaked or shredded coconut, chopped walnuts, sunflower seeds, wheat germ, soy meal, almonds, and dates may be added to provide a variety of granola cereal products which are characterized as chewy, ready-to-eat granola cereal products.

The milk product portion of the food bar comprises a sweetened concentrated milk product which is low in moisture content. It is prepared by evaporating whole milk to remove approximately 60% of the moisture content of the whole milk. The final moisture content of the milk concentrate is approximately 30 to 50% of the total product. Honey, molasses or sugar is added as a sweetening and preservative agent and comprises between about 10 and 40% by weight of the concentrated milk product. The remaining components comprise 8 to 11% by weight of fat and nonfat milk solids ranging from 2 to 20% by weight of the product.

The granola cereal product, including any of the additive fruit and nut products and condensed milk are combined in proportions of about 4 parts by volume of granola cereal and one part by volume of condensed milk. The combination is effected by spreading the cereal in a substantially even layer in a suitable baking pan and applying the condensed milk evenly over the cereal layer. The condensed milk may be applied in any suitable manner such as by pouring or spraying the condensed milk substantially evenly over the cereal layer. As an alternative, however, the cereal and condensed milk can be premixed prior to placing the mixture in a suitable baking pan.

The toasted cereal-condensed milk combination is baked in an oven at approximately 350°F for 13 to 15 minutes to form the mixture into a coherent unit. Following baking and cooling the coherent unit may be cut into smaller bars for convenience in packaging and for ease in consumption. The finished food bar exhibits sufficient internal strength to enable it to be readily packaged and to withstand ordinary handling encountered in the store and at home. The moisture content of the finished unit is substantially low, on the order of 4% moisture. The finished unit has a pleasing taste and a chewy texture which is believed to be attributable to the texture of the toasted granola product and the fat and sugar contents of the condensed milk.

This food unit is preferably utilized as a ready-to-eat breakfast product which can be eaten as is without the necessity of the addition of milk or cream and sugar. Nutritionally the food unit provides the same nutrition that would be obtained by eating a bowl of the toasted cereal product with cream and sugar added. The food unit can be employed as a confectionary or candy substitute which can both satisfy the craving for sweets and serve as a valuable adjunct to the daily nutritional intake of an individual.

Example: To three parts of a toasted honey date granola product comprising rolled oats, honey dates and wheat germ toasted in soy oil were added one-half part chopped walnuts and one-half part shredded coconut. The ingredients were well blended to ensure good mixing of the walnuts and shredded coconut with the toasted cereal product.

The mixture was spread on a baking pan, which had been lightly coated with margarine as a release agent to form a granola layer having the thickness of about one-half inch. One part of sweetened condensed milk was evenly distributed over the cereal layer. The condensed milk had the following analysis:

	Percent
Total solids	68.71
Total carbohydrates	48.45
Fat	11.38
Protein	7.62
Moisture	31.29
Ash	1.26

Specific gravity, 1.294

The condensed milk worked its way substantially through the cereal layer, through the intricacies between the cereal particles. After distributing the condensed milk over the cereal layer, the milk-cereal combination was baked at 350°F for 13 to 15 minutes, removed from the oven, and allowed to cool. After cooling, the coherent unit in the baking pan was cut into convenient size bars which were ready to eat.

The bars thus produced were coherent and could be readily handled without crumbling or otherwise disintegrating. The bars had a pleasant and satisfying flavor and a chewy texture. The cereal portion of the food composition retained its substantially firm texture and was neither brittle nor mushy.

Balanced Diet Product

B.L. Brooking and W.F. Wright; U.S. Patent 3,851,083; November 26, 1974; assigned to The Pillsbury Company provide a method of forming a solid, flexible, water-dispersible, unitary food piece consisting essentially of an external phase and an internal phase, the external phase comprising a homogeneous dispersion of a hydrophilic film former, an edible humectant which has a boiling point and decomposition temperature in excess of 300°F in an amount ranging from about 1 to 70 parts by weight humectant for each 10 parts by weight hydrophilic film former and water in an amount of 1 to about 30 parts by weight water for each 10 parts by weight hydrophilic film former, the internal phase comprising edible fat globules. The fat globules are preencapsulated within a shell of a hardened hydrophilic film former. Additional fat globules (free fat) are dispersed in and encapsulated within a mixture of hydrophilic film former and water. The total fat content is present in an amount ranging from about 150 to 1 part by weight fat for each 10 parts by weight hydrophilic film former.

The fat globules are preencapsulated within a coating of a hardened hydrophilic film former. Additional fat globules (free fat) are dispersed in and encapsulated within a mixture of unhardened film former, the hardened coating may or may not be a coagulated form of a coagulable protein but must be resistive to dissolution when placed in the dispersion.

Concerning the ratio of free and nonfree fat, it has been found that from 25 to 75% of the fat should be precoated and preferably 75 to 25% should not be precoated. While any amount of precoated fat will produce some resistance to oiling out, about ¼ to ⅓ of the fat should be in this state to provide a noticeable effect. One preferred free fat is a plastic shortening with a Wiley melt index of about 99 ± 2°F. The encapsulated fat is normally a liquid and the free fat is normally a plastic shortening.

Concerning water content when corn syrup is used, 6 parts of water is used for each 1 part of humectant (glycerin). An effective amount of an emulsifier is added to the dispersion to prevent too tight an encapsulation of the free fat thereby reducing the loss of free fat when the pieces are formed.

It is essential that a stable dispersion containing the free fat, encased fat, film former, water and humectant be provided. Stability of the dispersion can be readily ascertained by mixing a drop of the admixture in 100 ml of hot water (130°F) and then observing whether or not fat separation results. A stable dispersion will not release the fat (i.e., fat lakes will not appear at the water surface).

A suitable method of providing the food pieces is to prepare the fat encased in hardened shells of hydrophilic film former by forming a stable dispersion, e.g., of sodium caseinate, corn syrup, citric acid and fat and encapsulating by spray drying at 400°F. These particles have an average size of about 30 to 90 μ. They are then mixed with the remaining edible fat and additional edible hydrophilic film former and a sufficient amount of water and edible humectant at a temperature sufficient to melt the fat and for a period of time sufficient to provide a stable dispersion consisting essentially of an external phase of hydrophilic film former, water, humectant and an internal phase of an edible oil.

The fluidity of the stable dispersion is maintained by elevating the temperature of the dispersion during mixing and extrusion. It is desirable to either refrigerate to set the dispersion or place the dispersion in a mold to permanently set it in the form of a food piece having the characteristics described.

Another method is to admix the fat with a heat coagulable film former and a sufficient amount of water and edible humectant at a temperature sufficient to melt the fat but below the coagulation temperature of the film former for a period of time to blend uniformly. The stable dispersion is then heated to a temperature and for a period of time sufficient to heat coagulate the film former. Suitable heat coagulable film formers for this method include animal albumins such as egg albumin. After heat coagulation, the stable dispersion may then be put into the desired size and shape and dried.

When fats which are normally solid at room temperature are employed, the aerated product and fat is maintained at a temperature greater than the melting point of the fat. Other additives such as sugar, ungelatinized starch, coloring, and flavoring agents, etc., may be admixed and uniformly distributed throughout the stable dispersion after formation of the stable dispersion. Advantageously, the stable dispersion containing other food additives is provided as an extrudable mass through a die orifice (preferably a nonadherent orifice such as a polytetrafluoroethylene orifice). By cooling the extrudate (e.g., in cool air), the present food pieces can be produced in a continuous cooling manner.

Drying the food pieces is conducted in a manner such that the resultant product has a moisture content of at least 7 weight percent and generally less than 20 weight percent. The preferred moisture level for the food pieces ranges from 8 to 15% by weight.

In a more limited aspect of the process, food pieces can be provided which contain a uniform distribution of proteinaceous and caloric food ingredients throughout. Based upon a food piece having a weight ranging from 350 to 1,000 grams, such food pieces are adapted to provide at least 2,800 kilocalories and at least 40 grams of protein containing the essential amino acids (i.e., the minimum daily adult male caloric and protein requirements). Advantageously, food pieces can be produced that range from 400 to 800 grams and preferably less than 600 grams which provide the minimum daily adult requirements in respect to protein and calories.

The prerequisite protein may be provided by employing proteinaceous materials as the hydrophilic film former such as egg albumin, hydrolyzed soy protein, corn germ, gelatin, etc. If nonproteinaceous film formers (e.g., carboxymethylcellulose, gelatinized starch, agar agar, dextran, polyvinyl alcohol, etc.) are primarily employed, the prerequisite proteinaceous requirements may be provided in the external phase by nonfilm forming food components such as torula yeast and denaturized egg albumin. Essential amino acids may be employed to provide the prerequisite protein requirements. Amino acid supplements may also be incorporated in the food pieces.

A major portion or all of the prerequisite caloric requirements in the food pieces may be provided by the two internal fat phases. Additional edible caloric ingredients such as torula yeast, dextran, gelatinized and ungelatinized starches, sugars or sugar bearing substances, mixtures thereof and the like may be incorporated into the external phase.

It is essential in preparing the food pieces to provide fat encapsulated in a shell of hardened film former as well as fat not encapsulated in a hardened shell, both of which are stable against fat separation when subjected to the stable dispersion test. To provide food pieces which are stable against fat separation, particular care to maintain the stable dispersion must be exercised throughout subsequent processing steps. Food pieces which are comprised of a substantial amount of other food additives (other than the fats, hydrophilic film former and water and/or humectant) are best incorporated into the food pieces by first providing the stable dispersion and then adding and admixing the other food additives for a period of time sufficient to homogeneously disperse the other ingredients within the stable dispersion. A substantial quantity of these other food additives may be incorporated into the stable dispersion as a solid or solute. Since the stable dispersion is not adversely affected by the addition thereto of additional water and/or humectant, additional water and/or humectant can be employed to facilitate the incorporation of the other food additives within the stable dispersion. When food particles are provided in the external phase, such food particles typically have a particle size of less than 150 microns.

The food pieces can be provided in various sizes and shapes such as cubes, sheets, bars, rods, etc. The food pieces are of unitary construction so that any given portion of the food piece (e.g., 300 mg portion) will have substantially the same uniform distribution of food constituents and nutritional value as another portion thereof. In general, specific density of the food pieces is most generally in the range of 1.2 to 1.4. All quantities mentioned are on a percent by weight basis as indicated.

The fat encapsulated within the hardened shells of film former provides one of the sources of fat and protein in the product. The primary purpose of the drying of the ingredient is to encapsulate the fat to thereby prevent separation during manufacture of the finished product. Moisture content of the finished dried particles should be between 1 and 3%, with 2.5 being typical. One preferred shortening to be used in the particles is a blend of vegetable oils to produce a consistency somewhat softer than hard butter and containing a small amount (0.10%) BHA as a freshness preserver. Its solid fat index is as follows:

°F	% Solids
50	30 ± 3.0
70	18 ± 3.0
80	13 ± 3.0
92	2 min
100	1.5 max

Example: Fat encapsulated in hardened shells is prepared as follows. 40 parts of vegetable fat having the solid fat index above, 25 parts sodium caseinate, 35 parts of corn syrup (DE 42), 0.25 part citric acid and 100 parts water are made into a dispersion and spray dried at about 400°F to form vegetable oil globules encapsulated within hardened shells of a hydrophilic film former composed of sodium caseinate and corn syrup. This premix is employed to form a food piece using the following formulation in parts by weight:

Encapsulated vegetable oil (spray dried)	54	Sodium caseinate	18
Corn syrup	99	Emulsifier (distilled monoglycerides)	1.8
Sucrose (powdered)	114	Chocolate flavor	30
Water	14	Free fat (Wiley MP 99 ± 2°F)	21.3
Humectant (glycerin)	8	Salt	0.8
Waxy maize starch	5	Nonfat dry milk	7.5

Using a suitable blender such as a ribbon blender, a preblend is made comprising one-half of the formula amount of powdered sugar, all of the starch, monoglycerides, cocoa, and salt. This will prevent lumping of the cocoa and the starch when they go into the slurry to form the dispersion. The ingredients should be sifted going into or out of the blender. To a covered, jacketed, stainless steel kettle equipped with a scraper-agitator add the ingredients listed above in the following order (a) corn syrup, (b) water and (c) glycerin; mix for 30 seconds and add the powdered, preblended starch, sugar, monoglycerides and flavor and heat with mixing to the proper transfer temperature (about 155°F minimum), to regulate the final batch temperature to between 123° and 129°F.

The free shortening is added while heating and blended to form a dispersion. The dispersion is transferred to a mixer such as a sigma blade mixer in which flavoring is added. To a ribbon blender add the remainder of the formula amount given above of the sucrose, sodium caseinate and spray dried encapsulated fat and dry blend. Add this blend to the dispersion in the sigma mixer while it is running and mix for about 3 to 5 minutes (30 rpm for a 1,000 pound batch sigma mixer). The final temperature should be 123° to 129°F to provide the proper forming and the shaping consistency. The product is then molded, for example, by extrusion, cooled and packaged.

The food pieces are characterized by better retention of chewiness and flexibility throughout storage without loss of oil when extruded, good impact strength against shattering, lack of hygroscopicity and a low permeability to gases and moisture. The food pieces are stable against substantial reduction or increased flexibility when subjected to humidity variations of the surrounding atmosphere. At elevated temperatures (e.g., 300°F) unwrapped food pieces will ultimately degrade by charring rather than separation of the internal phase from the external phase. Similarly, the food pieces are not deformed when subjected to elevated temperatures (e.g., 100°F). Since the fat is encapsulated in two ways and protected by the external phase, the pieces are not subject to rancidification (e.g., oxidative degradation).

Bar Product with Protein Rich Filling

P.D. Halladay and J.W. Dougherty; U.S. Patent 3,821,443; June 28, 1974; assigned to General Foods Corporation describe a highly palatable, protein nutritious, easy to handle and shelf stable food product. The prime components of the food bar are a creamy nutritious frosting-like confectionery component and a farinaceous component comprising cake or a cereal bound in a matrix comprising fat and sugar. The filling composition is based on a mixture of an oil, sugar, and a mixture of soy protein and egg white solids.

The filling may also contain sugar, vitamins, flavorings, colorings, stabilizers and the like. The filling is prepared by adding the protein source material, sugar and other ingredients to the oil or liquid fat, and mixing these vigorously to form a creamy dispersion of the ingredients in the fat. Under vigorous agitation, the confection exhibits a whipped character. This whipping property is due to the combination of hydrogenated vegetable oil and protein solids. The proteins hold the aeration and make possible the heating of the filling without excessive loss of aeration and running of the filling. Vegetable or animal oil exhibiting liquid properties at about 100°F and having bland flavor may be used. The oils may be partially or totally hydrogenated. The protein sources used are a mixture of egg white solids and soy protein. These materials may be used in the relative proportions of 30 to 70% by weight of the egg white solids and corresponding 30 to 70% by weight soy protein. The amount of the protein source combination employed by the confectionery composition may vary depending on the nutritional value desired. Generally speaking, these materials may be used at a level of about 10 to 40% by weight of the confection. Aside from the nutritional aspects, the egg white solids also impart whipping properties to the filling composition. This whipping property is due to the combination of the vegetable oil and the solids. The protein holds the aeration and makes possible the heating of the filling without excessive loss of aeration and the running of the filling.

The filling also contains a sweetener such as sugar present to suit taste. The sugar should be very finely granulated (6X) or in liquid form. Sugar may be present to suit taste and generally in the range of about 10 to 40% by weight of the filling composition.

Vitamins such as A, B_1, B_2, B_6, B_{12}, C, D, E and niacin may be added in appropriate amounts to supply any desired percentage of the minimum daily requirement. Minerals such as calcium, phosphorus, iodine, iron or magnesium may also be added. Where vitamins and minerals are both used in the formulation of a cereal bar containing a filling layer, it is desirable to include the vitamins in one phase, say the filling, and minerals in the other phase, i.e., the cereal binder. This segregation of these ingredients prevents the possibility of their degradation caused by the reaction of the vitamin compounds with the mineral source materials.

The filling may also contain additives which impart improved heat stability to the filling. For example, the incorporation of a mixture of silicon dioxide and a polyhydric alcohol or polyhydric alcohol ester bridging agent into a low melting point oil increases the high temperature stability of the oil and prevents the oil from running or weeping out of the filling composition after prolonged periods of storage at room temperature or temperatures of 70° to 110°F. The fat present in the filling may be so stabilized by incorporating in the fat from about 0.1 to 11% by weight of the silicon dioxide and from about 0.1 to 7% by weight of the bridging agent.

No water, milk or other aqueous ingredient is used in preparing the filling composition. The only moisture present in the filling is that which is present in the ingredients used in its preparation. Because of the very low moisture content, the filling exhibits shelf stability over a period of six months or more. In general, the moisture content of the filling is less than 5% by weight, preferably 2 to 3% by weight.

The filling composition is best prepared by mixing the dry components, i.e., the sugar, egg white solids, soy protein, and any other additives with the oil. The oil is preferably heated above about 110°F at the time of mixing, as this facilitates the aeration of the oil. The mixture is then aerated by subjecting it to vigorous agitation using a high speed mixer until a filling having the desired light, fluffy consistency is obtained.

In some instances, it has been found that the filling may have a tendency to become crumbly or mealy after being subjected to elevated temperatures for an extended period of time. The condition is believed to be the result of the absorption of the lower melting point fractions of the oil by the protein sources which causes the filling to lose its plasticity or creaminess. This condition may be overcome by thoroughly mixing the protein sources at ambient or elevated temperatures with a sufficient amount of oil to saturate the protein and form a paste, and then incorporating the oil saturated protein with the remaining oil and other ingredients and mixing as described above.

As indicated, the filling may be used in combination with a cereal bar type product, cake type product or other farinaceous component. A cereal bar may generally be prepared by combining commercially available cereal flakes with a liquid binder composition, thoroughly mixing the cereal with the binder and forming a sheet of the bound cereal. After permitting the cereal sheet to harden, the sheet may be coated with the filling; more of the bound cereal may be added on top of the filler to form a laminate of cereal, filling, and cereal.

Useful cereal binders may be made of sugar, polyhydric alcohol, oils, or combinations of these. The preferred binder comprises mainly a vegetable oil such as corn oil or cottonseed oil. It is not necessary that the fat or oil used in the binder be liquid at body temperature; fats having a Wiley melting point of up to 120°F may be used.

The binder may also contain sugar, salt, corn syrup solids and other ingredients such as minerals, vitamins and the like. The binder is thus prepared by adding sugar, minerals and other ingredients to liquid oil and mixing thoroughly at a temperature above the melting point of the oils.

The binder is then combined with cereal flakes in a ratio of about 20 to 80 parts of binder per correspondingly 80 to 20 parts of cereal. Preferably, the binder and cereal are combined in approximately 50:50 ratios. Materials are mixed by combining the cereal and liquid binder and gently agitating in a mixer until the cereal flakes are completely and thoroughly dispersed with the binder. Where the binder contains an oil, it is preferred to mix the cereal and binder at temperatures above 110°F or the melting point of the oil.

The cereal bar may be formed by placing the desired amount of the cereal/binder mixture into a mold having the desired dimensions and applying gentle and uniform surface pressure sufficient to compact the mixture without causing excessive fracturing of the cereal particles.

Where the binder contains a fat or oil, the temperature of the mixture prior to the molding operation should be such that the fat or oil is liquid. The filling layer is then applied evenly over the lower layer of compressed cereal and the top layer of cereal/binder mixture applied and compressed in the same manner as was the lower layer.

Best results in terms of bar appearance are obtained if the lower layer of bound cereal is quick cooled in order to solidify the fat present in the binder prior to the application of the filling, as this prevents substantial commingling of the filling and cereal layers. The filling may be applied at a temperature above the melting point of the fat or oil contained therein or it may be applied cold in the form of a solid sheet which has been precut to the appropriate dimensions.

Example: A nutritious aerated filling composition was prepared as shown below.

Food Bars

Ingredients	Parts
Hydrogenated vegetable oil	12.00
Soy protein isolate (95% protein)	4.50
Egg white solids	4.50
Sugar (6X)	6.40
Glycerin	0.13
Silicon dioxide	0.51
Flavor	0.01
Preservatives (BHA + EDTA)	0.02

The filling was prepared by adding the glycerin, silicon dioxide and preservatives to the oil at about 140° to 180°F and mixing for about 2 minutes in a mixer. The sugar, soy protein, egg white solids and flavoring were then added and the composition was mixed at high speeds for several minutes until a viscous, aerated frosting-like filling was obtained.

The filling composition was then poured onto a cool cookie sheet and cooled to about 40°F, well below the melting point of the oil. Rectangular sections of the filling having the approximate dimensions of $1\frac{5}{8}$" x $3\frac{9}{16}$" x $\frac{3}{16}$" were cut for use in combination with the cereal layers of the bar.

The cereal portion of the bar was prepared by mixing corn flakes sized through a U.S. No. 5 screen and retained on a U.S. No. 10 screen with an equal amount of binder. The binder was prepared by mixing the following ingredients at about 140°F:

Ingredients	Parts
Hydrogenated vegetable oil	19.04
Glycerin	0.39
Silicon dioxide	0.57
Sugar (6X)	9.52
Salt	0.12
Corn syrup	3.50
Minerals	1.90

About 20 grams of the cereal/binder mixture at a temperature of 140°F was placed in a wooden mold having an inner dimension of $1\frac{5}{8}$" x $3\frac{9}{16}$", leveled, and gently compressed using a plunger to a thickness of about $\frac{1}{4}$". A 16 gram sheet of the precut filling as prepared above was placed in the mold on top of the compressed layer of cereal and then a second layer of the cereal/binder mixture applied on top of it and compressed as above. The assembly was quick cooled to about 40°F and removed from the mold.

The finished bar has a cereal content of about 35.7%, a binder content of about 35.7% and a filling content of about 28.6% by weight. The overall moisture content of the bar is about 2.5%. The bar was packaged in a moisture impermeable wrapping material and exhibited shelf stability for a minimum period of at least 6 months. The oil component of the bar was found not to run even after prolonged exposure to temperatures in excess of the melting point of the oil.

The actual protein efficiency ratio (PER) for the filling composition is unexpectedly higher than the PER as theoretically calculated. PER being calculated:

$$PER = 5.264 \, (0.065\% \times \% \text{ deficit limiting amino acid})$$

The percent deficit limiting amino acid is determined by analyzing each protein source to determine the amount of each of the essential amino acids present. These values are also available in the literature. Using whole egg as a standard, the percent deficit of limiting amino acids is obtained by comparing the combined amounts of amino acids in the given product with the combined amounts in whole egg.

The actual PER is determined by rat feeding studies conducted over a 28 day period. In this test the amount of protein eaten (fed at 10% in the test diet) is related to the amount of weight gain by the rats during the 28 day period. Thus, a PER of 4.00 means that for every gram of protein consumed during the 28 days, 4.00 grams of weight were gained per day.

The calculated PER for the filling of this example is 3.81. The actual PER by 28 day rat feeding studies was 4.36. The filling is thus specifically formulated using the mixture of soy protein and egg white solids to give PER's in excess of 4.00.

High Protein Product

J.E. Morgan; U.S. Patent 3,814,819; June 4, 1974; assigned to The Pillsbury Company provides an improved protein fortified food bar with the following characteristics and advantages: (a) caloric content limited to 250 calories per meal, (b) provision of one-fourth of the recommended daily allowance of high quality protein, vitamins and minerals, (c) flavor and textural stability when stored at room temperature, (d) a pleasing taste and aroma, (e) the provision of a fresh flavor and texture which does not create a dry sensation in the mouth when eaten, (f) the provision of an effective means for preventing the sensation of dryness normally perceived when a powdered protein is eaten.

Such protein fortified food bars are composed of several wafers stacked one above the other each composed of cereal flour or cereal starch, added edible protein and a small amount of chemical leavening. A creamy substantially moisture-free filling is layered between the wafers. The filling is composed of shortening in which is distributed a finely divided protein such as milk protein and preferably a minor amount of flavoring such as sugar. A vitamin mineral mixture, when used, is also distributed in the filling. A coating such as a confectioner's coating can be applied to the composite bar if desired.

The bar is preferably composed of at least three crisp wafers stacked one above the other with the creamy filling between them. Typically, each wafer consists of 10 parts of cereal flour (e.g., wheat flour), 6 or more parts of added protein, e.g., the calcium caseinate or a lactalbumin-caseinate coprecipitate, about 0.8 part oil as a release agent and a small amount of chemical leavening.

The wafer is dry, crisp, relatively thin and is fortified with added edible protein. It consists of 10 parts of wheat or other cereal grain flour, a minor amount of shortening, e.g., 2 to 5 parts to act as a separating agent from molds in which the wafers are baked. One suitable shortening consists of about 0.7 part oil such as cottonseed oil and about 0.25 part soy lecithin. A minor amount of chemical leavening is also used, e.g., about 0.5 part when ammonium bicarbonate is used as the leavening agent.

Protein fortification is accomplished with any edible protein that does not impart an undesirable taste to the wafer. Examples are lactalbumin-casein coprecipitate, calcium caseinate, purified or refined grades of casein or mixtures thereof. Sodium caseinate and soy isolates, if used, should be used in conjunction with calcium ions, e.g., by adding about 0.5 part calcium lactate, calcium chloride or other calcium salt for each 10 parts of sodium caseinate. Of these, calcium caseinate is preferred because of cost and better characteristics at relatively high concentrations.

There is no minimum amount of protein that can be added since any additional amount will have a small but measurable effect upon increasing the protein content of the wafer. It has been found, however, that to meet the established nutritional standards, preferably over 25% of dry composition should be added protein. When lactalbumin-casein coprecipitate or calcium caseinate is employed, they can be used in the amount of about 0.2 to 10 or more parts for each 10 parts of flour with about 4 to 7 parts being preferred for each 10 parts of flour.

To prepare the wafers a batter is made by adding the dry ingredients in a ratio of 150 to 250 parts water for each 100 parts dry ingredients with 175 to 225 parts water being preferred. If soy protein or sodium caseinate is used, the calcium salt is added to the water before other dry ingredients. The protein is then added slowly to the water with high shear mixing. The remaining ingredients are then added with continued mixing. The batter is then poured into wafer molds of the kind employed in commercial baking of crackers and wafers and baked at 450°F for three minutes.

The filling is a water-free combination of about equal parts of shortening and edible protein in finely divided powdered form. To prepare the filling, the protein is added to the shortening and mixed vigorously until a stable cream (or dispersion) is formed.

The shortening is used in amounts up to about 40% of the filling. It can comprise any edible shortening which is plastic at room temperature. One suitable shortening is less than 50% solids and typically about 20 to 30% solids at room temperature. High melting point shortenings will not provide the proper eating characteristics and will not provide the required creamy texture. Of the proteins that can be used in the filling, the preferred protein is a lactalbumin-casein coprecipitate.

The coprecipitate is preferably resolubilized to such a degree that the water absorptivity thereof is increased sufficiently to remove the gritty mouthfeel when eaten but without sufficient additional resolubilization to absorb large quantities of water. It is preferred that the coprecipitate is resolubilized, for example, by redispersing the curd in water containing 2% sodium tripolyphosphate calculated on the dry weight of the curd. While calcium caseinate, sodium caseinate, soy proteins and other edible proteins can be used, the taste is not as good as with the milk coprecipitate.

To improve the taste of the filling, a minor amount of sugar can be added. Confectioners' sugar is preferred. The filling can contain, for example, about 10 to 30% sugar and other flavor. When the bar composition is to contain added vitamins and minerals, they are incorporated into the filling which has been found to stabilize them probably by protecting them from moisture and oxygen. To prepare the filling, all ingredients except the protein are added to the shortening and mixed to form a cream. The protein is then added with continued mixing to obtain a homogeneous creamy consistency. During this time, a certain amount of air may be incorporated into the composition which adds to its creaminess. The shortening is then spread and applied as a layer about $1/10''$ thick between the wafers.

In a preferred formulation, the filling makes up about half of the composition, the wafers about 30%, the confectioners' coating about 20%. A minor amount of granular topping can be applied over the coating for flavor and visual appeal. The bars are preferably of such dimensions that one serving of two bars provides $1/4$ of the Recommended Daily Allowance of high quality protein, vitamins, minerals and contains about 12 grams of protein, about 12 grams of fat, about 21 grams of carbohydrate and about 250 calories. The product is acceptable in flavor and textural quality after storage at 70°F and 12 months as judged by standard taste panel tests.

The success of the product in providing a shelf stable protein fortified food bar is due in large part to the provision of two phases, one solid and one plastic with added protein present in both phases. In this way the wafer is prevented from being tough as it would be if all of the added protein were placed in the wafer. On the other hand, if all the protein had been placed in the filling, much more shortening would be required which would defeat the limited calorie objectives. Because the protein present in the filling is protected from hydration in the mouth when eaten, the characteristic drying of the mouth due to the absorption of moisture by protein is avoided.

The shelf stability of the bars is exceptional. This stability is believed to be in large measure due to the exclusion of water from the overall formulation without sacrificing the creamy eating quality of the bar. In this way the eating quality, characterized by the sharp textural diversity between the crisp wafer and creamy filling, is maintained through extended periods of storage. Furthermore, the stability of the vitamins present in the bar is outstanding. This is apparently due to the fact that the vitamins are not exposed to water in the filling and additionally are shielded from ambient oxygen and moisture by the protective shortening matrix of the filling.

Example: A filling is made up having the following composition:

Ingredients	Percent
Plastic shortening (vegetable)	35
Milk protein (casein-lactalbumin coprecipitate)	34
Powdered sugar	20
Vitamin and flavor preblend containing	10
Vitamin and mineral mixture, 44%	
Powdered sugar, 38%	
Caramel flavor, 10%	
Salt, 4%	
Vanilla flavor, 2.5%	
Butterscotch flavor, 1.5%	
Color	0.6
Emulsifier (lecithin)	0.4

The vitamin and flavor preblend is dry blended until homogeneous. The shortening, caramel color and emulsifier are placed in a horizontal dual sigma mixer and run at high speed until the texture is creamy and uniform; approximately three minutes. The vitamin flavor preblend is then added together with the powdered sugar and mixing is continued until a uniform texture is obtained; approximately three minutes on high speed. The milk protein is then added to the mixer and mixing is continued until a uniform color and texture is achieved; approximately another three minutes on high speed. Mixing temperature should be about 75°F. The wafers are prepared in accordance with the following formula:

	Percent
Wheat flour	62.25
Milk protein (casein-lactalbumin coprecipitate)	35
Cottonseed oil	2
Lecithin emulsifier	0.5
Ammonium bicarbonate	0.25

This composition is mixed with about 200 parts water for each 100 parts dry mix. The batter is then poured into wafer molds and baked for about 3 minutes at approximately 450°F. The filling is then spread to a thickness of about $1/10''$ and a complete bar is formed by providing three wafers measuring about $1\frac{1}{2}'' \times 3\frac{1}{2}''$ separated by two layers of filling. A small amount of flavored confectioners' coating is applied to the finished bar.

DEHYDRATED RECONSTITUTABLE BARS

Directly Edible, Readily Hydratable Product

G.R. Schafer and A.R. Rahman; U.S. Patent 3,882,253; May 6, 1975; assigned to U.S. Secretary of the Army provide a method of making compacted and dehydrated food bars which may be directly eaten without prior rehydration or which may be rapidly rehydrated in bar form in cold water, particularly water at room temperature or at the ambient temperature.

The compacted, dehydrated food bars are prepared by incorporating potato particles, preferably flavored and diced, which have been blanched, freeze-vacuum-dehydrated to a moisture content below 4% by weight, and thereafter equilibrated with water until they reach a moisture content of 5 to 15% by weight, in a food bar preparation mixture in a proportion by weight of 10 to 20% potato based on the freeze-dehydrated form to 90 to 80% of the nonpotato food bar forming ingredients.

The mixture of the potato particles with the nonpotato food bar forming ingredient mixture is then compressed into a bar and the compressed food bar is redried under vacuum to a moisture content below 4% by weight to produce compacted and dehydrated food bars having densities of from 1 to 1.4 g/cc. The compression of the food bars is carried out at 800 to 1,500 psi, using a dwell time of 5 to 20 seconds.

Example: Raw U.S. No. 1 grade Idaho Russet potatoes were washed, peeled and submerged in an aqueous solution containing about 1.0 gram of sodium metabisulfite per gallon to prevent darkening of the peeled potatoes. The peeled potatoes having sodium metabisulfite solution over their exterior surfaces were diced in a potato dicer to form substantially cube-shaped particles or dice of about 0.375 inch on each side and the dice were immediately submerged in an aqueous solution of sodium metabisulfite of the same concentration as above. The potato dice were removed from the aqueous solution of sodium metabisulfite and blanched for 1.5 to 2 minutes by submerging them in an aqueous solution of a flavoring ingredient described below at 170° to 212°F. The blanching solution had been brought to a boil and had been removed from the source of heat immediately prior to submerging the potato dice therein. The flavoring agent employed was lemon juice crystals, and was employed to mask the natural potato flavor in the potato dice. It was employed in a concentration of about 6 ounces of lemon juice crystals per gallon of water.

The blanched potato dice were removed from the hot aqueous solution after the blanching period and immediately cooled in a cold chamber to 40° to 50°F. The flavored aqueous solution used in blanching the potato dice was retained and permitted to cool to 40° to 50°F. The cooled potato dice were then returned to the cooled, flavored aqueous solution and permitted to soak therein for 2 to 4 hours to absorb more of the lemon flavor without being cooked. The potato dice were then removed from the flavored aqueous solution and drained free of excess solution, then freeze-vacuum-dehydrated in a conventional manner employing a shelf or platen temperature in the vacuum dehydrator of about 80°F, the potato dice having their moisture content reduced during the freeze-vacuum-dehydration to about 2%.

The freeze-dried potato dice were then sprayed with sufficient water to impart to the dice, upon equilibration, a moisture concentration of 12%. The dice were enclosed in airtight containers and permitted to stand for a period of time sufficient to permit the moisture to equilibrate throughout. This required 3 hours, but could be extended to assure the utmost in uniformity of distribution of the moisture throughout the potato dice. Uniformity of moisture distribution throughout the previously freeze-dried potato dice is important in determining how well the potato dice when mixed with the nonpotato food bar forming ingredients would retain their identity through compression into food bars and rehydration thereof. The better the retention of identity and particle discreteness, the more rapid the rehydration of the food bars prepared from freeze dried, remoistened dice. A cherry food bar preparation mixture was prepared by mixing the following ingredients in the percentages by weight thereof shown in the table.

Ingredients	Percent by Weight
Applesauce, dehydrated (noncaking)	25.8
Sugar	22.7
Potato dice, lemon-flavored, freeze-dried	15.6
Texgran soy protein, sour cherry-flavored	15.1
Almonds, slivered	10.9
Cherry powder, freeze-dried	4.5
Cherries, maraschino, dry	3.9
Silicon dioxide anticaking agent (Syloid 244)	1.5
Red Lake Blend No. 9443 color,	
0.044 part per 100 parts of mixture	

30 grams of the mixture were formed into each bar 3" long by 1" wide and compressed at room temperature and at 950 psi with a 10 second dwell to produce a bar of about 0.5 inch thickness. The resulting cherry food bars were dehydrated in a vacuum oven at about 100° to 120°F to a moisture content of about 2.0%

by weight and having a bulk density of 1.2 g/cc. The bars were subjected to technological panel testing both dry (i.e., without prior rehydration) and rehydrated by adding to each 30 gram bar 50 ml of water at approximately room temperature and permitting the water to soak into the bar for 10 minutes.

Test results showed that the food bars had good acceptability both in the dry (unrehydrated) state and after rehydration in water at about room temperature for only 10 minutes. Without the potato dice in the food bars, it would have been impossible to have rehydrated bars made in a similar manner within any reasonable time period and it would have been virtually impossible for a person to have bitten through such bars in the dry state.

Even after storage of the above described cherry food bars containing potato dice while hermetically sealed in moisture-proof containers for as long as one year at 100°F, the cherry food bars were quite acceptable with respect to color, flavor, and texture both dry and rehydrated by soaking for 10 minutes in water at about room temperature.

Compressed Compounded Reconstitutable Product

H. Corey, A. Bakal, K. Konigsbacher and D. Schoenholz; U.S. Patent 3,812,268; May 21, 1974; assigned to Foster D. Snell, Inc. have found that compounded food products, especially suited for compression, may be produced from a dry mix of ingredients comprised of at least 18% gluten or other vegetable protein and a relatively high percentage of a polyhydric alcohol (at least 10%), the percentages being calculated on the total weight of the product. When this mixture is mixed with water to produce a doughy mass which is baked and dried in the process, an open cellular product is obtained having a density of 12 lb/ft^3 or more, depending on the relative ratio of the ingredients and the processing conditions employed. Usually such products have densities of 10 to 40 lb/ft^3.

Such products after being compressed to a small fraction of their original volume will recover their original volume, geometry, and structure upon being immersed in water or other suitable liquid, or upon being moistened with any of these liquids and then heated in an oven at a suitable temperature above ambient, or, if the formulations contain a suitable amount of hard fat or other solid but meltable plasticizer, upon heating in an oven as above. Such food products are particularly advantageous for pet foods, for foods for military and space operations and for rations in any situation where small volume is important or where the expansion mechanism may be advantageous.

A typical production of such products is carried out by mixing the ingredients with appropriate amounts of water to produce a doughy mass. Depending on the desired final shape the dough is cut into pieces or forms and baked in an oven or cooked, thus causing expansion of the system as well as a locking-in of the structure.

In this manner, a sponge type structure is obtained. The density of the product can be controlled by the baking temperature, the aeration given to the dough prior to baking and the presence of leavening agents, if any, or by controlling the pressure upon the product during baking. Thereafter, the baked or cooked product is dried by any suitable dehydration method (air drying, freeze drying, vacuum air drying, etc.) to a moisture content of 4 to 8% by weight. This level of moisture is a key factor for successful compression of the product. Too low moisture content results in shattering and cracking during compression, while too high moisture content results in permanent deformation or even flow of the product under compression. The compression pressure (2,000 to 5,000 psig) results in a 20 to 80% reduction of the original volume. The compressed product is then locked into this compressed state by drying to a moisture content of 2% or less. Such food products can be stored at ordinary temperature or under refrigeration if protected from moisture, or in the frozen state for prolonged periods of time.

The key to the structural fidelity and the behavior of these products is associated with the relatively high vegetable protein content as exemplified by gluten, soybean protein and the like. Also animal proteins can be incorporated in the products in lieu of gluten, such as albumin, collagen, gelatin and whey. These materials are composed of high molecular weight molecules existing in long chains which become intermeshed in random distribution to form a web or interlaced network of crossed fibers which provide structural fidelity to the compressed food product and enable it to return to its original geometry and size.

Also essential in the food products is a plasticizer such as a polyhydric alcohol, such as glycerol, propylene glycol, mannitol or sorbitol, which serves as a plasticizer for the protein molecules and enables them to be compressed and yet return to their original symmetry and form on admixture with water. The polyhydric alcohol must, of course, be water-soluble and edible. Other plasticizers can be used in baked products which are insoluble in water, such as edible mono- and diglycerides, for example, glycerol mono- and distearate.

Example 1: Compressed beef was produced from the following:

Components	Percent by Weight
Gluten	15
Soy protein (Promine D)	11
Propylene glycol	7
Beef steak	10
Water	57

The beef steak was fried and then ground in a meat grinder. It was dispersed in water in a Waring blender. Then with continuous mixing the propylene glycol was added, followed by the gluten (wetted with alcohol) and the soy protein. The entire dough mix was kneaded for approximately 5 minutes and shaped into the desired form, and left to relax for approximately 15 minutes. The specimens were then baked in a preheated oven at 350°F for 2 hours. They were removed and air-dried with moisture level of not more than 2% by weight. To facilitate drying in some cases, the outer cooked layer of the baked product was removed.

The dried specimens were then rehumidified in a steam environment to a moisture level of 4.5%. They were then compressed under a pressure of 2,000 psi, resulting in a three to one size reduction. The products were then air-dried at room temperature to a moisture content not greater than 2%. The food products thus prepared could be stored at room temperature for an indefinite period. They were reconstituted by immersion in cold water and in hot water, each specimen expanding to its original size and form. The time required for full expansion varied from several seconds in hot water up to 5 minutes in cold water. Alternatively, the food products were expanded in a steam atmosphere and in hot oil. In each case, the product expanded to its original size and geometry.

Example 2: Compressed meat products prepared as in Example 1 with a moisture content of 5% were coated with ice so that upon thawing the moisture content of the product increased to 40%. The specimens were frozen to 0°F and then dipped in ice water. The operation was continued until a desired amount of ice coated each specimen. The products can be stored indefinitely in a freezer and upon thawing, either at room temperature or in a low oven, the specimens expanded to their original form and shape in periods of time varying from 1 to 5 minutes, depending upon the size of the sample and the thawing temperature.

Directly Edible Compacted Dehydrated Fruit Product

A.R. Rahman and G.R. Schafer; U.S. Patent 3,705,814; December 12, 1972; assigned to U.S. Secretary of the Army describe a process for producing directly edible, compacted, dehydrated fruit bars which are relatively soft and chewy which are comprised of one or a plurality of fruits suitably subdivided and coated with a lecithin or modified lecithin containing composition and dried to a moisture content of 7 to 14% on a weight basis, then compressed at a pressure of 200 to 3,000 psi into bar form of such dimensions as to facilitate the direct eating of the bar without prior rehydration thereof.

Apparently a relatively small quantity of lecithin or a modified lecithin, usually less than 5% by weight, when well distributed through a fruit bar on the surfaces of the subdivided particles that are compressed together to form the fruit bar produces a change in the texture of the fruit bar such that the resulting compacted fruit bar can be easily bitten through and chewed.

The lecithin may be derived from various natural sources, but those produced from the natural lecithin of soybeans have been found to be particularly effective for this purpose. In general, lecithins are phosphatides and more particularly diglycerides of aliphatic acids linked to the choline ester of phosphoric acid. The modified lecithin may, for example, be a hydroxylated lecithin. The lecithin or modified lecithin may be applied to the particles of subdivided fruit as a solution, such as soybean oil solution, or as a spray, such as an aerosol spray employing a nontoxic propellant.

Generally speaking, the fruit is subdivided to form particles of $\frac{1}{8}$" to $\frac{1}{2}$" in the longest dimension and the particles are dried to 7 to 14% moisture content by weight prior to the application of the lecithin or modified lecithin containing composition thereto. A sufficient amount of the solution or suspension of the lecithin or modified lecithin is applied to the particles of fruit to obtain a reasonably uniform coating on the particles of about 1 to 5% of lecithin or modified lecithin on a weight basis. About 2% has been found to be particularly effective.

In general, if the fruit particles are dried to less than 7% moisture content before the application of the lecithin thereto and the compression thereof, the compressed fruit bar will be too hard for ease or comfort in eating the bars directly even though lecithin has been added. On the other hand, if the moisture content of the fruit particles is greater than about 14%, the fruit is difficult to compress into bars because of its tendency to be extruded from the mold when the moisture content of the fruit is too great. In general, if less than about 1% of lecithin is applied to the fruit, it will be insufficient to render the compressed dehydrated fruit sufficiently mealy in texture to permit one to bite a compacted fruit bar without danger of damaging the teeth. On the other hand, if more than about 5% of lecithin is applied, the fruit pulp is inclined to be extruded from the mold, much as when the moisture content is greater than 14%.

The pressure required in compressing the subdivided fruit coated with lecithin or modified lecithin will, in general, depend on the amount of moisture in the fruit. The lower the moisture content of the fruit down to as low as 7%, the higher the pressure required, up to 3,000 psi, to obtain a fruit bar of the proper degree of adhesion. The higher the moisture content of the fruit, up to as high as 14%, the lower the pressure required, down to 200 psi, to obtain a fruit bar of the proper degree of adhesion. The type of fruit has some effect on the pressure required, figs and pears in general requiring higher pressures than most other fruits.

The process has been found to be particularly effective with dried dates, raisins, cherries, figs, and pears. However, it may also be applied to other fruits; also other components, such as edible seeds and nuts, may be added to the fruits in order to impart variety and interest to compressed fruit bars. Also, cereals, proteins, fats, chocolate, spices, and various other flavoring or chemical additives may be incorporated in the compressed fruit bars in minor proportions in relation to the fruit components.

Example: Dates were diced to form particles having a maximum dimension of about 0.5 inch. The particles of diced dates were air dried to a moisture content of about 8%, then spread out in a pan and spray-coated as uniformly as possible over the surfaces of the particles with Pam, an aerosol solution of lecithin, until an add-on of about 2.0% by weight was obtained. The particles coated with the lecithin solution were placed in a mold and compressed at 400 psi pressure to form a bar of the dimensions 3" x 1" x 0.5". The bars were stored overnight in a closed airtight container, then tested with an Instron Universal Testing Apparatus using a 500 kg cell.

The bars were penetrated at 50% of their initial thickness at a speed of 2 cm/min using a cylindrical, flat-surfaced punch with a diameter of 0.75 cm. The results obtained are given below. The sample numbers represent individual bars; the letters following the sample numbers represent replicate penetrations of the same bar. Firmness is shown by force at 50% penetration; toughness by work expended in penetrating to 50% of initial thickness; and hardness by the maximum force applied during the penetration.

Sample	Firmness, kg		Toughness, kg-cm		Hardness, kg	
	With Lecithin	Without Lecithin	With Lecithin	Without Lecithin	With Lecithin	Without Lecithin
1a	3.4	5.6	2.94	4.32	4.4	7.0
1b	3.1	5.4	2.60	4.30	4.0	7.4
2a	4.8	5.8	3.33	4.80	4.8	6.0
2b	5.3	7.6	4.48	5.45	6.2	7.6
2c	5.6	7.0	4.26	4.80	6.0	7.0
3a	5.2	9.0	4.21	6.13	5.8	9.0
3b	6.0	9.0	4.01	7.25	6.0	10.0
3c	7.4	10.2	5.12	7.30	7.4	10.2
Average	5.1	7.4	3.86	5.53	5.6	8.0

EGG AND WAFFLE PRODUCTS

EGGS, OMELETS AND PANCAKES

Cooked Frozen Egg Products

S.D. Latham and R.D. Seeley; U.S. Patent 3,769,404; October 30, 1973; assigned to Anheuser-Busch, Incorporated describe a composition for making cooked frozen omelets and other egg products which includes egg, water, a combination of cellulose gum derivatives, ethoxylated monoglyceride, and a chemical leavening system. Other ingredients include potato flour and nonfat milk solids and citric acid.

The egg composition is particularly useful in precooked frozen omelets. However, the product can be utilized in the production of a frozen uncooked batter, or it can be utilized by allowing the chef to mix the ingredients himself.

From 60 to 80% whole egg and 5 to 25% added water by weight are used. Whole fresh eggs, frozen egg and reconstituted egg can be used. The preferred product uses frozen whole egg. In this formulation about 70% whole egg and about 15% added water are used. The additional water is for the purpose of replacing water lost during cooking, thus reducing dryness and improving the eating quality of the product. The eggs are pasteurized to prevent spoilage.

The potato flour and nonfat milk solids are added to improve water holding capacity and to improve eating quality. These additives make the egg feel soft and creamy in the mouth. Up to 4% potato four and 3% nonfat milk solids can be used. These percentages are by weight of the final egg composition. In addition to potato flour other suitable carbohydrates, such as, corn starch, rice flour, wheat flour, pregelatinized wheat, tapioca, and potato starch can be used in whole or in part as a substitute. Liquid or dried skim milk, liquid or dried whole milk and nondairy milk substitutes can be substituted for all or part of the nonfat milk solids.

From 0.05 to 0.20% citric acid is added to improve cooked egg color. The citric acid brightens the yellow color of egg products and retards ferrous sulfide greening that often occurs when eggs are held at steam table temperature over extended periods. Other edible acids or acid salts, such as malic, fumaric, lactic or monosodium phosphate can be substituted for all or part of the citric acid.

The carboxymethylcellulose (CMC) is used as a thickening agent in the uncooked omelet batter which aids in suspending added ingredients. Other common thickening agents, such as alginates, carrageenan, locust bean, guar and cellulose gums, may be used for this viscosity control.

The other cellulose gum derivatives, namely hydroxypropylcellulose (Klucel) and methylcellulose (Methocel) are thermosetting gums. These gums are used to give strength to the coagulated egg protein structure during the cooling process after cooking. This results in an increased stability of omelet shape and volume after removal from the cooking utensil and upon cooling. Omelets cooked without the presence of these cellulose gums shrink very rapidly when cooled, thus lacking volume and eye appeal.

When one or more of these gums are removed from the composition, decreased volume of the cooked omelet product results. Thus the combination of gums is important. The reason for this increased volume stability is probably because the cold-water-soluble cellulose gum derivatives intimately associate with the egg proteins before cooking. During cooking the egg proteins coagulate, and the hydroxypropylcellulose becomes insoluble and the methylcellulose gels.

The coagulated protein is believed to associate with the insoluble and gelled gums, thus increasing the strength of the protein fiber during the cooling period. When the cooked product is cooled the hydroxypropylcellulose redissolves and the methylcellulose gel disassociates. But at the cooled temperature the egg proteins have sufficient strength to maintain the cooked omelet shape and volume.

Other compounds having properties similar to hydroxypropylcellulose and methylcellulose will function similarly in this composition. Other gum-like materials that do not become insoluble and/or gel at temperatures between $100°$ to $200°F$ do not act in this composition in the same fashion or achieve the same results as the aforementioned gums. The hydroxypropylcellulose and methylcellulose also act to increase the viscosity of the batter. All of the cellulose gums reduce syneresis which often results from freezing and thawing products.

From 0.10 to 0.5% hydroxypropylcellulose and from 0.05 to 0.45% by weight methylcellulose are added to the egg composition. From 0.07 to 0.15% carboxymethylcellulose is added.

These gums are identified as thermosetting and for this process thermosetting and heat precipitable gums, i.e., gums which gel or precipitate at about $100°$ to $200°F$, are satisfactory.

From 0.03 to 0.10% by weight ethoxylated monoglyceride (EMG) is added to soften and tenderize the omelet. Higher amounts do not detract from the eating quality of the product but do not improve it measurably. Omelets containing the cellulose gums alone are slightly hard and mealy when compared with those containing the cellulose gums plus EMG. Taste panel results indicate this tenderizing effect is a meaningful improvement. While EMG has been used previously in bakery products, it has not been used in precooked egg products. The egg omelet formulation uses a chemical leavening system which includes from 0.40 to 1.5% sodium bicarbonate and an amount of leavening acid sufficient to neutralize the sodium bicarbonate. Preferably this leavening acid is sodium aluminum phosphate which is used on a 1:1 weight basis. The chemical leavening system is used to increase the volume of the omelet during the cooking process. The chemical leavening system adds volume to the omelet mix during cooking and holds this volume on cooling. The increase in volume is about 40 to 50%.

For best results the chemical leavening should be of the type which gives off some CO_2 on mixing of the ingredients, some on standing, and some on heating. This results in a fluffy final cooked omelet. In mixing and cooking the omelet it is important for optimum quality that no more than about 90 minutes elapse between mixing stops and cooking starts. If substantially more time elapses, the action of the chemical leavening will be dissipated before cooking starts and an unsatisfactory omelet may result.

A small but effective amount of salt and pepper is used in the formulation strictly as seasonings. The formulation shown below may be modified to incorporate various flavoring ingredients or adjuncts to form various flavor varieties. These include meats, cheeses, peppers, mushrooms, and other conventional omelet additives. Up to about 50% flavoring ingredients can be added to the base formulation.

Optimum Plain Omelet Formulation

Ingredients	Percent
Whole egg	79.89
Water	14.82
Potato flour	1.56
NFMS	1.09
Citric acid	0.05
Carboxymethylcellulose	0.08
Hydroxypropylcellulose	0.15
Methocel	0.10
Ethoxylated monoglyceride	0.05
Sodium bicarbonate	0.75
Sodium aluminum phosphate	0.75
Salt	0.65
Black pepper	0.06

The foregoing preparation is made as follows: The egg is placed in a Waring blender or any other suitable mixer along with the added water and dissolved EMG. A small portion of the added water is heated and used to dissolve the EMG. The dry ingredients, except for the leavening system and seasoning are weighed and mixed together. The mixer is started and the speed adjusted to create a vortex. The dry ingredients are slowly sifted into the vortex. A total of about 2 minutes mixing is sufficient.

For optimum viscosity development and omelet quality this mixture is held at refrigerated temperature for 15 to 20 minutes. After this time the leavening and seasoning are added by mixing as described above for the dry ingredients. The resulting omelet batter is again held at refrigerated temperature for 15 to 20 minutes before cooking the omelets. The leavening and seasoning may be added with the dry ingredients and the hold periods reduced or eliminated, however, optimum quality is not achieved.

The omelets may be cooked by placing a measured quantity of the above omelet batter in a preheated omelet pan and cooked until the egg composition is about one-half coagulated. At this point the omelet may be folded. If flavored omelets are being made, the flavoring ingredients may be added before folding. In some cases, such as with egg foo yung omelets, the flavoring ingredients may be mixed with the batter before being deposited in the pan. After folding the cooking is continued until the egg composition is completely coagulated. The omelet may then be consumed or it may be frozen and packaged.

Controlled Portion Product

A.B. Rogers and M. Sebring; U.S. Patent 3,697,283; October 10, 1972; assigned to Armour and Company describe a method for making a food product in portions of controlled size and shape. In the process, gelatin in the amount of at least about 0.5% by weight is incorporated into a liquid uncooked food of the class consisting of pancake batters, egg batters and egg omelets. This liquid food containing gelatin is then placed into a mold which is chilled to a temperature sufficiently low to cause the gelatin to set and gel the food. The gelled food is then cut into portions of predetermined size and cooked, thereby obtaining cooked portions having controlled size and shape.

In one preferred aspect, a pancake batter may be prepared from typical ingredients such as pastry flour, corn flour, sugar, salt, milk, eggs, oil and water. Gelatin is added to the pancake batter. The gelatin may be added to the batter in the dry form or it may be dissolved in water and added to the batter with the water ingredient.

The amount of gelatin added may be varied depending upon the particular food product being made, the gel strength of the gelatin and the like. When using high strength gelatin of about 275 bloom, the incorporation of 0.5 to 2.5% of such gelatin gives very satisfactory results. Amounts in excess of 2.5% may be used although it is then preferred to use gelatin of lower strength, for example, about 75 bloom. Use of gelatin in amounts less than 0.5% may be ineffective to hold the slices intact. Adding the gelatin in the amount of from about 1.5 to 2.0% is especially preferred.

The uncooked, liquid food product with the gelatin added is placed into either a rigid mold, or a flexible mold, such as a flexible casing of the type generally used in the manufacture of sausage products. For ease of handling and slicing, it is preferred to place the batter into a flexible casing.

The encased batter is then chilled to a temperature sufficiently low to set the gelatin. By "set" is meant the semirigid rubbery state which is attained by chilled gelatin at temperatures above freezing. The temperature at which the gelatin will set may vary within fairly wide ranges depending upon the bloom strength of the gelatin used, however these temperatures are preferably in the range of 30° to 40°F.

After the food product has been chilled to set the gelatin, the product is in a semirigid rubbery state in which it can be easily sliced and handled. The product

Egg and Waffle Products

is then either removed from the mold for slicing, or in the case of a flexible casing type of mold, the product may be sliced directly in the casing in a manner similar to sliced bologna and the like. Since the product is in a semisolid condition, no special equipment is required to slice and it may be sliced on an ordinary meat slicer. The product when sliced holds together extremely well and the individual slices may be handled without breaking, running or falling apart.

It is also possible to eliminate the slicing or subdividing step by placing the liquid food with added gelatin into a mold of about the same size as would be obtained by slicing. Thus, a mold having a diameter of about 4 inches and a thickness of about one quarter of an inch would be suitable for the pancake batter.

After slicing to the desired proportions, the product may be placed into a frying pan or onto a grill for cooking in the normal manner employed in the cooking of pancakes, eggs and so forth. As the food product is heated to cooking temperatures it passes initially into a liquid state and then back into a semisolid or solid state as the food product coagulates due to cooking. The cooking step alters the physical characteristics of the food ingredients and the gelatin so that the presence of gelatin is not apparent in the finished, cooked product. That is, there is no change in the natural flavor and texture of the product as a result of the gelatin.

Pancakes and eggs made by the method when cooked will exhibit the natural flavor and texture of pancakes and eggs, and no change in these characteristics is noted as a result of having had the gelatin incorporated into the batter.

Example: A pancake batter was prepared according to the following formulation.

Ingredient	Weight Percent
Pastry flour	26.5
Corn flour	2.5
Granulated sugar	1.5
Corn syrup solids	1.5
Salt	1.0
Nonfat dry milk	5.4
Soda	0.9
Levair	1.2
Whole egg	10.0
Oil	3.0
Water	~45.0

To the batter was added 1.5% of 275 bloom gelatin and the batter was poured into a flexible sausage casing and tied. The encased product was chilled to about 35°F to allow the gelatin to set. The batter was then sliced into pancake sized proportions and cooked on a grill. The cooked product had the natural flavor and texture of a pancake, with no alteration of the natural flavor and texture due to the presence of gelatin in the cooked product.

WAFFLES

Apparatus for Making Waffles

A method is provided by *D.C. De Jersey; U.S. Patent 3,780,193; Dec. 18, 1973;*

assigned to C.L. De Jersey & Sons Proprietary Limited, Australia for making waffles and like food products in the form of a continuous strip which is subsequently severed into suitable individual waffle units. The method comprises moving a succession of complementary pairs of waffle molding and cooking plates which have opposed waffle molding faces and are arranged in side-by-side relationship so as to form upper and lower continuous stretches of plates between which the continuous waffle strip can be molded and cooked.

A waffle-making dough mixture is fed between the opposed waffle molding faces of the plates at the tail end of a stretch of plates which are heated whereby the dough mixture is molded and cooked between the opposed faces of the plates so as to form a continuous waffle strip. The continuous waffle strip is discharged from between the moving stretch of plates at the lead end of these stretches of plates. The discharged continuous waffle strip is severed into selected waffle units. The patent itself provides a fully illustrated description of the operation of the apparatus.

Shelf Stable Product

M. Kaplow and R.E. Klose; U.S. Patent 3,753,734; August 21, 1973; assigned to General Foods Corporation prepare shelf-stable pancake batters and pancakes which may be stored for long periods of time without refrigeration in nonhermetic packages by including in the batter water-soluble solids at least equal to the moisture in the batter with edible polyhydric alcohols constituting the principal source of the water-soluble solids.

The term "pancake" and "waffle" as it is employed in this process is to be understood as meaning any kind or type of batter or cooked product thereof which contains a major portion of wheat flour, bleached and/or unbleached, a minor portion of corn flour and a leavening agent.

In general, the shelf-stable pancake and waffle products are formulated by preparing a batter containing egg, polyhydric alcohols, edible oils or shortening to a pancake mix, to which milk has been added, and cooking the pancake batter on a griddle to a dark brown color. The product is then allowed to cool to room temperature and is then packaged.

The batter employed to produce the shelf stable pancakes and waffles is formulated on the principles of A_w that is, the ability of the soluble solids of the batter to limit the amount of free water available to bacteria; the bacteria's inability to survive this condition; and the subsequent shelf stability or product stability obtained by virtue of this condition.

An A_w value is a direct measure of water vapor which is a function of unbound water. It is determined by dividing the mols of water plus mols of soluble solids into the mols of water. The lower the A_w value, the more stable the pancake and waffle products against microbiological decomposition, e.g., 0.80 in a product indicates more stability than 0.90 in a similar type product.

Some of the ingredients employed in the A_w emulsion of this process cannot be directly calculated for their effects on A_w because of the unknown quantities of soluble solids which they contain. Therefore, samples of pancakes and waffles measured electronically for A_w are usually found to have somewhat lower A_w

Egg and Waffle Products

values as compared to those calculated directly. To compute the complete A_w, the A_w lowering of the calculated ingredients are added together and subtracted from "1", "1" being equivalent to 100% water vapor or maximum water vapor which would be produced if none of the free water were bound by soluble solids. Thus a calculated A_w of 0.96 indicates an A_w lowering of 0.04.

The relative weight percent of water-soluble solids to the moisture content of the pancake and waffle products, when initially incorporated into the products during their manufacture and preparatory to packaging determines the ultimate functionality of the solids in providing the requisite bacteriostatic effect.

Usually the level of moisture will range from 14 to 40%. The level of water-soluble solids may be varied as may the level of moisture initially incorporated within the desired ranges. However, in varying these levels the relationship of the water-soluble solids in solution to the water should be controlled so as to afford the desired osmotic pressure. A good rule to observe in this connection is to be sure that the water-soluble solids available for solution are at least equal to the weight of moisture present, although in some cases it is possible that a lower level of water-soluble solids might afford some protection against microbiological decomposition provided an equivalent degree of osmotic pressure is available to protect the product.

It will be found, however, that the water-soluble solids here will constitute a major percent by weight of the pancake and waffle products.

The pancake and waffle products of this process when prepared in the manner disclosed, are characterized by their substantially complete resistance to bacterial decomposition, when the level of moisture in the batter and cooked products ranges from the abovementioned 14 to 40%, and the A_w ranges from 0.80 to 0.90 for the batter, and 0.65 to 0.75 for the cooked product; however, as a precautionary measure against the growth of yeast and molds certain antimycotic agents are incorporated in the batter at sufficient levels to prevent the growth of such organisms.

Sorbate salts such as potassium sorbate as well as sorbic acid can be used either separately or in combination. Propylene glycol which may be used alone or with other humectants like sorbitol to impart a degree of product softness or tenderness has also been found to serve as an antimycotic.

The amount of antimycotic agent added is selected so as to produce the desired results and will constitute a minor proportion of the product, from 0.1 to 2.5% of the total weight, depending on the particular antimycotic and the particular product composition, although even lower levels in the order of 50 ppm can be employed in the case of some antimycotics such as primaricin. Potassium sorbate in a water solution can be sprayed into the surface of the pancake or waffle product, or the product can be dipped in this solution. Cellophane and other enwrapments for the food can be spray-coated wtih a sorbic acid solution but impregnation or dusting with sorbic acid or potassium sorbate is preferred.

The shelf-stable pancake or waffle product which has been developed has an appearance, texture, color and aroma not unlike conventional pancakes and waffles. The product can be packaged using a nonhermetic packaging material such as cellophane. When removed from its pouch, the moist and soft product may be warmed just prior to consumption using a toaster or grill. The product has sufficient cohesive strength so that when it is removed from the toaster or grill, it will not tear, nor adhere to the toaster or grill. The dry ingredients chosen to produce the balanced shelf-stable pancake or waffle product will include pancake mix and preferably potassium sorbate. Nondry ingredients employed to prepare the shelf stable pancake or waffle product may include syrups, edible food oils or shortening, edible polyhydric alcohols, milk and egg.

Edible polyhydric alcohols constitute the principal source of water-soluble solids of the A_w emulsion and may range from 20 to 35% of the batter depending upon the particular polyhydric alcohol or polyhydric alcohol mixture, to provide the desired bacteriostatic protection. As the moisture content of the product increases in the intermediate moisture range, the level of a given edible polyhydric alcohol will correspondingly increase in order to maintain a sufficient bacteriostatic effect.

The quantity of edible polyhydric alcohols chosen will vary depending upon the presence and level of auxiliary soluble solids which produce a similar increase in osmotic pressure to the batter. Thus a variety of low molecular weight polyhydric alcohols having two or more hydroxyl groups, including glycerol, sorbitol, propylene glycol, mannitol, mixtures thereof and the like may be employed.

The polyhydric alcohols further assist in depleting the moisture of the pancake and waffle products by substituting for a portion of the moisture present in the interior of the product and causing moisture transfer to the exterior thereof.

Example:

Ingredients	Parts by Weight		Percent
Pancake Mix	140.0		29.4
Wheat Flour (Bleached)		43.0	
Wheat Flour (Unbleached)		20.0	
Corn Flour		16.0	
Sucrose		5.6	
Rice Flour		5.0	
Dextrose		4.0	
Salt		2.4	
Sodium Bicarbonate		2.0	
Sodium Aluminum Phosphate		2.0	
Milk	120.0		25.3
Glycerol	140.0		29.4
Egg	60.0		12.6
Cottonseed Oil	5.0		1.1
Propylene Glycol	9.0		1.9
Potassium Sorbate	1.5		0.3

Milk and glycerol were added to pancake mix in a mixer bowl and blended for 2 minutes at medium speed. Next, egg, cottonseed oil, propylene glycol and potassium sorbate were added and the mixture was mixed at high speed for 2 minutes to form a homogeneous batter. The batter having a moisture level of 14 to 40% was then cooked on a griddle at 375°F to form a dark brown product having the texture and appearance of conventional pancake products. The A_w of the batter was 0.83, and the A_w of the cooked pancake product was 0.74.

Microbiological evaluation showed standard plate, mold and yeast counts of less than 10 after 4 weeks storage in a nonhermetic package at 100°F. The test also proved negative for Salmonella.

FRUIT AND DESSERT TYPE ITEMS

FRUIT AND NUT PRODUCTS

Dehydrated Fried Snack Food from Apples

The process described by *T. Yamazaki and T. Hayashida; U.S. Patent 3,962,355; June 8, 1976; assigned to Kanro Co. Ltd., Japan* relates to a method for producing a snack food from fruits such as apples, or vegetables such as taros and potatoes. In the process, the raw materials are washed, pared, and cut into pieces of suitable shape and thickness. If necessary, the pieces are treated to inactivate the oxidase contained therein, and are then fried at atmospheric pressure or in a vacuum. The fried pieces are expanded to restore their original size and shape and hardened in a cold vacuum. Thereby, a snack food which is porous and palatable, and has its natural tint, can be produced.

Example 1: Jonathan apples and Ralls Janet apples are subjected sequentially to washing, paring, coring, cutting, seasoning, drying, frying and vacuum swelling. The apples are washed in a conventional manner and peeled. The cores of the peeled apples are removed and the flesh portions of the apples are cut into pieces of suitable shape and thickness. The thickness of the cut piece may be about 5 mm so as to prevent crumbling.

In order to prevent browning caused by the oxidase contained in the apple pieces, they are treated with 2 to 3% saline solution, and the prevention of browning can be enhanced by using vitamin C in the saline solution. Then, the pieces are soaked in sugar solution (sugar concentration: 30° to 40° syrup) at 65° to 90°C for about 15 to 20 minutes. This high temperature seasoning treatment is also effective for the inactivation of oxidase in the apples.

The seasoned pieces are laid on screens to drain excess sugar solution, and they are dried to 6 to 8% moisture at about 70°C in a hot air drier. The proper selection of the drying temperature is important to keep browning to a minimum. The dried pieces are fried in a mixture of coconut oil and palm oil at 155° to 165°C under atmospheric pressure for 3 to 4 minutes.

While the fried pieces are still hot, they are placed in a cold vacuum chamber and restored to their original size and hardened within the chamber. The pressure in the chamber should be between 0 and 160 mm Hg to cause expansion of the pieces. When the pieces are expanded and cooled, they are removed from the chamber and residual oil is removed.

If the apple pieces are blanched in hot water at about 90°C for about 2 to 3 minutes before seasoning by the sugar solution, the sugar solution can be used at room temperature, but the treatment time is to be increased to about 30 minutes. Crumbling of the pieces and coloring of the sugar solution by conversion is prevented at the lower treating temperature, and the sugar solution can be used repeatedly. The apple pieces fried under atmospheric pressure must be placed in the vacuum chamber as quickly as possible. Therefore, the frying treatment may also be carried out in the vacuum.

An oil vessel is placed in the vacuum chamber, and the dried pieces are fried at 120° to 130°C for 3 to 4 minutes. These conditions are mild as compared with frying under atmospheric pressure, and the consumption and degradation of the oil is reduced. In addition, the undesirable coloring of the apple pieces at the higher oil temperature is prevented. The fried pieces are withdrawn from the oil vessel and expanded and cooled within the vacuum chamber which must be provided with cooling means. The chamber pressure is preferably in the range from 0 to 160 mm Hg.

When frying and expanding are carried out in the same vacuum chamber, the natural color of the apple pieces is maintained, and productivity is very much increased. Alternatively, two vacuum chambers may be used and each chamber provided with an oil vessel. The two oil vessels are connected for transfer of the oil from one vessel to the other after frying, so that the temperature of the oil is not lowered much, and the operation can be carried out efficiently and economically.

Example 2: Well-shaped taros are selected and washed, pared and cut into pieces of appropriate shape and thickness (preferably 2 to 3 mm). The pieces are soaked in a sugar solution of 20° to 30° at 65° to 90°C for 15 to 20 minutes, whereby the sugar permeates the pieces. The pieces are then laid on screen plates to drain excess sugar solution and fried. The procedures for frying and expanding the pieces in a vacuum chamber are the same as in the case of apples, so that a detailed explanation is omitted here. However, the taro pieces are fried without drying, and because of the high water content of the pieces, frying for 10 to 15 minutes is necessary.

The product obtained from taros has a porous texture like the product from apples, and is palatable, having the natural taste and flavor of the raw material. The coloring or yellowing by oil scorch is slight, so that the product has the natural tint of the raw material. It can be seasoned to give it a sweet taste, sour taste and oil taste.

Dehydrated Fruit to Add to Powdered Instant Food

H. Murai; U.S. Patent 3,931,434; January 6, 1976; assigned to Nagatanien Honpo Co., Ltd., Japan describes a process for manufacturing dehydrated fruit used as an additive to instant food, particularly raw powdered instant food such as jelly,

Fruit and Dessert Type Items

sherbet or ice cream. Raw powders of, for example, instant jelly, sherbet or ice cream which are very hygroscopic, are generally sold sealed in a moistureproof bag. When prepared, the powders are dissolved in cold or hot water and cooled in a cup or mold.

Where such powders include dried fruit, the prepared food will have an increased flavor. However, if ordinary dried fruit which generally contains about 20% water is mixed with the raw powders, they then will become solidified by absorbing the water of the dried fruit. To avoid such inconvenience, the dried fruit has to be dehydrated to a water content lower than 6%.

It is therefore the object of this process to manufacture a dehydrated fruit which can be quickly dehydrated to a desired low water content without loss of color and flavor and moreover with the ability to regain its original condition instantly and reliably. The method of achieving this end comprises covering the surface of fruit preliminarily dried to a prescribed extent with granulated sugar, embedding the granulated sugar into the surface of the fruit by pressing it and finally dehydrating the sugar-coated fruit at a prescribed level of temperature until the granulated sugar melted by the water content of the fruit is again solidified.

The raw fruit may consist of various kinds of commercially available dried fruit such as apricot, raisin and pineapple. Such dried fruit is preferred to have a water content of 20 to 30%. If the water content exceeds this level, the fruit will have its outline considerably deformed and undesirably attach itself to the inner walls of a press by oozing water.

Raw dried fruit first has its surface coated with granulated sugar and then is flattened to a prescribed thickness by a press. At this time the granulated sugar is embedded in the surface of the fruit to prevent the fruit from sticking to the inner walls of the press with the resultant decrease in an area of contact between the surface of the fruit and the inner walls. Particles of the granulated sugar are preferred to consist of pure crystals whose particle size ranges between 40 and 65 mesh.

The preliminarily dried fruit is pressed to the proper thickness in consideration of its readiness to be restored to its original condition, when actually cooked. The coating of granulated sugar and the pressing of the fruit may be carried out simultaneously or repeatedly by turns until the fruit is reduced to a prescribed thickness.

The fruit coated with granulated sugar and thereafter pressed is thermally dehydrated. In this case, the particles of granulated sugar forced into the interior of the fruit from its surface act as a medium for helping the water contained in the fruit to be dispersed in the interior and also evaporated on the surface thereof, thereby reducing the time of dehydrating the fruit far more than when it is not coated with granulated sugar. With the process of dehydration, the dissolved granulated sugar is again solidified to provide desired dehydrated fruit. Samples of raw dried fruit used were cut pieces of apricot 1.3 mm thick containing 24% water. Comparison was made between the samples whose water content after dehydration roughly averaged 6%. The samples were dried by hot air at 60° to 100°C.

Results showed that fruit samples free from granulated sugar took several times longer to dehydrate than those coated with granulated sugar, and moreover were considerably deteriorated in quality, for example, lost flavor, turned brown and were hardened on the surface. In contrast, fruit samples coated with granulated sugar were very quickly dehydrated to a lower water content than 6%, and were little subject to quality deterioration. To avoid, however, the loss of vitamins, and flavor and discoloration, it is preferred that dehydration be carried out at a temperature of 60° to 80°C and for a length of time ranging between 90 and 150 minutes.

Fruit thus dehydrated is cut by a cutter into pieces having a desired size and sealed in a moistureproof bag with raw powders of jelly, sherbet or ice cream. The final step of cutting fruit should preferably be effected after completion of its dehydration, because this process prevents the cut pieces from sticking to the cutter blades.

At the time of cooking, cut pieces of dehydrated fruit are mixed with the above-mentioned powdered instant food in cold or hot water. In this case, solidified granulated sugar acts as a medium for quickly drawing cold or hot water from the surface into the interior of the cut pieces of the fruit so as to help them to be restored to the original condition, and at the same time is dissolved in the water. Further, numerous pores appearing on the surface of the cut pieces of the fruit increase the contact area between the water and the cut pieces, thus promoting the restoration of the cut pieces to the original condition.

The time required for the cut pieces of dehydrated fruit to regain the original condition varies with the thickness of the cut pieces. Raw dehydrated fruit used in the experiment consisted of cut pieces of apricot containing 6% water. The cut pieces were dipped in 200 cc of hot water at 90°C and considered to have regained the original condition when they became soft with 20 to 25% water content.

Results showed that cut pieces of apricot coated with granulated sugar took far less time in being restored to the original condition than those of apricot free from granulated sugar, and a difference in the time of restoration between the cut pieces of both types of apricot increased more prominently as the cut pieces grew thicker.

It has been experimentally found that the cut pieces of dehydrated fruit are preferred to have a thickness of 1.2 to 1.6 mm. If the thickness decreases from this range, the cut pieces will feel undesirably soft to an eater's teeth, rendering the dehydrated fruit less commercially valuable. Conversely, if the thickness exceeds this range, the cut pieces will consume too much time in being restored to the original condition to be used as an additive to instant food such as raw powders of jelly, sherbet or ice cream.

Example: 1,000 g of preliminarily dried apricot containing 24% water were pressed by roller while being coated with fine granulated sugar having a particle size of 40 to 65 mesh. The apricot was flattened to a thickness of 1.3 mm by being pressed twice. The apricot was dehydrated 90 minutes at 80°C to a water content of 5.8%, and thereafter cut into pieces each having a size of 1 cm^2. A few cut pieces of the dehydrated apricot were sealed in a moistureproof bag with 27 g (sufficient for six persons) of jelly powder having the composition shown on the following page. At the time of cooking, the jelly powder and the cut pieces of dehydrated apricot were mixed in 200 cc of hot water at 90°C.

The cut pieces were restored to the original condition in one minute and 45 seconds.

Raw Material	Percent by Weight
Gelatin	12.50
Table salt	0.50
Glucose	3.50
Sugar	80.00
Citric acid	1.40
Natural coloring matter	0.015
Flavoring agent	0.803
Others	1.282

It is possible to mix 6.0 g of cut pieces of this dehydrated apricot with the powders of sherbet having a composition shown below.

Raw Material	Percent by Weight
Sugar	79.47
Glucose	16.56
Citric acid	0.99
Table salt	0.33
Fruit juice flavoring agent	2.65

Nutmeat Confection Coating

M.J. Pichel; U.S. Patent 3,819,839; June 25, 1974; assigned to Swift & Company describes a method of preparing nutmeat-based coating compositions comprising a blend of nuts and a broad plastic range fat used for coating confections and dairy products.

Generally, the compositions comprise ground nutmeats and wide plastic range coating fat in combination to provide protein-rich coating compositions having low viscosity and a quick setting time. Plastic range of the fat in the coating composition is related to the amount of nutmeat present in the composition in a manner which insures that the composition is flowable and quick-setting, whether it contains a small amount of ground nutmeat or a major amount of ground nutmeat. The amount of fat in the composition and the consistency of the fat are determined by the amount of nutmeat in the composition. In all cases, however, the fat component of the coating material is a wide plastic range fat.

The coating composition is formulated to possess viscosity characteristics, permitting envelopment of the entire surface of the material being coated with a uniformly thin layer of the coating which has good plasticity during storage, yet melts at a sufficiently low temperature so that it does not seem waxy on consumption. Thus, the coating compositions are highly nutritious, have an appealing appearance and good flavor, and also, possess characteristics rendering them highly desirable insofar as manufacturing operations are concerned.

The coating compositions include preferably from 40 to 80% nutmeat and 20 to 60% wide plastic range fat. The plastic range of the fat is related to percent solids in the fat at given temperatures, and thus the characteristics of the fatty component of the coating composition for a given amount of nutmeat may be expressed in SFI units at given temperatures, usually at 50°, at 70° and at 92°F.

SFI (solid fat index) is an empirical measure of the solid fat content of fats and oils. It is calculated from the specific volumes of the fats and oils at various temperatures, and provides an excellent indication of the plastic range of a fatty material. Solid fat indexes may be determined by Tentative Method Cd 10-57 of the American Oil Chemists' Society. Solid fat index is essentially the same as percent solids, and these terms are used interchangeably.

In those cases where the composition contains a minor proportion of nutmeats in the range of about 10 to 40% nutmeats by weight, the SFI of the fat will be low as compared to the SFI of the fat utilized in a coating composition containing a predominant amount of nutmeats in the range of 50 to 80% nutmeats. The fat component of the nut coating composition is a wide plastic range fat, and is solid at room temperature (78°F) with a Wiley melting point of 100° to 120°F. The wide plastic range fats may be defined as fats exhibiting a variation of less than 15 SFI units with a temperature change of 9°F in the range of 50° to 150°F.

Ingredients such as flavoring agents, coloring agents, stabilizers, etc., may optionally be incorporated in the coating, as desired. Usually a small amount of sugar and salt will be used to enhance the nut flavor. In the preparation of the nutmeats as a component of the coating, the nuts are ground to a fine particle size and thoroughly admixed with the fat. Although the coatings can be made from a variety of cooked nuts such as almonds, walnuts, pecans and filberts, the process in its preferred form utilizes peanuts as the nut component because of the wide appeal of peanut-flavored and peanut-butter-containing confections.

Usually the peanuts are roasted, then crushed or ground to about the form of a paste similar to peanut butter, and then the fat component of the coating composition is combined with the ground peanuts to form a homogeneous mixture. It is recommended that the fat be heated to a temperature above the melting point of the fat prior to incorporation with the ground peanuts to insure uniform dispersion of the fat and peanut solids. It is also possible to first mix the fat and ground peanuts and then heat the mixture to obtain uniform distribution of the fat and solids. If the coating composition is to be packaged and shipped to the point of use, the mix can be chilled by conventional means and packaged for efficient handling, or packaged without cooling.

The coating compositions must have characteristics which permit their use on machinery used in the ice cream and confectionery industries. The coatings possess characteristics which allow for their use in coating frozen confections utilizing automatic stick confection machines.

In the operation of such machines, there is provided a bar coating station just after removal of the bars from the forming molds and just prior to the packaging or bagging device. Because of the high speed operation of the machines, only a short period of time, usually not more than about twenty seconds, is permitted between the time of removal of the bars from the coating bath and the bagging and discharge station.

Thus any coating applied to the surface of the bar must have hardened and be nontacky as the coated bar reaches the bagging station. This time interval after removal from the coating applicator includes what is referred to in the art as drip time and set dry time. The total elapsed time from application of the warm (105° to 115°F) coating to the surface of the bar to the point at which the coated

Fruit and Dessert Type Items

bar is dry to the touch and can be packaged should not exceed about fourteen seconds. The drip time is that period during which a very limited amount of the coating composition drips from the bar and the set time is that interval after cessation of dripping during which the coating becomes hard and nontacky.

When the coating is set, it feels dry to the touch and the coated bar can be handled and packaged without smearing of the coating or adhesion of the coating to the wrapping materials. The major part of the time period of about 9 to 18 seconds elapsed time between application of the coating and development of a nontacky smearproof surface is taken up by drip time with only a comparatively short time being required for drying.

Example: 69.5 lb of ground, roasted peanuts were placed in a kettle and 4.95 pounds of sugar and 0.75 lb of salt were added. 24.8 lb of hydrogenated soybean oil was heated to 130°F and the heated oil was added to the kettle and the contents agitated for 5 to 10 minutes until a smooth, uniform dispersion was formed. The hydrogenated soybean oil had a Wiley melting point of 120°F and had a plastic range represented by SFI values as follows:

$SFI_{50°F}$	65.0
$SFI_{70°F}$	55.0
$SFI_{92°F}$	38.0

Frozen ice cream bars were dipped in the coating composition which had been previously heated to 115°F. The bars were removed from the liquid coating bath and the time to cessation of dripping of the coating from the bar was noted. The time for setting of the coating to a hard, nonsticky, continuous surface was also noted. The drip time was 9 seconds and the set time was an additional 3 seconds. An elapsed time of 12 seconds from removal of the coated bar from the coating bath to the setting of a uniformly thin, continuous coating on the bar is sufficiently rapid to permit the use of the coating composition in automatic coating and packaging equipment.

Layered Jelly Dessert

T. Ikeda, S. Moritaka, S. Sugiura and T. Umeki; U.S. Patent 3,969,536; July 13, 1976; assigned to Takeda Chemical Industries, Ltd. and Nichiro Gyogyo Kaisha, Ltd., Japan disclose a process by which gelled sherbet, particularly multicolored assembled gelled foods, can be successfully prepared.

In the process, at least two of the same or different materials, each of which contains 0.5 to 5 weight percent of a thermally gelable polysaccharide composed predominantly of β-1,3-glycosidic groups, and each of which has been prepared separately by holding a dispersion containing the polysaccharide at a temperature of 55° to 80°C under stirring, are assembled in such a manner that they are present independently from each other but in intimate contact with each other. The assembly is heated to at least 60°C and subsequently cooled. The assembled foods have a strong adhesivity between component gel bodies.

The thermally gelable polysaccharides can be produced by cultivating a microorganism belonging to the genus Alcaligenes or the genus Agrobacterium according to the procedures described in U.S. Patents 3,754,925 and 3,822,250. For example, polysaccharides A, B and C employed in the following experiments and examples are elaborated by *Agrobacterium radiobacter, Alcaligenes faecalis* var *mixogenes,* and *Alcaligenes faecalis* var *mixogenes K* respectively. In the process, a material containing such a polysaccharide in a proportion of 0.5 to 5 weight percent is first prepared. This polysaccharide-containing material is prepared by retaining a dispersion of the polysaccharide at 55° to 80°C under constant stirring. This temperature is retained under constant stirring.

It is important to disperse the entire amount of the polysaccharide evenly in a suitable amount of water and, then, heat the dispersion to the required temperature since it is not suitable to expose the system to any temperature in excess of 80°C even transiently throughout the process of preparing the polysaccharide-containing material. The heating may be achieved by adding hot water (hot water pouring). Since the gel-forming property of the polysaccharide is materialized over a significantly broad pH range, i.e., between 2 to 9, no special attention need be paid to pH.

As a precaution, it is undesirable to add solid materials, e.g., natural fruits, etc., in excessive amounts. Thus these additives are preferably limited to an amount suitable for decoration, i.e., not more than about 10% by weight. In such instances, the proportionate amount of the polysaccharide may be reckoned from the total weight including the weight of such solid materials.

When a water-soluble food color is employed as a colorant, it could happen that the color migrates from the gel block or body containing it to another gel block adjacent thereto. If that is objectionable, a water-insoluble pigment such as a food color of the aluminum lake type or such a natural coloring material as β-carotene, chlorophyll, lycopene, or other similar substances may be successfully employed.

When it is desired to manufacture a gelled food incorporating a whipped (foamed) gel as a component gel block, a suitable foaming agent such as egg white, a vegetable or animal protein partial hydrolyzate, and a propylene glycol fatty acid ester is used.

While the polysaccharide-containing material thus far described is fluid when just prepared, it gains considerably in viscosity as it is allowed to stand and cool to 50° to 40°C and forms a gel as it is cooled to 40°C or less. This cooling operation must be performed without agitation. The cooling operation may involve allowing the system to cool spontaneously to room temperature or by forced cooling to a lower temperature, or by a combination of the two cooling methods.

Since the product has a high viscosity, though it has not undergone gelation, at the internal temperature of 50° to 40°C, the material should be quickly superimposed thereon. It is desirable to effect cooling to the internal temperature of 45° to 10°C. When the polysaccharide-containing material in liquid condition is directly put to use, it is dispensed into a suitable container to obtain the desired gel product.

The polysaccharide-containing materials which have been prepared separately or similarly in the above manner are assembled with each other in mutually discrete yet intimate relation. Then, the combined or assembled polysaccharide materials are heated to a temperature not lower than 60°C, and preferably from 60° to 70°C, when both materials are solid and there is a contact face between gels in the assembly, or to 65°C or higher when a liquid material is assembled with another liquid or a solid material.

If necessary, the assembled product is further heated to 80°C or higher, whereby the inherent thermal gelability of the polysaccharide is materialized to provide a thermally insolubilized gel or elastic product and, at the same time, pasteurization effects are accomplished.

After the above heat treatment, the product is cooled, preferably to a temperature not higher than 45°C whereby the gelled product is obtained. The cooling may be effected in the routine manner, or the product is chilled in a freezer in order to obtain a sherbet-like frozen food.

In preparing a frozen jelly, it is preferable, quality-wise, to carry out the heat treatment at a temperature of about 80°C or more as described above and freeze the resulting gel in which the inherent thermal gelability of the polysaccharide has been materialized.

Thus, there are obtained a variety of assembled foods with ease and at low cost. The gels are highly stable in a broad pH range, given jelly of good quality under acidic conditions (e.g., pH 2 to 3). Particularly, there is realized a firm bond between gels upon assembling, with the individual gel bodies being difficult to take apart, so that a delicious taste emanating from a subtle blend of textures of gels can be obtained.

Furthermore, by controlling the temperature of the resulting jelly product, a variety of foods such as cold jelly, warm jelly and frozen jelly can be obtained. For example, if a frozen laminar fruit jelly is served as such, it gives a taste and mouth-feel like that of a delicious sherbet but, if the frozen product is thawed, it reverts to a jelly. Thus, since freezing and thawing can be reversibly repeated, a large quantity of jelly can be safely stored in frozen condition.

Moreover, when the product is heated to a temperature of about 80°C or higher as described above, the inherent thermal gelability of the polysaccharide is materialized to yield thermally insoluble gels and an elastic product of such gel with an intimate bond. And the product, on freezing, yields an excellent frozen jelly. Thus, the product remains stable in quality even after a protracted time of storage.

Example: To a jelly composition of 25 g of sucrose, 20 g of glucose, 1.25 g of citric acid, 0.25 g of ascorbic acid, 0.5 g of orange flavor, 0.02 g of β-carotene and 2.5 g of powdery polysaccharide B, there was added 200 ml of water at about 30°C. After thorough mixing, the dispersion was heated under agitation to prepare a fluid with a temperature of about 65°C. The fluid was distributed into containers up to about half their capacity and allowed to stand and cool.

When the temperature of the fluid had reached about 40°C, a fluid prepared in the same manner as above and with a temperature of about 65°C (except that it contained 0.5 g of melon flavor and 0.15 g of chlorophyll instead of the orange flavor and β-carotene) was layered onto the above orange-flavored fluid up to the brim of the container to form an overlayer. Then, with the container covered, each product and container was heated in the routine manner. When the temperature of the product had reached about 80°C, the product and container was held at that temperature for 30 minutes. Then, the product was taken out and cooled in a refrigerator.

The jelly product thus obtained is of good quality consisting of two layers, i.e., an orange and a melon layer, and showing an excellent interlayer bond. When, after the above fluid-pouring procedure was repeated, the same heat-treatment was carried out at the last stage, there was easily obtained a multilayer (3- or 4-layer) jelly of good quality with firm interlayer bonds.

When, in the above cooling procedure, the product was directly frozen, there was readily obtained a delicious layered sherbet-like dessert. Upon thawing, the frozen product reverted to a multilayer jelly of good quality with a firm interlayer bond. Similar products were also prepared from polysaccharide A and polysaccharide C instead of polysaccharide B. The results were similar to the products obtained in the above example.

"INSTANT" AND "READY-TO-EAT" DESSERTS

Dessert Powder for "Instant" Cooked Pudding

Powdered desserts made from ungelatinized starch products, which have to be boiled to yield desserts, are well known. They contain as an essential ingredient starch which imparts texture to the prepared dessert and at the same time serves as a carrier for flavors and coloring matters. The amount of sugar necessary for sweetening the dessert as a rule has to be added by the consumer, but some powdered desserts are known which the sugar has already been added by the manufacturer.

Apart from these powdered desserts on the basis of ungelatinized starch, which have to be boiled during preparation for gelatinizing the starch, so-called "instant desserts" have been gaining ground which contain as a binder pregelatinized, cold-water-swelling starch. A disadvantage is connected with instant desserts in that during addition of the cold aqueous liquids, such as water or milk, bacteria may get into the dessert and cause food poisoning.

On the other hand, powdered desserts on the basis of ungelatinized starch products, which require boiling, have the disadvantage of having to be mixed with aqueous liquids while cold because otherwise unhomogeneous lumpy desserts would result.

H. Bohrmann and G. Schneider; U.S. Patent 3,928,650; December 23, 1975; assigned to CPC International Inc. describe a pasty dry product which does not have these disadvantages. A dessert is prepared from it by stirring it into boiling aqueous liquids, such as milk, fruit juice and/or water, and cooling. This pasty dry product is characterized in that it consists of triglycerides of the unbranched (i.e., linear) fatty acids naturally present in edible oils and edible fats, ungelatinized starch, at least one sugar, and one or more suitable emulsifiers, preferably monoglycerides or mono/diglycerides. The pasty dry product preferably contains 20 to 35% by weight of triglycerides, up to 5% by weight of mono- or mono/diglycerides, 15 to 35% by weight of starch and 30 to 35% by weight of sugars. Essential ingredients of the pasty dry product, apart from the ungelatinized starch, are the triglycerides as they impart to the product the texture necessary for filling in tubes and at the same time allow lump-free preparation by pressing the dry product into boiling aqueous liquids. Triglycerides preferably used for the purpose are vegetable oils and/or vegetable fats with a maximum melting point of about 40°C.

Products containing less than about 20% by weight of triglycerides are difficult to press out of a tube, whereas products containing more than 35% by weight of triglycerides are rather soft and an even higher fat content at the expense of the content of starch and sugar leads to a dessert with a creamy, very soft texture.

The mono- and/or mono/diglycerides impart to the pasty dry product a uniform, homogeneous texture. It is also possible to replace the mono- or mono/diglycerides in the pasty dry product with, or as an extra ingredient, lecithin and/or other suitable emulsifiers in an amount of up to about 5% by weight.

Any ungelatinized starch that may be used for a dessert starch is suitable as a binder for the pasty dry product, e.g., native cereal starches like corn and wheat starch as well as waxy starches, and/or tuber or root starches like potato and tapioca starch, and chemically or enzymatically modified starches like phosphate modified starches. The amount of starch used is determined not only by the texture the dessert is desired to have but also by the amount of triglycerides and sugars contained in the pasty dry product. The average starch content of the dry product is 15 to 35% by weight.

Sugar is usually employed in the form of sucrose, but any other kind of sugar like lactose, dextrose and dry glucose syrup, and/or sugar alcohols like sorbitol, xylitol or mixtures thereof may be used as well. The amount of sugar added is determined by the flavor the prepared dessert is desired to have. The average sugar content ranges from 30 to 50% by weight.

Any specific change in the texture of the dessert may be obtained by adding, as a binder (apart from starch), 0.2 to 2.0% by weight of vegetable binders like agar, alginate, pectin, carrageenan and carob kernel meal, and/or gelatin. Flavors, such as cocoa, vanillin, natural fruit powder and aromas, and natural and/or artificial coloring matters may of course also be added.

The pasty dry product for the preparation of desserts is manufactured in a fashion that the mono-, di- and triglycerides and, if desired, the lecithin and/or other emulsifiers are melted together at 50° to 60°C, and kneaded together with the starch, the sugars, flavors and coloring matters until a homogeneous mass is obtained, whereupon the product is vacuumized for a short time and then filled in tubes at 20° to 30°C.

To prepare a dessert a specific amount, depending on the composition of the pasty dry product, is pressed out of the tube into a boiling aqueous liquid (milk, water, and/or fruit juice), stirred in by whipping with a whisk and evenly blended. For cooling the mass is filled into bowls or jars and, if desired, unmolded after cooling. The amount of pasty dry product may be increased or reduced depending on whether a thick or thin texture is desired.

Example: The following ingredients are used to make the exemplary product of this process.

	Kilograms
Sunflower oil	24.80
Glycerin monostearate	0.25
Lecithin	0.50
Sucrose (powder)	39.20
Cornstarch	25.83
Cocoa (20 to 24% cocoa butter)	9.40
Vanillin	0.02

The sunflower oil is blended at 60°C with the glycerin monostearate and the lecithin, whereupon the starch, sucrose, cocoa and vanillin are kneaded into the mass until a homogeneous paste is obtained. This paste is then filled in tubes at 20° to 30°C and is ready for use.

To prepare a chocolate-flavored dessert about 130 g of the pasty dry product is pressed from the tube into 500 ml of boiling milk, whereupon the mixture is whipped with a whisk and stirred evenly. For cooling the mass is filled in bowls or jars. When cooled, the dessert may be unmolded. The example was repeated replacing the cornstarch with wheat starch, waxy maize starch, tapioca starch, and blends of the foregoing, with comparable results.

Spoonable Gelatin Dessert Concentrate

A.S. Clausi, M. Glicksman and E. Farkas; U.S. Patent 3,889,002; June 10, 1975; assigned to General Foods Corporation describe a process whereby a spoonable frozen or shelf-stable concentrate which when diluted with hot tap water and thereafter refrigerated produces a gelatin-type dessert.

It has been found that by soaking gelatin in a polyhydric alcohol of a temperature not exceeding room temperature for a specific period of time, a gelatin which is readily soluble and dispersible in hot tap water is obtained which, when mixed with other ingredients of a gelatin dessert-type nature and allowed to stand at room temperature for a short period, yields a spoonable gelatin dessert concentrate which may either be frozen or retained as a shelf stable product.

When dissolved in hot water and thereafter refrigerated, a completely gelled dessert is derived in about one quarter of the time required by the conventional gelatin dessert product due at least in part to having eliminated the need of dissolving the gelatin in boiling water.

The behavioral characteristics of gelatin with regard to its poor solubility in water indicates a fundamental arrangement of its molecular structure whereby the amino acid radicals are joined together by peptide linkages in chains of varying lengths and molecular weights. Due to this structural configuration therefore, the granulated gelatin when placed in cold water, tends to imbibe the same and remain as discrete swollen particles rather than dissolving therein.

This process is based on the fact that gelatin imbibes a cold polyhydric alcohol in much the same way as it does water which accounts for the low solubility of gelatin in the latter. To date, polyhydric alcohols have been regarded as poor dispersants for gelatin since they tend to dissolve hydrophilic colloids as a whole. However, it has been found that when the gelatin is allowed to absorb the polyhydric alcohol for a period of time sufficient for the gelatin granules to become

Fruit and Dessert Type Items

swollen but prior to actual dissolution in the alcohol, the gelatin, when dispersed in hot tap water is readily soluble and enjoys a degree of viscosity appropriate for use as a spoonable gelatin concentrate.

The composition is prepared by soaking a gelatin in a polyhydric alcohol, the temperature of the alcohol as well as duration of soaking being critical. It has been found that the gelatin must be soaked in a polyhydric alcohol not exceeding room temperature for a period of time sufficient to allow the colloid granules to imbibe the alcohol and assume the appearance of discrete swollen particles or beads which requires a minimum time of about one hour.

At the same time it is essential that the impregnating process not be so long as to allow the gelatin to appear solid and cohesive as this indicates that the gelatin has begun to dissolve in the alcohol. It is important that these parameters be strictly observed since an appreciable variance therefrom will result in a gelatin of either poor solubility and dispersibility or poor workability from a manufacturing as well as consumer standpoint.

For example, if gelatin is soaked in glycerin for appreciably less than one hour or alternatively allowed to dissolve in the glycerin, the improved solubility in hot tap water will not be derived. Similarly, if the gelatin is soaked in glycerin exceeding ambient temperature, a tough rubbery ball which is less soluble and difficult to handle is obtained, making use of the same as a spoonable concentrate infeasible.

The ratio of gelatin to polyhydric alcohol may encompass a wide range but a preferred ratio is 5:1 to 1:3 by weight of the gelatin to alcohol since the gelatin imbibes all of the alcohol and thus eliminates the need for subsequent removal of any remaining solvent, the final product having the appearance of a composition of discrete beads with the absence of any solvent.

Both the liquid polyhydric alcohols and solutions of normally solid polyhydric alcohols may be utilized to achieve the desired result but glycerin is particularly preferred since it demonstrates the least off-taste of this class of alcohols. The preferred embodiment is therefore a 5:3 weight ratio of gelatin to glycerin.

The other product ingredients of the gelatin dessert concentrate such as the sucrose, food acids, flavoring and coloring may be added either while the gelatin is soaking in the alcohol for the initial one hour period or may be added at the conclusion of that period, in both instances the mixture being allowed to equilibrate at room temperature for an additional period of time, usually an hour, being careful not to allow dissolution of the gelatin in the polyhydric alcohol to occur in either instance.

Example: A 3:5 weight ratio of gelatin to glycerin (30:50 g) was prepared and allowed to stand at room temperature for one hour during which time the following ingredients were added:

	Grams
Sugar	130
Citric acid	3
Water	70
Flavor and color q.s.	

At the completion of the first hour the entire mixture was allowed to stand for an additional hour at room temperature after mixing the gelatin/glycerol phase and ingredient phase together. The mixture was refrigerated at 0°F and thereafter 2 teaspoons (30 to 40 g) of the concentrate were stirred into 120 cc of hot tap water (125°F). The concentrate dispersed within 1 minute and gradually went into solution upon standing. It was then refrigerated and ready to consume as a gelatin dessert in 45 minutes.

Canned Fruit Pudding

Fruit puddings have customarily been prepared by mixing together water, sugar, starch and edible acids. To this basic mix was added, in varying amounts, a vegetable fat or oil, salt and flavoring and coloring ingredients. This mixture is stirred together and sterilized at 200°F. The sterilized mixture is thereafter poured into cans and allowed to cool while in the can. A more recent innovation has been the cooling of the sterilized mix prior to canning and thereafter aseptically canning the sterilized pudding.

This procedure, although commercially employed, includes certain disadvantages that increase the cost of the process as well as result in a less palatable product than should be the case. The use of starch in the mixture has as its purpose the maintenance of a suitably high viscosity of the resulting pudding. However, the effect of a heated acid on starch is to deactivate the starch's thickening property.

Thus, when the combined mix is sterilized, the elevated temperature of the mix, in the presence of the acid ingredient results in a partial deactivation of the thickening effect of the starch on the pudding mixture. To compensate, food processors add an excess of starch to get the desired viscosity of the pudding. The cost of this additional starch adds to the cost of making the pudding. Moreover, the pudding often takes on an undesirable starchy flavoring.

An additional disadvantage is the corrosive effect on the processing equipment caused by the presence of the edible acid, especially at elevated temperature. In view of the relatively large size equipment required, large additional costs may be incurred by employing corrosion resistant equipment. Alternatively, if no such precautions are taken, the expense of maintaining the large size equipment adds significantly to the preparation costs.

A.P. Stewart, Jr. and C.R. Dreier, Jr.; U.S. Patent 3,770,461; November 6, 1973; assigned to Allied Chemical Corporation overcome these drawbacks by a process in which a base mixture comprising sugar, starch and water is blended and sterilized and a flavoring mixture comprising an edible acid, flavoring and water is separately blended and sterilized. The two separately processed mixtures are cooled and are thereafter mixed together to form a sterilized fruit pudding, which is then preferably aseptically canned.

In more detail, the base mixture is prepared by blending sugar, starch and water together. A vegetable fat or oil may also be added. In addition, lesser amounts of salt and coloring agents are included in the mix. The composition of the base mixture in terms of the percentage of each of the above-mentioned ingredients varies in accordance with the flavor and quality of the fruit pudding to be produced. The percentage of starch in the base mixture is preferably in the range to produce a final fruit pudding with a starch concentration of 4 to 6% by weight. The ingredients are mixed together to form a homogeneous mixture. After mixing, the base mixture is heated to 120° to 150°F. This heating step reduces the steam load in the subsequent sterilizing procedure. The temperature of the base mixture is preferably maintained below 155°F. At a temperature greater than 155°F the starch constituent is activated. That is, the starch granules begin to swell. In this condition, the starch is more readily sheared when sterilized and tends to lose its effectiveness.

The heated base mixture is next sterilized. The sterilization step is preferably by steam injection. In steam injection sterilization, the base fruit pudding mixture is heated to about 280°F for 1 to 60 seconds by the injection of steam. Although steam injection sterilization is preferred, other methods of sterilizing the base pudding mixture may be substituted.

In a preferred embodiment, the hot, sterilized base mixture is conveyed, immediately after sterilization, into a flash tank. The flash tank is provided for the dual purpose of cooling the mixture as well as removing excess water contained in the mixture. The mixture is cooled to about 130° to 160°F. The excess water in the original blend as well as water added due to any condensation of injected steam is herein removed.

In a separate procedure the acid flavoring mixture is prepared. The acid flavoring mixture comprises a combination of an edible acid, flavoring and water. Once again, the relative composition of the constituents varies with the type and quality of fruit pudding to be produced. Of course, the flavoring added is dependent upon the type of fruit pudding to be prepared.

A change in the fruit flavoring employed will make necessary, at most, a small change in the percentage of the edible acid employed. In this regard, it is preferable that the percentage of edible acid in the final fruit pudding be about 0.4 to 0.5% by weight of the pudding. In terms of the resultant pH of the pudding, the edible acid constituent should result in a pudding having a pH below 5, and preferably 3.5 to 4.2.

The acid-flavoring mixture is sterilized upon completion of the mixing of the ingredients. There is no need to preheat the acid-flavoring mixture because of its relative small volume compared to that of the base mixture. Thus, the heat load is correspondingly reduced to the point where the preheating step does not involve significant savings in the heat sterilization step. The acid flavoring mixture is preferably steam sterilized to 180° to 200°F for 10 to 300 seconds. Again, sterilization by steam injection is preferably employed.

Immediately after sterilization of the acid-flavoring mixture, the mixture is cooled. The cooling procedure, preferably by passing the hot acid flavoring mixture through a double pipe exchanger in which cold water or the like is employed as a cooling medium, results in a reduction of the temperature of acid-flavoring mixture to 70°F or below. The temperature of the flavoring mixture may be as low as 40°F.

It should be appreciated that the corrosive effect of the acid-flavoring mixture on the processing equipment is directly proportional to the temperature of the mixture. Thus, the lower the temperature, the lesser the corrosive effect of the flavoring mixture. For this reason, cooling occurs immediately after sterilization of the flavoring mixture and occurs to as great a degree as is consistent with the equipment available.

The sterilized and cooled base mixture and the cooled sterilized acid-flavoring mixture are thereafter mixed together. Preferably this mixing occurs by pumping the two streams together. This procedure is often described as in-line mixing. The combined stream is thereafter cooled to a temperature below 120° and preferably about 80°F. The cooled fruit pudding is thereafter aseptically packaged.

Example: A lemon pudding base mixture is prepared by mixing together the following:

Ingredient	Amount, lb
66.5% sugar syrup	33.0
Starch	5.5
Salt	0.2
Sodium citrate	0.25
Vegetable oil	1.5
A trace amount of coloring	
Water	55.4

The mixture is blended, stirred and thereafter preheated in a double pipe heat exchanger to 145°F. The heated mixture is next sterilized by injecting steam into a mixture so that the total mass is at a temperature of 280°F for a period of about 60 seconds. Immediately after sterilization, the mixture is conveyed into a flash tank in which the mixture is cooled to 145°F and wherein the water resulting from the steam injecting into the mass is removed.

In a separate processing step, the following ingredients are mixed together:

Ingredient	Amount, lb
Citric acid	0.45
Lemon flavoring	0.95
Water	3.60

The mixed acid-flavoring aqueous mixture is heated to 200°F for 30 seconds by direct steam injection. The flavoring mixture is thereafter cooled in a double pipe heat exchanger to 70°F. The sterilized pudding base mixture and the sterilized acid-flavoring mixture are pumped together. The combined fruit pudding mixture is immediately thereafter cooled to 80°F and aseptically packaged.

BAKING AND BAKED PRODUCTS

Dough and Icing Combination Packaging Method

The packaging of unbaked dough products and icing or filling presents unique problems which are solved with particular efficiency by the process described by *C.H. Turpin; U.S. Patent 3,962,476; June 8, 1976; assigned to The Pillsbury Company*. Biscuit dough patties usually contain baking powder or a similar delayed action leavening agent. In order to facilitate depositing of the patties in the containers, the patties are usually cut so as to have a slightly smaller diameter. After the patties are in the cans, generation of leavening gas by the leavening agent causes the patties to rise or proof.

The containers are deliberately not air tight and the expanding dough expels the air from the container, totally filling the container and developing pressure when the surfaces of the dough pieces contact the inner surface of the container at which time the dough itself appears to seal the minute openings in the container thereby preventing leavening gas from escaping from the containers. The pressure of the dough, however, has in the past caused dough extrusion in some cases beyond the separator plate into the icing compartment and it is the triple seal of this process which prevents this.

The package is prepared by partially inserting the icing cup so that its upper end is even with the top of the can. The icing cup is then pressed to the bottom of the can. The end is then placed on that end of the can. The cup is then filled and the separator plate and dough are inserted and the can is sealed.

The two compartment package of this process comprises an outer spirally wound fiber can containing a dough product in one compartment separated from a second compartment by a flat separator member positioned transversely and engaging the inside wall of the container. On the other side of the separator is an icing cup which engages the walls of the container at its open end which faces the separator plate. A triple seal is provided, viz, between the container wall and the separator, between the wall and the cup and between the separator and the cup.

The dough container includes a multiple ply spirally wound tubular peripheral wall usually enclosed by an exteriorly decorative spirally wound removable label. A disc-shaped end closure is secured by crimping or other conventional means to one end of the wall to provide a bottom for the container. After filling the container with a product such as unbaked biscuit dough patties and a nondough food product such as icing, the container is closed by crimping or otherwise securing a disc-shaped top closure to the opposite end of the peripheral wall to define a product package.

This method provides the resistance to the extrusion of dough in addition to low cost since no new materials are required. The cup faces upwardly or toward the center of the container to permit the icing cup to be filled on the same assembly line as used to insert dough into the container. Additionally, the metal separator plate provides the strength to resist the expansion of the dough under pressure and also provides resistance to deformation which plastic resins alone cannot provide.

The process effectively prevents the extrusion of dough into the space between the icing cup and the can wall and this in turn virtually eliminates the possibility of mold and damage to the appearance to the bottom biscuit. The cup is tapered to facilitate the release of the cups from molds. A taper of about 1.5% with respect to the axis of the cup is satisfactory for this purpose.

The cup can be made of a variety of thermoplastic resinous materials including the polyolefins, polyethylene, polypropylene, high impact polystyrene and others of the well known thermoplastic resinous materials compatible with food products.

Flavor Bits for Cake Mixes

D.C. Weigle; U.S. Patent 3,794,741; February 26, 1974; assigned to The Procter & Gamble Company describes the composition of flavor bits for incorporation into culinary mixes which comprises 45 to 55% sugar, 0.1 to 10% water, 20 to 35% corn syrup, 2 to 8% of an edible cooking fat, at least 3% of a suspending agent, 0 to 2% of a food acid, 0 to 2% glycerin, 0 to 1% salt, 0.005 to 5% of a flavoring material, and 0 to 1% dye.

A process for producing such flavor bits comprises mixing sugar, water, corn syrup, and glycerin, and cooking these ingredients at 230° to 320°F; adding in a suspending agent and an edible fat; cooling the mixture to between 140° and 200°F; mixing in a flavor material; cooling the mixture until it becomes hard; and subdividing the hardened mixture into small particles. Highly volatile flavor material can be incorporated into these flavor bits without significant loss of such material. Furthermore, the flavor bits will remain dispersed throughout the finished culinary mix without settling out.

The flavor bits are made by using from about 30 to 40% sugar in the initial mix. The sugar can be sucrose, dextrose, and mixtures thereof. Some, but not all, of the sucrose and/or dextrose can be replaced by fructose, levulose, maltose, lactose, galactose, or other sugar. The sugar is present to provide sweetness and structure to the flavor bit. The preferred range for the use of sugar is 32 to 35%.

The flavor bits are made by using from about 20 to 30% water in the initial mix. The water is used as a solvent for the other ingredients so they can react with each other during cooking. It is preferred that 26 to 28% water be used. The flavor bits are made by adding from 20 to 30% corn syrup to the initial mix. Some, but not all, of the corn syrup can be replaced by invert sugar or glycerin. The corn syrup helps to retain moisture and prevents the formation of a crystalline structure such as occurs in fondants.

At least about 2.5% of a suspending agent must be included in the initial mix of the flavor bits. If less than 2.5% is used, the bits will settle out of the cake. Suitable suspending agents include hydrophilic colloids, water-soluble starch, gelatins, and gum. Sodium carboxymethylcellulose is the preferred suspending agent and the preferred concentration range for the suspending agent is from 4 to 6%.

Almost any flavoring material can be utilized in the process. The range of use generally is 0.005 to 5%, although some materials may have to be used in greater or lesser concentrations. Examples of flavor materials which can be utilized in the process are strawberry, blueberry, cocoa, chocolate liquor, nut flavors, and citrus flavors.

The flavor bits also can comprise from 0 to 2% citric acid to accentuate the flavor of the bit. Other food acids besides citric acid, such as malic, tartaric, and fumaric, can be used in the bits as long as their effect on sugar inversion does not exceed the effect of a 2% addition of citric acid. The flavor bits can also contain from 0 to 2% glycerin to help retain moisture and to make the bit more pliable if it is so desired. Salt can be added in the range from 0 to 1% to accentuate the flavor of the bit. Any necessary amount of dye can also be added to the flavor bits.

Example: Six different flavor bits are made by the following process. In each of the bits, a different level of carboxymethylcellulose is used (0 g, 15 g, 20 g, 25 g, 40 g, and 50 g corresponding approximately to 0%, 2%, 3%, 4%, 6% and 8%). The carboxymethylcellulose had a degree of substitution of 0.7 and a 1% solution had a viscosity of 4,000 cp at 25°C. The remaining ingredients are present in the following amounts in all of the bits:

Ingredient	Amount, g
Sucrose	215
Water	180
Corn syrup	160
Margarine	28
Strawberry flavor	12
Citric acid	10
Glycerin	8
Salt	5
Dye	1

The sucrose, corn syrup, water, salt, and glycerin are cooked to a temperature of 290°F in a quart Pyrex pot. The heat is removed and the margarine and carboxymethylcellulose are mixed in. The mixture is cooled to a temperature between 160° and 170°F and citric acid, strawberry flavor, and dye are stirred into the mixture. The mixture is then poured into a cold aluminum pie pan and frozen in dry ice. The frozen mixture is then cracked and milled with a Waring blender into bits, which are then sifted and collected on a U.S. Standard No. 12 sieve and dusted with cornstarch to prevent them from sticking together.

The bits are then incorporated into a strawberry cake mix with the following formula:

Ingredients	Percent by Weight
Sugar	44.5
Dextrose	1.25
Flour	39.5
Shortening	8
Leavening	2.5
Salt	0.75
Strawberry flavor	0.2
Strawberine dye	0.1
Strawberry flavor bits	3.2
	100.0

A strawberry cake containing the bits is then baked in a conventional manner. Tests indicated that levels of at least 3% carboxymethylcellulose are necessary to prevent settling out of the flavor bits, and 4% is preferred. All of the cakes had a very strong strawberry flavor.

POPCORN PROCESSES

FLAVORINGS

Flavored Popcorn Using Encapsulated Flavoring Substances

J.L. Caccavale, V.J. Pierce, R.W. Young and S.B. Prussin; U.S. Patent 3,961,091; June 1, 1976 provide a method and a composition for producing flavored popcorn which comprise in a broad aspect the combining of popcorn kernels in a cooking medium together with a flavoring substance and lecithin following which the contents of the vessel are heated to pop the kernels while at the same time they are being flavored.

In a preferred form of the process the lecithin is evenly coated on the surface of the flavoring substance when it is combined with the cooking medium. A feature of the process is the provision of a premix having both the foregoing contemplated cooking medium, flavoring substance, and lecithin to which the popcorn kernels can be added in the cooking vessel.

A further feature is the provision of a concentrated premix where less than all the cooking medium used to pop the kernels is mixed with the flavoring substance following which an additional amount of cooking medium necessary to pop the corn kernels is introduced into the vessel. It is contemplated in a commercial context that the flavoring substances, premix, or concentrated premix, depending upon the circumstances, may be sold to the consumer either separately, or with separately packaged popcorn kernels.

A preferred package includes flavoring substance with its surface coated with lecithin and includes separately packaged popcorn with instructions that the consumer provide and add the necessary cooking medium. The cooking medium is preferably an oil or semisolid or solid fat suitable for cooking purposes and particularly suitable for popping corn kernels.

In a preferred form of the process the flavoring substances are in the form of liquids encapsulated in a suitable encapsulating medium. It has been found that practically any liquid flavor capable of being encapsulated can be used. Preferred encapsulating media are acacia, starch and/or dextrins or other hydrocolloids and methylcellulose.

It is thought that the encapsulated flavors produce particular advantages because the encapsulating medium inhibits the flavor from being extracted and subjected to volatilization, fractionation, decomposition and the otherwise destructive temperatures of popping particularly from steam distillation which occurs when the pressure from superheated steam generated in the kernel exceeds the cohesive strength of the kernel shell material.

In a typical encapsulating process, the encapsulating medium is supplied as a gum which is dissolved in water. The flavoring substance is then added and suspended in the gum solution. In forming the encapsulated flavoring substance the gum solution is sprayed into a drying tower and the water driven off by a countercurrent stream of dry air. It has been found that ratios of gum to flavoring substance in the range from and including 90 to 10 to and including 60 to 40 parts by weight produce the best results.

Among the advantages of the process are the uniform distribution of flavoring. This is thought to be due to several factors present in the one step popping and flavoring process which causes intimate contact of popped and unpopped corn with the flavoring substances in their encapsulated form. The unpopped kernel is first soaked in the popping medium containing the encapsulated flavor which is further brought into contact with the expanding corn during the popping process. Because of its high surface area popped corn will adsorb the encapsulated flavor as well as absorb it when the popped corn cools and partial vacuums are created in the interstices thereof.

It is desirable to include an amount of lecithin in the cooking medium during the popping step. It is preferred that the lecithin be evenly coated on the surface of the flavoring substances when they are combined with the cooking medium. The lecithin helps maintain the dry flavoring substance in its particulate form preventing or minimizing agglomeration when it is dispersed in the oil cooking medium. The popcorn also helps promote dispersion of the flavor ingredients by agitation as a result of the high velocity movement of the popping kernels.

It has been found that the amount of lecithin to give good results is dependent in part upon the weight of popcorn kernels present in the cooking medium. The water present in the corn kernels forms a lecithin stabilized emulsion with the oil which might normally be expected to foam excessively as the water and oil boil to form a stable froth which would deleteriously impede the movement of kernels in the cooking medium as noted.

It has been determined that an amount of lecithin below that which will cause foaming is nevertheless satisfactory to prevent agglomeration or "clumping" of the flavoring substance. Preferred ranges of the lecithin, based on weight percent of popcorn kernels are 0.02 to 0.2%.

Example: The following ingredients were mixed and introduced into a cooking vessel with 2.3 oz corn oil and heated to popping temperature. Upon popping the dispersion of the flavoring was observed to be excellent. There was a slight foam at the time of popping, but it was observed to break as fast as it was formed.

	Grams
Imitation bacon flavor	8.00
Salt	5.00
Monosodium glutamate	0.20
Lecithin	0.05
Popcorn	86.75

Popcorn Flavored by Using Oil-in-Water Emulsion Containing Flavor Ingredient

P. Kracauer; U.S. Patent 3,704,133; November 28, 1972 describes a product made of corn kernels which upon popping in the ordinary manner, i.e., a closed container, results in popcorn which is uniformly flavored with either shortening and salt, sugar, candy flavor or cheese. This is accomplished by mixing the corn kernels with shortening, a lipophilic surfactant and with water prior to the popping.

The key to obtaining uniform flavoring of all of the kernels as they are popped is the use of water, which is used in a fairly substantial amount. The water is used with a shortening and a lipophilic surfactant so that a water-in-oil type emulsion of the shortening is obtained which carries with it and uniformly coats the popcorn not only with the shortening but also with the flavoring.

In one variation, the corn kernels can be coated with the emulsion of the flavoring, shortening, water and surfactant. The coating is achieved by a normal tablet coating procedure in which the corn kernels are rotated in a coating pan along with the emulsion.

In another version, particularly where the popcorn is to be made in the home in aluminum containers, the corn kernels are not uniformly coated with emulsion, but the emulsion is merely mixed therewith. Substantially similar flavoring results can be obtained in this way; however, larger amounts of the emulsion, and larger amounts of the flavoring portion of the emulsion may be used than in the case of the individual coating of the corn kernels. In the case of coated corn kernels, for salted popcorn, the proportions of the components, other than the corn kernels are generally as follows:

	Percent by Weight
Shortening	50-60
Water	5-10
Lipophilic surfactant	7-12
Salt	20-30

The ratio of corn to the above emulsion, for the coating of the corn is about 100 parts of corn to about 20 to 40 parts of the emulsion. All parts are by weight. In the case of sweetened popcorn, all of the proportions are substantially as indicated above, except that the salt is replaced by sugar, and the amount of sugar is about 30 to 35% of the emulsion.

In the case of candy flavored popcorn, the ratios are substantially the same as for the sweetened popcorn given above, except that some of the sugar may be replaced by the candy flavor, e.g., chocolate, (preferably in the form of chocolate liqueur), maple, butterscotch, strawberry, cherry, cinnamon, etc. In the case of a cheese flavored popcorn, the proportions of the components remain about the same with two exceptions. The salt is partly replaced by cheese, the amount of which is about 15 to 25% by weight, and the amount of lipophilic surfactant is reduced to about 3 to 10% by weight.

In the case of simple mixing of the corn kernels with the emulsion, rather than individual coating of the corn kernels, the proportions of the components, other than the corn, are as follows:

Sweetened Popcorn

	Percent
Shortening	15–35
Sugar	45–70
Water	8–18
Lipophilic surfactant	0.5–4

For candy flavoring, a small amount (0.5 to 1%) of flavoring is added to the basic mix above.

Cheese Flavored Popcorn

	Percent
Cheese	20–30
Shortening	40–60
Water	6–22
Surfactant	0.5–5
Salt	8–15

In all of the above compositions, the amount of emulsion mixed with the amount of kernels will vary widely depending upon the particular type of flavored popcorn to be produced. In the case of the sweetened popcorn, the preferred proportion is 70 parts of emulsion to 35 parts of kernels; in the case of the cheese flavored popcorn the preferred amount is about 80 to 100 parts of corn kernels to about 60 to 80 parts of emulsion.

The compositions can of course have ordinary preservatives such as sodium benzoate added thereto, as well as coloring agents, e.g., turmeric, dyes, etc.

These mixtures are formed into water-in-oil emulsions due to the action of the lipophilic surfactant. The water which is present in the composition, and which is actually essential in order to permit uniform distribution of the flavoring on the popcorn, does not adversely affect the corn kernels so that the kernels pop in normal manner and become coated with the flavorings contained in the emulsion. Thus, the heating of the corn kernels and emulsion result not only in popping of the corn but also in breaking up of the water-in-oil emulsion so that the oil becomes separated from the other ingredients and the kernels become coated with the flavoring.

The emulsion which is produced from the compositions set forth above is preferably in a paste-like semisolidified form, which is then mixed with the kernels, and it is during heating, as explained above, that this paste-like emulsion breaks up, the oil separating and actually covering the bottom of the container to prevent burning of the kernels and other ingredients therein, and all of the ingredients coating the resulting popped corn.

Example: 55 parts by weight of hydrogenated vegetable oil, 7 parts by weight of water, and 10 parts by weight of Atmul 124 (mono- and diglycerides of edible fats or oils) are mixed in a kettle and heated to about 80°C. The mixture is stirred at room temperature, after which 28 parts by weight of salt are stirred in. The mixture is stirred until somewhat solidified.

100 parts by weight of corn kernels are placed in a rotating pan of the type used for tablet coating, and 35 parts by weight of the above emulsion are added thereto. The pan is rotated until the kernels are uniformly coated. For best results a small amount of calcium phosphate is introduced into the pan to act as antisticking agent.

The coated kernels when heated in a closed container for popping purposes provide uniformly fatted and salted popcorn. When the popping is carried out in a closed aluminum pan with an expansible aluminum top, uniformly flavored popcorn is obtained.

PACKAGING METHOD AND POPPING APPARATUS

Popcorn Package

G.B. Bourns; U.S. Patent 3,969,535; July 13, 1976; assigned to American Home Products Corp. describes a popcorn package having a poppable popcorn composition contained in a metal foil pan which is closed by an expansible clear plastic cover. The package comprises a gasket of particular configuration disposed adjacent the plastic cover to support the plastic cover during expansion to prevent tearing.

The popcorn package, a metal pan typically of aluminum foil, contains a composition of poppable corn dispersed in cooking fat and other materials in which the corn may be heated to cause expansion, or popping, and may also be flavored or colored at the same time. An expandable cover, or bonnet is attached over the pan by crimping the edges of the foil pan over the cover.

The cover may be made of any stretchable plastic which meets the approval of the FDA. It is preferred that the cover be spirally wound or swirled. A transparent plastic permits the progress of popping to be viewed during the heating process and is especially advantageous. Preferably, the plastic has "memory" so that once the swirl is set at elevated temperature, the plastic tends to retain the swirled position assuring a tight, attractive package. The plastic is preferably one mil or less in thickness so that it will expand under pressure and preferably resist heat up to 460°F.

A wire handle which is a substantially circular piece of wire having a radially extended portion may be applied. The circular segment is substantially coextensive with the rim of the metal pan and is connected to it by crimping the metal foil rim over the wire. The radially extended portion serves as a handle.

An annular gasket adjacent the plastic cover prior to crimping the metal pan may be on either side of the plastic, relative to the pan but preferably on top. The outer periphery of the annular gasket is substantially coextensive with the rim of the pan so as to be firmly connected to it by the crimping process. The inner diameter of the annular gasket is sufficiently large to provide a clear view of the contents through the transparent plastic cover. The annular gasket is preferably formed of light paperboard.

The gasket has an annular score between its inner and outer diameters. The diameter of the score is substantially less than that of the rim of the metal pan so as not to interfere with the crimping operation. The score may be on the bottom surface of the assembled gasket and extend partly through the gasket. Preferably the score is intermittent, cut through with small uncut portions holding fingers to the rest of the gasket.

A plurality of radial scores extends completely through the gasket from its inner diameter to the annular score. The radial scores define an equal number of tapered segments, or fingers, which are adapted to bend around a hinge defined by the radial score. The radial scores are preferably twelve in number. In a typical package the pan has a diameter of 6 inches. The fingers are preferably about 2 inches long.

Each of the fingers is attached to the adjacent plastic surface by an adhesive. The adhesive is applied on the finger so as to leave a clear area around the periphery of the finger. The clear areas prevent adjacent fingers from being inadvertently joined together by the adhesive. Also, care is taken that the adhesive does not extend into the folds of the cover formed by the spiral winding. The adhesive may be any heat resistant type which is approved for use with foods and has a high melting point, preferably above 250°F. A typical adhesive is a water base, formulated resin emulsion which sets to a tough flexible film.

Separately Packaged Popcorn Confection for Making Popcorn Balls

B.E. Tomlinson; U.S. Patent 3,950,567; April 13, 1976 describes the preparation of a nonsticky popcorn ball confection by cooking a confection including sweetener, fat, water and gelatin which may be prepackaged and later used by merely heating in the package, pouring the cooked confection over popped popcorn and forming balls.

In the process gelatin and fat are used as ingredients in addition to those which have in the past been found in most popcorn ball confection recipes. The gelatin is utilized to keep the confection in a soft pliable state prior to use much in the manner that it does in marshmallows. In fact, marshmallows can be utilized to provide all of the ingredients but the fat and part of the sugar. The fat may be provided as butter, margarine or some other suitable substitute. A typical recipe for the confection for use with about 12 to 14 quarts of popped corn is as follows:

Gelatin	¾ oz
Margarine	¼ lb
Sugar	2½ cups
Corn syrup (glucose)	1½ cups
Corn starch	1 oz
Water	⅔ cup
Salt	2 tsps
Vanilla extract	2 tsps
Citric acid and a flavor extract may be added if desired	

To prepare the confection the gelatin is thoroughly mixed in ⅔ cup of cold water and the water heated to dissolve the gelatin. To this is added 1 cup of sugar and the heat increased to bring the mixture to a rolling boil whereupon it is removed from the burner and 1½ cups glucose and 1 oz corn starch added and well mixed and cooked to 200°F. ¼ lb of margarine is then added and the mixture allowed to cool. The remainder of the ingredients are then added. Desired special flavoring or coloring may be inserted at this time.

The resulting confection is packaged and cooled for storage. It is preferred to use heat resistant transparent envelopes or pouches for storage of the type which can be heat-sealed and later subjected to boiling water without damaging, such as the polystyrene pouches of about 2 mil film thickness commonly used for storage and cooking of frozen vegetables. The confection may be packaged before or after cooling. When at room temperature it is soft and pliable much like putty.

To prepare the packaged confection for use while the popcorn is being popped the closed pouch of confection is placed in a pan of boiling water and heated until the confection has a consistency suitable for pouring. After removal from the pan the heated pouch is cut open at one end or corner and the confection conveniently poured therefrom directly onto the freshly popped corn while the corn is stirred to mix the hot confection with the corn. Then handsful of the confection-laden popcorn are shaped into balls in the normal manner or molded in other fashion. However, during this ball forming operation the fat present in the confection prevents sticking thereof to the fingers.

In the above described recipe the amounts of sugar and glucose may be varied somewhat for individual taste and the cooking starch is not essential. The gelatin and much of the sugar and glucose may be provided by marshmallows of the conventional type made from corn syrup, sugar, gelatin and albumin.

Automatic Popcorn Popping Method

A.M. Day and G.D. Browning; U.S. Patent 3,697,289; October 10, 1972; assigned to Compupop, Inc. provide a popping machine and method of operation with fully automatic functions controlled in accordance with a predetermined program providing an optimum popcorn product of uniform flavor, tenderness, and appearance. The corn is popped in hot oil enabling the use of a lower popping temperature. A closed popping pot reduces the possibility of contaminants mixing with the product and affords removal of objectionable steam and waste oil effluent. The material supplies corn and salt precisely metered in a predetermined quantity for each popping cycle which are conveyed into the pot by an air current removing objectionable moisture therefrom and providing a positive hopper air pressure at all times.

The raw corn is fed from a large bin at the base of the machine upwardly to a supply hopper above the pot by an air conveyor. Seasoning oil contained in a supply at the base of the machine is delivered upwardly to a metering reservoir above the pot by a pump in the oil supply through a telescoping supply tube and support. Heating means are provided to melt that portion of the solidified oil adjacent the pump inlet and telescoping tube for rapid start-up. As the oil is consumed, the pump melts additional oil and moves downwardly with the level of the solidified oil. An oil metering device is provided measuring the precise quantity of oil required for each pop by filling up above a predetermined level in the reservoir, drawing down the oil to a level which is vertically adjustable, and then injecting the charge of remaining oil into the pot. The oil level in the reservoir is electronically sensed to signal the control circuit for continued cycling, or oil resupply, as required.

A rotary valve disc is indexed in accordance with a predetermined program and exposes a series of inlets and outlets including the inlets for air, corn and salt supplies, outlet to the condenser, and product outlet for communication between the pot interior and display case. A deflector plate is disposed below the air inlet for directing the air current into a path around the inner periphery of the pot for carrying the popped corn upwardly to a discharge tube for delivery to the display case.

In a modified form the unpopped corn or "old maids" are removed from the popped corn by a trap and delivered through a discharge chute for subsequent removal. During a popping cycle the steam and vaporized oil are removed from the pot by a vacuum created by a venturi in a self-cleaning condenser. In another modified form a major portion of the steam is condensed within an exit conduit having a dome disposed above a gutter receiving the condensed water and preventing it from draining back into the pot.

An agitator blade in the pot has a configuration with its leading edge defining a forward rake to sweep the popped corn radially inward for evacuation into the discharge opening. The drive for the agitator includes a spring-biased driving shaft mounted from above and interfitting with a socket in the agitator base permitting easy opening and closing of the agitator and hotplate for cleaning purposes.

An electronic control circuit is provided to correlate the various machine processes, provide automatic warning of insufficient material supplies, provide a visual indication of machine cycling, provide selective variation of material supplies and popping times for maximum popcorn volume, tenderness, flavor and appearance, provide either continual popping or a selected number of pops at any desired rate, and automatically count the number of pops for supply and usage control.

SPECIALIZED PROCESSES

Popped Corn in Dough Matrix Snack Food

J.M. Rispoli and A.C. Capossela, Jr.; U.S. Patent 3,719,501; March 6, 1973; assigned to General Foods Corporation describe a snack food product made from popped popcorn in a dough matrix containing flours and starch. The snack food product preferably contains comminuted popcorn in a cooked dough matrix of tapioca flour, corn flour and potato starch, and is deep fat fried.

The dough matrix, as abovementioned, contains a mixture of flours and starch. Although flours obtained from a variety of cereals, grains and tubers, may be readily employed, it has been found that the combination of tapioca flour and corn flour provides a snack food product with very desirable flavor, texture and appearance.

It has been found that tapioca flour results in good texture in the final product and has the advantage of permitting puffing during deep fat frying which is also advantageous. Moreover, because of its bland flavor, tapioca flour generally does not mask the flavor impact of the other principal ingredients of the snack food product. The use of corn flour is advantageous in that since popcorn is an essential ingredient of the snack food product, corn flour provides, together with popcorn, an overall predominating corn flavor and texture.

Although corn puffs and corn chips are well-known, such products are usually prepared from corn grits and/or corn masa flour which, while they may be used in minor amounts in the matrix, are not as essential as corn flour. Further, even though it is possible to employ any one or more of a large number of food starches, such as waxy maize, corn, rice, tapioca, etc., potato starch, more particularly a pregelatinized potato starch, provides extremely desirable characteristics in the snack food product.

In making the dough matrix, it has been found advantageous to employ the preferred combination of starches and flours within a certain range. A ratio of 1:1:1 of tapioca flour to corn flour to potato starch furnishes very desirable characteristics in the final product.

Popped popcorn may be incorporated into the dough matrix, preferably after the matrix has been cooked to gelatinization temperatures. The popcorn may be either whole or comminuted, that is, discrete exploded kernels may be used or popcorn which has been chopped, sliced, ground or otherwise subdivided, may be employed. It has been found advantageous to use a ratio of popped popcorn to dough matrix of 2:1, on a dry weight basis.

It appears that with lower ratios of popped popcorn to dough matrix, fat pickup during final processing, e.g., in deep fat frying, may be excessive. The use of comminuted popped popcorn is especially desirable since the final snack product is seen to be somewhat less fragile and in-processing difficulties are avoided because of the higher density of the comminuted popped popcorn.

In making the dough matrix, the ingredients of flours and starch are preblended and then introduced to a suitable cooking vessel containing water. The preblend may contain other ingredients such as salt and other flavor adjuncts, but it is obvious that such ingredients may be incorporated into the cooking water. The cooking of the mixture of the ingredients can be accomplished by any one of a number of known cooking methods. Generally, the amount of water employed in cooking of the dough would be from one to four parts per part of preblended ingredients. Cooking is carried out at 170° to 200°F for 5 to 60 minutes. Following cooking of the dough, popped popcorn is blended with the matrix and thoroughly distributed therein.

Subsequently, the popcorn-containing cooked dough is then shaped and formed either into the general shape desired for the end product or into a shape for permitting later additional shaping and forming. The popcorn-containing matrix may be extruded and sheeted, extruded and sliced, rolled into sheets and later cut and formed into desired shapes such as chips or otherwise processed to permit ease in handling as well as to provide shapes of different kinds which would be desired for the final snack food product.

The shaped and formed mixture is then cooled and dried to a moisture content of about 8 to 12%. During this part of the process, conditioning and/or tempering of the dough matrix may take place but it is apparent that conditioning and/or tempering may be done prior to shaping and forming the popped popcorn-containing dough matrix.

The dried, shaped and formed intermediate product may then be shipped and stored as such. Alternatively, the final step of the process may be carried out by immersing the intermediate product in an edible hot oil for brief periods of time to finish-cook and puff the product. The oil temperature may range from 350° to 425°F and the time interval may range from 5 to 45 seconds.

Alternatively, roasting, fluidized bed, and other methods of finish-cooking the product may be used. Generally, deep fat frying is employed inasmuch as the flavor, texture and appearance characteristics appear to be very well developed with such technique.

Following deep fat frying, the snack food product, having a moisture content of approximately 1 to 4%, is coated with salt or other flavor adjuncts, such as spices, sauces, condiments and the like. Such flavor adjuncts as well as foodstuff pieces may, however, also be blended into the dough matrix at the time the popcorn is incorporated therein.

Example: Ingredients, in parts by weight, and processing conditions for a snack food product containing whole popped popcorn are as follows:

Popcorn-Containing Dough

	Parts	Percent
Popped popcorn	2,540.0	34.7
Dough Matrix		
Tapioca flour	380.0	5.2
Corn flour	380.0	5.2
Potato starch, pregelatinized	380.0	5.2
Salt	12.8	1.7
Water	3,500.0	48.0

Finished Snack Food Product

Solids from popcorn-containing dough phase	61
Fat	35
External salt	2
Moisture	2

Water is added to a steam jacketed mixer and is brought to a boil. A dry-blended mixture of tapioca and corn flours, potato starch and salt is then added to the mixer and the mixture is gelatinized by cooking for about 5 minutes. The popped popcorn is then slowly added to the cooked dough and blending is continued for about 5 minutes. The popcorn-containing dough is then removed from the mixer and extruded into ¼ inch thick sheets in an extruder. The sheets are then passed through rollers to obtain ⅛ inch thick flaked sheets which are subsequently air dried to a 10% moisture content. The dried flaked sheets are broken into strips which are then deep fat fried in a hot (375°F) oil bath for 30 seconds until cooking and puffing are complete. The puffed snack food product is removed from the bath, cooled, dusted with salt and packaged.

Sugar Coated Popcorn Coating Method

According to the process described by *I. Grunewald-Kirstein; U.S. Patent 3,843,814; October 22, 1974* popcorn coated with a substantially continuous layer of sugar or caramel is manufactured in the following manner.

First, a liquid coating mass is prepared by heating edible oil or fat to form a hot liquid. Sugar or syrup is then added to the hot liquid. The sugar or syrup dissolves in the hot liquid substantially instantaneously. The amount of sugar or syrup is chosen so that it comprises at least one half of the liquid coating mass thus obtained. Raw corn kernels are then added to this liquid coating mass while the coating mass is at a temperature above the popping temperature of the kernels but at least about 20° to 30°C below the boiling temperature of the mass. The kernels are thus popped and coated with the mass.

Since the kernels contain an appreciable amount of water, they are maintained in the hot coating mass until the moisture in the kernels has evaporated. Experience has indicated that within about 2 to 4 minutes the water in the kernels has disappeared. In a preferred embodiment the kernels are thus maintained within the hot coating mass for 2 to 4 minutes. Generally, 3 minutes are sufficient.

A preferred temperature for the coating mass is between 180° to 220°C, excellent results being obtained at 200°C. The exact temperature to be chosen will, of course, be somewhat dependent on the nature of the edible oil or fat and the amount of sugar or syrup. The edible oil or fat is preferably a vegetable oil or fat. Preferably sugar instead of syrup such as corn syrup is added to the oil or fat.

In the most desirable procedure the coating mass is prepared from 250 to 300 parts by weight of edible oil or fat such as a suitable vegetable oil or fat and 550 to 700 parts by weight of sugar or syrup. 300 to 400 parts by weight of raw corn kernels are then added to this coating mass. The coating mass may, of course, also contain flavoring substances and/or food colorants.

From a practical point of view, the fat or oil is first heated and the sugar or syrup is dissolved in the hot fat or oil. It has been found that the sugar dissolves almost instantaneously and the resulting coating mass is thus tantamount to a hot liquid bath. The raw kernels are then fed into the hot bath.

Extensive tests indicate that this coated popcorn has a significantly longer shelf life than coated popcorn produced according to conventional methods. Further, a more even and uniform coating of the kernels is accomplished. While conventionally produced coated popcorn loses its crispiness after a storage period of about 3 months, and has a tendency to become soggy and rancid, coated popcorn produced in this manner can be successfully stored for at least 12 months without affecting the initial crispiness. Moreover, no rancidity could be detected after a storage period of 12 months.

Example: 270 grams of unhardened vegetable fat were heated to about 200°C. 630 grams of sugar were added to the fat bath under stirring. The sugar dissolved substantially instantaneously in the liquid fat. The temperature was maintained at 200°C and 350 grams of raw corn kernels were added to the coating mass consisting of the sugar enriched fat bath, under agitation. The temperature of the mixture thus obtained was maintained at the 200°C value for about 3 minutes whereupon the mixture was allowed to cool. Caramel coated popcorn completely devoid of moisture was obtained.

The above experiment yields substantially the same results if the conditions are varied as follows:

Edible oil or fat	250 to 300 grams
Sugar	550 to 700 grams
Corn kernels	300 to 400 grams
Temperature	180° to 220°C

Time period within which kernels are maintained within hot coating mass: 2 to 4 minutes.

ETHNIC AND SPECIALTY FOOD ITEMS

FRIED PRODUCTS

Fried Tofu

"Tofu" is one of the most popular traditional soybean foods in Eastern Asia and is an important protein source for people living in that region. It is a watery, white, jelly-like fragile product having a moisture content as high as 88 weight percent. In most cases, tofu is prepared by complicated manual processes. In a typical process, soybeans, as the raw material, are soaked in water for prolonged periods (e.g., about 8 hours during the summer months and 22 to 24 hours during the winter months) and the soaked soybeans are ground to form a slurry thereof. This slurry is heated to extract the soy protein (i.e., the soy protein becomes dissolved in the water phase) and then filtered through a coarse cloth to remove insoluble soybean refuge, consisting mainly of pulverized cellular substances commonly like "okara."

The filtrate or soy milk is coagulated to form a curd by adding a coagulating agent, such as a nontoxic water-soluble alkaline earth metal salt (e.g., calcium sulfate, calcium chloride or magnesium chloride) and the whey is separated from the tofu curd by draining. In some processes, certain organic gamma or delta lactones of aldonic and uronic acids, such as D-glucono-δ-lactone, are used as the coagulating agent and the necessity for whey draining is eliminated. Notwithstanding this improvement, processes used for making tofu still require many laborious, time-consuming steps and generally are not adaptable for automated mass production.

Tofu is used as a foodstuff in several different forms. In Eastern Asia, it is commonly consumed as a fried product. Today, about one-third of the tofu consumed in Japan is in this form.

"Aburage" (often referred in shortened form as "age") is one of the most common forms of fried tofu. It is generally square-shaped and is prepared by slicing tofu curd into relatively thin slices, pressing the slices to adjust the moisture content therein to about 80 to 82% and then deep frying in two successive stages. Aburage is consumed chiefly in a cooked state or in a toasted state with appropriate condiments and/or seasonings.

Occasionally, aburage is also consumed as an edible casing or wrapping for other foodstuffs. This aburage casing is prepared by diagonally cutting a square piece of the aburage to form two triangular pieces. Each triangular piece is then slit open along the cut edge to form a bag. "Sushi" is prepared by stuffing the aburage bags with various foodstuffs. For example, "inarizushi," a particular kind of sushi, is prepared by stuffing the aburage bags with a vinegared rice. Daily dishes can be prepared by stuffing bags formed from aburage with various comminuted vegetables and fastening the stuffed bags with an edible string or cord, such as "kanpyo" (made from the fruits from certain convolvulacean and lagenarian plants). Aburage can be cut into two rectangular pieces, each of which are slit open along the cut edge to form a bag which is used in a similar manner.

Because of the laborious and time-consuming manual steps typically required by these methods for preparing fried tofu products, economical mass production of such products has not been possible in the past. Tofu formed by the lactone coagulants mentioned above generally are not acceptable for preparing a fried tofu product because of the difficulty of draining whey to reduce the moisture content to the desired level of 80 to 82%. Also, the tofu is acidified by these coagulants and tends to reduce the flexibility of the fried product. Consequently, preparation of fried tofu products generally are restricted to the use of a tofu curd formed with an alkaline earth metal salt. The presence of these salts in the fried product has several disadvantages.

First, it is often desirable to freeze the fried fu products for prolonged storage. This is particularly true for "ganmodoki" which retains a considerable amount of moisture even after frying (because of its thickness as compared to the thin aburage) and therefore, tends to putrefy within a relatively short time unless frozen. While being stored in a frozen state, the alkaline earth metal salts present in the fried products tend to accelerate the denaturation of soy protein. This denaturation causes the thawed product to have a porous texture (i.e., honeycomb-like) and unsatisfactory mouthfeel or chewiness. Second, unless extreme care is exercised during frying, these salts tend to leach out onto the frying oil and cause a deterioration thereof.

Third, it is desirable to incorporate egg ingredients (egg yolk, egg white or whole egg) into the fried products to improve their flavor and/or food value. It is difficult to do this with prior processes, particularly when aburage is being prepared. If the egg ingredient is added to the heated soybean slurry prior to filtering, the egg protein may be filtered out with the soybean refuge because it tends to coagulate at temperatures below which the slurry must be heated to extract soy protein. If the egg ingredients are added to the soy milk before curd formation, some of the egg protein may not be coagulated by these salts and, consequently, is drained away along with the whey. Therefore, the above-discussed processes generally are not acceptable for preparing fried tofu products (particularly aburage) also containing egg ingredients.

T. Katayama and Y. Ishiwatari; U.S. Patent 3,950,550; April 13, 1976; assigned to Fuji Oil Co., Ltd., Japan describe a method for making a fried tofu product comprising kneading a mixture containing a heat-coagulable soy protein and sufficient water to form a plastic-like, moldable soy protein dough. The soy protein dough is shaped and deep-fried. The deep-frying step includes successive first and second stages with the temperature of the frying oil for the first stage ranging between 100° and 135°C and the temperature of the frying fat for the second stage ranging between 135° and 200°C. The soy protein mixture contains 20 to 40 parts by weight of heat-coagulable soy protein and 11 to 60 parts by weight of an edible oil or fat per 100 parts by weight of water. The mixture may further include an egg ingredient in the form of egg white, egg yolk, whole egg or mixtures thereof, the amount, as egg protein, being 1 to 10 parts by weight per 100 parts of water.

Example 1: 2 kg of commercially available isolated soy protein (a sodium proteinate), 0.3 kg of potato starch and 6.6 kg of water were admixed and kneaded together to form a homogeneous mass. This mass was extruded through an annular orifice of an auger-type extruder having a 27 mm i.d. and 33 mm o.d. to form an endless tubular extrudate. The tubular extrudate was continuously and successively introduced in two frying oils. The temperature of the first and second frying oils were about 110°C and about 170°C, respectively, and the frying time in each was 3 minutes and 4 minutes, respectively.

The resulting fried tubular product had a texture and flexibility acceptable for aburage. It was cut into 12-cm-long sections which were stuffed with vegetables. The opposite ends of each tubular section were sealed closed with a conventional heat-sealing device used for sealing thermoplastic films. This unexpected capability of the fried aburage to be sealed in this manner makes it adaptable for high-speed production of such stuffed foods.

Example 2: A kneaded protein dough prepared in the same manner as in Example 1 was extruded through a rectangular orifice (3 mm x 25 mm) of an auger-type extruder and the extrudate was continuously introduced into a continuous deep fat fryer having an increasing temperature gradient, 100°C at the inlet and 150°C at the outlet. The fried product was cut into 16-cm-long sections. Each fried section was slit open with a slender, flat spatula to form a hollow tubular body which was stuffed with a skinless sausage.

Apparatus for Dough Sheets for Rolled Foods

Raw dough sheets used for wrapping of certain Japanese foods have been traditionally made by hand. Higher speeds of production and uniform quality of such products are strongly desirable today. In frying a product using a raw dough sheet containing much water, if the water is not sufficiently removed, the cooked food will not taste good. In addition, the water contained in a raw dough sheet causes bacteria to grow in the food, which is undesirable, and the food cannot be kept for long periods of time.

Therefore, *N. Ohkawa; U.S. Patent 3,930,441; January 6, 1976; assigned to Daieigiken, Inc., Japan* sets out to provide a device for forming such dough sheets with high speed. The device also allows for continuously baking the above-mentioned dough sheets which contain little water. These primary points are accomplished in a device having a flat nozzle which oscillates in the longitudinal direction, and moves toward and away from a rotating drum at intervals when dough is injected from the flat nozzle on the outer circular surface of the drum which has a heater in it. Dough sheets containing little water and having uniform quality can be produced continuously with this device.

The device for producing dough sheets and baking them has a hopper, a gear pump, a flat, slit nozzle, a rotating drum and a releasing plate. The pump and the nozzle are connected by a flexible tube. A heater is equipped in the inner circular surface of the drum and a large gear is fixed to the back of the drum. An adiabatic insulating material is inserted between the drum and the gear.

The center of the back of the drum is supported by a shaft so that it can rotate freely. A motor is provided above the device. A smaller gear or pinion, fixed to the shaft of the motor, is engaged with the large gear. The drum is rotated by a reduction gear connected to the motor, actually constituted by the above-mentioned gears.

The flat nozzle is fixed to one end of a supporting arm of the device, leaving a clearance with the drum, so that an outlet orifice of the nozzle faces the outer circular surface at the bottom of the drum. The arm has a structure to be described later. The clearance is adjustable by means of a mechanism which will also be explained later.

A short shaft is fixed to both upper sides of the nozzle horizontally, and an eccentric roller is connected with each side of this shaft at a small distance, and a cylindrical member is attached to each roller. The cylindrical member can rotate coaxially outside the roller. It should be noted that the latter is fixed to the short shaft by means of a screw so that it cannot rotate; the cylindrical member which rotates in unison with the drum is not fixed to the roller. The cylindrical member is contacted with the outer circular surface of the drum. An operating knob having a large diameter is provided at the outside portion of the roller, and the screw is used in this knob.

The clearance is adjusted by the rotation of the roller. When the desired clearance is obtained, the roller is fixed to the shaft by tightening the screw into or against the shaft. A connecting mechanism is secured to the other end of the arm (the earlier-mentioned end has the flat nozzle attached to it). The mechanism includes a vertical shaft and a rotating member into which latter the shaft is inserted together with a bearing.

The shaft is fixed to the arm, and the rotating member is fixed to a horizontal rod. The arm is freely movable relative to the rod within a horizontal plane but they move together within a vertical plane. The rod is inserted into a bearing secured to the device. The other end of the rod is connected with a vertical rod. The other end of this latter rod is pulled by a spring to give an upward movement to the flat nozzle. The cylindrical member is contacted with the drum by the tension of this spring.

A round projecting member is attached by a shaft to the rod at a location lower than the center of its length, and a rotating cam is provided in a manner so that it contacts the member. A projecting portion of the cam pushes the vertical rod rightward when the cam rotates. At this moment, the horizontal rod, fixed to the vertical rod and cooperating with the arm, moves the flat nozzle downward from the drum.

One end of a connecting rod is connected near the center of the arm by means of a ball joint, and the other end of the rod is orthogonally connected with a drive shaft. The rod is connected to the shaft by an eccentric shaft secured to the drive shaft with a ball joint inserted between them. When the shaft rotates, the eccentric shaft gives a horizontal reciprocal movement to the connecting rod and the supporting arm connected to the rod. It will be understood that the connecting mechanism and the parts described in connection therewith constitute the means for intermittently reciprocating the nozzle toward and away from the periphery of the drum, while the connecting mechanism and the parts connected to it constitute the means for intermittently reciprocating the same nozzle substantially parallel to the drum periphery, for the purposes explained above where the primary points of the process were described.

A cooling-water tube provided along and extending from the outlet orifice of the flat nozzle prevents the dough from sticking fast to the flat nozzle heated by the drum on account of the heater.

The rotation of the gear pump forces the dough from the hopper into the nozzle through the tube. The dough is then injected onto the outer circular surface of the drum. The thickness of the dough sheet thus obtained depends upon the clearance. If the latter increases for a moment, the dough sheet will be interrupted. Therefore, each downward movement of the nozzle at appropriate intervals makes individual dough sheets having the same constant length, and this is done by the operation of the cam which moves the rod and the associated connecting mechanism at intervals.

The dough sheet discharged from the nozzle sticks to the drum and is baked by the heat, which ranges approximately between 70° and 230°C. If the outer circular surface of the drum is finished on a lathe, the dough sheet baked on it has numerous grooves, and they are easily broken. Uneven baking will be caused if the drum is heated unevenly.

The eccentric shaft is fixed to the drive shaft, which gives a horizontal reciprocal movement to the supporting arm in a way that the dough sheet discharged from the nozzle is vibrated, so that no grooves are made on the sheet and no uneven baking occurs. The dough sheets consecutively baked are released from the drum by a releasing plate, the end rim of which contacts the outer circular surface of the drum.

Frittaten

The process described by *A. Ruhdorfer; U.S. Patent 3,830,946; August 20, 1974* relates to the production of "Frittaten" (thin pancakes cut into little strips like noodles and used in soups or other food products), in which a mass of dough baked on both sides is cut up into Frittaten-shaped pieces and is subsequently dehydrated.

In the case of known processes, dough baked on both sides is produced by inserting Frittaten dough between two revolving heated drums. The mass of dough is subsequently cut into pieces of 50-cm width. These pieces are dried for 1 to 2 days in order to facilitate the cutting. They are cut and subsequently dried in a hot air current, for example, in the manner of noodles. This drying out is necessary to avoid spoilage of the goods which will reach the market ready-packed.

The customary manner of drying out is cumbersome and, moreover, leads to end-products of an inferior quality. This process avoids these disadvantages because it provides for the dehydration to be accomplished in such a manner that the Frittaten are put into hot oil or fat, the temperature of which is preferably 120°C, where they are left until they reach a water content preferably below 2% by weight.

Preferably the freshly cooked dough should be fed continuously to a cutting installation which has separating disks between guides, which guides revolve with the speed of the mass of dough. Behind the disks are provided one or several rotating knives guided against a fixed knife.

Liquid batter or dough is fed continuously from a container to the upper of the two rollers and is carried along by the roller. The composition of the batter used is one that is suitable for the production of pancakes or waffles, for example, a mixture of 56% by weight water, 40% by weight wheat flour, 2.5% by weight powdered milk and 1.5% by weight of powdered whole egg seasoned with salt. Both rollers are heated so that the mass of batter is baked on both sides when reaching a conveyer belt. A superficial drying of the mass of dough is accomplished by a hot air blower system. In the case of a speed of movement of 1 m/min, the drying time is about one minute.

The cutting up of the mass of dough in a half-dried state will be facilitated through the fact that the guides for the mass of dough move with the same speed as the latter, therefore, with the peripheral speed of the drums. Immediately after the mass of dough is broken up by the separating disks revolving between the belts, the individual strips of dough are broken up finely by means of a knife revolving with a roller and acting against a fixed knife.

The half-dried Frittaten are immediately guided to a bath of vegetable cooking oil which heats the Frittaten and as a result of that, drives out the remaining water. The temperature of the vegetable oil used was about 120° to 150°C.

The oil or fat used for heating and dehydrating the precooked dough may be any edible oil or fat known to be useful for frying and cooking of food products. Vegetable oils are particularly useful, especially those that are processed and blended for good heat stability.

The described process results in thin pancakes cut into strips of about 30 to 40 mm length and 2 to 3 mm width, which have been baked to a golden brown and are crisp and crunchy. They are suitable particularly for use in soups but also as tidbits. They differ from the prior known Frittaten, especially through their high fat content which usually lies between 25 to 50% by weight of the total product weight. The analytical data for a typical product are (data in percent by weight):

	Percent
Ash	1.86
Common salt	1.35
Starch	35.17
Total fat	47.32
Milk fat	2.69

TORTILLAS

Shelf Stable Tortillas

A typical process for preparing corn tortillas is initiated by immersing the whole corn kernels in a mixture of water and lime which is heated to about 180°F, the corn being allowed to soak in the water and lime mixture for a suitable period, for example overnight, such that the desired reaction may take place to break down the corn kernels. The excess water-lime fluid is then drained off the corn and the corn is thereafter ground, resulting in a tortilla dough commonly referred to as masa having about 50 to 65% moisture content. The tortillas may then be made directly from this dough, or the moisture may be removed from the dough product by suitable known drying techniques to produce a dry corn flour which may be stored for subsequent use by adding water to produce the desired masa or dough for making tortillas.

The masa dough in bulk form is fed into a tortilla oven, the dough being fed through extruding rollers or the like to produce the desired flat sheets. The dough rollers are also provided with means for cutting the flattened dough into the desired tortilla shape. The oven is operated at about 750°F to bake the tortilla. This baking process takes less than 1 minute, e.g., about 45 seconds, and the tortilla exits the oven with an internal temperature of 212°F with a moisture content of 40 to 50%.

Normally, these tortillas are then processed in different manners. In the most common process, the tortillas are sent along a conveyer belt which is long enough to permit the hot tortillas to cool down sufficiently so that they may be easily handled by workers who collect the tortillas into a suitable number, for example, one dozen, and package these tortillas in a suitable container such as a plastic bag. However, these tortillas are not sterile and so in the most common usage the packaged and sealed tortilla is refrigerated. This refrigerated product is then maintained refrigerated in the retail grocery outlet, commonly in the compartments with the milk and cheese products, until sold to the consumer. The consumer maintains the product refrigerated until use. Like most refrigerated products, the storage time of the packaged tortilla is limited to, for example, 1 or 2 months after which the spoilage sets in and the tortilla becomes unsatisfactory for the consumer.

In a second process, the tortilla, immediately after being packaged as described above, is frozen and the frozen tortilla product is then maintained frozen and sold with the frozen foods in the grocery store and kept in the consumer's freezer. The frozen tortilla has a substantially longer lifetime than the refrigerated product although freezing adds to the expense and inconvenience of shipping and storage.

Approximately 90% of the refrigerated and frozen packaged tortillas produced by these two processes are utilized in the home in making enchiladas and tacos. Typically, the tortilla is unpackaged, preferably after thawing the product in the case of the frozen product, and the tortilla is fried in hot frying oil. The tortilla is then removed from the hot oil and the excess oil is removed. The desired meat or meat and bean filling is then placed on the fried tortilla, the tortilla is rolled or folded, suitable sauces or the like may be spread on the product, and the product is then placed in an oven for baking and subsequent serving.

To produce this end product, the tortilla must be flexible for rolling and must remain rolled during the preparation and baking process.

In a third process, the tortilla may be fried and filled. Immediately after packaging, the filled tortilla product is frozen and maintained frozen in the retail stores and in the consumer's home freezer until its final preparation for consumption.

In a fourth known process, the tortilla is cut into small triangular chip-size pieces which are then deep-fried for about 30 seconds, or more, to produce a tortilla chip much like a potato chip. The end product, after frying, has a very low moisture content such as 2 to 4%. These chips are then placed in bags and sold off the shelf in the stores with the other crisp chip products. Because of the very low moisture content, there is no problem with spoilage or the like and these tortilla chips are shelf-stable.

In a fifth process, the whole tortilla is fried for about 30 seconds or more in a U-shaped form until the moisture content is very low as with the chips to form a rigid and brittle taco shell.

The process described by *P.H. Mattson; U.S. Patent 3,930,049; December 30, 1975; assigned to S & W Fine Foods, Inc.* provides a tortilla product and process whereby a prefried, shelf-stable, flexible tortilla is made and packaged for sale off the dry grocery shelf to the end consumer, the tortilla being ready for filling and baking by the consumer without refrigeration or the added step of frying the tortilla. In this process, the tortilla is prepared from the masa by forming and baking in the tortilla ovens as before.

The tortillas exit the oven with a moisture content of from 40 to 50% and at a temperature above 180°F, for example an internal temperature of up to 212°F. While still hot from the oven, the tortillas are fried lightly by being immersed in frying oil which is at about 275° to 300°F to 400°F. The tortillas remain in the frying oil for a limited time, e.g., between 2 and 20 seconds. The tortillas are then removed from the frying oil at an elevated temperature, e.g., an internal temperature of up to 212°F. The excess oil is drained or otherwise removed from the tortillas.

The temperature of the frying oil and the frying time is selected to limit the dehydration of the tortilla. In other words, the frying conditions are mild enough that the tortilla retains sufficient moisture for it to remain flexible (e.g., in excess of 13.5%). There is a direct relationship between the moisture loss, the time and temperature of frying, and flexibility.

The oil content of the fried tortilla does not significantly affect its flexibility. Longer frying times produce higher oil contents up to a typical maximum of 20 to 25%, depending on the type of oil and absorptivity of the tortilla. Thus, the oil content is determined by the degree of frying required for the desired moisture content. Typical oil content may range from 5 to 24%.

The tortillas, while still at a sterile, elevated temperature, are rolled into tight rolls of spiral slightly flattened cross section and inserted into a strong moistureproof bag which is immediately sealed to maintain the sterility of the tortillas. From 8 to 12 tortillas are packaged in each bag.

Although the tortillas have a relatively high moisture content, typically from 15 to 35%, the tortillas processed and packaged in this manner are shelf-stable in the retail store for up to one year or more without refrigeration. This stability is due to the packaging of the product while the temperature is still elevated due to heat retained after frying and without the introduction of any contaminant.

The end user, when preparing, first places the unopened bag in boiling water for about 10 minutes to insure that, upon opening the bag and removing the tortillas, they will be limber and will unroll, without cracking, to be filled, rerolled and baked.

Extending Shelf Life of Tortillas

Tortillas and tortilla dough are made from corn which is steeped in calcium hydroxide or sometimes in sodium hydroxide or the like, to produce a reaction with the corn known as nixtamalizing. The nixtamalized corn having a chemical combination with calcium hydroxide or the like is then ground into corn flour which is combined with water to make tortillas.

This steeping during which the reaction occurs is done at an elevated temperature of 80°C and thus it can also be properly said that there is cooking at this time. In addition to the reaction already mentioned and its important general effect on the product that is involved, the steeping has the effect of softening the hull, thus allowing the water to penetrate through the hull into the corn, and also of causing a reaction specifically between some of the calcium and at least some of certain of the oils originally present in the corn to produce special compounds which add to the taste.

This steeping reaction with alkali such as calcium hydroxide produces a product having the ingredients of the corn combined with calcium hydroxide or the like, leaving some alkali free and producing in the tortilla dough, if no additive is used, a pH in the range of 6.5 to 6.7, there having been a washing operation after the steeping.

M.J. Rubio; U.S. Patent 3,730,732; May 1, 1973 has found that if a water-soluble alkali such as sodium hydroxide or the like is added to the tortilla dough in controlled proportions, it will not only increase the yield of tortilla dough and tortillas, but will also retard microbiological spoilage of the tortillas and tortilla dough.

At the same time, if this alkali is added after the washing, it has none of the effects already mentioned as occurring during the nixtamalization, the softening and the reaction already mentioned having already taken place at the time of the nixtamalization.

The results indicate that the sodium hydroxide or the like if used in the correct quantities produces these different effects because at the dough stage it no longer reacts with the corn in the same way that the calcium hydroxide, sodium hydroxide or the like reacted with the corn during steeping.

Tortillas, when normally prepared without additives of any kind, have a maximum shelf life of 12 to 15 hours. After such time they are spoiled by microorganisms and become hard or stale.

Ethnic and Specialty Food Items

It is known that tortillas when kept under conditions in which no moisture is lost, nevertheless become hard and inflexible with the passage of time and break or crumble easily when flexed or bent. This effect increases with time. Freshly made tortillas are very flexible but lose their flexibility with the passage of time. Hardening is appreciable after 24 hours, marked after 48 hours and almost complete after 72 hours if the product is kept at room temperature. It should be noted that the hardening or staling effect increases with decreasing temperature. At temperatures below room temperature, therefore, hardening proceeds at a faster rate than at room temperature and vice versa. Hardening becomes still faster when you go from temperatures in between ordinary room temperature and freezing temperature to temperatures below the freezing point of water in the tortillas.

The additive imparts the property of retarding the loss of flexibility of tortillas with time. It must be mixed with the dough used for making tortillas, although the mixture may be achieved in various ways.

These alkaline materials may be incorporated as dry powders with the tortilla flour used in making up the dough or they can be dissolved in the water used in making the dough or they can be added in solution to incorporate with the dough, due allowance being made for the water which is introduced.

The effect of certain alkalizing substances in increasing the shelf life of tortillas at 25°C is shown below.

Type of Additive and Dose	Shelf Life, hours
Calcium hydroxide, 0.3%	48
Calcium hydroxide, 0.5%	72
Sodium carbonate, 0.4%	24
Control	12

Further study by *M.J. Rubio; U.S. Patent 3,694,224; September 26, 1972* revealed that an aliphatic polycarboxylic acid or its anhydride having 3 to 6 carbon atoms in its carbon chain would also be an effective agent in extending the shelf life of tortillas.

In addition *M.J. Rubio; U.S. Patent 3,709,696; January 9, 1973* found that incorporating hydrophilic inorganic gels in making the tortilla dough would also retard the staling and microbiological spoilage of tortillas.

PEANUT PRODUCTS

Peanut Flakes

Sliced almond for decorating bakery and confectionary products can be obtained by slicing almond kernels with a slicing machine in a direction parallel to its major axis with no marked difficulty. However, cultivation of the almond is largely limited to the southwestern part of North America; therefore, the price of the almond markedly fluctuates and is relatively high. Contrary thereto, since the peanut is cultivated in most tropical and mild temperature regions, there is small possibility of fluctuation of the price of the peanut and the peanut is available at a lower price than that of the almond because of the high absolute yield.

Furthermore, because the peanut is an annual plant, different from the almond, planted acreage thereof can be easily changed according to the variation of the demand. Thus peanuts are superior from the standpoint of a stable supply. Accordingly, utilizing the peanut, cheap and stable in supply, instead of the almond, expensive and unstable in supply, becomes beneficial for both manufacturers of bakery and confectionary products and consumers.

However, considering the peanut's utility as a substitute for the sliced almond, we may find two difficulties to be solved. Namely, one of the difficulties involves the fact that the peanut has an approximately circular section to its major axis passing through the embryo and this is quite different from the almond. The other difficulty involves the fact that it has a peculiar grassy taste and flavor. Due to the former fact, a peanut kernel tends to rotate about the major axis passing through the embryo when it is to be sliced at an angle transverse of the plane of the confronting surface of both fractions of the peanut kernel. Therefore, slices of the peanut kernels can hardly be obtained in uniform and relatively large size unless the peanut kernel supplied to a slicing machine happens to be positioned in such a manner that the confronting surface thereof becomes parallel to the cutting blade.

Consequently, the yield of the peanut slices having a commercially acceptable value will be relatively small. A problem of how to slice peanut kernels in a direction parallel to the confronting surface should, by all means, be solved to enable peanut flakes to be manufactured on an industrial scale, or otherwise development of the peanut slices will not be achieved.

I. Ohta, A. Matsunobu, M. Nishizawa, H. Kubota and K. Sakamoto; U.S. Patent 3,928,635; December 23, 1975; assigned to Ton Co., Ltd. and Fuji Oil Company, Ltd., Japan developed a method for producing peanut slices which involved separating a pair of fractions of a peanut kernel from each other and then slicing each peanut fraction. Combination between the fractions of one peanut kernel is so comparatively loose that they can be easily separated from each other by simple mechanical means and each of the peanut fractions thus separated has an approximately semicircular section to its major axis.

Each peanut fraction assumes an optimum position for slicing since each peanut fraction will be obviated from free rotation during slicing operation and then the slicing will, in most cases, be done parallel to the confronting surface of the fractions of each peanut kernel. This was accomplished by use of a commercially available rotary slicer.

However, in the course of the experiment, it has been found that the moisture content in each peanut fraction prior to being sliced is an important factor to be considered to obtain a good result, and that if the moisture content is below 6 or over 14%, the yield of peanut flakes of relatively large size having a minimum diameter of 7.5 mm will be small and that the best result will be obtained when the moisture content is within the range of 9 to 11%.

Change in the yield from different moisture contents appears to be due to (1) change in the texture of the peanut and (2) physical correlation between the cutting blade and the texture of the peanut. However, the change in the peanut texture seems to be most responsible.

Experimental data showed the use of the fractioned peanuts as the raw material and control of the moisture content within a specific range in each fraction of the peanuts to be effective.

Raw peanuts, however, possess a grassy taste which seems to be caused by lower to higher saturated or unsaturated aldehydes or ketones. Therefore, in order to market them, this undesirable taste should be removed. Peanuts, when roasted, generate specific fragrance which does not last long and would hinder the use of the sliced peanuts as a substitute for sliced almonds. Various deodorizing methods instead of roasting were tried and steaming was found to be most effective. In cases where suitable steaming was done, not only peculiar taste and odor of the peanuts almost vanished, but also the product became one with an almond-like texture in the mouth.

It was found that the grassy taste decreases as the steaming temperature is raised, but too high temperatures or too long steaming cause bitterness and further cause the texture and color to worsen. Although there can be seen little bad influence on the texture and color at 90°C it seems to be uneconomical since it takes a long time for the removal of the grassy taste.

On the other hand, a higher temperature such as 120°C will effect rapid removal of the grassy taste, but readily causes generation of the bitterness and also stimulates the deterioration in the texture and color. Heating at 100° to 110°C for 1 to 5 minutes appears to be optimum. However, in practice, it should empirically be determined in consideration of various working conditions such as size, thickness, amount, etc. of the slices to be deodorized.

As the result of further study, it was found that an ethanol treatment to the raw material, either raw peanuts, separated fractions thereof or slices of the latter, not only accelerates the removal of the grassy taste by the steaming, but also imparts sweetness to the product.

In practice, each of large-sized peanuts (as large as possible) is skinned, dried, divided into two fractions, moistened with addition of a predetermined amount of water, allowed to stand in a closed atmosphere and sliced with a slicing machine, when the moisture content attains a constant value, to provide slices of a predetermined thickness. The slices are then classified and the classified slices are put in an autoclave, steamed at a predetermined temperature for a predetermined period of time, and dried with hot air and, further, preferably, with microwave radiation until the moisture content thereof attains 3%. The classification with a sieve may be carried out after the drying has been finished.

The ethanol treatment may be applied during any of the above steps. However, to fully exploit the removal of the grassy taste with ethanol, it has been empirically found that it would be better that the slices be as thin as possible and the treatment period be as long as possible so as to allow perfect penetration of ethanol solution or vapor into the material to be treated. The amount of ethanol to be added is sufficient if it is preferably over 1.0% relative to the weight of the material to be treated. However, in the case where the ethanol is added at the time of the steaming, an amount over 5% is preferable, because the lower concentration will not cause sufficient permeation of the ethanolic vapor even though a higher temperature is used, since the steaming time is short. Similarly, somewhat higher concentration of ethanol to be added is desirable in the case where the ethanol treatment is carried out subject to the nonfractioned peanuts or fractioned peanuts compared with one to the slices. The addition of ethanol to the peanut fractions may be done simultaneously or separately with the moistening.

The generation of sweetness by the ethanol treatment appears to be an enormous effect. The sliced peanuts thus obtained have a mild texture in the mouth and a pleasant chewiness and can broadly be applied in confectionary products. The thickness of each peanut slice may be changed as desired according to its purpose by adjusting the distance between the slot and the tip of the blade of the machine. However, in general, 0.8 ± 0.1 mm in thickness is preferable.

Example 1: 100 kg of large-sized peanuts was skinned by a wet process and dried by hot air at 70°C until the moisture content thereof attained 6% and each peanut was divided into fractions with a dividing machine. 4.2 kg of water was sprayed to the fractioned peanuts which were then allowed to stand overnight in an airtight vessel. Next morning, the moistened peanut fractions were taken out of the vessel and allowed to stand on a shelf to allow the water attached to the surface of each of the peanut fractions to evaporate (moisture content: about 10%).

Thereafter, the moistened peanuts were sliced with a slicing machine wherein the distance between the cutting blade and the slot was adjusted to 0.8 mm. The slices thus obtained were put into an autoclave and steamed for 5 minutes at 105°C by injecting superheated steam thereinto. The steamed slices (moisture content: about 12%) were taken out of the autoclave, dried for 10 minutes with hot air heated to 70°C until the moisture content attained 6%, and then dried for 8 minutes in a continuous high-frequency drier (output: 4.5 kw; frequency: $2,450 \pm 5$ MHz) to obtain peanut slices having a moisture content of about 3%. The product was then classified with a 7.5-mm, rotary shifter. 62 kg of finished peanut slices having the minimum diameter over 7.5 mm could be obtained.

Example 2: 12 kg of the peanut fractions obtained as in Example 1 were divided equally into six samples which were then autoclaved for 2 minutes under 1.4 kg/cm². At the autoclaving, these samples were added with 0, 10, 20, 40, 100 and 200 ml of ethanol, respectively. After steaming, the individual samples were dried as in Example 1 to obtain peanut slices each having the moisture content of 3 to 4%. The organoleptic test showed the following results.

Ethanol Added, ml	Grassiness	Roughness	Bitterness	Sweetness
0	+	+	−	−
10	+	+	−	−
20	+	+	−	−
40	±	+	−	±
100	−	−	−	+
200	−	−	−	+

Peanut Butter

Peanut butter consists essentially of ground roasted peanuts, sugar (dextrose and/or sucrose) and salt. Because this product exhibits gravitational instability (oil layer separating on top of the product) it has become regular practice to add relatively high-melting fat components to the hot (about 170°F) peanut butter prior to filling the product into jars. This high-melting fat component usually has a melting point in excess of 110°F, about less than 160°F, and may be: a partially hydrogenated fat, a completely hydrogenated fat, monoglyceride and diglyceride esters of saturated fatty acids or mixtures of these stabilizing agents.

These high-melting fat components, when added in small amounts, (viz, 1 to 3% of the peanut butter), may be introduced as a supplement to the ground roasted peanuts or when added in larger amounts (viz, 5 to 10% of the peanut butter), may be introduced after an equivalent amount of liquid peanut oil in the ground roasted peanuts has been removed. The added hard fat is believed to form a continuous or semicontinuous structure within the final peanut butter during the cooling of the product and in so doing prevents oil from separating from the peanut butter.

The sugar and salt flavorings are added in the peanut butter manufacture in total amounts usually less than 5% and this addition may be balanced if desired with an equivalent addition by weight of liquid nonhydrogenated vegetable oil or the stabilizing agent previously mentioned. During the roasting of the peanuts, the moisture content is reduced so that the final product will contain less than 4% moisture.

Oil separation can easily be prevented by the use of a sufficient amount of a completely saturated fat or other stabilizers. This, however, leads to a sacrifice of low-temperature spreadability and the development of waxy mouthing properties. The delicate balance required to prevent oil separation without sacrificing too much temperature spreadability and incurring too waxy mouthing properties is difficult to attain and almost impossible to maintain in the day-to-day manufacture of peanut butter.

The well-known determination of solids content index (SCI) applied to the extracted fat from heated peanut butters provides a good method for correlating the spreadability and stability of peanut butters with the amounts and kinds of stabilizers used in the peanut butters. The SCI of the fat may be determined by the dilatometric method described by Fulton et al *(JAOCS* 31, 98, 1954). The less solids the fat contains at 50°F, the more spreadable is the peanut butter. On the other hand, there must still be a sufficient solid fat content at 100°F if oil separation is to be avoided. Thus, the higher the SCI values at about 100°F, the better is the tendency of the peanut butter containing the oils to resist oil separation.

C.M. Gooding; U.S. Patent 3,882,254; May 6, 1975; assigned to CPC International Inc. has found that an unhydrogenated fraction of palm oil is capable of immobilizing the oil phase of peanut butter without undue drag in the mouth. This property is very likely related to the composition and structure of the glycerides contained in the hard fraction of palm oil which, itself, is high melting but not so high melting as the usual hydrogenated and partially hydrogenated fats. Furthermore, the hard fraction of palm oil contains a significant amount of polyunsaturated acids, in fact, as much as 3 to 5 times the amount usually present in butter fat and as much as twice the amount usually present in cocoa butter. Thus, while the hard fraction of palm oil is the hard or high-melting fat, it owes its high melting point to the peculiar glyceride structure of that fraction of palm oil rather than to the presence of large amounts of stearic acid or hydrogenated fat stabilizers used in the prior art which, incidentally, contain no or insignificant amounts of polyunsaturated acids.

The unhydrogenated hard fractions of palm oil utilized are easily prepared simply by allowing whole, refined and bleached palm oil to partially crystallize while slowly stirring at temperatures between about 85° and 105°F or even as high as 108°F. The simplicity of separation of the partially crystallized palm oil by filtration provides an abundant source of stabilizer. At the same time the process yields a soft or liquid fraction of palm oil suitable for many edible uses. In fact, the soft fraction is more useful for many such applications than is whole palm oil.

Example 1: 800 lb of refined and bleached palm oil was partially crystallized with slow stirring for 45 hours at 95°F. Filtration through a filter press with air-blowing of the filter cake produced 12.8% of hard fraction having the following characteristics.

Melting Point 130.8°F, Iodine Value 32.6

		SCI Values		
50°F	70°F	80°F	92°F	102°F
90.9	80.7	78.5	77.9	75.1

		Fatty Acid Composition %			
Myristic C14	Palmitic C16	Stearic C18	Oleic C18:1	Linoleic C18:2	Linolenic C18:3
1.4	65.8	5.3	21.4	5.7	0.3

Example 2: The filtrate of Example 1 was used to prepare a second crop of hard fraction through randomization by ester interchange. The randomized filtrate was partially crystallized after the manner in which the first crop of hard fraction was obtained from the whole palm oil in Example 1.

	Melting Point °F	Iodine Value	SCI Values				
			50°F	70°F	80°F	92°F	102°F
(a) Filtrate before randomization	86.4	57.1	27.6	7.2	2.3	0.0	0.0
(b) Filtrate after randomization	108.1	56.7	17.9	10.3	11.0	9.3	7.7
(c) Filtrate from crystallized, randomized (b)	86.2	62.8	20.5	8.2	3.2	0.1	0.1
(d) Hard Fraction from randomized, crystallized (b) yield 18.7%	129.2	30.1	61.8	61.2	61.7	60.5	56.5

Peanut butter was prepared in which the sole stabilizer was the hard fraction obtained from whole refined and bleached palm oil. Preliminary exploration of SCI values contributed by the hard fraction in peanut oil solutions indicated that 3.4% of the stabilizer in peanut butter would provide the desired degree of stabilization. This concentration corresponds to 6.8% in the peanut oil solutions of the pilot exploration.

Combination Nut and Jelly Spread

The packaging of a combination product wherein the components are in contiguous contact has not previously met with total success since during normal storage periods, there occurs moisture diffusion from the second food spread phase into the nut component phase. This moisture diffusion causes an unsightly dark bank at the interface between the phases and results in the texture of the nut component becoming soggy and objectionably heavy, while that of the second food spread can become grainy and crystalline.

The products of a process described by *P.J. Tiemstra; U.S. Patent 3,969,514; July 13, 1976; assigned to Swift & Company* are combinations of a spreadable nut component in discrete relationship with a second food spread which may be a gelled fruit spread, a marshmallow spread, or a flavored starch-based spread. The method includes either or both of the steps of raising the water activity and raising the oil content of the nut component, and may or may not include lowering the water activity of the second food spread.

The term water activity used herein characterizes the physical property of a solute or mixture of solutes in an aqueous solution and can be used interchangeably with terms such as osmotic pressure and equilibrium relative humidity. As used herein, water activity is precisely defined as the relative humidity of the adjacent atmosphere at equilibrium, expressed as a decimal.

It has been determined that the production of a nut butter or spread and second food spread combination in the same package has been unsatisfactory because moisture from the second food spread transfers into the nut butter or spread after a relatively short period of time, causing browning through what is thought to be a Maillard-type reaction. It has been found that the rate of moisture transfer is directly proportional to the difference between the water activity of the second food spread phase and that of the nut component phase. This moisture transfer is inversely proportional to the amount of fat in the nut component phase. To lessen moisture transfer, the water activity difference between the phases is lowered and/or the fat content of the nut component phase is raised.

The discretely phased products of the process include a nut component that has been formulated to inhibit moisture transfer into the nut component from the other component, a second food spread. The process includes preparing a spreadable nut component including one or more of the steps of adding water such that the water content thereof is relatively high, adding oil such that the oil content thereof is relatively high, or including a quantity of nuts such that the nut content thereof is relatively low. This nut component is combined in discrete phases with a second food spread and packaged for shelf storage at room temperature.

Many commercially marketed products that may be utilized as the second food spread phase have a relatively large water activity (on the order of 0.85 to 0.90). The water activity of commercially marketed peanut butter is usually less than 0.15, roughly corresponding to an approximate water content of 0.5% by weight of the nut component. This difference between the water activities of the second food spread and of the nut component may be lowered in accordance with this process by utilizing a nut butter or a nut spread having a water content in the range of about 2 to 6% by weight, which corresponds to an approximate water activity range of 0.40 to 0.70. Thus the difference between the respective water activities is reduced. It has been determined that a water content in the spreadable nut component that exceeds about 6% by weight is not desirable, this being the level at which browning is initiated.

The combination food product contains approximately 25 to 75 weight percent of the spreadable nut component. The spreadable nut component is an intimately mixed composition of minute particles of protein and carbohydrate suspended in an oil base that is spreadable and which contains significant amounts of ground nuts. The spreadable nut component may also include ingredients such as natural or hydrogenated, saturated or unsaturated fats or oils, peanut oil, butter or margarine. The spreadable nut component will also contain water and a relatively small quantity of salt, generally not more than 1.5% by weight of the nut component.

The second food spread may be a marshmallow spread or a flavored spreadable starch gel. This spread has a consistency and texture that resembles pudding. The second food spread may also be a gelled fruit spread, preferably having a normal commercial water content of approximately 30 to 35 weight percent. The second food spread can be unmodified in its normal commercial water content, which can be as high as approximately 30 to 35 weight percent, corresponding to a water activity range of about 0.85 to 0.90.

More particularly, in making the spreadable nut component, ground nuts are prepared by milling nuts in a conventional apparatus, the amount of ground nuts added being approximately 60 to 98% by weight of the total nut component. Additional oil or fat may be added as peanut oil, vegetable oil, margarine, butter or the like, so that the oil content of the final nut component is within the approximate range of from about 50 to about 65% by weight. Also, water may be added to achieve a water content of the nut component of about 2 to 6% by weight. The preparation of the nut component is accomplished at a temperature of about 130° to 190°F.

If a marshmallow spread is to be utilized as the second food spread, it is prepared and processed as follows. A syrup is prepared by heating or boiling to dissolve in water sweeteners, thereby forming a solution of about 70 to 75% solute in water, and adding to this solution prewetted gelling and whipping agents. The temperature should be high enough to dissolve and liquify the ingredients but not so high as to denature the egg albumin. The moisture content of the marshmallow syrup should be at the desired level for the finished product. The material can be whipped in any conventional equipment with or without cooling to obtain an overrun of 100 to 400% of original volume. The aerated product will be layered or swirled with the nut component in the manner described herein at a temperature not to exceed 100°F.

When the second food spread is prepared as a spreadable starch-based gel, the gelling starch is blended with any one or a combination of sweeteners. Sufficient water is added by heating or boiling to prepare a smooth spread of 80 to 85% solids content.

When the second food spread is to be a gelled fruit spread, it is prepared by boiling sugar, a fruit acid and water to form a sugar solution. Fruit pectin or some other gelling agent is presoaked in water with a sugar, and the presoak is added to the boiling sugar solution until the pectin is dissolved, after which is added any fruit flavoring agent, such as a fruit juice. The temperature is then lowered to a point suitable for filling but preferably not so low as to promote gelation. Generally, incipient setting takes place at a temperature below 170°F; however, when the partially set solution is cooled with stirring to a temperature within the range of about 90° to 150°F, it will pour and set to a firm, clear, gelled product.

The combined food product can be produced by any number of methods. One such method is the filling of a container with alternate quantities of the spreadable nut component and of the second food spread. If this method of filling is used, the ingredients must be preconditioned so that they set up quickly. Generally, this may be done by either blowing a cold blast of gas, such as air or nitrogen, over successive quantities of each product immediately after pouring into the container, or by supercooling the ingredients prior to pouring.

For example, the nut component may be supercooled in a heat exchanger such as a Votator at a temperature between about 70° and 100°F so that it sets within a few seconds. Further, the second food spread can be made to set within 30 seconds if also subjected to supercooling conditions similar to those produced by a heat exchanger such as in a Votator, where heat is exhausted rapidly by thin-film agitation. Temperatures are determined by the composition of the second food spread, but generally the temperature may be reduced 10° to 20° toward the normal setting temperature with a resultant quick set when removed from the supercooling conditioner.

Various means may be used to combine the spreadable nut component and the second food spread so that they are in contiguous association yet possess a definite and distinct configuration. In one method a manufacturing line is set up in which there is, in order, the nut component heat exchanger drawing from a supply kettle of fluid nut component, and a second food spread heat exchanger drawing from a supply kettle of hot second food spread material. The nut component and the second food spread flow from their respective heat exchangers to filling machines in such a fashion that a quantity of nut component is poured into a jar followed by a quantity of the second food spread and then by a quantity of the nut component, and so forth, until the desired number of quantities are filled into the jar.

Between the nut component filling apparatus and the succeeding second food spread filling apparatus may be chill means to chill the quantity of second food spread before the product being produced receives the next quantity of nut component. The packages are capped and labeled by means of conventional equipment.

Example: A peanut spread was prepared by preparing an intimate mixture of 87.0% by weight of ground peanuts, 2.0% by weight hydrogenated vegetable oil, 1.0% by weight salt, 6.0% by weight peanut oil and 4.0% by weight water. This peanut spread was containerized into glass jars, in contiguous contact with an unmodified commercially marketed jelly having a moisture content of 32% and a water activity of 0.87, to form a combined peanut spread and jelly food product. The jars were stored at room temperature. No discoloration of the peanut spread or liquid migration was observed until after 4 months had elapsed. Even then, evidence of water migration was slight.

VEGETABLE AND SALAD PRODUCTS

Stable Avocado Base

F.E. Latimer; U.S. Patent 3,958,036; May 18, 1976; assigned to Cav-Pro, Inc. describes a method by which a stable avocado base is prepared. The avocado base will remain stable for extended periods of time under those conditions of storage and transportation which are required for products that are widely distributed and sold in retail grocery stores. The avocado base is stable both by itself and when admixed with other ingredients, such as mayonnaise, spices, vegetable flakes, starches and the like.

In the process, the avocado flesh, water, vegetable gums and other ingredients, if desired, are thoroughly and intimately admixed so as to produce a fine dispersion which is stable and from which water does not separate under conditions of storage and transportation for extended periods of time.

The intimate and thorough admixing of the avocado flesh, water and vegetable gums is accomplished in equipment which is designed to produce fine uniform dispersions, such as, for example, homogenizers, colloid mills and emulsifiers.

The avocado flesh varies somewhat in its properties depending upon the variety, the climate, the soil and the specific growing conditions under which that avocado was grown. For these reasons it is not possible to predefine exactly the conditions which will in each instance produce a fine dispersion of optimum stability. In general, when the admixing is accomplished in a homogenizer, the pressure should be at least 500 lb/in^2 to produce the stable fine dispersion. Pressure in excess of 2,000 lb/in^2 may be employed if desired; however, no substantial benefits are obtained by using such pressures.

When a colloid mill is used, the setting should be about 0.001 to 0.050 inch to produce a fine stable dispersion. In general it is not possible to produce a dispersion fine enough to be stable under conditions of storage without using special mixing equipment capable of producing a fine dispersion, such as that produced by a homogenizer at a pressure of at least 500 lb/in^2.

The skins of the avocado may be incorporated with the avocado flesh to replace a portion of the vegetable gums. When used, the skins are cleaned, heated, ground and then intimately admixed with the avocado flesh before it is dispersed. The vegetable gums which may be used include gum tragacanth, carrageenan, guar, gum arabic, locust bean, alginates, starches, pectin and the like.

Water is added to the avocado to facilitate its dispersion and may be used in quantities from 35 to 65% by weight of the admixture. The vegetable gums may be used in an effective amount ranging from 0.5 to 1% by weight of the total admixture.

The stabilized avocado base remains stable under many different conditions.

The stable avocado base, for example, may be frozen and thawed, and the thawed product will remain stable. Likewise, the stable avocado base may be dried by freeze or spray drying techniques, and when admixed with water, it will again be stable. The avocado base may be admixed with other ingredients, for example, mayonnaise, vegetable flakes, sour cream and the like. The resultant admixture will be stable under conditions of storage and transportation. The admixtures are stable for long periods of time, i.e., about three months.

Other ingredients besides avocado flesh, water and vegetable gums may be added and taken through the intimate admixing step. Other common ingredients include, for example, salt, vegetable flakes, spices, coloring agents, flavor additives, lemon juice to stabilize the color of the avocado and the like.

The avocado flesh, water and vegetable gums may be premixed under conditions which are less rigorous than those of the intimate admixing so as to provide a premix. The premix may be frozen for storage and transportation purposes, if desired. The premix is then thawed and subjected to the intimate admixing step to produce a fine uniform dispersion. The characteristics of the fine dispersion are substantially unaffected by the freezing and thawing cycle of the premix. The ability to utilize previously frozen avocado flesh makes this method amenable to a year-round practice. If it were not possible to utilize previously frozen and thawed avocado flesh, then the process could only be practiced during or shortly after the avocado harvesting season when fresh avocados are available.

Example: The composition of the avocado material used in each run of this example is as follows:

> Run 1—A mixture of 40 weight percent avocado pulp, 55 weight percent water, 4.5 weight percent of an admixture of lemon juice, salt, ascorbic acid, onion, garlic, pepper, chili powder and vegetable flakes and 0.5 weight percent vegetable gum.
>
> Run 2—The composition is the same as in Run 1.
>
> Run 3—The composition is the same as in Run 1 with the addition of 0.4 weight percent vegetable gum.
>
> Run 4—The composition is the same as in Run 3.
>
> Run 5—The composition is the same as in Run 3.
>
> Run 6—The composition is the same as in Run 3.
>
> Run 7—The composition is the same as in Run 3.

Separate portions of the avocado material are given various treatments to produce dispersions of varying characteristics. The conditions and results are recorded in the table on the following page. The avocado material of Run 1 is not treated in any way to reduce the particle size of the fat globules before it is examined microscopically.

The particle size of the fat globules in each run is determined by diluting one part by weight of the dispersed product with 99 parts by weight of water. The dilutions are then examined under a microscope with a field 150 microns in diameter. The number of particles found in this field for each run is recorded in the table.

Convenience Foods

	\- Run Number \-						
	1	2	3	4	5	6	7
Treatment of Avocado Material	None	Case Emulsifier	Colloid Mill Set at 0.030 inch	Homogenizer, 750 lb psi	Homogenizer, 1,500 lb psi	Homogenizer, 2,000 lb psi	Homogenizer, 2,500 lb psi
Consistency at End of Run	Liquid, Water Separation	Thick, Slight Water Separation	Thick, No Water Separation	Heavy, Heavier Than No. 3	Heavy, Heavier Than No. 4	Very Heavy	Very Heavy
Micron size of fat globules:							
30 and under	3	15	0	0	0	0	0
25 and under	-	-	0	0	1.2%	0	0
20 and under	50%	10	0	0	0.6%	1%	1%
15 and under	-	-	1%	2.5%	0.6%	5%	7%
10 and under	49%	99%	8%	7.5%	7.5%	16%	22%
Under 5	-	-	91%	90%	90%	78%	70%
Weight	5	4.5	4.25	5	1	0.5	0.5
Penetration, inches	-	-	-	-	Stopped	Stopped	Stopped
Time in seconds	2	120	120	60	120	120	120
Viscosity, cp	-	-	6,250	8,000	9,500	10,000	11,500

The depth of penetration of a predetermined weight into the dispersed product in a measured period of time is determined. This is an indication of the stability and viscosity of the product. The weight used weighs ⅜ of an ounce and consists of a right circular conical head having a 45° angle and a diameter at the base of ¾ inch, and a ¼-inch-diameter straight shaft. The weight is symmetrical about any plane including the axis of the cone. The point of the cone is brought to rest on the surface of the sample, and it is allowed to settle point first under the urging of gravity into the sample. The times and depths of penetration are recorded. In Runs 5, 6 and 7 the weight penetrates to the indicated depth in the indicated time and then stops. All of the penetration tests are conducted at 40°F.

The sizes of the fat globules in Runs 4, 5 and 6 tend to be very uniform. In these runs less than 10% of the total number of globules differ in their diameters by more than about 10 μ. In Run 7 the globules are clustered so that an accurate determination of their size and number is difficult to make. The globules of Run 3 are not as uniform as those in Runs 4, 5 and 6.

The product of Run 1 is not acceptable for sale because water separates out of it immediately upon standing. The product of Run 2 is not acceptable for sale because water soon separates out of it upon standing. The product of Run 3 is acceptable for sale where it will not be required to stand for more than 30 days. This product tends to separate after about 30 days.

The product should have fat globules of a substantially uniform size, that is, at least 80% of the globules should not differ in diameter from one another by more than 10 μ. At least 90% of the fat globules should have diameters of less than 10 μ. At least 70% of the fat globules should have diameters of less than 5 μ.

Ethnic and Specialty Food Items

The ⅜-ounce weight which is used to determine the depth of penetration into the dispersed product should take at least about ½ minute to penetrate 5 inches into the fine dispersion of avocado at 40°F. It is preferred that at least 90% of the fat globules will have diameters which do not differ by more than 10 μ from the average globule size. It is also preferred that the ⅜-ounce weight should take at least 1 minute to penetrate 5 inches into the fine dispersion. At least 95% of the globules should preferably have diameters of less than 10 μ.

The viscosity of the fine dispersion of this stable avocado base should range from 5,500 to 15,000 centipoises. Preferably, the viscosity should be at least 6,000 centipoises.

The fine dispersion of avocado will preferably contain substantially no globules having diameters larger than 25 μ. The blending of the avocado product should be sufficient to produce a fine dispersion in which none of the fat globules have diameters in excess of 30 μ.

Dehydrated Ready Mix Tabouly Salad

E.A. Slyman; U.S. Patent 3,917,857; November 4, 1975; assigned to Slymans Lebanese Foods, Mfg. Co., Inc. provides a dehydrated Tabouly salad mix to which is added water, oil and fresh chopped tomatoes.

The preferred formulation for the Tabouly salad mix consists essentially of on a weight basis 76% No. 2 grade cracked wheat, 3.3% dehydrated parsley, 11.8% dehydrated onions, 0.7% red pepper, 0.7% green pepper, 0.18% mint, 0.6% black pepper, 4.6% salt and 2.4% citric acid.

The citric acid employed may be either the monohydrate or the anhydrous acid form. Also, instead of the acid, the sodium salt of the acid may be used. Therefore, when citric acid is used herein, it is meant to include these various forms as well as all other equivalent forms.

The salt utilized is ordinary table salt. The black, red and green pepper and mint employed are also staple articles of commerce. They may be prepared in the customary manner, as, for example, by dehydration or freeze drying.

In order to prepare a salad mix from the above components the following procedure has been utilized. About 225 grams of a Tabouly salad mix having the foregoing formulation is mixed with 2 cups of water and ⅓ cup of oil. To this mixture is added 3 or 4 freshly chopped tomatoes. The mixture is then stirred thoroughly and permitted to stand for several hours, or preferably overnight, in a refrigerator. The mixture will be thin at first but after standing in the refrigerator it will thicken. The resultant mixture will serve approximately 6 to 9 people. The final product may be eaten in this form or it may be added to a lettuce salad.

French Fried Onion Product

J.B. Shields; U.S. Patent 3,705,812; December 12, 1972; assigned to American Potato Company describes the production of an onion product which comprises distinct pieces of dehydrated onion which are partially reconstituted with an edible liquid in the presence of mildly flavored starchy food substances or other binders with flavorings to make a dough which can be shaped and then fried in hot fat to produce a fried onion product with the following advantages.

(1) Onion solids of the mix can be varied to produce a product of desired strength. Onion solids and flavor far in excess of that resulting from the use of 100% raw onions can be obtained. In the dehydration of onions, about 90% of the raw weight is removed as water. By using dehydrated onion pieces as a major ingredient, only a portion of the water removed by dehydration needs to be added to form a workable dough.

(2) The product is relatively homogeneous and does not contain fragile crusts.

(3) The moisture content of the dough is regulated far below that of raw onions so that the fried product does not have soggy centers when the exterior is properly fried.

(4) The product can be held after frying without becoming limp or soggy.

(5) Flavorings can be uniformly distributed throughout the product instead of being concentrated on the surface.

(6) The product can be made in any desired size or shape and is not limited by the natural ring construction of onions.

(7) The product has firm textured onion bite and is accepted as an onion product—not an onion-flavored product.

A series of tests was conducted in which the percentage of dehydrated onion pieces in the dry mix was varied. The purpose was to determine the amount necessary to result in an accepted onion product rather than an onion-flavored product and to determine the onion level preferred by a panel. Doughs were made from the following mixes and formed and deep fat fried.

Dry Ingredients	Percent		
	Sample 1	Sample 2	Sample 3
Chopped onion	9.1	20.0	25.1
Potato granules	87.3	76.4	71.3
Salt	1.8	1.8	1.8
Guar gum	1.8	1.8	1.8

Sample No. 1 was judged to have too few onion pieces and bite to be considered an onion product. Sample No. 2 was judged to have very good flavor and texture. Sample No. 3 was judged excellent in texture and flavor and was preferred over a product made from raw onion. In general, it has been found that where the dry formulation contains 10% or less of dehydrated onion pieces, the panel eating the above product thought of it as a French fry containing onion pieces.

It has been found that when the dry formulation contains 15% or more dehydrated onion pieces, the panel eating the fried pieces refer to them as onion sticks or rings. Further, it has been found that the optimum range of onion content in the dry formulation seems to be from 20 to 40% dehydrated onion pieces by weight in the dry formulation. Conversely, the maximum level of binder used with this product is limited only by the ability of the product to make a dough that can be formed and fried in a single unitary piece.

Another series of tests was run to determine the significance of the particle size of the dehydrated onion used in the standard formula. Lots were produced using three sizes of commercial dehydrated onion at a level of 18.6% by weight of the dry mix as onion.

Sample Number	Type of Dried Onion Used	Dried Onion Mesh Size
4	Special chopped	−5+10
5	Minced onion	−10+20
6	Ground onion	−20+40

Sample No. 6 was judged to have a strong onion flavor but no bite. Onion particles were not noticeable in the fried product. Sample No. 5 was judged to have very good flavor and texture. Onion pieces were evident and this product was considered an onion product; however, the panel consensus was that pieces any smaller would not be acceptable. Sample No. 4 was also judged to have excellent flavor and bite. The onion pieces were quite evident and the product was considered an onion product.

The tests indicated that discernible pieces of onion were required and that the pieces before the addition of liquid should be larger than 20 mesh. Although any size larger than 20 mesh was rated good, further tests showed that dried onion pieces larger than 5 mesh or long pieces caused problems when the dough was extruded through dies of about ¼ to 5/16 inch diameter. Further tests using ground potato flakes to substitute for part of the potato granules and using dried sweet dairy whey at a concentration of 1.6 to 8.3% by weight of the dried mix were equally acceptable when the moisture and guar gum levels were adjusted to get a dough of the desired handling qualities. A typical process yielding the desired end product follows.

Example: A uniform dry mix was made of the following ingredients:

	Grams
Dehydrated minced onion	70
Potato granules	152
Potato flakes (ground)	40
Dried sweet dairy whey	10
Salt	3.2
Guar gum	3.2

The dry ingredients were mixed until uniform. 500 ml water at 70°F was added and the blend was mixed to a uniform dough. The dough was allowed to stand at least 5 minutes. The dough was then extruded through a 5/16-inch-square die and cut to about 4-inch lengths. The extruded dough sticks were deep fat fried for 60 seconds at 350° to 360°F. The fried product was judged excellent in onion flavor, texture and bite. The firm textured bite and the unique release of onion flavor noted during chewing was strongly preferred over regular fried onion rings which have an undesirable mushy texture and mouth feel.

SNACK PRODUCTS

Heat-Sensitive Condiment-Containing Fatty Particle

R.E. Cermak; U.S. Patent 3,796,814; March 12, 1974; assigned to SCM Corporation describes the preparation of condiment-containing fatty particulates with a substantially continuous fatty matrix phase at the surface. The composite particles are prepared by contacting a heat-sensitive condiment with preformed fatty matrix particles at a temperature not substantially above the Wiley melting point of the matrix particles for a time sufficient for the condiment to be absorbed. Agglomerates of the composite particles can be formed.

The condiment can be any heat-sensitive liquid or solid phase seasoning ingredient suitable for producing or enhancing a flavor and/or a colorant for edible products. The condiment includes solid condiment, flavoring oils, essences, extracts and other zesty flavorings. By heat-sensitive, it is meant to refer to those condiments, e.g., flavorings or colorants used as a seasoning in making food products which are susceptible to organoleptic degradation at temperatures in excess of about 120°F at atmospheric pressure.

There are many examples of heat-sensitive condiments either in solid or liquid form, and they include the imitation fruit flavors, oleo resin of paprika, cinnamon, anise seed or oil, natural cranberry, imitation flavorants or colorants containing acetaldehydes, cinnamaldehyde, caprylic aldehyde and lower alkanols. These compositions, when exposed to temperatures of 120°F, tend to undergo degradation often because some of the more volatile components in the flavors evaporate during the manufacturing process. Some undergo a color change. Paprika, when exposed to high temperatures, e.g., above 120°F, for a period of time, has the tendency to discolor to a brownish color as opposed to its normal reddish color.

The heat-sensitive condiment or condiment mixture employed is enrobed by the fatty matrix so as to substantially encapsulate it and protect it from contaminating ingredients.

By a fatty matrix particle is meant an ostensibly solid (nonsticky to and not readily deformed by touch at room temperature of 75°F) small particle of fatty material such as one of a triglyceride fat, fatty acid, etc., suitably of edible quality and capable of being preformed into small matrix particles which remain substantially discrete from each other and readily pourable at room temperature (75°F) from a conventional 100 ml beaker which has been loosely filled at such temperature with the matrix particles in uncompressed bulk condition.

The fatty matrix particle can be preformed into the shape of a bead, flake, a chip or the like. It can be colored and/or flavored or otherwise compounded if desired or necessary. Fundamentally, the composition of the matrix particle should be of a composition distinguishable from the condiment composition applied to it, enrobed by it or sorbed into it.

Materials which can also be included as a fraction (ordinarily a minor fraction) of the fatty matrix particle include emulsifying materials, fungistats, bacteriastats, silicone oil, tints, dyes, colorants, flavorants, odorants and antioxidants. When incorporating such materials into the matrix particle, they are generally proportioned in useful ratios for their end purposes. Thus, for example, one can use in a typical formulation 0.1 to 30% (by weight of the matrix particle) of conventional emulsifiers and stabilizers; colorants are useful in about the same proportion to yield the desired color in the resulting particle or in the end product to which it is to be added.

The matrix particle advantageously is a fat which can be any neutral edible triglyceride or mixture of triglycerides such as one having a Wiley Melting Point about 120°F. A fatty core particle such as fat in straight or compounded form should have a melting point sufficiently high so that conventionally made beads thereof (from a spray chilling operation and passing a sieve from about 30 mesh and retained on a 60 mesh U.S. Standard Sieve) will be substantially resistant to uncontrolled agglomeration (not over 25% of its weight agglomerated into multiparticle aggregates) when standing at 85°F in unpacked, loosely loaded condition in a conventional 100-ml beaker.

Vegetable fats (including nut fats) and animal fats or mixed vegetable and animal fats, generally hydrogenated and often rearranged, are suitable for making the matrix particle. Among the most desirable fats here are the so-called confectioners' hard butters because of their desirable mouthing characteristics.

By a hard butter is meant a broad class of triglycerides having physical properties and performance properties permitting their use in confectioners' coatings as a replacement for cocoa butter. Suitable hard butters should have a Wiley Melting Point between 90° and 120°F and should diminish fairly sharply in their ratio of solid to liquid fraction at a temperature of about 75°F, preferably at about mouth temperature. An example of especially useful hard butter is one derived from hydrogenated palm kernel oil.

By judicious selection of such melting point, the temperature for release of the condiment in or on the baked goods can be regulated. For example, a condiment having fungistatic or fungicidal action is sorbed into or enrobed by a fatty matrix having a high melting point; it can be made to delay its release from the matrix during a dough processing cycle until after useful action of yeast for proofing or the like has taken place, typically at a temperature lower than such melting point.

In practice the matrix particle is preformed prior to its blending with the condiment or condiment mixture. Preferably the preforming operation is accomplished by spray chilling the molten fatty substance or mixture to form a bead. A beaded matrix is substantially spherical. However, the shape is not critical. Generally, the advantageous size of the beaded matrix particle is between 30 and 60 mesh.

The condiment-containing particulate is formed by intimately contacting the condiment with the preformed fatty matrix particles at a temperature below the Wiley Melting Point of such matrix particles. If a plurality of matrix particles of different Wiley Melting Points are used, then the lowest of such melting points is the limiting one on the preferred contacting operation. A solid phase condiment, when in extremely finely divided form (all passing a 150 mesh U.S. Standard Sieve, typically with at least about 95% by weight being retained on the mesh screen), yields a discrete composite particle with the condiment sorbed into or onto the matrix particle.

The matrix particle and condiment mixture can be efficiently contacted by blending in conventional blending equipment. A double-motion paddle mixer (bakers' type) is preferred. Vapor phase or entrained liquid phase droplets or fog of condiment can be blended with the matrix particles by fluidized or moving bed techniques, for example where the matrix particles make up the bed and the condiment is carried upwardly therethrough in a noncondensible gas stream such as air or nitrogen, which can be recirculated. Blending times of 5 to 15 minutes are used to promote efficient union of the feeds and obtention of the desired particles.

A typical contacting or blending operation is done at about room temperature. However, the contacting operation can be conducted at substantially lower temperatures or even at somewhat higher temperatures for a limited time where necessary or desirable so long as formation of discrete composite particles occurs without substantial uncontrolled agglomeration (about a maximum of 25% of the mass by weight) of the matrix particles or resulting particles one to another. Agglomeration is suppressed by contacting the matrix particles and condiment particles in a sorption zone at a bulk temperature not exceeding the Wiley Melting Point of the matrix particles and an average holding time of at least about a second.

Example 1: A fatty particulate containing an imitation fruit flavor, i.e., strawberry, is prepared as follows: 35 parts beaded hard butter particles, 10 parts imitation strawberry in powdered form and 0.2 part of a plasticizing fat-soluble edible oil are blended in a conventional double-motion paddle mixer (bakers' type) at room temperature (75°F) and at atmospheric pressure for about 10 minutes. The beaded hard butter particles are preformed by spray chilling molten fat to a particle size between 30 to 60 mesh (U.S. Standard Sieve). The hard butter has a Wiley Melting Point of 120° to 121°F, a Solid Fat Index of 58 to 64% total solids at 100°F, 70 to 76% total solids at 92°F and 75 to 82% total solids at 80°F.

The plasticizing oil is made from refined and rearranged domestic vegetable oils, namely soybean and cottonseed, has a Wiley Melting Point of 63° ± 4°F, an Iodine Value between 74 and 81 and a Solid Fat Index of 3% total solids at 70°F. The plasticizing oil and heat generated in the sorption zone of the mixer by agitation softens the beaded hard butter matrix particulates to allow the fat to sorb and enrobe the imitation strawberry flavor. The temperature, holding time, speed of mixing and proportion of plasticizing oil interacting can be controlled to suppress the formation of large agglomerates in the sorption zone until virtually nil.

Discrete composite particles comprising the strawberry flavor and hard butter are produced in about 10 minutes. About 1% ultrafine powdered silicon dioxide then is blended with the discrete product for a few minutes to render the product substantially free-flowing. The resulting discrete particles are beads, the vast preponderance of which are between about 10 and 20 mesh (U.S. Standard Sieve).

The product is then applied to the top of a hot vanilla cookie wafer. The fat melts and flows into the cookie surface and releases the flavorant providing for excellent taste.

Example 2: A cinnamon-containing fatty particulate is produced by blending in the mixer of Example 1 at 70°F and at atmospheric pressure 74 parts of beaded hard butter and 10 parts of cinnamon (ground) and 10 parts butter flavor for 1 minute, then adding 25 parts of very finely divided cinnamon powder and continuing to blend for 9 minutes. The beaded hard butter is the same as that described in Example 1.

On blending, the finely divided cinnamon is sorbed into the matrix of hard butter, forming a discrete composite particle of cinnamon and hard butter. The discrete particle then can be applied from a dispersion to a piece of toast just from the oven. The toast possesses the characteristic butter cinnamon flavor.

Dough Covered Nutmeat Snack Food

E. Turitz; U.S. Patent 3,787,588; January 22, 1974 has developed a dry edible food product for use as a snack food which comprises a nut core and a crisp and crunchy edible shell covering for the nut core, the edible shell being formed of an essentially unleavened dough containing both wheat and corn flours. The dough preferably comprises 15 to 65% by volume corn flour and 85 to 35% by volume of wheat flour based on the total amount of flour used.

While the core is preferably a whole nut, such as a peanut, cashew, pecan, walnut, filbert, etc., fruit may also be used as the core, such as a prune, raisin, dried cherry, etc. In addition, while the nuts are, as indicated above, preferably used whole in all sizes from small to jumbo or fancy, they may also be chopped or in various sized pieces. In addition, the nuts may be used in either raw or prepared (cooked) form.

It was found that when a combination of corn flour and wheat flour in an essentially unleavened dough was utilized, a shell formed on the nut core which was tasty, crisp and crunchy, was easy to handle and to apply to a nut, even with the skin left thereon, and formed a thin shell of relatively uniform thickness. It is important for the corn flour to be of the extra-fine ground variety, such as Masa Harina. This type of corn flour is very different from the relatively coarse corn meal, corn hominy or corn grits most often used in the United States. Extra-fine ground flour is that used in Mexico, for example, to make tortillas, and unexpectedly gives excellent results when mixed with wheat flour in the proper proportions.

It will be understood, therefore, that the term corn flour means extra-fine ground corn meal. The flour portion of the dough must comprise 15 to 65% by volume corn flour and 85 to 35% by volume wheat flour. Preferably the compositions are between 20 to 60% corn and 80 to 40% wheat.

The basic dough recipe includes additional percentages, based on 100% by volume of flour, of salt (about 5%), sugar (about 15 to 60%), oil or other shortening (about 15 to 25%) and whole egg (about 5%), all based on percents by volume. In addition, further coloring and flavoring ingredients may be added. Many additional flavoring materials may be added such as cheese, chili, onion, garlic, spice, peanut butter, ground nuts, etc.

In general, the snack food is prepared by mixing the dough, kneading the dough until it becomes pliable and forming a sheet of the dough, and wrapping the dough about the nut core. Of course, other methods of providing the dough coating may be used, such as dipping or otherwise coating.

If desired, the snack food may then be provided with a glaze coating or dip as an optional step prior to cooking or freezing. At any rate, the dough which is wrapped or coated around the nut or other core forms a shell or hard, crisp crust when baked or deep fat fried.

Under certain conditions it is desirable to provide a preliminary treatment prior to cooking the snack food. Thus, after the nut has been coated with the dough, it may be blanched in boiling water prior to baking. One particularly desirable method involves dipping the snack food in a mixture of boiling water and oil prior to baking, this procedure providing a satisfactory oil coating on the product.

Example 1: The following example constitutes a basic dough mix and its typical use. One-fourth of a cup (2 fluid ounces) of extra-fine ground corn (e.g., instant Masa Harina) was mixed with 1 cup (8 fluid ounces) all-purpose white flour, 1 tablespoon (½ fluid ounce) salt, ¼ cup (2 fluid ounces) granulated white sugar, ¼ cup (2 fluid ounces) brown sugar or corn syrup, 3 to 4 tablespoons (1½ to 2 fluid ounces) oil (depending upon the grade of flour used), 1 tablespoon (½ ounce) of whole slightly beaten egg, 2 to 3 tablespoons of water (also depending on the grade of flour used), ¼ teaspoon of imitation butter flavoring, ½ teaspoon monosodium glutamate, and a dash of yellow food coloring. The dough was kneaded or worked until pliable, approximately ½ minute. Shelled raw peanuts were used for the core and the dough was wrapped about each nut.

The dough was easy to handle and readily adhered to the skin of the nut. A thin (approximately 1/16 inch) uniform shell could be placed on each nut, which shell would stay intact about the nut throughout the cooking process.

The coated peanuts were then dipped in a liquid mixture of 1 tablespoon whole egg, 4 tablespoons water, 1½ tablespoons oil, ¼ teaspoon salt, ⅛ teaspoon monosodium glutamate and food coloring. The snack food was then baked in a moderate oven until the artificial shell was crisp and crunchy.

With regard to the above basic formulation, it will be understood that the quantity of sugar or corn syrup may be varied, and that other shortening in place of oil may be used, such as oleo, butter or mixtures. In addition, prebaked peanuts may be used, or any other nuts such as shelled filberts. In addition, the basic procedure may be altered for freezing before baking, in which case the dip will not contain egg but will contain an additional half teaspoon of oil.

Example 2: This example shows the preparation of a fruit-center snack product. A composition comprising ¾ cup fine ground corn, ½ cup all-purpose white flour, 1 tablespoon salt, ½ cup granulated white sugar, ¼ cup brown sugar, 2 tablespoons oleo and 2 tablespoons oil, 1 tablespoon whole slightly beaten egg, 2 to 3 tablespoons water, 1 teaspoon almond flavoring, ½ teaspoon artificial butter flavoring, ½ teaspoon monosodium glutamate and food coloring was used as the dough mixture. 6 ounces of raisins were blanched with boiling water and 1 teaspoon of orange flavoring and 3 tablespoons of honey were added to the raisins.

Several raisins were used as cores and were wrapped with dough. The dough was then dipped in a liquid dip of 4 tablespoons water, 1 tablespoon oil, 1 tablespoon whole egg, ⅛ teaspoon almond flavoring, ⅛ teaspoon lemon flavoring and food coloring. The covered raisins were then baked in an oven at approximately 325°F. The raisin-coated snack food may be prepared for freezing by eliminating the egg from the dip and increasing the oil by ½ teaspoon.

MISCELLANEOUS PROCESSES

SPECIALTY PRODUCTS AND PROCESSES

Quickly Soluble Gelatinized Powdered Starch

J. Minami, M. Takatsu, M. Terada, T. Takeuchi and Y. Takagi; U.S. Patent 3,930,029; December 30, 1975; assigned to Nissin Shokuhin Kaisha, Ltd., Japan describe a procedure which is useful for manufacturing a quickly soluble, gelatinized starch for use in potages, stews, curries, etc. capable of being prepared by merely pouring into boiling water.

In the process, water containing dissolved proteolytic enzyme compositions including amylase and protease and common salt is added to powdered grain such as wheat flour and rice and white potato starch and the mixture is mixed at a given temperature to effect zymolysis.

Suitable enzyme compositions include those which are commonly employed for the production of gelatinized flour, e.g. thermoase (Daiwa Kasei Co.), an enzyme preparation derived from a strain of *Bacillus stearothermophilus,* also known as *Bacillus thermoproteolytica Rokko.* Other suitable enzymes include thermoase, papain, and bromelain.

After enzyme treatment, the resultant product is then formed into a strip-like shape ready to fry. Prior to frying, it may be steamed and/or boiled. It is then fried by fatty oils or fats to dehydrate. Suitable oils or fats include palm oil, lard, cottonseed oil or other animal or vegetable oils. The resultant product is then comminuted in a conventional manner.

The product, with the addition of common salt, compared with no salt, imparts a smooth sensation to the tongue and aids in recovery and dispersion as well. Such trend, when over 2% of salt is added, is especially significant. The formation of a thin strip is substantially the most efficient means to secure uniform dehydration in a short time during frying by fatty oils and fats. This rapid dehydration causes swollen particles of powdered starch to become porous so that they can be easily shattered. Fatty oils and fats freed of water during drying, prevent caking and formation of small grains when the product is added to boiling water and in addition functions effectively to improve dispersion.

Example: 1 kg of soft wheat flour is put into a heat-retaining mixer, to which is gradually added water in which 50 g of common salt and 2 g of enzyme (thermoase) is dissolved. This mixture is mixed for 20 minutes while maintaining a temperature of 30°C and is then rolled into strips with 1 to 2 mm of thickness. The thus-formed strips are steamed and boiled by a steaming device for one minute. The steamed strips are fried by fatty oils and fats heated at 140° to 145°C to dehydrate them and are then comminuted to approximately 100 mesh.

Distributing Food Dye on Protein Seed

A.A. Levinson and K.B. Basa; U.S. Patent 3,769,041; October 30, 1973; assigned to National Can Corporation describe a procedure for incorporating coloring matter on the surface of vegetable seed protein particulates which would achieve even distribution of color on the product using a minimum of dyeing material and furthermore, not require large volumes of water which would have to be removed by a subsequent drying step.

The process comprises incorporating coloring matter in a polyhydroxy alcohol carrier and applying the resulting carrier admixture to the vegetable protein particulate with agitation until distribution on the surface of the particulates is essentially complete.

The distribution and fixing of the coloring matter uniformly throughout the vegetable seed protein material is done by compaction of the resulting colored particulate under conditions of heat and pressure to produce a uniformly colored proteinaceous vegetable seed meal based protein product. The product is resistant to color extraction under aqueous food processing conditions customarily involved in further cooking and sterilization in preparation for consumption.

The vegetable protein starting materials used are vegetable protein containing seed meal materials in particulate form such as soybean meal, cotton seed meal, sunflower seed meal, and peanut meal, of which soybean meal is the most preferred. Preferably the vegetable protein seed meals are those which have been defatted and/or dehulled. They are customarily sold in the form of grits, meals or flakes having a particle size of −10 to 40 mesh. The polyhydroxy alcohols are nontoxic food grade materials preferably selected from the group consisting of glycerin, propylene glycol and butylene glycol or mixtures thereof.

The food colors are approved nontoxic FD&C dyes and vegetable colors (caramel color). Caramel color in combination with the dyes utilized is particularly desirable to simulate the brownish red colors of beef which often require dye admixtures which, when utilized by themselves to color the product without the use of the caramel color can permit color changes when such dyed or colored product is subject to processing (autoclaving, etc.).

Generally speaking, these dyes are incorporated into the carrier in concentrations ranging from 1 to 10%, although this is dependent on the solubility thereof. The carrier containing the dye is applied to the vegetable seed meal particulate preferably by permitting a fine stream of spray of the dye solution to be applied to a mass of vegetable seed meal particulates during agitation of the mass followed by further mixing after the desired quantity of dye and carrier has been incorporated therein. The ratio of carrier-color admixture to particulate vegetable protein seed meal is from about 2 to 5 gallons per ton of seed meal material.

Caramel colorants are characteristically very sticky, readily ball and if used alone to color seed meal material are extremely difficult to distribute and result in a product having unacceptable color distribution. If, on the other hand, sufficient water is utilized with such caramel color to achieve distribution over the seed meal material, problems associated with the necessary removal of the attendant moisture arise.

By employing caramel color in the polyhydroxy alcohol carrier color distribution is markedly enhanced without such problems. After the distribution, the products are compacted by passage through a high-pressure extruder-plasticator machine.

The product by virtue of the compaction step has color uniformly distributed throughout the final material. Furthermore, the compaction process results in a fixing of the color to render it resistant to water extraction during further processing. It should be understood the products after compaction are used as vegetable protein foods which may or may not be mixed with other materials such as meat. The products are especially useful as protein food sources when mixed with other protein materials as pet foods.

For consumer appeal to simulate meat they are desirably colored. Since processing of the materials involves heating, reconstitution, retorting and/or sterilizing in the presence of moisture, it is important that the coloration added to the products be resistant to extraction by water. This is accomplished by this process.

Food Preservation by Immersion Cooking in Stabilizing Solution

M. Kaplow and J.J. Halik; U.S. Patent 3,745,027; July 10, 1973; assigned to General Foods Corporation describe a process for the preservation of foods such as meat, fruit and vegetables. The process involves immersion cooking the food in an aqueous microbiologically stabilizing solution for a period of time sufficient to deplete the moisture in the food to 15 to 45% of the food weight. The microbiologically stabilizing solution has a weight of from 1.5 to 4 times the weight of the food and consists essentially of an aqueous solution of:

(1) a polyhydric alcohol selected from the group consisting of glycerol, sorbitol, mannitol, propylene glycol and mixtures thereof in an amount ranging from 25 to 90% by weight of the stabilizing solution;

(2) solutes comprised of mixtures of sucrose, dextrose and edible organic and inorganic salts; and

(3) an antimycotic agent selected from the group consisting of sorbic, propionic, benzoic acids and their salts and esters in an amount ranging from 0.5 to 1.0%. The moisture content of the stabilizing solution is less than that of the food being treated and the stabilizing solution infuses the food and replaces a major weight percentage of the original moisture present in the food causing the polyhydric alcohol to be present in the thus-treated food at an effective level, ranging from 10 to 40% of its weight to impart microbiological stability to the food.

The treated food is then removed from the resulting water-enriched stabilizing solution. The treated food has a moist eating quality and is essentially stable against microorganic decomposition, such that the need for any further treatment to provide bacteriostasis and protect against development of yeast and/or molds is avoided.

Basically, the process involves the treatment of foods, having a moisture content substantially approximating their pristine condition and typically in excess of 50% moisture, by immersing them in a cooking solution containing at least 5% polyhydric alcohol, and preferably high in concentration of other stabilizing solutes, selected from a class consisting of sugars, salts and mixtures thereof.

The solution will typically contain glycerol as the preferred polyhydric alcohol, and treatment in the solution will be for a sufficient period of time to at least thermally deactivate any latent enzymatic and pathogenic activity. The solution used is in an excess amount to immersion cook the foodstuff and cause it to undergo a water substitution by the stabilizing solution, such that the polyhydric alcohol and preferably the sugars, and/or salts as well replace a substantial and usually a major part of the percent by weight of the original moisture content of the food, until such time as the food itself has been caused to undergo a moisture reduction to between 25 and 35%.

In this condition, the polyhydric alcohol will generally infuse the produce at a weight level in excess of 5% and will generally be present at a level usually in excess of the moisture level, although lower levels of polyhydric alcohol will be practical at terminal produce moistures below 20%. In this latter instance the level of polyhydric alcohol will commonly exceed 10% and be complemented by other stabilizing solutes.

Cooking is carried out by immersing the foodstuff in an excess of heated cooking solution, which solution per se has a moisture content essentially less than the major weight percent of the stabilizing solutes therein and less than the intended final moisture in the food. The relative concentration of the polyhydric alcohols and the sugar and/or salt solutes of use will in large measure be dictated by the flavor requirement for the food being so treated.

In the case of fruits such as apples, it may be desirable to employ a higher concentration of sugars than in the treatment of meats and vegetables; in the case of produce such as carrots, the use of a significant amount of stabilizing sugars will be practical, since this will not be offensive to taste.

The process therefore essentially results in dehydration, wherein moisture present in the food is progressively depleted and at least partially substituted for by the polyhydric alcohol; the polyhydric alcohol infusion in combination with the moisture retained provides desired softness and pliability to the food for organoleptic acceptability, and imparts a sensation of moistness that is quite reminiscent of higher moisture cooked foods despite the moisture reduction produced.

The polyhydric alcohol or mixtures thereof, such as glycerol, or glycerol mixed with other polyhydric alcohols, serves as stabilizing solute in conjunction with any sugar and/or salt present, and necessarily is present with such other solutes in a sufficient concentration to substantially increase the osmotic pressure of the resulting solution infused in the food solids. By immersing the foodstuffs in an excess of the stabilizing solution, any sugar and/or salt in solution is also infused together with the polyhydric alcohol to effectively permeate the foodstuff in a practical period of time, the extent of infusion being dependent upon the morphology of the food itself.

Treatment by the stabilizing solution will preferably involve an initial cook wherein such solution will be elevated in temperature above 160°F and the foodstuff immersed therein for at least 5 minutes and preferably for at least a more prolonged period, say 10 to 15 minutes, until the degree of cooking or heat treatment required for softening and microorganic inactivation takes place.

During this operation not all of the stabilizing solute needed to achieve bacteriostasis may migrate throughout the food and so a continued immersion in the stabilizing solution will be called for until such time as the requisite concentration of such solutes in the food is effected. In the case of most food that has been cooked, say for 15 minutes, in the stabilizing solution, it may be allowed to stand for anywhere from 2 to 4 hours and longer until such time as the stabilizing solutes (glycerol or a glycerol-salt-sugar solution) will penetrate and infuse the interior of the produce and be present in this diffused state in a sufficient concentration, relative to water present, that microorganic stability is obtained.

During this entire immersion treatment the polyhydric alcohol will serve to deplete the moisture content of the foodstuffs by substituting for a portion of the moisture present in the interior of bean, fruit, vegetable or meat and causing moisture transfer to the exterior thereof.

The rate of infusion will be determined by the concentration of polyhydric alcohol and any salt and/or sugar solutes in the stabilizing solution; the higher the concentration of these solutes the greater the rate of infusion thereof, and hence the less the period required to effect substitution of water in the foodstuff by the polyhydric alcohol. The concentration of such solutes in the cooking solution and the cooking time will be predetermined by the requisite terminal moisture in the produce, such moisture being dictated by the stability and texture requirement for the produce.

The process will find its widest application in the treatment of fresh vegetables and raw meats which are destined to be packed aerobically, i.e., cold packed under less than commercial sterilization conditions. Thus, a meat such as beef or a fresh vegetable such as carrots, peas and the like, will be boiled by immersion in an excess of the cooking solution for that period of time required to essentially inactivate any latent enzymic activity and any pathogens that may be present. Preferably this will be for a period of time usually exceeding 5 minutes at a temperature in the neighborhood of 200°F for 15 to 30 minutes, or until the food has been cooked.

Thereafter, the meat or vegetable may be further immersed for a protracted period of time depending upon the relative concentration of polyhydric alcohol, salt and/or sugar solutes and the target terminal moisture desired for microorganic stability. Foods so treated will offer a desirable texture and flavor approaching that of food which has been cooked by immersion in boiling water. Advantageously, the polyhydric alcohol substituted for water naturally occurring will provide a plasticity and softening of texture to the produce and act in combination with the balance of moisture left in the foods such that the produce can be eaten as is, rewarmed or immersed in an excess of water for further moistening preparatory to consumption.

Products stabilized by the process will generally be of two types. The first type will be products destined for consumption as such, being merely warmed in those instances where heat enhances the acceptability of the product. The second type will be those which are intended to be mixed with other foods and further hydrated to undergo a desirable reduction in concentration of solutes present with the food. Representative of the latter class of foods will be stabilized meat cuts or vegetables intended for dilution as part of a soup or other fluid preparation, wherein the solutes are desirably at a lesser concentration for organoleptic acceptability.

Example 1: Immersion Cook Infusion of Fresh Chicken — Chicken pieces (½" to 1" dimensions) were immersion cooked (210° to 220°F) for 15 minutes in the stabilizing solution described below and soaked for six hours therein under refrigeration and drained. Chicken so prepared had acceptable eating qualities when eaten cold or when warmed.

Formula for Immersion Cook Infusion of Fresh Chicken

	Percent Solution	Percent Final Product
Fresh chicken solids	–	40.0
Glycerol	71.5	29.7
Water	16.7	25.3
Chicken soup base (including salt, sugar, monosodium glutamate)	8.9	3.7
Propylene glycol	2.2	1.0
Potassium sorbate	0.7	0.3
Total	100.0	100.0

NOTE: Preparation used 100 g fresh chicken and 164 g solution.

Example 2: Immersion Cook Infusion of Fresh Carrots — Diced carrots (⅜" by ⅜" by 3/16") were cooked (210° to 220°F) for 15 minutes in the following stabilizing solution and soaked for six hours therein under refrigeration and drained. Carrots so prepared had acceptable eating qualities and microorganic stability.

Formula for Immersion Cook Infusion of Fresh Carrots

	Percent Solution	Percent Final Product
Glycerol	88.6	46.4
Water	5.6	35.5
Fresh carrot solids	–	15.1
Salt (NaCl)	3.7	1.9
Propylene glycol	1.6	0.8
Potassium sorbate	0.5	0.3
Total	100.0	100.0

NOTE: Preparation used 100 g fresh carrots and 142 g solution.

The preparations are infused with a potassium sorbate which serves as an antimycotic. The stabilizing solution will preferably contain such an antimycotic when product terminal moisture is at a comparatively high moisture level, generally in excess of 20%, the need for and the level of antimycotic being dependent upon the level of total solutes infused. At a high solute infusion level, such as when the level is substantially in excess of the product moisture level, an antimycotic need not be employed. Generally any antimycotic may be used such as sorbic, propionic, benzoic acids and their salts and esters.

FLAVORINGS

Potato Chip Flavor Concentrate

M.R. Sevenants; U.S. Patent 3,857,982; December 31, 1974; The Procter Gamble Company describes a process of preparing a potato chip flavor concentrate comprising a sequence of steps including: (1) heating a potato source material; followed by (2) extraction; (3) cation-exchange treatment; and (4) elution of the adsorbed flavor ingredients.

In the first step, a potato source material is subjected to heating until uniformly brown in color. The potato source material from which the potato-chip flavor concentrate is prepared can include raw whole potatoes or parts thereof, such as potato sprouts or potato peels. Potato-derived materials can also be employed such as dehydrated flakes, granules or flour, doughs prepared from dehydrated potatoes, and cooked potato forms such as potato chips, French fries and the like. Thus, any potato or potato-derived source of potato-chip flavor precursors can be suitably employed.

The potato material may be heated without further treatment but preferably it is comminuted to insure uniform heating exposure throughout the raw material. Thin potato pieces, such as sliced, flaked or sheet-like pieces are preferably employed to ensure maximum flavor conversion during the heating step. Normally the potato source material will be heated in a form which permits the development of flavor materials from precursor compounds and which minimizes the loss of flavor materials by dissipation into the heating medium. An advantage of the process is that it allows the utilization of all potato parts including those which normally would constitute wastage, for example, skins, sprouts and dehydrated potato dough scraps.

The potato source material is subjected to heating until a uniformly browned potato material is obtained. During the heating step the potato constituents will react to form the desirable flavoring ingredients together with a multitude of undesirable by-products. The heating is excessive by reference to the conditions (time and temperature) prevailing during the manufacture, for example, of commercial potato chips. Accordingly, a marked degree of transformation of the potato product occurs and provides a material having a taste and aroma barely recognizable as having a potato origin.

The heating operation is carried out under inverse time/temperature conditions, i.e., an increase in one parameter calls for a decrease of the other parameter. Time and temperature conditions are employed so as to avoid charring due to excessive heating. Obviously too-low temperatures or too-long heating times are to be avoided. Preferably the potato source material is heated at at least 300°F for 10 seconds to 2 hours, more preferably at 375° to 500°F. During the heat treatment, the potato source material is dried and completely cooked. Potato-chip flavoring compounds will result from the reaction of the amino acids and the reducing sugars present in the potato raw material.

The reaction completeness, with respect to the flavoring ingredients, depends upon the operating conditions and can be optimized through the proper selection of temperature and time. Numerous side reactions take place as well and confer undesirable taste and flavor characteristics to the potato-chip material. Thus, the desirable and flavorful components characteristic of fried potato products may be completely or partially masked in effect by these side products. It will be appreciated, however, that the heating step provides a high level of the flavoring compounds which impart a potato-chip flavor to commercially available potato-chip products.

The heating can be applied using any of a variety of known heating methods including electrical, infrared, hot-air or contact heating. The heating process can be performed in a continuous or semicontinuous operation. Preferred are continuous processes such as infrared and fluidized bed heating methods (jet zone heating). The heating step produces a high amount of desirable flavoring ingredients in combination with many undesirable side-products which have to be separated prior to isolating the desirable flavor fraction.

The browned product of the heating step is extracted by contact with a solvent, e.g., water, a lower C_1 to C_4 alcohol or a mixture thereof. The browned potato material can be extracted without further treatment but preferably is pulverized, ground, or otherwise reduced in size to facilitate the extraction operation. The extraction solvent is normally used in a weight ratio of solvent to browned potato material of from 2:1 to 1000:1. It will be appreciated that higher solvent/potato material ratios can be used, although they might be less desirable from an economical point of view. Preferred solvent/potato material weight ratios range from 10:1 to 100:1. Preferred are mixtures of water and methyl or ethyl alcohol in a weight ratio of from 1:50 to about 50:1.

The extraction is preferably carried out under agitation at ambient temperature or at a higher temperature up to the boiling point of the particular solvent. Preferred extraction temperatures range from ambient temperature, i.e., 68° to 140°F. The extraction can be carried out in a continuous or batch operation and, if desired, pressure may be applied. The extraction time can easily be optimized for a particular set of extraction conditions. For example, extraction of browned potato material, employing a potato material to solvent ratio of about 1:20, the solvent being a 1:1 by weight mixture of water and methanol, is substantially completed within a period of from 1 to 10 minutes at room temperature.

Upon completion of the extraction, the extract is preferably separated from the suspended water-insoluble materials by, for example, filtration, decantation, centrifugation, or any other technique known to be suitable for such purpose. The resulting extract normally will contain desired flavoring components in combination with certain undesirable side products capable of virtually completely masking the potato-chip flavoring ingredients. The desired flavoring ingredients can be separated and isolated from the undesirable by-products by submitting the extract to a cation exchange treatment. Apparently, the potato-chip flavoring ingredients are cationic in nature and, accordingly, become adsorbed, affixed, or otherwise bound to the active groups of a cation-exchange resin.

Suitable ion-exchange resins for effecting the separation of desired potato-flavor compounds from undesirable side products include any of a variety of ion-exchange resins which, in general, are comprised of a structural portion (polymer matrix) and a functional portion (ion-active group). Suitable ion-exchange resins herein are the strong-acid cation-exchange resins which are best exemplified by the principal sulfonated styrene-divinylbenzene copolymer products.

Application of the extract to the ion-exchange resin can be carried out by admixing the extract with the resin material, or more usually, by passing the extract through a bed of the resin. The ion exchange can be conducted in a continuous process or in a batch operation. It can be performed in a single step or in a multiple operation employing a series of columns filled or partially filled with the particular exchange resin. Subsequent to the extraction, the adsorbent ion-exchange resin is preferably rinsed several times to eliminate undesirable by-products which are not adsorbed by the resin.

The potato-chip flavoring ingredient is then eluted from the cation-exchange resin by means of a suitable eluent. Preferably, a strong acid or strong base is employed. Partially or completely neutralized salts (e.g., sodium, lithium, calcium, magnesium salts) of these can also be used. Salts of food-compatible metals will be employed. The elution is performed by contacting the flavor-laden resin with the eluent. For example, this can be done by using a column packed with the flavor-laden resin or by treating the flavor-laden resin in a batch of said eluent.

The eluate containing the potato-chip flavoring components is preferably, and if needed, neutralized to a pH of about 7. It may also be desirable to concentrate the flavoring solution. To that end, all concentration techniques known in the art suitable for that purpose can be used. Examples thereof include thin layer distillation, conventional distillation, freeze drying or vacuum concentrating techniques.

Example: Seven pounds of raw sliced potatoes were heated at 400°F for 40 minutes in a conventional infrared oven, resulting in 1.4 pounds of browned potato material. The potato material was then comminuted in the presence of 100 pounds of warm water in a blender for about five minutes, followed by centrifugation to separate the potato solids from the extract. The flavor-containing extract was then passed through a column packed with a cation-exchange resin (AG 50W-X8, Bio-Rad Laboratories) and having a cation-exchange capacity of 510 meq per 100 grams of cation-exchange material to adsorb the flavoring ingredients onto the resin.

The flavor laden resin was then rinsed by passing water through the columnar bed until the rinsing solution remained clear. An aqueous alkaline solution (2 N sodium hydroxide) was passed through the column to elute the adsorbed flavoring materials. The resulting eluate containing the desirable flavoring ingredients was then neutralized with hydrochloric acid to a pH of about 7. This flavor concentrate was added to a potato dough prepared by mixing water with the dehydrated potatoes that had been obtained from 335 pounds of raw potatoes. From the dough were prepared 67 pounds of potato chips by conventional processing techniques. The resulting potato chip products had greatly improved flavor and good eating quality by reference to comparable commercial potato chips to which no flavor was added.

Similar results are also obtained when the raw sliced potatoes are replaced with a potato dough prepared from dehydrated potatoes and in the form of sheets or flakes, or diced or slabbed raw potatoes. Equivalent results are also obtained when instead of the conventional infrared radiation oven, one employs a fluidized bed with hot-air heating.

A similar potato chip concentrate can also be prepared when the extraction solvent is a mixture of water/methanol; water/ethanol; water/isopropanol; water/n-propanol; or water/butanol and where the weight ratio of water/alcohol for each combination is any one ranging from 50:1 to 1:40.

Substituting the sodium hydroxide eluent by an equivalent quantity of potassium hydroxide, ammonium hydroxide, sulfuric acid, hydrochloric acid, phosphoric acid, sodium or potassium chloride or potassium sulfate, respectively, will produce a similar flavor concentrate.

Potato Chip Flavor and Aroma

S.S. Chang and B.R. Reddy; U.S. Patent 3,814,818; June 4, 1974; assigned to Research Corporation describe the preparation of a flavor material reminiscent of potato chips and potato. In the snack food industry, it is desirable to produce a flavor material capable of imparting to food a potato chip flavor. For example, it would be particularly desirable to be able to impart a potato chip flavor and aroma to snack foods prepared from starch, meal or flour, particularly snack foods prepared from cornstarch, potato starch, waxy maize starch, tapioca, corn meal, wheat flour, soy flour, soybean protein and/or amylopectin which may or may not be pregelatinized, since these foods when prepared by baking or by deep fat frying do not possess to the desired extent a potato chip flavor or aroma.

It has been discovered that methionine or methionine in admixture with a reducing sugar, such as glucose, when subjected to heating, such as heating in the presence of oil, e.g., deep fat frying, produces a flavor and aroma reminiscent of potato and potato chip. It has also been observed that the produced flavor possesses a tomato flavor note which is more noticeable when the flavor is produced according to this process at the lower temperature range.

In the preparation of the potato and potato chip flavor and aroma substantially any oil may be employed. The potato and potato chip flavor and aroma appears to be brought about by the heating of methionine in the presence of oil, in the presence of water and with some access to or in contact with air or in a nitrogen or other substantially inert atmosphere, usually at a temperature of about 185°C.

If desired, there may be admixed with the methionine a minor amount of a reducing sugar, such as glucose, although the presence of a reducing sugar for the production of the desired potato chip flavor and aroma is not essential. Some desirable results are obtained, particularly with respect to the quality of the food material processed, when the methionine contains a reducing sugar admixed therewith.

The temperature requirements to produce the desired flavor and aroma when methionine is heated in the presence of oil as opposed to methionine when heated in oil under deep fat frying conditions are somewhat different. For example, when methionine or a mixture of methionine and a reducing sugar, is suspended

Miscellaneous Processes 315

in oil or added to oil, and the oil then heated with agitation either in the presence of air or in a substantially inert atmosphere, such as in the presence of nitrogen, which may be bubbled through or swept over the heated oil to carry away the resulting produced odor and flavor materials, a good aroma and flavor is produced at a temperature as low as 50°C. The aroma and flavor become more intense as the temperature is raised. At 110°C a strong odor and aroma are noticeable. At a temperature of above about 130°C under these conditions it appears that the quality of the aroma and flavor begins to deteriorate.

When methionine is heated in oil under deep fat frying conditions, temperatures above 100°C in deep fat frying temperature range are employed, for example a temperature of about 180°C. When methionine or a mixture of methionine and a reducing sugar, such as glucose, dissolved and/or suspended in water is applied to cotton balls and the resulting wetted cotton balls then immersed in oil under deep fat frying conditions a good aroma and flavor are generated. It would appear that equivalent results would also be obtained if an aqueous solution and/or dispersion of methionine was added directly to the heated oil maintained at deep fat frying temperature.

The flavor and aroma generated by heating methionine or an admixture of methionine and a reducing sugar in the presence of oil or under deep fat frying conditions can be recovered and added to food products to enhance and to improve their aroma and flavor and/or to impart a potato and potato chip flavor and aroma thereto.

The production and recovery of the flavor can readily be carried out by subjecting methionine to deep fat frying followed by recovery of the resulting volatilized or vaporized materials. The vaporized and volatilized materials either before or after fractionation may be incorporated in a suitable carrier, liquid or solid, and then applied to foods or employed in the preparation of foods so as to impart a potato and/or potato chip flavor and aroma thereto.

An oil employed in the heating of methionine can be further treated by removing therefrom the more volatile components. The resulting oil can be subjected to steam distillation, preferably vacuum steam distillation. An oil so treated, although evidencing a reduced strength in its aroma and flavor, nevertheless shows an improved quality with respect to its aroma and flavor.

The aroma and flavor of the oil becomes even more pleasant and desirable. The resulting oil can be used to produce food products with a potato and potato chip flavor. It may be used as the frying medium for potato chips and other snack foods and it may be used to spray on food products prepared as a substitute for potato chips. It may also be used as a salad oil and as an ingredient of salad dressings and soups.

Furthermore, a food product possessing a potato and potato chip flavor and aroma may be prepared by incorporating methionine or an admixture of methionine and a reducing sugar in a food product during processing and then subjecting the food product to heating, such as by baking or by heating in the presence of oil or under deep fat frying conditions in order to develop the desired aroma and flavor therein. In another variation, a cooking oil can be prepared which has dissolved and/or dispersed therein a sufficient amount of methionine or methionine and a reducing sugar, so that upon heating the oil an aroma and flavor reminiscent of potato and potato chips is produced.

Methionine does not lead to or cause formation of a dark brown color when heated in oil under deep fat frying conditions. At a concentration sufficient for the generation of a strong aroma and flavor reminiscent of potato and potato chips only a light yellow color is developed in the material containing methionine when subjected to heating, such as heating in the presence of oil. Even in combination with glucose the color developed during heating in oil or in deep fat frying can be reduced to a light yellow by controlling the amount of glucose admixed with the methionine.

In practice, only very minor, almost slight, amounts of methionine or methionine and a reducing sugar are required to impart or to generate the desired flavor and aroma. Usually an amount of methionine in the range 0.025 to 0.1% when incorporated in oil or an amount in the range 0.001 to 4.0% by weight on a wet food basis when incorporated in a food product, is sufficient to generate and produce a flavor and aroma reminiscent of potato and potato chips. When glucose is employed in admixture with methionine, the amount of glucose is usually substantially less than that of methionine, such as 10 to 20% by weight based on the weight of the methionine.

Example 1: This example illustrates the generation and production of an aroma and flavor reminiscent of potato and potato chips by heating methionine under conditions of deep fat frying. Corn oil in an amount of 2,300 ml was heated in a household deep fat fryer to 185°C and maintained at this temperature. A saturated solution of methionine in water containing approximately 2.7% by weight methionine was prepared.

Twenty cotton balls were each moistened with 1.5 ml of the saturated aqueous methionine solution and these cotton balls were then deep fat fried in the heated corn oil for three minutes. The deep fat frying was continued until a total of 180 cotton balls were fried. The volatile flavor and aroma ingredients produced during the deep fat frying were collected and the collected flavor and aroma ingredients had a strong pleasant aroma reminiscent of potato and potato chips.

Example 2: This example is illustrative of the preparation of a cooking oil having a potato and potato chip flavor and aroma. The cooking oil used in Example 1, after deep fat frying of the methionine-containing cotton balls, was vacuum steam distilled at a temperature of 150°C for one hour at a vacuum of 0.02 mm Hg. The oil after vacuum steam distillation possessed a pleasant and desirable aroma and flavor reminiscent of potato and potato chips.

Example 3: This example is illustrative of the generation of a potato and potato chip flavor and aroma by heating a mixture of methionine and glucose under conditions of deep fat frying. Corn oil in an amount of 4.5 pounds was heated in a household deep fat fryer to a temperature of 185°C and maintained at this temperature. A saturated aqueous solution of methionine was then prepared and to each 100 ml of this solution 0.37 gram of glucose was added.

Twenty cotton balls were then moistened with 1.5 ml of the resulting methionine-glucose solution and the cotton balls were then deep fat fried in the corn oil for 30 minutes. The frying was continued until a total of 180 cotton balls were fried. There were developed in the corn oil an aroma and flavor reminiscent of potato and potato chips. Further, the cotton balls after frying evidenced a potato and potato chip flavor and aroma.

Example 4: This example is illustrative of the use of methionine to improve the flavor of potato chips. Two batches, a control batch and a test batch, of potato chips were prepared under the same conditions using the same raw materials. No additive was employed in the preparation of the control batch. In the preparation of the test batch 20 mg of methionine were added for each 100 g of potato slices. The two batches of potato chips were then organoleptically evaluated by a panel of eight members. There was a clear indication that the panel evaluated the test batch of potato chips prepared with added methionine as superior in flavor to the control batch.

Example 5: Potato chips were prepared from regular, commercially available corn oil and potato chips were prepared from a corn oil prepared in accordance with the treatment described in Example 2. Upon evaluation by an organoleptic evaluation panel it was found that the potato chips prepared from a corn oil treated in the manner described in Example 2, i.e., corn oil which had been subjected to deep fat frying conditions in the presence of methionine, were preferred over those potato chips prepared from regular commercial corn oil.

Popcorn Flavorant

T.H. Parliment; U.S. Patent 3,840,675; October 8, 1974; assigned to General Foods Corporation describes the preparation of a substance having a taste and aroma virtually indistinguishable from that of freshly-popped popcorn which is produced by reacting a compound selected from the group consisting of glyoxal, glycolaldehyde and combinations thereof, with a sulfide source at elevated temperatures. The reaction is preferably carried out in the presence of water at relatively high pH. After cooling, the reaction mixture is acidified and aged, and a characteristic, pleasant popcorn flavor and aroma develops.

The glyoxal, represented by the structural formula

$$O=\overset{H}{\underset{}{C}}-\overset{H}{\underset{}{C}}=O$$

and the glycolaldehyde represented by the structural formula

$$H-\overset{H}{\underset{HO}{C}}-\overset{H}{\underset{O}{C}}$$

are well-known, commercially available materials and can be prepared according to procedures well known in the art. Although simple, readily available inorganic sulfides are preferred as the sulfide source, any compound which releases $S^=$ or HS^- ions at reaction conditions and does not impair the quality of the final product may be employed.

For example, organosulfur compounds may be employed providing they release sulfide under the reaction conditions. However, since the inherent potency of any unreacted organosulfur compound may overpower the delicate popcorn character, these compounds are not considered preferable sources of sulfide. Exemplary of the inorganic sulfides which may be employed are hydrogen sulfide, alkali metal sulfides and hydrosulfides, ammonium sulfide, and alkaline earth metal sulfides and hydrosulfides. Ammonium sulfide is particularly preferred.

The reaction is generally carried out in a hydroxylated solvent such as water alone or in combination with another solvent. The solvent is preferably present in an amount ranging from 0.1 to 100 times the total weight of the reactants with 10 times the total weight being particularly preferred. The glyoxal, the glycolaldehyde or a combination of the two, is preferably added in an equal molar amount relative to the sulfide source. However, the molar ratio of the glyoxal or the glycolaldehyde to the sulfide may be from 1:10 to 10:1.

The reactants are admixed with solvent and the reaction mixture is preferably brought to a relatively high pH by adding a sufficient amount of a suitable base such as sodium hydroxide. The exact order of adding these reactants and the base is not critical. The reaction is preferably carried out at a pH of above 7 and desirably close to 12.

However, the reaction can be carried out at a pH value as low as 3 with somewhat diminished results. The reaction mixture is then heated to an elevated temperature, with the boiling point of the reaction mixture at atmospheric pressure being preferred. Higher temperatures may be employed but necessitate the use of pressure equipment, whereas lower temperatures may also be employed but require extended periods of heating.

The reaction is generally completed within about 10 minutes to 2 hours. Preferred reaction times range from 15 to 30 minutes. A change in the color of the reaction mixture from light to dark brown generally indicates completion of the reaction. After completion of the reaction, the reaction mixture is acidified with a sufficient amount of a suitable acid such as HCl and agitated to expel excess H_2S. The pH is preferably brought to below 3. After acidification, the reaction mixture is allowed to age for from ½ to 2 days during which time the reaction product develops the desired flavor and aroma of popcorn. Longer aging periods can be employed if desired.

Example 1: A reaction mixture is prepared by combining 9 ml of water, 0.1 g of glycolaldehyde and 1 ml of a 20% aqueous solution of ammonium sulfide in a wide mouth jar. Sufficient concentrated NaOH is added to the reaction mixture to raise the pH to 12.5. The reaction mixture is then heated at 100°C for 60 minutes. After cooling, sufficient concentrated HCl is added to the reaction mixture to reduce the pH to 3. The acidified reaction mixture is stirred at room temperature to expel excess H_2S and allowed to age for two days. After aging, the reaction mixture was found to possess a nice, freshly-popped popcorn aroma and taste.

Example 2: This example illustrates the effect of pH and the sulfide reactant on the final popcorn flavor. In each of the 9 experiments listed below, a reaction mixture was prepared by combining 0.5 ml of a 40% aqueous solution of glyoxal, 10 ml water and 0.5 g of the indicated inorganic chemical and adjusted to the indicated pH with either HCl or NaOH as required. In each case the reaction mixture is heated at 250°F for 1.5 hours and then cooled to room temperature. The pH of each reaction mixture is then adjusted to a pH of 3 with sufficient HCl where required and stirred to expel excess H_2S. The mixtures are allowed to age for 24 hours and then tasted to provide the results summarized in the table below.

Inorganic Reagent	Reaction pH		
	3	7	12
$(NH_4)_2S$	Corn, popcorn	Nutty popcorn	Nice, slightly charred popcorn
Na_2S	Meaty, weak popcorn	Burned meat	Freshly-popped popcorn
NH_4Cl	Weak, nondescript	Weak, nondescript	Weak, brownish

Thus it can be seen that inorganic sulfides, particularly $(NH_4)_2S$, give the desired popcorn flavor and aroma over a wide pH range when reacted with either glyoxal or glycolaldehyde, whereas an inorganic ammonium compound not containing sulfur failed to give the desired results. Moreover, it can be seen that the reaction mixture should preferably be basic during the heating step with a pH of about 12 being particularly preferred.

ADJUVANTS

Salts of Acetyl Amino Acids as Water Binders

H.H. Friedman and V. Moreno; U.S. Patent 3,944,681; March 16, 1976; assigned to General Foods Corporation disclose a process which relates to water binders, and more specifically to compositions employing a specific group of compounds having the ability to bind large amounts of water. The composition of this compound defined by the formula

$$CH_3-\underset{\underset{O}{\|}}{C}-\underset{\underset{H}{|}}{N}-\underset{\underset{H}{|}}{\overset{\overset{R}{|}}{C}}-C\overset{\diagup O}{\diagdown OM}$$

wherein: R is a member selected from the group consisting of $-(CH_2)_n-CO_2M$, $-(CH_2)_n-NO_3$, $-(CH_2)_n-SO_3M$, and $-(CH_2)_n-NH_2$; n is an integer from 1 to 4; and M is an alkali metal.

Exemplary of water binders defined by the above formula are the alkali metal salts of N-acetylated amino and imino acids. Examples of the latter series of compounds are the sodium and potassium N-acetyl-L-glutamate, the sodium and potassium salts of N-acetyl lysine, and the sodium and potassium salts of N-acetyl aspartic acid.

All of these compounds are commercially available in the acid form. Alternatively, they can be prepared by methods well known to the art. For example, N-acetyl-L-glutamic acid can be prepared by acetylating L-glutamic acid in aqueous solution with acetic anhydride. The resulting N-acetyl-L-glutamic acid is then purified in known manner.

Any of the alkali metal salts of these compounds can be used. The sodium and potassium salts are preferred. These salts can be easily prepared by neutralizing the acid form of these compounds with any suitable base containing the appropriate alkali metal cations. For example, the sodium salts of these compounds can be prepared by neutralizing the acid with a slight excess of sodium hydroxide, and the potassium salt with a slight excess of potassium hydroxide.

These salts are employed in any amount which is effective to bind water and reduce the tendency for water loss from the composition. Typically, these alkali metal salts will be employed in amounts greater than 0.5% by weight of the composition. Preferably they are employed at levels of 1 to 5% by weight of the composition. Their use in food is limited by the levels of the alkali metals employed and the resultant salty taste of the composition.

In use, the water binder is added to the edible material. It may be employed in preparing intermediate moisture food products such as meat, fish, poultry, fruit and vegetable products. When added to vegetable products, the natural basic characteristic of the vegetables can aid in neutralizing the acid form of the water binding compounds to the salt form. In food products, the water binders aid in reducing the tendency of the products to support microbial growth.

Example: Fresh carrots are infused with a stabilizing solution at just below boiling for a period of about 18 hours. The carrots are peeled and trimmed before treatment in the following stabilizing solution:

Ingredient	Percent
Glycerol	85.0
Water	5.5
Sodium chloride	3.7
Disodium N-acetyl-L-glutamate	5.3
Potassium sorbate	0.5

The carrots thus treated are more stable against microbial attack.

Hydrocolloidal Food Thickener

Starches have often been used for various thickening applications. For example, the most common method normally employed in the home for thickening food products involves the use of a starch, such as, flour or cornstarch. There are various disadvantages for using a starch as a thickening agent.

For example, starches must be premixed with a liquid in order to insure a lump free consistency; starches are normally dependent upon temperature for their thickening action; a starch cannot be utilized for many products which require thickening; carbohydrates found in starches contribute abour four calories per gram and thus products thickened with a starch cannot usually be considered to be low calorie; starches generally present storage problems since insects may be attracted to the starch; and in commercial applications relatively large amounts of space are required for the storage of starches.

The process described by *L.E. Rigler, G.H. Taki and N.G. Spirtos; U.S. Patent 3,928,252; December 23, 1975; assigned to Adolph's Ltd.* relates to a versatile general purpose hydrocolloidal thickening agent which has a low calorie content which is particularly desirable for use in food preparations. The thickener also allows instant solubilization over a wide pH range in both hot and cold media and also allows an initially thickened solution to be made more viscous by the addition of more dry thickener. Also, the thickener substantially overcomes the lumping problems generally associated with prior art gums or hydrocolloidal thickeners.

In its basic form the product comprises sodium carboxymethylcellulose which is combined with a halogen donating compound (e.g., sodium chloride, potassium chloride, ammonium chloride, potassium iodide, etc.) and with sodium bicarbonate and an organic acid (e.g., citric, adipic or tartaric). It is believed that the addition of a halogen contributing compound increases hydration and, therefore, yields faster and more complete solubilization of the sodium carboxymethylcellulose and makes it somewhat more dispersible.

Since sodium carboxymethylcellulose and other hydrocolloids are generally hydrophilic, it has been observed that when sodium carboxymethylcellulose is slowly added to water, even with stirring, clumps tend to form. The formation of clumps has been a definite disadvantage of hydrocolloids, as previously discussed.

This process resolves the dispersion problem by utilizing what is believed to be the bursting action of the carbon dioxide produced when the product thickener is used. The carbon dioxide is formed by the reaction of sodium bicarbonate and an organic acid, such as citric, adipic or tartaric. The dispersing action which is believed to be caused by the formation of carbon dioxide is an added factor to the improved rate of solubility achieved by the presence of the halogen contributing compound.

In addition, to the above basic constituents, certain optional but preferred constituents, such as anticaking agents and wetting or surfactive agents can be used to further improve the overall properties of the thickener. The thickening agent is substantially instantly soluble in water, milk, and other hot or cold media over a pH range of about 2.4 to 12.6 and displays a stable viscosity. No time consuming preblending operation is required and the thickener donates a negligible amount of calories.

The basic formulation which is required to yield the overall properties described is as follows:

Ingredient	Percent by Weight	Percent by Weight of Preferred Composition
Sodium carboxymethylcellulose	50 - 75	54.0 ± 4
Halogen donating compound	15 - 25	24.3 ± 0.7
Sodium or potassium bicarbonate	10 - 15	13.5 ± 1.5
Organic acid	3 - 10	8.2 ± 1.5

While satisfactory results have been obtained throughout the ranges recited above, during experimentation it was found that a thickener having the above preferred composition yielded particularly excellent results over a wide range of pH (i.e., about 2.4 to 12.6) and for various hot and cold media.

SPECIALTY NUTRITIVE PRODUCTS

Encapsulated Nutrients

The primary purpose of the products of the process disclosed by *S. Katzen; U.S. Patent 3,962,416; June 8, 1976* is to supply the body with its necessary nutritional needs and those products are such that can be stored without detrimental effects to the nutrient materials therein.

A high protein vegetable encapsulating agent and at least one nutrient are admixed together. The cereals or other vegetable encapsulating agents are gelatinized or polymerized under elevated pressure and at elevated temperatures. The process causes the nutrients to be encapsulated (coated or protected) by the gelatinized or polymerized encapsulating agent.

When cooled and the pressure removed, the resultant product is dry and can be stored for extended periods of time. Storage can easily be for four months or more with nearly complete retention of nutrient potency. The encapsulation prevents the nutrients from being oxidized, reduced, solubilized, sublimated or otherwise diminished in potency which would occur if left in an unprotected state.

The product can be sized, if desired or necessary by any convenient means such as grinding. The rate of release of the encapsulated nutrients can be varied according to the solubility of the gelatinized or polymerized encapsulating agent. The time in the digestive tract may vary from one to eight hours, with four hours being normal. Digestion depends upon enzyme action as well as acid hydrolysis. Digestion begins in the mouth by action of salivary amylase (ptyalin) with an optimum pH of 5.5 to 6.5. The stomach pH is 0.85 to 1.00. There are no carbohydrate enzymes in the stomach, but the small intestine contains many enzymes in addition to pancreatic amylase.

The high protein vegetable agent can only contain up to 40% by weight of nonprotein material such as starch or nonprotein nitrogenous material (for example, ammonium phosphate). Preferably, 100 parts by weight of the encapsulating agent are admixed with 40 to 50 parts by weight of the nutrients. The broad range of nutrients admixed with 100 parts by weight of the encapsulating agent is from 1 to 40 parts by weight. That weight range for nutrients includes such additives as surfactants, preservatives, etc.

The encapsulating agent is normally gelatinized or polymerized preferably at about 350°F. The temperature utilized must be such that the potency of the nutrients and/or additives is not seriously impaired. The pressure utilized will be above atmospheric and will vary with the type of encapsulating agent, nutrients and additives and the operating temperature. The preferred operating pressure is 1,000 psi. The time of product formation at those pressures and temperatures is about 10 seconds.

If the encapsulating agent is made viscid for the admixing and encapsulating steps by the addition of water, or like material, the end product is made dry by the flashing off (evaporation) of the entrapped water as steam when the product exits from the extruder or expander. The resulting expanded product has air spaces which make the product brittle and easily ground. This is the preferred method and product. (The end product can be further dried before or after the encapsulating step, if necessary.)

The resultant product can have any shape and is often an irregular shape due to its method of manufacture. The irregular shape is within the scope of the process because during polymerization or gelatinization of the carrier the nutrients were completely encapsulated. Complete encapsulation of the nutrients is not based on the use of a carrier as a viscid state when the two are admixed.

Thus it is seen that the nutrients may be in a dry particulate form for use. To assure encapsulation the nutrients should have a particle size of about 20 to 200 mesh. If desired, before encapsulation, several types of nutrients may be coparticulated so that each type of nutrient used is contained in each encapsulated unit. The term nutrient(s), within the scope of this process, encompasses hormones, enzymes, pigments, lipids, plasma proteins, inorganic salts, vitamins, and so forth, that are necessary for a proper diet.

High Protein Chocolate Snack

A. Rebane; U.S. Patent 3,901,977; August 26, 1975; assigned to Sandoz Inc. provides a nutritious, stable, high protein chocolate snack which contains preferably 40% chocolate, 15 to 30% protein and 0.5 to 2.5% calcium caseinate. (All percentages are by weight based on the final weight of the chocolate snack.) The chocolate portion normally consists of 15 to 25% milk chocolate and 15 to 25% dark chocolate. The milk chocolate contains at least 10% chocolate liquor according to the Federal Standards of Identity and the dark chocolate contains at least 15% chocolate liquor. The chocolate snack of the instant process contains about 4.8 to 6.3% chocolate liquor in all.

The majority of the protein in the chocolate snack is provided by proteinaceous ingredients such as sodium caseinate, which contains about 90% by weight protein, and is present in the chocolate snack at levels of 15 to 20%, and peanut butter which contains about 25% by weight protein and is present in the chocolate at levels of 15 to 20%. These proteinaceous ingredients comprise about 25 to 40% of the contemplated chocolate snack. In addition to these ingredients, protein is also provided by the milk chocolate and dark chocolate which contains about 7.5 to 8.0% protein based on the weight of the chocolate and by the calcium caseinate which is about 88% protein.

Sweetener such as sugar in the range of 10 to 15% and corn syrup at levels of 3 to 5% are used in the chocolate snack. In addition, vitamins and minerals which are compatible with the ingredients of the snack can also be added if desired to further enhance the nutritional value of high protein chocolate snack. A typical formulation and range of ingredients for the chocolate snack is as follows:

Ingredient	Range, percent
Milk chocolate	15 – 25
Dark chocolate	15 – 25
Cocoa butter	5 – 15
Sodium caseinate	10 – 20
Calcium caseinate	0.5 – 2.5
Sugar	10 – 15
Corn syrup	3 – 5
Peanut butter	15 – 20

The above formulation provides chocolate snacks having a protein content ranging between 15 to 30% by weight.

The process is carried out as follows: (a) A mixture which contains 15 to 25% milk chocolate, 15 to 25% dark chocolate and 5 to 15% cocoa butter is slowly heated to 130° to 150°F and is mixed until uniform. (b) The mixture is cooled to 80° to 100°F with continuous stirring. (c) 0.5 to 2.5% calcium caseinate and 25 to 40% proteinaceous ingredients are added. (d) The mixture is stirred until uniform while maintaining the temperature between 80° to 100°F.

It is preferred that this procedure be carried out between 85° to 98°F. The sweetener and corn oil normally incorporated in the chocolate snack are usually added along with the peanut butter in the form of a peanut crunch in step (c). Following step (d), the melted composition, after mixing, can be formed into any of the conventional chocolate snack forms using standard techniques.

For example, the melted chocolate can be spread out in sheets as thin as desired, chilled to 65° to 70°F and then cut to the desired size and shape and packaged. Alternately, molds of various shapes can be filled with the melted chocolate, which can then be chilled to 45°F, after which the finished product is removed from the mold and packaged. The melted chocolate can also be extruded through a specific orifice, e.g., rod, ribbon, etc., cooled to 45° to 55°F in a cooling tunnel and packaged.

Example: The following ingredients were used in the preparation of a high protein chocolate bar having a protein content of approximately 23%.

	Percent
Milk chocolate, 7.6% protein	19.90
Dark chocolate, 7.9% protein	19.90
Cocoa butter	8.20
Sodium caseinate, 90% protein	15.74
Calcium caseinate, 88% protein	1.13
Granulated sugar	13.00
Corn syrup	4.55
Peanut butter, 25.5% protein	16.98

The chocolate and cocoa butter are heated slowly to 135° to 140°F. The mixture is then cooled with stirring to 81° to 82°F. A peanut butter crunch mixture is prepared from sugar, corn syrup and peanut butter by heating the sugar and corn oil to 305°F and the peanut butter is added and mixed. The chocolate phase is reheated to 95° to 98°F and then cooled to 88°F at which point the sodium caseinate, calcium caseinate and peanut butter crunch are added.

The mixture is under continuous stirring during the addition of the ingredient, and stirring is continued after addition is completed until a uniform mixture is obtained. The mixture is then spread on aluminum foil with a Teflon covered surface to a thickness of ¼ to ½ inch and cooled to 65° to 70°F. The chocolate formulation is then cut into bars 3½ inches by 1⅝ inches and packaged in tinfoil.

The bars are stored under ambient conditions for a period of 248 days and at intervals of 30 days the bars are checked for flavor and texture. It is found that over this period the bars retain their excellent flavor and texture. Similar chocolate bars, but without the calcium caseinate, are also prepared and tested. These bars show signs of deterioration after seven months and began losing texture after eight months.

Protein Enriched Low Shortening, Low Sugar Baked Product

C.C. Tsen and W.J. Hoover; U.S. Patent 3,883,669; May 13, 1975; assigned to Kansas State University Research Foundation describe a protein fortified composition and premix for preparing wheat flour based, low shortening and low sugar, baked and fried goods, and a method of incorporating protein supplements into the ingredients of such products without adversely affecting the volume, texture, shelf life, crumb grain or organoleptic properties of the finished goods.

The method comprises adding to the original ingredients of a selected product from 0.1 to 3% by weight, based upon the total weight of the wheat flour content, of an additive selected from the group consisting of the edible alkali and alkaline earth metal salts of the acyl lactylates of C_{16} to C_{18} fatty acids, with the average number of lactylic groups in the additive ranging from 0.5 to 4. In preferred forms, the additive is a member of the group consisting of the sodium and calcium salts of the acyl lactylates of C_{16} to C_{18} fatty acids, and the protein supplement is defatted soy flour.

The defined additives permit incorporation of significant amounts of soy flour in various products as a protein supplement therefor, and undesirable taste properties associated with the latter are effectively masked in low sugar, low shortening baked or fried products such as breads or oriental noodles.

Incorporation of an additive of the class described, and preferably sodium stearoyl-2-lactylate (SSL) or to a lesser degree calcium stearoyl-2-lactylate, permits supplementation of the wheat flour based doughs or the like with any one or more of a number of protein additives.

These may for example be selected from the group consisting of soy flour, soy isolates, nonfat milk solids, whey products, fish protein concentrates, cottonseed flour, chickpea flour, sesame seed flour, corn-soy-milk blend flour, wheat protein concentrate, wheat gluten, defatted wheat germ, torula yeast, wheat soy blend flour, edible single cell proteins, and mixtures thereof. Generally speaking, the wheat based, low shortening, low sugar compositions referred to herein contain from about 0 to 8% (baker's weight) of sugar and from 0 to 6% (baker's weight) of shortening.

Example 1: The effect of SSL on bread quality of breads containing either defatted soy flour or full fat soy flour using a no-time straight dough process is illustrated in this example. The bread formula, on a flour basis, calls for 100% flour (14% moisture basis), 12% (variable) of soy flour or other protein-rich foodstuffs, 3% yeast, 5% sugar, 2% salt, variable water, variable bromate, and 0.5% sodium stearoyl-2-lactylate.

All the ingredients are combined at room temperature in a vertical mixer, equipped with a MacDuffee type bowl and fork, and mixed at first speed (low) for one minute and then at second speed (medium) to optimum dough development. The dough is then scaled into 500-g pieces, rounded, and let rest for 40 minutes at 86°F and 85% relative humidity. The doughs are then molded, panned, and proofed at 96°F and 92% relative humidity to height (1.5 cm) over the pan. Baking is at 425°F for 25 minutes. Loaf weight and volume were measured within 10 minutes after bread was removed from the oven and averaged from duplicates.

Specific loaf volume (cc/g) was then calculated from the average loaf weight and volume. Specific loaf volume is an important parameter of bread's marketability. Generally, specific volume of marketable bread (1-lb loaf) should be at least 6.00 (2,722 cc) with acceptable appearance, crumb texture, and grain. Breads were scored 18 hours after baking. Finished bread that scored below 5 was regarded as unsatisfactory. Most of the baking tests were repeated at least once on a different day to substantiate results. The results are given below.

Effects on Baking Quality of Fortifying Wheat Flour with Indicated Percentages of Defatted Soy Flour or Full-Fat Soy Flour

Fortificant, %	SSL, %	Avg Specific Loaf Volume, %	Grain Score
Defatted soy flour			
12	0	4.54	4
16	0	4.14	3
20	0	3.40	2
24	0	3.17	2
28	0	2.94	2
12	0.5	6.22	8
16	0.5	5.76	7
20	0.5	5.05	6
24	0.5	4.25	5
28	0.5	3.38	3
Full-fat soy flour			
12	0	4.90	4
16	0	4.58	4
20	0	4.24	3
24	0	3.82	2
28	0	3.22	2
12	0.5	6.62	9
16	0.5	6.34	8
20	0.5	6.24	8
24	0.5	6.03	7
28	0.5	5.82	7

Results indicate that SSL improves the baking performance of fortified flour in low shortening, low sugar breads. Its improving effect is greater for full-fat soy flour than for defatted soy flour, so more full-fat than defatted soy flour can be used to prepare acceptable high protein bread.

Example 2: Organoleptic tests were conducted to compare bread fortified with defatted soy flour containing 0.5% sodium stearoyl-2-lactylate against soy flour fortified bread which did not include the additive. The baking procedure used was as described in Example 1. In the first study, ten persons were asked to rate appearance, flavor, texture, and overall acceptability of bread fortified with 12% defatted soy flour containing 0.5% SSL in one instance and without SSL in another instance. The samples were coded and the compositions or purpose of the test were not known by the panelists. The test panel was asked to score for appearance and palatability on a scale of:

Highly desirable	5
Desirable	4
Acceptable	3
Fair	2
Unacceptable	1

The test panel was asked to score for overall acceptability on a scale of:

Would occasionally purchase and consume	4
Would purchase and consume but less frequently than 4	3
Would consume product if it was available but would not purchase	2
Would neither purchase nor consume product	1

The mean values obtained from this test panel scoring were as follows:

	No SSL	0.5% SSL
Appearance	2.0	3.9
Flavor	2.8	3.0
Texture	2.1	3.6
Overall acceptability	2.0	3.3

Subsequently, in another evaluation eight panelists (most of whom comprised the original panel) were asked to evaluate their preference between bread fortified with 16% defatted soy flour and containing no SSL versus 16% defatted soy flour fortified bread containing 0.5% SSL. The results of this test were scored on the same basis as previously described.

	No SSL	0.5% SSL
Appearance	1.9	3.0
Flavor	2.5	2.9
Texture	1.5	2.8
Overall acceptability	1.8	2.9

The results of these organoleptic evaluations reveal not only the beneficial effects of SSL on the texture and appearance of soy fortified low shortening, low sugar breads, but also indicate the improvement of taste or flavor when SSL is used.

Hydratable Translucent Proteinaceous Product

L. Sair and D.W. Quass; U.S. Patent 3,968,268; July 6, 1976; assigned to The Griffith Laboratories, Inc. describe the preparation of edible, hydratable, proteinaceous products capable of withstanding retorting conditions used in food processing to yield a food product having structural integrity suitable for use as a food or food supplement for humans. Moist, hydratable, proteinaceous food material having suitable moisture is subjected to elevated mechanical pressure and suitable temperature and pH conditions to convert the protein material under non-puffing conditions to a dense, substantially homogeneous, translucent to glassy, coherent, bonded, proteinaceous product of desired size and shape. The material is thereby bonded together so as to be capable of withstanding the disruptive deterioration and loss of structural identity caused by subjecting the proteinaceous material to retorting conditions such as used in food processing. The translucent to glassy, proteinaceous product yields hydrated food products having structural integrity and desired textural characteristics.

The hydrated product has desired textural characteristics as such or, if the hydrated material is too tough, upon being suitably or coarsely ground, comminuted or otherwise subdivided to a particular form for use in coarsely ground meat products such as meat patties, hamburger, meat loaf or the like. When proteinaceous material is puffed from an extruder, the cells tend to be fragile. This reduces the structural integrity of such materials when added to foods which are later cooked, hydrated or retorted. Furthermore, the puffing tends to cause the proteinaceous material to lose structure. By avoiding puffing it was found that this product can be hydrated to more closely simulate the textural qualities of natural foods.

The proteinaceous material used in the process requires hydration. It may be a hydrophilic protein material such as a vegetable protein or defatted (solvent-extracted) oil seed protein such as obtained from defatted soybean having a protein content (dry basis) of at least 40%, preferably 70%. Soy protein concentrates may be used which are soluble or insoluble and have a high or low nitrogen solubility index.

To produce a bland, proteinaceous product, the proteinaceous material should be substantially pure and have a high protein content. Thus, when soy protein material is used, it is desirable to use a bland neutralized, soy protein concentrate having a protein content of at least about 70% (on a dry basis).

The material may include a desired, controlled, edible amount of a suitable cereal, starch, sugar, coloring material, seasoning or flavoring ingredient, hydrolysate, nutrients, or the like. Those materials may be present in or blended with the proteinaceous material before the resulting blend is converted to the dense, substantially homogeneous, translucent to glassy form or before or after the translucent to glassy product is subjected to hydration in the presence of added water.

The proteinaceous material is in a substantially uniform state and has a controlled effective amount of water when it is subjected to effective mechanical pressure under conditions which cause the protein material to be converted to the glassy form. The moist material must be subjected to treatment under conditions, including sufficient elevated mechanical pressure and satisfactory temperature and pH conditions, which result in its being converted to a workable, substantially homogeneous, deformable, flowable, coherent plastic mass which forms a dense, translucent to glassy product that is not puffed as a result of that treatment.

The controlled amount of water must be sufficient to enable that material to convert to a plastic state. For most purposes, it has been found that water in the range of 12.8 to 40 parts of water per 60 parts of solids or approximately 12 to 13 to 40 parts of water per 60 parts of dry protein material (regardless of whether or not the water is wholly or partly present as added water) is satisfactory when conventional compaction rolls or extruders are used. It has been found, for example, that it is desirable to use an amount of water, preferably

Miscellaneous Processes 329

within the range of 20 to 35% in order to convert the protein material satisfactorily in a conventional extruder and obviate discoloring the material or forming undesired flavor-conferring material.

A variety of devices may be used to apply mechanical pressure. One may use, for example, a press, commercial rolls or pellet mill, or extruder which subjects the moist material to sufficient pressure and temperature conditions and forms a product of desired size and shape (e.g., sheets, discs, pellets, rods, strings or bars). When an extruder is used, it is essential not to discharge or eject the extrudate under puffing conditions, so that extrusion does not subject the material to simultaneous puffing which normally results from the rapid or sudden release of water vapor from the mass when or as the discharged or ejected extrudate enters a zone of lower pressure.

The moisture content of the product can be reduced to the desired moisture level, i.e., 20%, by conventional means such as air drying, with air at room temperature or hot circulating air preferably within the range of 130° to 150°F. The following example is illustrative only and parts of the example indicate process conditions or material(s) which should be avoided.

The example illustrates that merely using compaction pressure, either with or without heat, is not enough to produce a dense, translucent to glassy product. Furthermore, it has been found that merely producing a translucent to glassy product may not produce a product meeting the requirements of structural integrity or good structural integrity when that product is hydrated under retorting conditions such as used in the processing of canned food. The retorting of the translucent to glassy product is more disruptive to the product than merely placing the product into warm water.

The laboratory Brabender extruder in the example had a 1:1 transfer screw which rotated at 100 rpm and a barrel which was heated with circulating hot oil which was fed to a jacket which surrounded the barrel. The barrel was connected to or communicated with a die at which pressure was applied upon the material fed to it by the screw. The die had a restricted extrusion opening and was heated to selected temperatures by electrical means. The buildup of material transferred to the die by the transfer screw caused significant pressure to be applied to the material at the die.

The material which was fed through the die opening (after the application of mechanically applied pressure) was fed directly into a connecting or communicating tubular die extension which was threaded into the die opening at the inner end of the extension. The extension consisted of an elongated tubular nozzle about 7 inches long. The entire length of the extension, as originally made, had an inner diameter of $1/4$-inch and an outer diameter of $1/2$-inch; however, about 6 inches of the outer discharge end of the tubular extension had been flattened so as to eject or issue extrudate in the form of a ribbon about $1/8$-inch high and about $1/2$-inch wide. The flattened extension was used in all of the runs.

The die extension was air-cooled sufficiently to avoid puffing the extrudate; however, in some instances the extension was electrically heated to facilitate plastic flow of material through the extension, but in no such instance was the temperature of the heated extension high enough to allow the extrudate to puff. The extrusion temperatures refer to the temperature of the die at or near the point where the material is discharged from the die into the extension and represents the highest temperature the material was treated at or heated to prior to being discharged through the extension.

In determining the existence or extent of structural integrity of the extrudate in the example, 15 g of the treated protein material which had been cut into ribbon-shaped chunks (e.g., about ½ + ½ + ⅛ inch chunks) were added with 60 milliliters of water to a 3-ounce can. The can was then sealed and the contents retorted at 230°F for 90 minutes.

The can was opened after being cooled. If the resulting hydrated protein product, although swollen to an increased size by contact with the heated water, had essentially retained its chunky shape and structure (structural identity) and had an essentially clear broth, then it was deemed to have or to have retained its structural integrity; however, if the resulting hydrated proteinaceous product disintegrated to the extent that it had the consistency of porridge or was mushy and had not substantially retained its coherent, self-supporting, chunky shape and structure (structural identity) and had a very milky broth, it was deemed not to have or not to have retained its structural integrity.

The product must retain more than 50% of its shape and structure (excluding swelling) before it is herein considered as having good or excellent structural integrity. The percent water absorption or hydration value expressed in the example is based upon the grams of water retained per gram of dry material and was determined as follows:

$$\% \text{ Water Absorption} = \frac{\text{Grams of Water Retained}}{\text{Grams of Dry Material}} \times 100\%$$

NSI is the ratio of the weight of soluble to total nitrogen of the proteinaceous material and was calculated as follows:

$$\% \text{ NSI} = \frac{\text{Soluble Nitrogen}}{\text{Total Nitrogen}} \times 100\%$$

The NSI determination is conducted at a pH of 6.8.

Example: Moist soy flour which had been defatted or solvent-extracted was subjected to extrusion at various temperatures. The resulting products were examined, cut into chunks about ½ inch x ½ inch x ⅛ inch, and air-dried to a moisture content of 8 to 13%. Fifteen grams of the material were then placed with 60 ml of water into individual 3-ounce cans. The cans were sealed, the contents of the cans were retorted for 90 minutes at 230°F, the cans were allowed to stand overnight, and the cans were opened and the contents examined. The soy flour used had an NSI of 50% and a protein content of 52%.

In the first series of runs, sufficient water (without any additive) was added to produce moist soy flour having a moisture content of 35.4%. The pH of the moistened soy flour was 6.7. The moistened soy flour was extruded at temperatures of 180°, 210°, 230°, 260°, 280°, 300°, and 320°F. The materials extruded at 180° and 210°F were compacted, but were not translucent or glassy. The material extruded at 230°F was compacted, nonhomogeneous and only slightly translucent. The material extruded at 260°F was compacted and had about 50%

translucency, whereas the material extruded at 280°F had about 90% translucency. The materials extruded at 300°F and 320°F had complete translucency and were completely converted to the homogeneous glassy form.

The extruded materials were then subjected to retorting (i.e., in the can) at elevated temperatures. When the materials extruded at 180°, 210° and 230°F were retorted, the retorted material which had been extruded at 180°F disintegrated and had a consistency resembling porridge and the materials extruded at 210° and 230°F formed heavy pastes and had no structural integrity. The material extruded at 260°F, when retorted, had some structural integrity and retained about 50% of its chunky shape or structure and the hydrated chunks had a water absorption value of 372%.

The materials extruded at 280°, 300° and 320°F, when retorted, each had excellent structural integrity and had water absorption values of 341, 317 and 298%, respectively. More specifically, the retorted material which had been extruded at 280°F had a clear broth; the retorted materials which had been extruded at 300° and 320°F had good texture, almost resembling that of mushrooms, and had progressively clearer broths.

The second series of runs involved first adjusting the pH of the soy flour to 7.4 with sodium hydroxide equal to 0.5% of the weight of the soy flour. The material had a moisture content of 34.7%. The moist, neutralized material was then subjected to extrusion and retorting as described above.

The materials extruded at 180°, 210° and 230°F were compacted but were not translucent to glassy and, upon being subjected to retorting, completely disintegrated and resembled porridge. The material extruded at 260°F showed definite conversion to the glassy form and, upon being subjected to retorting, had about 40% breakdown or loss of structural integrity and a somewhat milky broth. The material extruded at 300°F was converted to an excellent glassy form and, upon being retorted, had excellent structural integrity, a clear broth, and a water absorption value of 375% (as compared to 317% obtained during the first series of runs).

In the third series of runs, an aqueous solution having calcium chloride and trisodium phosphate equal to 2 and 0.5%, respectively, of the weight of soy flour used was added to the soy flour. The resulting moist flour had 34% moisture. The pH of the material was 6.3. A higher extrusion temperature was found to be necessary in order to convert the treated soy flour to the glassy form.

The material extruded at 230°F was compacted and not translucent to glassy and, upon being retorted, completely disintegrated. The materials extruded at 260° and 280°F were compacted and nonhomogeneous and, upon being retorted, substantially disintegrated.

About 80% of the material extruded at 300°F was converted to the glassy form and, upon being retorted, showed some lack of structural integrity. The material extruded at 320°F was completely converted to the glassy form and, upon being retorted, had excellent structural integrity, a clear broth, and a water absorption value of 273% (as compared to a value of 298% obtained during the first series of runs).

COMPANY INDEX

The company names listed below are given exactly as they appear in the patents, despite name changes, mergers and acquisitions which have, at times, resulted in the revision of a company name.

Adolph's Ltd. - 320
Allied Chemical Corp. - 258
American Frozen Foods Corp. - 125
American Home Products Corp. - 268
American Potato Company - 63, 95, 110, 114, 121, 297
Anheuser-Busch, Inc. - 237
Armour and Company - 166, 240
Beatrice Foods Co. - 67, 73, 187
Borden, Inc. - 74
CPC International Inc. - 69, 254, 289
Cav-Pro, Inc. - 294
Compupop, Inc. - 270
Corporate Foods Ltd. - 52, 77
Daieigiken, Inc. - 278
C.L. De Jersey & Sons Proprietary Ltd. - 242
Dragoco Spezialfabrik Konz, Riech- und Aromostoffe Gerberding & Co. GmbH - 198
Frito-Lay, Inc. - 54
Fuji Oil Co., Ltd. - 277, 286
G.T. Products, Inc. - 134
General Foods Corp. - 8, 22, 43, 92, 116, 162, 163, 172, 201, 203, 224, 242, 256, 271, 307, 317, 319
General Mills, Inc. - 24, 49, 62
Gerber Products Co. - 14, 16, 19, 217
Cie Gervais-Danone - 207
Grain Processing Corp. - 173
Griffith Labs., Inc. - 145, 148, 327
Haberstroh Farm Products, Inc. - 185
H.J. Heinz Company - 197

Hercules, Inc. - 194
ICI America Inc. - 10
Instituent Voor Bewaring En Verwerk- ing Van Landbouxprodukten - 56
J.D. Jewell, Inc. - 184
Kanro Co. Ltd. - 245
Kansas State University Research Foundation - 325
Kikkoman Shoyu Co., Ltd. - 149
Lever Brothers Company - 192
Martin, Robertson & Bain Ltd. - 128
Merck & Co., Inc. - 175
Nabisco, Inc. - 2, 6, 41, 45
Nagatanien Honpo Co., Ltd. - 246
National Can Corp. - 306
National Starch and Chemical Corp. - 178
Nibb-It Products Association Ltd. - 59
Nichiro Gyogyo Kaisha, Ltd. - 251
Nissin Shokuhin Kaisha, Ltd. - 18, 305
Ordena Lenina Institut Elemento- organischeskikt Soedineny - 153
Ore-Ida Foods, Inc. - 117
Pate Foods, Inc. - 61
Peavey Company - 139
Pillsbury Company - 4, 105, 107, 155, 158, 220, 228, 260
Procter & Gamble Company - 30, 47, 64, 101, 120, 262, 311
Quaker Oats Company - 11, 12, 21, 23, 32, 36, 39, 44, 148, 160
Ralston Purina Co. - 27, 86, 89, 142, 190, 196

Company Index

Research Corporation - 314
SMC Corporation - 299
S & W Fine Foods, Inc. - 283
Sandoz Inc. - 323
Slymans Lebanese Foods, Mfg. Co., Inc. - 297
Foster D. Snell, Inc. - 233
A.E. Staley Manufacturing Co. - 79, 168
Ste. d'Assistance Technique pour Produits Nestle SA - 82
Swift & Company - 185, 209, 212, 249, 291
Takeda Chemical Industries, Ltd. - 251
Ton Co., Ltd. - 286
U.S. Secretary of Agriculture - 98, 113, 118, 131
U.S. Secretary of the Army - 177, 180, 231, 235

INVENTOR INDEX

Abe, S. - 80
Adams, P.F. - 52, 77
Aonuma, T. - 149
Baggerly, P.A. - 43
Bakal, A. - 233
Basa, K.B. - 306
Beall, N.J. - 49
Beck, R.G. - 121
Bedenk, W.T. - 30
Bernotavicz, J.W. - 160
Billerbeck, F.W. - 217
Blagdon, P.A. - 89
Boettger, R.M. - 178
Bohrmann, H. - 254
Bonner, W.A. - 23
Boroshok, M.J. - 175
Bourns, G.B. - 268
Boyce, F.O. - 197
Bressler, M.A. - 182
Bretch, E.E. - 74
Brooking, B.L. - 220
Brown, A.V., Jr. - 86, 196
Browning, G.D. - 270
Bumbiers, E. - 24
Bundus, R.H. - 187
Burgess, W.B. - 190
Caccavale, J.L. - 264
Campbell, G.M. - 62
Capossela, A.C., Jr. - 116, 271
Carasso, D. - 207
Carpenter, R.P. - 192
Carroll, L.P. - 32
Cermak, R.E. - 299
Chang, S.S. - 314

Cheng, H. - 168
Clausen, E.E. - 172
Clausi, A.S. - 256
Cloud, L.L. - 14, 16
Cloute, J.R. - 196
Collins, J.J. - 85
Connick, F.G. - 185
Conway, R.F. - 189
Corey, H. - 233
Cox, J.M. - 128
Cox, J.P. - 128
Cremer, C.W. - 79
Curry, A.D. - 47
D'Arnaud Gerkens, D.R. - 59
Davis, E.E. - 189
Day, A.M. - 270
Decelles, G.A. - 4
De Jersey, D.C. - 241
Devero, J.E. - 85
Dougherty, J.W. - 224
Dreier, C.R., Jr. - 258
Durst, J.R. - 155
Duvall, L.F. - 36
Dwyer, C.J. - 182
Eastman, J.E. - 79
Elofson, G.L. - 49
Epstein, E. - 67
Ershova, V.A. - 153
Farkas, E. - 256
Flier, R.J. - 142
Fogel, H.P. - 162
Foster, H.G., Jr. - 209
Frederick, C.D. - 209
Friedman, H.H. - 319

Inventor Index

Fritze, H.-J.F.G. - 34
Fujiwara, H.K. - 89
Galle, E.L. - 158
Ganske, W.L. - 155
Ganz, A.J. - 194
Gellman, G. - 6
Glasgow, C.F. - 61
Glicksman, M. - 256
Gooding, C.M. - 289
Gould, M.R. - 23
Grunewald-Kirstein, I. - 274
Haas, G.J. - 22
Halik, J.J. - 203, 307
Halladay, P.D. - 224
Halligan, J.F. - 116
Hammes, P.A. - 175
Harkey, C.N. - 184
Harmon, J.F. - 114
Harms, V.D. - 69
Harris, N.E. - 177, 180
Harwood, C.C. - 148
Hautala, E. - 98, 118
Hayashida, T. - 245
Henthorn, L.J. - 11, 44
Hilton, B.W. - 54
Hollis, F., Jr. - 92
Homnick, D.N. - 131
Hoover, W.J. - 325
Huelskamp, H.J. - 85
Huessy, E.G. - 139
Hunter, J.E. - 64
Huth, H. - 198
Huxsoll, C.C. - 131
Hyldon, R.G. - 21
Ikeda, T. - 251
Ishiwatari, Y. - 277
Izjumov, D.B. - 153
Jensen, E.R. - 69
Johnson, E.A. - 196
Johnston, R.D. - 114
Johnston, R.J. - 41
Kaplow, M. - 203, 242, 307
Katayama, T. - 277
Katzen, S. - 322
Kellermeier, R.J. - 117
Kelly, M.H. - 92
Kelly, V.J. - 14, 16, 19
Keyser, W.L. - 39
Kincs, F.R. - 44
King, D.M. - 172
Kings, F.R. - 11
Kiploks, E.M. - 105
Kleiner, F. - 162

Klose, R.E. - 242
Knight, J.T. - 117
Knipper, A.J. - 2
Kolosky, J.F. - 158
Konigsbacher, K. - 233
Kortschot, C. - 52, 77
Kracauer, P. - 266
Kubota, H. - 286
Lach, J.H. - 114
Langan, R.E. - 69
Larson, V.M. - 4
Latham, S.D. - 237
Latimer, F.E. - 294
La Warre, R.W., Sr. - 73
Lee, C.R. - 172
Lee, F.H. - 180
Levine, L. - 47
Levinson, A.A. - 306
Liedman, S.G. - 62
Liepa, A.L. - 64
Liggett, J.J. - 150
Loepiktie, S.F. - 142
Lowrey, E.R. - 120
Luft, L.R. - 173
Lundy, C.N. - 45
Lyall, A.A. - 41, 45
Lynch, M.J. - 10
Magnino, P.J., Jr. - 190
Maher, R.H. - 217
Makaron, L.S. - 116
Malzahn, W.R. - 27, 89
Mangiere, R.J. - 182
Marotta, N.G. - 178
Matsunobu, A. - 286
Mattson, P.H. - 283
McCabe, D. - 127
McKay, W.C. - 185
Merriam, C.J. - 145
Metz, F.E. - 197
Meyer, R.R. - 190
Mikkelson, M.O. - 158
Miller, R.C. - 6
Milling, T.E. - 23
Minami, J. - 18, 305
Moegle, V.L. - 161
Mone, P.E. - 212
Moore, C.O. - 168
Moreno, V. - 319
Morgan, J.E. - 228
Moritaka, S. - 251
Murai, H. - 246
Murphy, T.L. - 114
Murray, D.G. - 173, 178

Nishizawa, M. - 286
Nonaka, M. - 98, 113, 118
Novotny, J.C. - 32
Noznick, P.P. - 187
Oborsh, E.V. - 86, 196
Ode, V.H. - 219
Ohkawa, N. - 278
Ohnishi, F. - 18
Ohta, I. - 286
Parliament, T.H. - 317
Pavey, R.L. - 212
Payne, B.M. - 196
Pedersen, D.C. - 107
Petersen, W.D. - 24
Pichel, M.J. - 249
Pierce, V.J. - 264
Poat, J.G. - 12
Prakash, V. - 82
Pratl, F.J. - 166
Prussin, S.B. - 264
Purves, E.R. - 30, 101
Quass, D.W. - 148, 327
Rahman, A.R. - 231
Rebane, A. - 323
Reddy, B.R. - 314
Reesman, S.H. - 8, 201
Reinhart, R.D. - 49
Reinhart, R.R. - 148
Richards, A.W. - 32
Rigler, L.E. - 320
Rispoli, J.M. - 271
Rogers, A.B. - 240
Rose, D.W. - 47
Rosenquest, A.H. - 2
Rossen, J.L. - 6
Rubio, M.J. - 284, 285
Ruhdorfer, A. - 280
Rusch, D.T. - 10
Rydeski, R.R. - 189
Sair, L. - 148, 327
Sakamoto, K. - 286
Sautier, P.M. - 107
Schafer, G.R. - 231
Schanefelt, R.V. - 79, 168
Schneider, G. - 254
Schoenholz, D. - 233
Schum, H. - 198
Schwab, E.C. - 24
Sebring, M. - 240
Seeley, R.D. - 237
Segmiller, J.L. - 197
Sevenants, M.R. - 311
Shatila, M.A. - 63, 95, 110, 121
Shields, J.B. - 297

Sijbring, P.H. - 56
Slonimsky, G.L. - 153
Slyman, E.A. - 297
Smalligan, W.J. - 14, 16, 19
Smith, G.M., Jr. - 148
Smith, N.F. - 12
Snively, C.O. - 101
Spiel, A. - 136
Spirtos, N.G. - 320
Steljes, B.E. - 117
Stewart, A.P., Jr. - 258
Stone, C.D. - 36
Straughn, R.O. - 49
Sugiura, S. - 251
Takagi, Y. - 305
Takatsu, M. - 18, 305
Takeuchi, T. - 305
Taki, G.H. - 320
Terada, M. - 305
Terrell, R.M. - 110
Tiemstra, P.J. - 291
Toei, R. - 149
Tolson, R.C., Jr. - 134
Tolson, R.C., Sr. - 134
Tolstoguzov, V.B. - 153
Tomlinson, B.E. - 269
Tompkin, R.B. - 185
Tsen, C.C. - 325
Turitz, E. - 303
Turpin, C.H. - 260
Umeki, T. - 251
Von Der Lieth, W.H. - 114
Waitman, R.H. - 92
Watanabe, H. - 149
Weaver, M.L. - 98, 113, 118
Weddle, R.B. - 192
Weigle, D.C. - 262
Weis, V.E. - 120
Weiss, V.E. - 62
Westover, J.D. - 105
Wheeler, F.G. - 166
Willard, M.J. - 50
Wilson, G.L. - 62
Wisdom, L.W. - 54
Wood, F.W. - 192
Wood, R.W. - 2
Wright, W.F. - 220
Yamazaki, T. - 245
Young, R.W. - 264
Yuasa, T. - 149
Zielinski, W.J. - 39
Zobel, F.A. - 163
Zukerman, H.W. - 125

U. S. PATENT NUMBER INDEX

3,694,224 - 285	3,767,825 - 175	3,835,222 - 54
3,697,283 - 240	3,769,027 - 182	3,840,673 - 52
3,697,289 - 270	3,769,029 - 194	3,840,675 - 317
3,698,914 - 77	3,769,035 - 162	3,843,814 - 274
3,698,915 - 61	3,769,041 - 306	3,843,815 - 201
3,703,378 - 74	3,769,042 - 203	3,843,827 - 172
3,703,382 - 184	3,769,404 - 237	3,845,232 - 8
3,704,133 - 266	3,769,438 - 10	3,846,457 - 120
3,705,812 - 297	3,770,461 - 258	3,846,572 - 118
3,706,573 - 134	3,780,193 - 241	3,849,582 - 89
3,709,696 - 285	3,782,963 - 36	3,851,072 - 139
3,709,698 - 189	3,787,588 - 303	3,851,081 - 67
3,711,296 - 73	3,790,690 - 34	3,851,083 - 220
3,717,469 - 153	3,792,183 - 45	3,851,084 - 6
3,719,497 - 158	3,792,956 - 21	3,852,491 - 27
3,719,501 - 271	3,793,467 - 187	3,852,492 - 86
3,725,084 - 189	3,794,741 - 262	3,857,982 - 311
3,726,693 - 177	3,794,742 - 180	3,862,344 - 163
3,729,323 - 118	3,796,811 - 198	3,862,345 - 105
3,730,732 - 284	3,796,814 - 299	3,864,505 - 64
3,732,109 - 12	3,806,613 - 32	3,865,964 - 117
3,745,019 - 131	3,812,268 - 233	3,868,468 - 185
3,745,027 - 307	3,812,274 - 98	3,868,471 - 4
3,753,729 - 69	3,812,775 - 56	3,872,229 - 155
3,753,734 - 242	3,814,818 - 314	3,873,748 - 24
3,753,735 - 59	3,814,819 - 228	3,873,749 - 192
3,754,930 - 149	3,814,822 - 44	3,873,755 - 185
3,754,931 - 92	3,814,824 - 30	3,876,811 - 23
3,759,715 - 142	3,819,839 - 249	3,879,566 - 128
3,761,284 - 209	3,821,443 - 224	3,881,028 - 116
3,764,715 - 11	3,830,941 - 173	3,882,253 - 231
3,767,823 - 166	3,830,946 - 280	3,882,254 - 289
3,767,824 - 39	3,833,739 - 107	3,883,669 - 325

3,883,671 - 63	3,925,563 - 49	3,956,510 - 49
3,885,048 - 150	3,925,565 - 148	3,956,515 - 168
3,886,291 - 50	3,925,566 - 148	3,956,517 - 47
3,887,714 - 19	3,925,567 - 80	3,958,032 - 145
3,889,002 - 256	3,927,222 - 2	3,958,036 - 294
3,890,453 - 114	3,928,252 - 320	3,959,498 - 41
3,895,122 - 95	3,928,635 - 286	3,959,501 - 95
3,896,716 - 207	3,928,650 - 254	3,959,515 - 127
3,901,977 - 323	3,930,027 - 16	3,961,087 - 125
3,903,308 - 219	3,930,029 - 305	3,961,091 - 264
3,903,313 - 217	3,930,030 - 197	3,962,355 - 245
3,904,772 - 161	3,930,049 - 283	3,962,416 - 322
3,904,775 - 148	3,930,441 - 278	3,962,476 - 260
3,904,776 - 190	3,931,434 - 246	3,966,990 - 79
3,911,142 - 85	3,934,046 - 113	3,968,260 - 110
3,912,824 - 136	3,935,322 - 62	3,968,265 - 121
3,914,454 - 18	3,937,848 - 62	3,968,268 - 327
3,917,857 - 297	3,944,681 - 319	3,968,269 - 196
3,917,866 - 101	3,946,116 - 98	3,969,514 - 291
3,917,876 - 148	3,950,550 - 277	3,969,534 - 212
3,920,852 - 22	3,950,567 - 269	3,969,535 - 268
3,922,353 - 160	3,955,000 - 43	3,969,536 - 251
3,922,370 - 82	3,956,506 - 14	Reissue 27,531 - 178

NOTICE

Nothing contained in this Review shall be construed to constitute a permission or recommendation to practice any invention covered by any patent without a license from the patent owners. Further, neither the author nor the publisher assumes any liability with respect to the use of, or for damages resulting from the use of, any information, apparatus, method or process described in this Review.